DATE DUE

Health Care in America

Health Care in America

Separate and Unequal

Kant Patel and Mark E. Rushefsky

M.E.Sharpe
Armonk, New York
London, England

Library of Congress Cataloging-in-Publication Data

Patel, Kant, 1946–
  Health care in America : separate and unequal / by Kant Patel and Mark E. Rushefsky.
    p. cm.
  Includes bibliographical references and index.
  ISBN 978-0-7656-1661-6 (cloth : alk. paper)
  1. Minorities—Medical care—United States. 2. Health and race—United States.
  3. Discrimination in medical care—United States. 4. Equality—Health aspects—United States.
  5. Medical policy—United States. I. Rushefsky, Mark E., 1945– II. Title.
  [DNLM: 1. Healthcare Disparities—United States. 2. Health Policy—United States.
  3. Health Services Accessibility—United States. 4. Health Status Disparities—United States.
  5. Minority Groups—United States. 6. Socioeconomic Factors—United States. W 84 AA1
  P2847h 2008]

  RA448.4.P38 2008
  362.1089—dc22   2008009083

In memory of Kahlua
—KP

To Echo and Damian, may you not face any health disparities
—MER

Contents

List of Tables

Preface and Acknowledgments

We have had a long, rewarding friendship dating back to 1985, when Rushefsky came to what was then called Southwest Missouri State University and is now simply Missouri State University. The friendship and collaboration has produced five books (counting the copy in your hand) or nine books (if you count subsequent editions) and several articles. This has occurred because of common interests in sports (as spectators) and despite differences in work habits and family situations. Patel is impeccably neat and well-organized. Rushefsky, as we have discussed in our previous books, has been married over thirty-nine years, has two daughters and two grandchildren. The grandchildren, four and two, are the delight of their grandparents and can do (almost) no wrong. Rushefsky is less well-organized and considerably less neat than Patel. However different our work habits, family, and other activities, the collaboration has worked out well.

The present book focuses on health care disparities. The inspiration for the project came from Patel. Our *Health Care Politics and Policy in America* (now in its third edition) covers some of this ground, but not nearly enough for our satisfaction. The United States has a wonderful health care system, especially in terms of its capabilities. But it is not equally available to all. It is an expensive system and highly fragmented. Although it works for many of us, it does not work for all. That is what we try to get across through this book. There are many explanations for these disparities. Some are the characteristics of the health care system. Some are related to who has political power. Some are based on socioeconomic differences. Some are based on discrimination, both past and present. Some reside within ethnic and racial communities, such as distrust of the system. There are multiple problems with multiple possible solutions. Even if the United States adopted some form of universal, national health care, some disparities would still remain. Addressing those disparities, especially in an era of deep concern about the costs of care, is one of the great projects of the American way of health care.

As is typical of any book, this one is not the product of its authors only. We would like to thank Patricia Kolb, editorial director at M.E. Sharpe, for her continued support of our work, as well as her assistant, Makiko Parsons. Thanks are also due to Henrietta Toth, production editor, and to her staff for the copyediting. Of course, any remaining errors are ours.

Health Care in America

1

The American Health Care System

Separate and Unequal

American Democracy and Equality

American democracy is characterized by many contradictions and paradoxes. The United States is the richest country in the world, yet it also suffers from high rates of poverty, infant mortality, homicides, and economic inequality compared to other advanced democracies (Halstead 2003). Michael Harrington (1971) in his book *The Other America* pointed out the existence of two Americas. One is the affluent America that is the most visible and celebrated in speeches and advertised on television. The other America is invisible and is impoverished. It is made up of millions of people who are poor, dispirited in mind and body, and exist without adequate housing, education, and health care. Two decades after President Johnson declared war on poverty, poverty still persisted (Harrington 1983) and it continues to exist today.

The United States spends more money per capita on health care than any other country and has the best medical care, yet around 45 million people do not have health insurance. The United States remains the only industrialized country in the world without a national health insurance system. Some believe that such a bifurcated condition is a necessary and acceptable tradeoff for national prosperity, while others believe that the very idea of a necessary tradeoff between social and economic well-being is un-American because it runs against the idealistic foundation on which the American republic was built (Halstead 2003). One of the most important ideals promoted by American democracy is that of equality. Here again we see a paradox. The American ideal of equality confronts the reality of inequality that persists in American democracy.

The Declaration of Independence proudly proclaimed: "We hold these truths to be self-evident, that all men are created equal." However, this declaration of equality presumably did not apply to slaves nor to women. Thomas Jefferson, who wrote these eloquent words himself, was a slave owner. While he opposed slavery, he lived off slave labor, and expressed doubts that blacks could be intellectually equal to whites. Upon his death, only a few of his slaves were emancipated (Manley 1990). Edward Coles, a protégé and family friend of Thomas Jefferson, inherited slaves from his father and was considering setting them free. In the summer of 1814 he wrote to Jefferson seeking his advice. Jefferson, in his reply, scolded Coles for having even considered abandoning his property. Jefferson insisted that even though he abhorred slavery and foresaw its eventual demise, until that day came, it was the duty of every slaveholding gentleman to shoulder the ancestral burden as best he could, for the good of both races (Goodheart 2005).

Thomas Jefferson also felt that women had no place in politics and public meetings. He argued that women should not "mix promiscuously" with men in public meetings "to prevent depravation of morals and ambiguity of issues" (Lipscomb 1903–1904, 72). When a general's daughter wrote to him about the Constitution, he told her not to worry because "the tender breasts of ladies were not formed for political convulsion" (Sochen 1974, 73).

The issue of slavery was still alive eighty-six years after the Declaration of Independence. Abraham Lincoln on September 22, 1862, issued the Emancipation Proclamation declaring that on January 1, 1863, he would issue an order freeing the slaves in the states in rebellion. In July of 1863, Lincoln invoked the words of the Declaration of Independence in his Gettysburg Address when he said, "Four score and seven years ago our fathers brought forth on this continent a new nation, conceived in Liberty, and dedicated to the proposition that all men are created equal." However, Lincoln's views on slavery had evolved over time. Even though he did not approve of slavery, he did not think that blacks and whites could live with equality. During the Lincoln-Douglas debates at Charleston, South Carolina, on September 18, 1858, Lincoln stated that

> I am not, nor have I ever been in the favor of bringing about in any way the social and political equality of the white and black races—that I not nor have ever been in favor of making voters or jurors of Negroes, nor of qualifying them to hold public office, not to intermarry with white people. . . . There must be a position of superior and inferior, and I. . . . am in favor of having the superior position assigned to the white race. . . . (Johannsen 1965, 162)

According to historian Richard Current (1967, xvi), even though slavery was evil, Lincoln tolerated it for three reasons. One, the Constitution did not give him the power to act against slavery within states. Second, even if the federal government had the power to act and had acted, abolition would have created more problems than it would have solved. Third, Lincoln felt that the institution of slavery would eventually die of its own weight if it were confined to the Southern states. Lincoln's challenge was to balance his opposition to slavery and his fidelity to the Constitution (White 2002). Thus, before his presidency, Lincoln endorsed a "middle position" on slavery, arguing it could remain legal in the South but not be allowed to spread to new territories. However, one can see a shift in his position when on March 4, 1865, he gave his Second Inaugural Address in which he condemned slavery as a grievous national sin that had prompted a just God to deliver upon the United States a punishment in the form of a devastating Civil War (White 2002). Black abolitionist Frederick Douglass, who did not begin as an admirer of Lincoln, had become one. In a speech delivered eleven years after Lincoln's death he stated that "viewed from the genuine abolition ground, Mr. Lincoln seemed tardy, cold, and indifferent, but measuring him by the sentiment of his country, a sentiment he was bound as a statesman to consult, he was swift, zealous, radical, and determined" (Douglass 1962, 485).

As Barry Schwartz (1996) has pointed out, even the meaning of the Gettysburg Address has changed as successive generations have interpreted it in light of new circumstances and challenges. Originally it was viewed by its supporters as a call to arms. It was recognized for its esthetic appeal, but rarely commemorated. During the Progressive era in the early twentieth century, it came to be interpreted as a symbol of industrial democracy, regional solidarity, and patriotism. In the background of the civil rights movement of the 1960s, the Gettysburg Address came to be interpreted as a plea for racial integration, egalitarianism, and equality. For example, at the 1963 Gettysburg Address Centennial, Secretary of State Dean Rusk reminded and urged his audience to remember that Lincoln's reaffirmation of the American commitment to the preposition that "all men are created equal" was preceded by the Emancipation Proclamation.

The post–Civil War Amendments—Thirteenth, Fourteenth, and Fifteenth—abolished slavery, gave black men the right to vote, and prohibited states from denying equal protection and due process of the laws to its citizens. Women won the right to vote in 1920 after a hard-fought struggle. Yet, by the 1950s, the equality of men envisioned by the Declaration of Independence was far from reality in America. On August 28, 1963, on the steps of the Lincoln Memorial, in his famous "I Have a Dream" speech, Martin Luther King evoked the name of Lincoln when he said:

> Five score years ago, a great American, in whose symbolic shadow we stand today, signed the Emancipation Proclamation. This momentous decree came as a great beacon light of hope to millions of Negro slaves who had been seared in the flames of withering injustice. It came as a joyous daybreak to end the long night of their captivity.
>
> But one hundred years later, the Negro still is not free. One hundred years later, the life of the Negro is still sadly crippled by the manacles of segregation and the chains of discrimination. One hundred years later, the Negro lives on a lonely island of poverty on the midst of a vast ocean of prosperity. One hundred years later, the Negro is still languishing in the corners of American society and finds himself an exile in his own land. So we have come here today to dramatize a shameful condition. (King, August 28, 1963).

The slow progress in achieving equal rights gave rise to the civil rights movement following World War II. In 1954, a unanimous Supreme Court ruled that racial segregation in the public schools was unconstitutional. The early 1960s witnessed direct action undertaken by the civil rights movement, such as marches, protests, boycotts, and sit-ins, which led Congress to pass the Civil Rights Act of 1964, the Voting Rights Act of 1965, and the Fair Housing Act of 1968. These laws helped end a wide range of discriminatory practices and helped make significant progress in the area of political equality for African Americans.

Of course, African Americans were not the only group seeking equality and justice. The civil rights legislation of the 1960s also benefited Spanish-speaking people and other minorities. César Chávez was the early leader of civil rights involved in helping raise the standard of living for Mexican American farm workers and helped organize the National Farm Workers Association in 1962. Today, a variety of groups speak for the rights of Spanish-speaking people.

Another minority group that has struggled and fought hard for equal rights is Native Americans. At times, Native Americans have turned to militant action and have organized demonstrations, marches, and sit-ins and fish-ins, and confronted government officials to meet their demands as exemplified in the takeover of the abandoned government prison on the island of Alcatraz in San Francisco in November 1969, and the takeover of the village on the Pine Ridge Reservation–Wounded Knee, South Dakota, in February 1973. Today, a number of Native American groups work toward strengthening tribal governments, legal reforms, and educational and financial advancement to help rebuild Native American communities.

It was not too long ago that women did not enjoy the same political and economic rights as men. The passage of the Nineteenth Amendment in 1920 giving women the right to vote was the first step toward achieving political equality. The reemergence of the women's rights movement in the 1960s has worked to promote gender equality in the areas of equal pay, property rights, reproductive choices, and fighting the glass ceiling.

Since the 1960s, the civil rights movement and the women's rights movement have brought about some progress, especially in the area of political equality. However, as Theda Skocpol (2004) has argued, American civil life was transformed between the 1960s and 1990s from large, broad-based membership organizations to professionally run advocacy groups. This has been both a blessing and a curse. It created another paradox in American democracy. It gave fresh voices to women and minorities and helped raise important issues. However, it has also marginalized masses of Americans and caused their interests to be not as well represented in the American democratic process. Professionally run advocacy groups have relied on foundations and computerized direct-mail appeals to affluent Americans for financial support and in the process have failed to mobilize and bring into democratic politics masses of Americans from low on the ladder of socioeconomic status. Thus, in another irony, while progress has been made in the area of political equality, there is evidence of rising social and economic inequality in the country.

Rising Economic Inequality

> Give me your tired, your poor, your huddled masses yearning to breathe free,
> The wretched refuse of your teeming shore.
> Send these, the homeless, tempest-lost to me,
> I lift my lamp beside the golden door.
>   (From Emma Lazarus's 1883 "The New Colossus" sonnet engraved on a plaque
>   and placed in the pedestal of the Statue of Liberty in 1903)

A recent report titled "American Democracy in an Age of Rising Inequality" by the Task Force on Inequality and American Democracy of the American Political Science Association (2004) concluded that the American ideal of equal citizenship is threatened by rising inequality reflected in disparities of income, wealth, and access to opportunities. After carefully examining the evidence on citizen participation, government responsiveness, and patterns of public policy making and their consequences, the report argues that today the voices of American citizens are raised and heard unequally. On the one hand, many previously marginalized groups have gained rights to full participation in American institutions and U.S. society has become more integrated across the past barriers of race, ethnicity, gender, and other forms of social exclusion. On the other hand, American society has experienced growing gaps of income and wealth and many African Americans, Latinos, and women who head families are losing ground (American Political Science Association 2004).

During the postwar period, income shares have been highly unequal in the United States compared to other industrial nations. Furthermore, inequalities of income and wealth are heightened by race and ethnic distinctions (Goldsmith and Blakely 1992). Poor families are disproportionately headed by women, and this is compounded by the fact that African American families overall are more likely to be headed by women. High proportions of African Americans and Hispanics live below the poverty line, and minority households have rates of poverty two to three times as high as whites. Occupational segregation by race and gender also contributes to low income for minorities and women because they are generally employed in low paying occupations.

There has also been a geographic concentration of poverty. In 1959, most poor people (57 percent) lived in rural areas and small towns. However, by 1985 large portions (43 percent) of the poor were living in central cities (Goldsmith and Blakely 1992). Patterns of economic inequality have become more evident in major cities. Between 1980 and 1990, in the hundred largest cities in the United States, the percent of census tracts living below the federal poverty level (defined as at least 40 percent of all residents living below the federal poverty level) increased from 9.7 percent to 13.7 percent (Kasarda 1993).

It is also clear that exposure and susceptibility to disease are distributed according to social, political, and economic patterns. Nearly one in five (20 percent) of all U.S. children under the age of eighteen live below the poverty level. The poverty rate among black children in 1997 was 37.2 percent and among Hispanic children it was 35.8 percent (Sherman 1997). Among children, most prevalent mortalities and morbidities are associated with poverty (Whiteis 2000). Similarly, death rates among individuals with low incomes are much higher than individuals with high incomes (Pappas et al. 1993).

Disparities in wealth and income have grown more sharply in the United States than in Canada, France, Germany, Italy, and many other advanced industrial democracies, and these disparities are even more striking across races. Even though the absolute economic conditions of minorities have improved, between 1913 and 1998, the median white household earned 62 percent more income and possessed twelve times more wealth than the median black household. Nearly two-thirds of black households (61 percent) and half of Hispanic households lacked any financial assets as compared to only a quarter of their white counterparts. Blacks still earned 20 percent less income than whites (American Political Science Association 2004).

Nor has everyone shared equally in the economic prosperity of the country; in fact, poverty in America is actually getting worse. More than 37 million Americans live in poverty (individuals under the age of sixty-five earning less than $9,800 a year, and $14,689 for a family of three, are considered poor). The poverty rate of 12.7 percent (measuring a poverty rate is controversial and, depending on how it is measured, the numbers may vary) is the highest in the developed world and more than twice as high as in most other industrialized countries. Twenty-four percent of blacks, American Indians and Alaska Natives, and 22 percent of Hispanics live in poverty compared to 8 percent of whites (Alter 2005).

It is the existence of such sharp economic inequalities along racial lines that leads some to argue that there have been two visions and two political, economic, and cultural agendas in American history related to the concepts of race and citizenship. One vision conceives of this nation as won by right of conquest and settled by mainly Anglo-Saxon ancestry—a country whose bounty should benefit white elites alone. The second vision conceives of this nation as embodying the premise and possibility of freedom and equality across racial and gender boundaries. Many of the progressive political and social movements, such as the antislavery movement, the women's movement, the civil rights movement, and other populist movements in American history, have been inspired by this second vision (Hudson 1995).

Economic and social inequalities are also related to levels of political participation in American democracy. Those who enjoy higher income, occupational success, and formal education are more likely to participate in politics and make their demands known to the government compared to those who come from low socioeconomic status. For example, nine out of ten individuals in families with incomes over $75,000, compared to only five out of ten in families with incomes under $15,000, reported voting in presidential elections (American Political Science Association 2004). The concerns of lower or moderate income Americans, racial minorities, and legal immigrants are less likely to be heard by government officials because they are also less likely to be involved in electoral campaigns, join organized interest groups, make campaign contributions, and other forms of political participation. As a result, government policies are more responsive to more affluent citizens.

The gains made by African Americans, women, and other minorities in outlawing discrimination and winning the right to vote and run for office, for example, have considerably narrowed voter-turnout among African Americans, women, and whites. The reduction in overt discrimination has been marred by growing economic inequality and is undermining the economic progress and political inclusion of minorities and women (American Political Science Association 2004). As the current George W. Bush administration is engaged in a neo-Wilsonian campaign to spread democracy abroad, the reality of widening economic disparities at home is becoming a threat to American democracy's ideal of equality and justice for all—another paradox of American democracy.

John Manley (1990) has argued that three dreams run through American history: the democratic dream, the elitist dream, and the American dream. The democratic dream does not argue that all people are equal in ability or talent. It argues that equality is a necessary condition for independence and freedom. Any society that is sharply divided between rich and poor cannot be democratic. Some inequality may be tolerated, but the general social objective is a dominant middle class. The elitist dream envisions an America of the superior few and inferior many. Such elitist beliefs have accommodated/supported slavery, subjugated women, and justified displacement or annihilation of Native Americans. The American dream is essentially a compromise between the democratic and the elitist dreams. On the issue of economic equality, the American dream is elitist. It promises equal opportunity but not social and economic equality. The American dream supports legal and political equality. Maxwell Geismar (1970) calls the American dream our "ruling myth," embodied in all major statements and political and cultural documents for more than two hundred years and still persisting as a cultural ideal in mass media and popular notions of American democracy.

American Public Opinion and Equality

The Indians will perish in the same isolated condition in which they have lived; but the destiny of the Negroes is in some measure interwoven with that of the Europeans. These two races are attached to each other without intermingling; and they are alike unable to entirely separate or to combine. (Tocqueville 1961, 423–24).

The moderns, then, after they have abolished slavery, have three prejudices to contend against, which are less easy to attack, and far less easy to conquer, than the mere fact of servitude: the prejudice of the master, the prejudice of the race, and the prejudice of colour. (Tocqueville 1961, 416)

According to public opinion polls, Americans (much more so than Europeans) are willing to accept considerable disparities of income and wealth because unequal economic outcomes are seen as a legitimate result of differences in individual talent and effort and not a result of any flaws in the economic system. Americans strongly support rights to private property and free enterprise, and they also expect the government to ensure equal opportunity for all so that everyone has an equal chance to get ahead. Americans also strongly support equal democratic rights—political and legal rights—the idea that every citizen should have a voice in representative government (American Political Science Association 2004). This is consistent with the American dream discussed above. Polls also suggest that Americans are increasingly concerned about disparities in participation and government responsiveness and believe that special interests exercise too much influence on government (American Political Science Association 2004). However, they often fail to recognize, as the above discussion suggests, that economic inequality may make it difficult to achieve political equality.

At a theoretical level, Americans are generally very supportive of the idea of providing equal opportunity for everyone including minorities. For example, public opinion has shown increased support for the idea of equal opportunity. In 1944 only 45 percent agreed with the statement that blacks should have as good a chance as white people to get any kind of job. Three decades later, 97 percent agreed with this statement (Page and Shapiro 1992).

Most Americans believe that racial discrimination is still a problem facing American society. In a 1999 poll of a nationwide sample of 1,107 adults, 68 percent believed that blacks suffered discrimination "a lot" or "somewhat" in American society (ABC News/Lifetime Television Poll 1999). In a 2003 Gallup poll (2003) only 19 percent of blacks and 41 percent of Hispanics felt that they had never experienced discrimination in public life because of their race. In 2005 when poll respondents were asked if they had personally felt discriminated against because of race, 81 percent of whites said no while 54 percent of blacks responded affirmatively (ABC News Poll 2005). Thus, perceived racial discrimination against minorities still remains a major problem in American society.

Americans' attitudes about social welfare and other policies directed at addressing the problem of inequality tend to be inconsistent and contradictory. Americans generally accept the idea that blacks and other minorities have suffered from discrimination and verbalize an absolute commitment to equal opportunity, yet, whites often oppose specific policies (such as busing and affirmative action) designed to assure equal opportunity (Kluegel and Smith 1986).

One of the major tools to promote equal opportunity for minorities and women in American society is affirmative action programs. In a 2000 CNN/Gallup/*USA Today* Poll (2000) 58 percent of the respondents indicated that they favored an affirmative action program for women and minorities. However, by 2003 support for affirmative action programs seemed to have declined. In a Gallup poll (2003), overall only 49 percent of respondents favored affirmative action programs and 43 percent were opposed. The major difference in opinions of whites, blacks, and Hispanics is significant. Of the total, only 44 percent of non-Hispanic whites favored an affirmative action program compared to 70 percent of blacks and 63 percent of Hispanics. Thus, whites and racial minorities often have a very different perception about issues of equality, discrimination, and methods for promoting equality in American society.

Americans' attitudes toward social policies are rooted in ambivalence regarding individual self-reliance, collective social responsibility, and limited government. Thus, on the one hand, Americans express support for equal opportunity, while on the other hand they also favor ideals of self reliance and limited government (Jacobs and Shapiro 1998).

Opinions about equal opportunity also vary. For example, among low-status whites, a majority rate opportunity for average Americans as good or very good and believe that they have had a fair chance to make the most of themselves. In contrast, a substantial majority of low-status blacks believe that they have not had a fair chance to make the most of themselves as individuals (Kluegel and Smith 1986). Similarly, women have a consistently less optimistic assessment of opportunity in general and personal opportunity in particular than men at each status level (Kluegel and Smith 1986).

This racial divide is reflected in opinions about the government's handling of the devastation caused by hurricane Katrina in August of 2005 in Louisiana, Mississippi, and Alabama. In a 2005 ABC News/*Washington Post* Poll (2005) respondents were asked whether they thought the federal government would have responded more quickly to rescue people trapped by flood water if more of them had been wealthier and white than poorer and black. Overall, 64 percent said that race did not affect the speed of rescue effort while 31 percent said it did. However, when responses are broken down by race, dramatic differences emerge. Of the total respondents, 73 percent of whites believed that race had no effect while 76 percent of blacks believed that race was a factor. In the same poll, 73 percent of whites said that problems with the hurricane relief effort were not an indication of racial inequality in the country while 63 percent of blacks felt that it was indication of racial inequality. Similarly, 65 percent of whites said that President Bush cares about the problems facing black people in the country while 68 percent of blacks indicated that President Bush does not care about the problems facing black people.

Other polls have reported similar results. In a 2005 *USA Today*/CNN poll (Page and Puente 2005) six in ten African Americans said that the fact that most hurricane victims were poor and black was one reason that the federal government did not come to the rescue more quickly. Nine out of ten whites rejected that idea. In the same poll, whites by 50 percent to 44 percent stated that most people shown on television involved in grabbing food, water, and TV sets were criminals taking advantage of the situation. In sharp contrast, blacks by 77 percent to 16 percent said that they were mostly desperate people trying to find a way to survive.

In another 2005 poll (Murray 2005) only 37 percent agreed with the statement that the Bush administration would have responded with greater urgency had the affected areas been mostly white suburban communities. However, a huge gap is found when responses are broken down by race. Seventy percent of African Americans agreed with the statement, while 67 percent of whites disagreed (Murray 2005). While it is true that most of the people affected by Katrina were black and poor, the fact remains that St. Bernard Parish in Louisiana, which is largely made up of white poor, suffered equally. This tends to suggest that the slow government response perhaps had more to do with lack of foresight, planning, and emergency preparedness by all three levels of government than race.

However, what is true is that whites and racial minorities often tend to view American society and its problems through different color lenses. The same kind of racial divide is found with respect to the American health care system. Whether such divergent views are grounded in reality or not is not as important as the fact that such different perceptions do exist and in politics, perception often shapes reality.

American Health Care, Equality, and Public Opinion

One of the devastating effects of hurricane Katrina was the damage it caused to the city of New Orleans' health system of public and private hospitals. Many of the hospitals were so badly damaged that they may never reopen (Manning 2005). Also, many health experts believe that many of the storm-related deaths resulted not from trauma or drowning but from lack of medicine and treatment of people with chronic illnesses such as diabetes, heart disease, and hypertension. Most of the victims of hurricane Katrina were poor people at risk before the storm hit New Orleans because of health disparities related to poverty and race (Payne 2005).

According to a poll of 680 randomly selected evacuees from New Orleans living in the Houston area conducted by the *Washington Post,* the Henry J. Kaiser Family Foundation, and the Harvard School of Public Health, six in ten evacuees had family income of less than $20,000 in 2004. A large majority of evacuees did not have a bank savings or checking account or any usable credit cards. One in eight was unemployed when the storm hit and seven in ten had no insurance to cover their losses. Half did not have any health insurance and for the majority of those who did have health insurance, Medicare or Medicaid was the main source of health insurance. Four in ten suffered from a variety of health problems such as heart disease, diabetes, or high blood pressure or had a physical disability (Henry J. Kaiser Family Foundation 2005b; Morin and Rein 2005).

Statewide disparities in health related to race and incomes are documented by Louisiana's Department of Health and Hospitals in annual health report cards. For example, according to the 2004 Louisiana Health Report Card, statewide about 11.9 percent of African Americans have diabetes compared to 7.2 percent for whites.

Around 15.8 percent of those who lived in households with an income of less than $15,000 per year had diabetes. The prevalence of diabetes steadily decreases as family income rises. Only 4.8 percent of people who lived in households with an income of more than $50,000 had diabetes (Payne 2005).

Louisiana is not unique with respect to health care inequalities. Health care disparities are common nationwide. There is also considerable variation in the levels of health care disparities between states and within states ("US Health Care: A State Lottery?" 2004). Health disparities in the United States have been called a "national embarrassment" (Mourey et al. 2005). Similarly, Senator Edward Kennedy (D-MA) has called the state of U.S. minority health "an embarrassment to the nation" (Kennedy 2005, 457). Former U.S. surgeon general David Satcher has placed the human cost of this racial health gap at 84,000 premature deaths a year (Szabo 2005).

What is ironic is that despite the well-documented and publicized prevalence of health disparities, many Americans seem unaware of them. A poll conducted by Lake, Snell, Perry & Associated, Inc., commissioned by the Harvard Forum on Health, found that U.S. blacks and Hispanics are much more likely than whites to recognize that minorities do not always receive an equal level of health care. About 65 percent of blacks and 41 percent of Hispanics believe that minorities receive lower-quality care while only 22 percent of whites believed it to be the case. The polls also found that 57 percent of blacks and 49 percent of Hispanics felt that health care providers treated minorities differently while only 21 percent of whites believed this to be the case (Lake, Snell, Perry & Associates 2003). Whites and minorities also assess their own health very differently. In a National Health Interview Survey, when respondents were asked to rate their own health as excellent, very good, good, fair, or poor, American Indians/Native Alaskan adults and black adults were substantially less likely than white adults to assess their own health as excellent or very good. Over 65 percent of whites rated their own health as excellent or very good compared to only about 50 percent of American Indians/Alaskan Natives and blacks ("QuickStats" 2005).

Public opinion about health care in general again illustrates Americans' ambivalence toward social policy. Polls consistently show that Americans indicate a high and stable level of personal satisfaction with their own health care. At the same time, they express considerable dissatisfaction and anxiety about the price of that care, the future of health care, and support extending health insurance to the uninsured, guaranteeing health care for all Americans, and overhauling the current health care system. However, the American public is also predisposed to hang on to the status quo because of satisfaction with their own personal situation and apprehension about an increased government role (Jacobs and Shapiro 1998). The failed effort of the Clinton administration to overhaul the U.S. health care system stands as a testimony to Americans' desire for reforming the system at a theoretical level and failure to support major reforms in practice because of multiple and competing considerations.

Inequalities in the American Health Care System

> Despite being the most expensive health care system in the world, the U.S. health care system fails to provide care to all our citizens and the care actually delivered is substandard. Perhaps most concerning, our health care system remains largely separate and unequal. (Editorial 2004, 815).

Since the 1990s the issue of health inequalities in American society based on race/ethnicity, gender, age, and geographic location has begun to receive serious and systematic scholarly attention. With respect to race and health, African Americans, Hispanics, and American Indians/Alaskan Natives minorities fare much more poorly than whites. Women do not do as well as men. The young and the old experience more health disparities compared to any other age group. Individuals living in central cities and rural areas do not do as well as individuals living in urban areas and suburbs. Health care inequality is reflected in access to care, treatment and quality of care received, and health outcomes.

While Medicare and Medicaid have increased access to care for the poor and minorities, these programs have not erased disparities in health care access, the quality of care received, or health status/outcomes. Health care providers, individual or institutional, provide different care to minorities than they do to whites (Watson 2001). Health inequalities in the United States continue to be strongly linked to race and income. The homicide rate for blacks is six times and the AIDS death rate five times higher than for whites (Mitchell 1997). Black infant mortality is nearly twice as high as white infant mortality. Overall in the United States, mortality rates are 52 percent higher for blacks than for whites (Whiteis 2000). The death rate for Hispanics is 53 percent higher than for non-Hispanic whites (Mitchell 1997).

Minority Americans have significantly higher rates of cancer, strokes, heart disease, AIDS, diabetes, and other health problems. Minorities have fewer doctor visits and receive less primary care. Also, uninsured blacks and Hispanics are less likely than whites to have private physicians (Watson 2001). Hispanics and American Indians are less likely than whites to receive cardiac bypass surgery and angioplasty (Watson 2001). AIDS fatalities are disproportionately high among Hispanics and African Americans (Nemecek 1999).

According to the National Congress of American Indians, Indian reservations have a 26 percent poverty rate and a disproportionately high unemployment rate. Moreover, their health, income, and education statistics are among the worst in the nation (National Congress of American Indians n.d.).

A report by the American Lung Association showed that African Americans are more likely to develop and to die of lung cancer while Hispanics have the highest death rate from the respiratory disease (Ozols 2005). Black patients in Medicare managed-care plans receive worse care than white patients (Schneider, Zaslavsky, and Epstein 2002). Black patients also receive fewer interventional cardiac procedures than whites in health care plans that provide similar benefit packages (Petersen, Wright, and Peterson 2002). Also, blacks, Hispanics, and those who speak limited English are less likely than whites to be screened, diagnosed, and appropriately treated for diseases such as breast cancer (Thomas 2005).

One thing is clear from the proliferation of studies and reports on racial and ethnic differences in access to and use of health services—race makes a difference. Minority groups experience a substantial disadvantage when it comes to patterns of health services use and health outcomes (Lew and Weinick 2000).

Women continue to suffer inequalities in the workplace and the labor market in America. Women fill low paying and traditional jobs in the labor market such as preschool and kindergarten teachers, secretaries and administrative assistants, receptionists, and nurses, among others. Women's earnings in 2002 were only 77.9 percent of men's (Sieber 2005). Women are more likely to develop depression and anxiety disorders compared to men and women's bodies have become the battleground of religious and ideological warfare between supporters and opponents of abortion (Sieber 2005). High costs are increasingly acting as a barrier to health care for many women, and women who are sick face more obstacles than men in obtaining health care (Salganicoff and Wyn 2005). Based on an analysis of data from the National Registry of Myocardial Infarction, a recent study found significant sex and racial differences for rates of reperfusion therapy, use of aspirin, use of beta-blockers, and coronary angiography (Vaccarino et al. 2005). White women are more likely to get breast cancer, and women of color, in particular black women, are more likely to die from it, most likely due to later detection (Thomas 2005). There are some very notable differences in health status between white women and women of color. Women of color are more likely to report that they are in fair to poor health. One-fifth of African-American women and 29 percent of Hispanic women assess their own health status as fair or poor compared to 13 percent of white women. Incidences of chronic illnesses also vary for women by race and ethnicity (Henry J. Kaiser Family Foundation 2004).

One of the major problems confronting the U.S. health care system is the large number of uninsured people. A study that used data from the Centers for Disease Control and Prevention's 2003 Behavior Risk Surveillance System found that more than 20 million working adults lacked health insurance ("Uninsured Working Adults" 2005). In early 2004, 16.8 percent of the U.S. noninstitutionalized population (around 48.3 million individuals) were uninsured (Rhoades 2005a). Minorities are substantially more likely than whites to lack health insurance. For example, among people under age sixty-five, 36.2 percent of Hispanics or Latinos and 21.9 percent of blacks lacked health insurance compared to 14.5 percent of white non-Hispanics (Rhoades 2005a). In 2004, 11.7 percent (8.5 million) of children under the age of eighteen were uninsured. Between 1996 through 2004 Hispanic or Latino children were more likely than children of any other racial/ethnic groups to be uninsured. In 2004, 21.8 percent of Hispanic or Latino children and 10.5 percent of black and 8.4 percent of whites were uninsured (Rhoades 2005b).

Individuals without health insurance are less likely to have regular access to health care and are more likely to suffer from health problems. Minorities typically have less access and use health services less (Ozols 2005).

A report by the U.S. Department of Health and Human Services (DHHS) (1985) Task Force on Black and Minority Health in 1985 had raised national awareness of about 60,000 excess deaths resulting from health disparities, especially among African Americans. The issue of racial/ethnic disparities in health received a great deal of attention when, in 1999, the Henry J. Kaiser Family Foundation (1999) released the first edition of *Key Facts: Race, Ethnicity, and Medical Care*. The U.S. Department of Health and Human Services (2000) report, *Healthy People 2010: Understanding and Improving Health*, included eliminating health disparities as one of the major goals of the nation's public health agenda.

The Healthcare Research and Quality Act of 1999 assigned the Agency for Healthcare Research and Quality (AHRQ) of the U.S. DHHS the task of supporting the improvement in quality of care by developing annual reports to the nation regarding health quality and disparities (Poker, Hubbard, and Collins 2004). It directed the AHRQ to produce two annual reports for Congress: (1) the National Health Care Quality Report (NHQR), and (2) the National Healthcare Disparities Report (NHDR). The NHDR tracks racial, ethnic, and socioeconomic disparities in care across rural, urban, and inner-city areas and among people of low income, women, children, and others. The AHRQ commissioned the Institute of Medicine (IOM) to produce two separate versions for each of these reports (Poker, Hubbard, and Collins 2004).

After the study committee of the Institute of Medicine reviewed more than a hundred studies that assessed the quality of care for racial and ethnic minority groups, it issued its report, *Unequal Treatment: Confronting Racial/Ethnic Disparities in Healthcare* (Smedley, Stith, and Nelson 2002). The report found many racial/ethnic health disparities, and more importantly, it argued that such disparities were associated with worse health outcomes. The report also argued that racial/ethnic disparities in health care occurred in the broader context of social and economic inequality. The report further suggested that the health care system, health care providers, patients' mistrust, utilization managers' bias, stereotyping, and prejudice may contribute to racial/ethnic health care disparities. The report made a series of recommendations to address the problem of racial/ethnic disparities. Some of the major recommendations include the following: (1) collect and report health care access and utilization data by patient's race/ethnicity, (2) encourage use of evidence-based guidelines and quality improvement, (3) support the use of language interpretation services in clinical setting, (4) increase awareness of racial/ethnic disparities, (5) increase the number of under-represented minorities in the health care workforce, (6) include cross-cultural education in the training of health care professionals, and (7) conduct further research to identify sources of disparities.

The literature since the 1980s has also pointed out that racial/ethnic disparities occur not only in health but also in health care, that is, in the quality of care. Thus, for example, research has shown that minorities receive a lower quality of care when they are in the health care system even when controlling for social determinants and insurance status (Betancourt and Maina 2004). A report by the Applied Research Center and Northwest Federation of Community Organizations (2005) documented the persistent problems experienced by persons of color attempting to access health care services across the nation. The report describes the institutional and structural barriers that block access to quality care for persons of color. The report helped reinvigorate the debate over one of the greatest public health challenges confronting the country—how to close the gap in health inequalities. Its recommendations for closing the health disparity gap included (1) eliminating disparities in access to health insurance, (2) tracking racial disparities in health care provisions, (3) providing medical interpretation services for all clinical encounters, and (4) developing health care institutions that are more sensitive to different races.

Similarly, an issue brief by the Henry J. Kaiser Family Foundation (2005a) recommends expanding health coverage, improving the number and capacity of providers in under-served communities, increasing the knowledge base, and improving health care quality as a way of closing the racial/ethnic divide in health care. Other recommendations to reduce racial inequalities in health include implementing race-sensitive policies, recruiting more minority physicians, improving health outcomes for children, and addressing inequalities in medical care (Williams 2001).

The U.S. Department of Health and Human Services (DHHS) has launched a number of new initiatives/programs designed to address the problem of minority health disparities. Some of these initiatives include the following: It created a Council on Health Disparities to coordinate and unify the department's actions on disparity issues. The Consolidated Health Center Program is designed to create community health centers to deliver preventive and primary care to patients regardless of ability to pay. Health Disparity Collaboratives seek to close the disparity gap by making sure that patients receive evidence-based care. Other initiatives include the National Diabetes Education Program, the Diabetes Detection Initiative, Closing the Gap/Take a Loved One to the Doctor Day, Racial and Ethnic Approaches to Community Health, and the National Breast & Cervical Cancer Early Detection Program (NBCCEDP), among others (U.S. Department of Health and Human Services 2004).

According to Lurie (2001), the DHHS has adopted four main strategies in an effort to eliminate health inequalities. These include expanding access to care for low income and minority, populations, improving health care quality and health outcomes, developing intersectoral and preventive approaches at the community level, and creating a scientific knowledge base to better understand the relationship between socioeconomic status, race, prevention, and health. The State Children Health Insurance Program (SCHIP), started in 1998, and the Community Access Program, started in 2000, exemplify the first strategy. Under the second strategy, the Healthcare Financing Administration (now called the Centers for Medicare and Medicaid Services) began a program to examine and improve the quality of care for minority beneficiaries in Medicare. The Racial and Ethnic Approaches to Community Health (REACH) program led by Centers for Disease Control and Prevention (CDC) is an example of the third strategy. This program is designed to test best practical approaches to eliminating health disparities at the community level. Under the fourth strategy, the Minority Health and Health Disparities Research and Education Act of 2000 created the National Center on Minority Health and Health Disparities at the National Institutes of Health. Furthermore, the Agency for Healthcare Research and Quality (AHRQ) established eight Centers of Excellence in minority health (Lurie 2001; Hofrichter 2003).

Despite all these initiatives, very limited progress has been made in closing the gap in health care disparity. The Agency for Healthcare Quality Research (2004) in its 2004 *National Healthcare Disparities Report* concluded that disparities are pervasive in the United States. According to the report, African Americans received poorer quality of care than whites for about two-thirds of quality measures and had worse access to care than whites for about 40 percent of access measures in the study. For Hispanics, the quality of care was lower for about half of quality measures and 90 percent of access measures.

Other studies have also reported very little progress. One study examined data for nine surgical procedures for men and women enrolled in Medicare from 1992 to 2001. The study concluded that the difference between the rates among whites and blacks increased significantly for five of the nine procedures, remained unchanged for three procedures, and narrowed significantly for one procedure. The authors of the study concluded that for the decade of the 1990s, they found no evidence that efforts to eliminate racial disparities nationally or locally were successful (Jha et al. 2005). Another study that measured quality of care for elderly Medicare beneficiaries in managed-care plans found that during the seven-year study period (1997–2003), clinical performance improved on all measures for both white and black enrollees. Racial disparities declined for most, but not for all Health Plan Employer Data and Information Set (HEDIS) measures the authors studied (Trivedi et al. 2005). Some recent evidence also suggests that the so-called treatment gap for women with heart disease, that is, the tendency for doctors to treat women less aggressively than men, may be narrowing (O'Neil 2005).

Thus, it is clear that health inequality remains a major public health challenge facing the United States ("Disparities Remain a Major Public Health Challenge" 2005). In January 2005, thirty private and state medical groups announced an initiative aimed at stemming a widespread shortfall in medical care received by racial minorities. It promised to begin a nationwide educational campaign to increase cultural sensitivity in doctors' offices, hospitals, and medical schools (Zwillich 2005).

The Relationship between Socioeconomic Status and Health Inequality

There has been a significant amount of research that has explored the relationship between socioeconomic inequality and health. A great deal of research has focused on examining the determinants of population health by asking why some societies are healthier than others. Such analyses deal with aggregate national level data to figure out what factors affect population health. Such a broad view of the determinants of health has led many scholars to examine health inequalities between and among different societies. For example, Wilkinson (1996), in his book *Unhealthy Societies*, using examples from the United States, Britain, Japan, and Eastern Europe, argues that healthy, egalitarian societies are more socially cohesive, with stronger community life, and they suffer from fewer of the corrosive effects of inequality because in such societies the public arena provides a supportive social network rather than stress and potential conflicts. In such societies, individualism and values of the free market are restrained by a social morality. Research in different countries has shown a correlation between life expectancy and various measures of social status—income, education, occupation, and residence (Wilkinson 1992). In other words, health status is correlated with socioeconomic status (Evans 1994).

Several other studies have made the claim that income inequality is an important determinant of a population's health. This claim is supported by evidence that repeatedly shows a statistically significant relationship between income inequality and aggregate measures of health across different countries (Waldman 1992; Wilkinson 1992; Wilkinson 1996). Andrain (1998) has argued that healthy societies have higher income equality and as the national income gap widens, health inequality increases. Daniels, Kennedy, and Kawachi (2000a) have argued that wealthy countries with more equal income distribution have higher life expectancies. They have also argued that the health of the population is affected not just by the size of the economic pie but how the pie is shared. Others have argued that policies that produce high levels of income inequality are also associated with systematic under-investment in human, physical, social, and a health infrastructure (Kaplan and Lynch 2001). Thus, many scholars consider income inequality to be a major public health problem (Kawachi and Kennedy 1997; Kennedy et al. 1998). This has led Daniels and Kawachi (2000), and Daniels (2002) to argue that we should view health inequalities that derive from social determinants as unjust and that justice requires flattening socioeconomic inequality.

However, the findings demonstrating a repeated association between income inequality and aggregate health outcomes across countries and in the United States have been challenged by many scholars. Critics argue that such studies imply causation when the only thing scholars have demonstrated is a statistically significant association (i.e., connection) between income inequality and aggregate measures of health. Furthermore, they charge that most of these studies examine only a single cross section of data and employ none to few control variables. Mellor and Milyo (2001) argue that the "income inequality hypothesis" is not well supported by evidence. They assert that the evidence of an association between inequality and health is more limited and mixed. However, they concede that they themselves could not prove that there is no causal relationship between inequality and health.

After reviewing ninety-eight aggregate and multilevel studies examining the association between income inequality and health, Lynch et al. (2004a) conclude that overall there seems to be little support for the idea that income inequality is a major, generalizable determinant of population health. In fact, the authors conclude that the evidence suggests that income inequality is not associated with population health differences, at least among wealthy nations. However, the authors (Lynch et al. 2004a) concede that in aggregate-level U.S. studies, there appears to be a robust association between income inequality across states and metropolitan areas and a variety of health outcomes, especially when measured at the state level. The link between income inequality and population health is strongest within the United States based on evidence from cross-sectional studies.

Lynch et al. (2004b) further concede that the largely negative finding for the direct health effects of income inequality does not in any way contradict the ample evidence that suggests that at the individual level people with higher income also are healthier. Income inequality is a characteristic of a social system and as such determinants of income inequality are different from those of individual income, which is a characteristic of an individual person. Individual income is partly determined by a person's education, skills, and other factors, while income inequality at a societal level is determined by history, politics, and economics (Lynch et al. 2004a).

Thus, it is important to remember that looking at health from the standpoint of society rather than of the individual can lead to a very different view of the determinants of health. For example, a great deal of research that looks at health from the standpoint of society, as discussed above, has focused on the relationship between income inequality in society and its relationship to societal or population health. Looking at health from the standpoint of the individual leads one to examine relationships between factors such as individual income, education, genetics, and lifestyle and health. Researchers often use income, education, and occupational status as the main attributes of person's socioeconomic status (Williams and Jackson 2005).

Andrain (1998) has argued that individuals who rank low in the social stratification system are more likely to experience illness than those who rank high. Individuals who live unhealthy lifestyles that include things such as smoking, alcohol abuse, and lack of exercise and good nutrition are more likely to suffer from illness. Unemployed people are generally poor and they are more likely to live in an overcrowded, unsanitary environment. Favorable genes can help lengthen life expectancy when they interact with health-inducing behaviors (Andrain 1998).

Other scholars have argued that both income and education appear to be important determinants of individual health (Wilkinson 1996). Researchers have found that education and income are directly related to health status because education produces several lifetime advantages such as greater social and psychological resources. Thus, well-educated persons are more likely to engage in positive health behaviors. However, researchers generally have not attempted to differentiate the effects of education from the effects of income on health status (Budrys 2003).

Overall, a great deal of research has tended to focus on the relationship between individual income and health status.

Ethnic stratification also shapes health through its close relationship with socioeconomic status. Overall, ethnic minorities and migrant workers generally experience low socioeconomic status in American society. They generally achieve less formal education, earn lower wages, occupy less prestigious jobs, work in more unsafe occupations, face higher unemployment, and live in overcrowded and damp housing. They also experience poor health, suffer from frequent disabilities, have difficulty securing prenatal care, and have high infant mortality rates (Andrain 1998). Poverty also afflicts female headed families, many children, the elderly on fixed income, and individuals living in central cities and rural areas; they also experience more health problems.

In the past, biology was seen as the source of racial differences in health. However, scientific evidence clearly shows that racial categories do not capture differences in health. Racial categories are more alike than different in terms of genetics (Williams 2001). However, race is often a crude indicator of differences in economic circumstances. Social class may offer a far better explanation for variation in health than race. In fact, socioeconomic status is a strong predictor of individual health. The distribution of wealth in the United States is extremely unequal, with the top 1 percent owning about 40 percent of the marketable wealth. The United States is one of the most economically unequal countries in the world (Budrys 2003). Kawachi, Daniels, and Robinson (2005) argue that both class and race matter in explaining health care disparities and both should be addressed simultaneously if we are to succeed in reducing health disparities.

There is no question that poor people experience poorer health and higher mortality that the non-poor. Wilkinson's (1996) analysis of American data covering some 300,000 white men in the Multiple Risk Factor Intervention Trial (MRFIT) demonstrated that death rates are related to the average household incomes of the U.S. ZIP code areas in which they live. With regularity, death rates decline with increasing income (Budrys 2003). Analysis of geocoded public health surveillance data including events from birth to death linked to 1990 census tract poverty data for Massachusetts and Rhode Island showed that for virtually all outcomes, risk increased with census tract poverty, that is, increased risk is associated with living in increasingly poor census tracts (Krieger et al. 2005).

Analysis by Williams (2001) revealed a clear relationship between socioeconomic status and health status for both racial groups—whites and blacks. There is an inverse relationship between income and heart disease for both blacks and whites. That is, among both blacks and whites, persons of lower income have higher rates of heart disease. Similarly, socioeconomic status is responsible for much of the racial differences in health. Furthermore, racial differences in heart disease persist at every socioeconomic level (Williams 2001). Death rates from heart disease are two to three times higher among low-income blacks and whites compared to their middle-income peers. In addition, for both males and females at every income level, blacks have higher coronary heart disease death rates than whites (Williams and Jackson 2005). Other studies have suggested that women with low income residing in metropolitan areas are less likely to be screened for breast cancer than more affluent women residing in the same area. A study by the Centers for Disease Control and Prevention (CDC) that analyzed the percentage of women who had a mammogram by using individual data—household income and education level—found that among women in thirty-five statistical metropolitan areas (SMAs), those with annual income of less than $15,000 were less likely to have had a mammogram than more affluent women. Similarly, those without high school education were less likely to have had a mammogram than women with more education ("Breast Cancer Screening" 2005).

A large body of evidence now supports the possibility that ethnic inequalities in health are largely a consequence of socioeconomic differentials or at least the proposition that inequalities in socioeconomic position are related to ethnic inequalities in health (Nazroo 2003). Yet, the role that socioeconomic position may play in explaining health care inequalities still remains a subject of considerable debate. Some claim that socioeconomic inequalities make a minimum or no contribution to ethnic inequalities in health (Wild and McKeigue 1998).

Another study that included individual family income and county-level poverty rates to assess whether documented effects of income inequality on health are consistent across demographic subgroups of the U.S. population concluded that conditional effects of inequality were restricted to certain subgroups. The study found that African Americans are likely to be most affected by the geographic manifestations of income inequality (LeClere and Soobader 2000).

Critics charge that statistical artifacts have often been mistaken for real effects. Others have suggested that the correlation between inequality and health is, in fact, not causal but spurious. In other words, third factors/variables such as habits, limited opportunities, risky behavior, schooling, and the like may lead to poorer health (Fuchs 1993; Eberstadt and Satel 2004).

The Politics of Health Care Inequality

As the above discussion has illustrated, most explanations of health care inequalities/ disparities center on income inequality at the aggregate level (national, state, or local) or socioeconomic status, that is, income/wealth and education at the individual level. Other explanations have tended to focus on the role that genetics, environment, culture, race, gender, age, and lifestyle habits and behavior play in producing health care inequalities. Most discussion of health and health inequalities, whether in the scholarly literature or the media, has tended to ignore or rarely touch on political conflicts and the politics of health policy making that may produce health care inequalities.

As Starr (1993, 23) has argued, the politics of a health system that is 90 percent public and 10 percent private is very different from a health system that is 90 percent private and 10 percent public. The first can be called a "broad-based, two-tier coverage" while the second can be called a "narrow-based, two-tier coverage." He further suggests that the main danger of a two-tier system is the segregation of the poor in a lower tier or base that over time may become inferior. Such deterioration is more likely if the lower tier is largely serving the poor through public sector programs because the middle class who are served by the private sector insurance coverage will resent paying the taxes to support the base and will insist that the public sector offer the minimum to the poor. In contrast, if middle-class voters are getting their health insurance through the public system, they are more likely to be generous and not begrudge the poor getting equal access to that system. The U.S. health care system comes closer to a "broad-based, two-tier system" in which a large majority of individuals receive health insurance coverage through the private sector while the public sector programs such as Medicaid and Medicare provide health insurance coverage to the eligible poor. Nonetheless, millions of people still slip through the cracks and have no or partial health insurance coverage during any given year. The failure to reform the U.S. health care system to provide universal health insurance coverage can be attributed to fundamental political ideological differences between liberals and conservatives about the role of the public and private sector in health care (Patel and Rushefsky 1998).

Furthermore, even though, historically, major advances in health status have come about as a result of public health initiatives such as improved sanitation, safe food, improvements in living and working conditions, and the like, the United States fails to invest adequately in public health (Patel and Rushefsky 2005). Similarly, the United States spends very little on primary care and the American health care system is not centered around primary care infrastructure. This is despite the fact that evidence suggests that the health care systems organized around strong primary care infrastructure enhance health equity more effectively and efficiently (Starfield 2004). Again, politics and political power have a lot to do with this.

The part that power, politics, ideology, and conflicts play in influencing health policy making and creating inequalities has not received a great deal of attention. At times, independent of individual behavior, the characteristics of the political system structure the possibilities for health and illness. Hierarchical structures of power and inequality based on race and gender can influence life chances and opportunities. For example, racial and gender discrimination can play a role in creating health care inequalities (Hofrichter 2003). Political power is also related to political participation. Policy makers are more likely to listen to and respond to those who vote or contribute financially to a campaign than to those who do not. Individuals of low socioeconomic status are less likely to vote and make financial contributions to a campaign and thus their voice is often more likely to be ignored.

The Plan of This Book

The purpose of this book is fourfold: (1) to examine the problem of health care inequality in the American health care system based on race, ethnicity, gender, age, and geographic location; thus, the purpose of the book is broader than just examining health care disparities based on race and ethnicity; (2) to analyze factors associated with health care inequalities with respect to access, quality of care, and health outcomes; (3) to examine efforts made and initiatives undertaken to reduce health care disparities; (4) to analyze reasons for successes and failures in reducing health care disparities.

The book's focus is on examining health care inequality within the American society at the individual and group level. The book does not focus on relationships between economic inequality and health inequality at a macro level across countries. Chapters 2, 3, and 4 examine inequalities experienced by African Americans, Hispanics, and American Indians and Alaska Natives in the American health care system. Chapter 5 looks at health care inequalities based on gender. Chapters 6 and 7 explore health care inequalities related to age—children and the elderly, respectively. Chapter 8 examines health care inequalities related to geographic location, with emphasis on central cities and rural areas. Chapter 9 provides a summary and some concluding thoughts about inequalities in the American health care system.

Each chapter examines the issue of health care inequalities from the perspective of the four purposes outlined above.

References

ABC News/Lifetime Television Poll. 1999. Online at www.PollingReport.com/Race.htm. Accessed on 9/17/2005.

ABC News Poll. 2005. Online at www.PollingReport.com/Race.htm. Accessed on 9/17/2005.

ABC News/Washington Post Poll. 2005. Online at www.PollingReport.com/disasters.htm. Accessed on 9/17/2005.

Agency for Healthcare Quality and Research. 2004. National Healthcare Disparities Report 2004. Rockville, MD: U.S. Department of Health and Human Services. Publication Number 05–0014.

Alter, Jonathan. 2005. "The Other America: An Enduring Shame." Time, September 19: 42–48.

American Political Science Association. 2004. American Democracy in an Age of Rising Inequality. Report by the Task Force on Inequality and American Democracy. Online at www.apsanet.org/section_256.cfm. Accessed on 9/16/2005.

Andrain, Charles F. 1998. Public Health Policies and Social Inequality. New York: New York University Press.

Applied Research Center and Northwest Federation of Community Organizations. 2005. Closing the Gap: Solutions to Race-Based Health Disparities. Online at www.arc.org/Pages/pubs/closinggap.html. Accessed on 7/21/2005.

Betancourt, Joseph R., and Angela W. Maina. 2004. "The Institute of Medicine Report 'Unequal Treatment' Implications for Academic Health Centers." Mount Sinai Journal of Medicine 71, no. 5 (October): 314–21.

"Breast Cancer Screening and Socioeconomic Status—35 Metropolitan Areas, 2000 and 2002." 2005. Morbidity and Mortality Weekly 54, no. 39 (October 7): 981–85.

Budrys, Grace. 2003. *Unequal Health: How Inequality Contributes to Health and Illness.* New York: Rowman & Littlefield.

CNN/Gallup/*USA Today* Poll. 2000. Online at www.PollingReport.com/race.htm. Accessed on 9/17/2005.

Current, Richard N. Ed. 1967. *The Political Thoughts of Abraham Lincoln.* Indianapolis: Bobbs-Merrill.

Daniels, Norman. 2002. "Justice, Health, and Health Care." In Rhodes Rosamond, Margaret P. Battin, and Anita. Silvers, eds., *Medicine and Social Justice: Essays on the Distribution of Health Care,* 6–23. New York: Oxford University Press.

Daniels, Norman; Bruce Kennedy; and Ichiro Kawachi. 2000a. *Is Inequality Bad for Our Health?* Boston: Beacon Press.

Daniels, Norman; Bruce Kennedy; and Ichiro Kawachi. 2000b. "Justice Is Good for Our Health: How Greater Economic Equality Would Promote Public Health." *Boston Review.* Online at bostonreview.net/BR25.1/daniels.html. Accessed on 10/15/2005.

"Disparities Remain a Major Public Health Challenge." 2005. *Nation's Health* 35, no. 3 (April): 6.

Douglass, Frederick. 1962. *The Life and Times of Frederick Douglass.* New York: McMillan.

Eberstadt, Nicholas, and Sally Satel. 2004. "Health, Inequality and the Scholars." *Public Interest* no. 157 (Fall): 100–118.

Editorial. 2004. "Inequality in Health Care: Unjust, Inhumane, and Unattended." *Annals of Internal Medicine* 141, no. 10 (November): 815–17.

Evans, Robert. G. 1994. "Introduction." In Robert G. Evans, Morris L. Barer, and Theodore R. Marmor, eds., *Why Are Some People Healthy and Others Not? The Determinants of Health of Populations,* 3–26. New York: Aldine De Gruyter.

Fuchs, Victor R. 1993. "Poverty and Health: Asking the Right Questions." In David E. Rogers and Eli Ginzberg, eds., *Medical Care and the Health of the Poor,* 9–20. Boulder, CO: Westview.

Gallup Poll. 2003. Online at www.PollingReport.com/Race.htm. Accessed on 9/17/2005.

Geismar, Maxwell. 1970. "The Shifting Illusion." In David Madden, ed., *American Dreams, American Nightmares,* 9–20. Carbondale: Southern Illinois University Press.

Goldsmith, William W., and Edward J. Blakely. 1992. *Separate Societies: Poverty and Inequality in U.S. Cities.* Philadelphia: Temple University Press.

Goodheart, Adam. 2005. "Setting Them Free." *New York Times Book Review,* August 7: 1, 10–11.

Halstead, Ted. 2003. "The American Paradox." *Atlantic Monthly* 291, no. 1 (January): 123–25.

Harrington, Michael. 1971. *The Other America: Poverty in the United States.* Baltimore: Penguin Books.

Harrington, Michael. 1983. *The New American Poverty.* New York: Holt, Rinehart, and Winston.

Henry J. Kaiser Family Foundation. 1999. *Key Facts: Race, Ethnicity & Medical Care.* Washington, D.C.: Henry J. Kaiser Family Foundation.

Henry J. Kaiser Family Foundation. 2004. *Issue Brief: Racial and Ethnic Disparities in Women's Health Coverage and Access to Care Findings from the 2001 Kaiser Women's Health Survey.* March. Online at www.kff.org/womenshealth/7018.cfm. Accessed on 10/3/2005.

Henry J. Kaiser Family Foundation. 2005a. *Policy Challenges and Opportunities in Closing the Racial/Ethnic Divide in Health Care.* Online at www.kff.org/minorityhealth/index. cfm. Accessed on 7/21/2005.

Henry J. Kaiser Family Foundation. 2005b. *Survey of Hurricane Katrina Evacuees.* September. Online at www.kff.org. Accessed on 9/16/2005.

Hofrichter, Richard. 2003. "The Politics of Health Inequities." In Richard Hofrichter, ed., *Health and Social Justice: Politics, Ideology, and Inequity in the Distribution of Disease,* 1–56. San Francisco: John Wiley & Sons.

Hudson, Blaine J. 1995. "Simple Justice: Affirmative Action and American Racism in Historical Perspective." *Black Scholar* 25, no 3 (Summer): 16–23.

Jacobs, Lawrence R., and Robert Y. Shapiro. 1998. "The Politicization of Public Opinion: The Fight for the Pulpit." In Margaret Weir, ed., *The Social Divide: Political Parties and the Future of Activist Government,* 83–125. Washington, D.C.: Brookings Institution Press.

Jha, Ashish K.; Elliot S. Fisher; Zhonghe Li; E. John Oray; and Arnold M. Epstein. 2005. "Racial Trends in the Use of Major Procedures among Elderly." *New England Journal of Medicine* 353, no. 7 (August 18): 683–91.

Johannsen, Robert W. Ed. 1965. *The Lincoln-Douglas Debates of 1858.* New York: Oxford University Press.

Kaplan, George A., and John W. Lynch. 2001. "Is Economic Policy Health Policy?" *American Journal of Public Health* 91, no. 3 (March): 351–53.

Kasarda, J.D. 1993. "Inner-City Concentrated Poverty and Neighborhood Distress: 1970 to 1990." *Housing Policy Debate* 4, no. 3: 253–302.

Kawachi, Ichiro, and Bruce P. Kennedy. 1997. "Health and Social Cohesion: Why Care About Income Inequality?" *British Medical Journal* 314, no. 7086 (April 5): 1037–40.

Kawachi, Ichiro; Norman Daniels; and Dean E. Robinson. 2005. "Health Disparities by Race and Class: Why Both Matter." *Health Affairs* 24, no. 2 (March–April): 343–52.

Kennedy, Bruce P., and Ichiro Kawachi. 2001. "How Income Inequality Affects Health: Evidence from Research in the United States." *Report–National Policy Association,* no. 299: 16–28.

Kennedy, Bruce P.; Ichiro Kawachi; R. Glass; and D. Prothrow. 1998. "Income Distribution, Socioeconomic Status, and Self-Rated Health in the United States." *British Medical Journal* 317, no. 7163 (October 3): 917–21.

Kennedy, Edward M. 2005. "Perspective: The Role of the Federal Government in Eliminating Health Disparities." *Health Affairs* 24, no. 2 (March–April): 452–58.

King, Martin Luther, Jr. 1983. "I Have a Dream." American Rhetoric: Top 100 Speeches. Online at www.americanrhetoric.com/speeches/mlkihaveadream.htm. Accessed on 5/15/2005.

Kluegel, James R., and Eliot R. Smith. 1986. *Beliefs about Inequality: Americans' Views of What Is and What Ought To Be.* New York: Aldine De Gruyter.

Krieger, Nancy; Jarvis T. Chen; Pamela D. Waterman; David H. Rehkopf; and S.V. Subramanian. 2005. "Painting a Truer Picture of US Socioeconomic and Racial/Ethnic Health Inequalities: The Public Health Disparities Geocoding Project." *American Journal of Public Health* 95, no. 2 (February): 312–23.

Lake, Snell, Perry & Associates, Inc. 2003. "Americans Speak Out on Disparities in Health Care." Online at www/phsi.harvard.edu/health_reform/Poll_media_report_disparities.pdf.

LeClere, Felicia B., and Mah-Jabeen Soobader. 2000. "The Effects of Inequality on the Health of Selected US Demographic Groups." *American Journal of Public Health* 90, no. 12 (December): 1891–97.

Lew, Nancy D., and Robin M. Weinick. 2000. "An Overview: Eliminating Racial, Ethnic, and SES Disparities in Health Care." *Health Care Financing Review* 21, no. 4 (Summer): 1–7.

Lipscomb, Andrew A. Editor-in-chief. 1903–1904. *The Writings of Thomas Jefferson.* Washington, D.C.: Thomas Jefferson Memorial Association, Monticello Edition.

Lurie, Nicole. 2001. "Eliminating Inequalities in the U.S. Health Care System: Efforts of the U.S. Department of Health and Human Services." In James A. Auerbach and Barbara K. Krimgold, eds., *Income, Socioeconomic Status and Health: Exploring the Relationships,* 91–100. Washington, D.C.: National Policy Association.

Lynch, John; George D. Smith; Sam Harper; and Marianne Hillemeier. 2004a. "Is Income Inequality a Determinant of Population Health? Part 2. U.S. National and Regional Trends in Income Inequality and Age- and Cause-Specific Mortality." *Milbank Quarterly* 82, no. 2 (June): 355–400.

Lynch, John; George D. Smith; Sam Harper; Marianne Hillemeier; Nancy Ross; George A. Kaplan, and Michael Wolfson. 2004b. "Is Income Inequality a Determinant of Population Health? Part 1. A Systematic Review." *Milbank Quarterly* 82, no. 1 (March): 5–99.

Manley, John F. 1990. "American Liberalism and the Democratic Dream: Transcending the American Dream." *Policy Studies Review* 10, no. 1 (Fall): 89–102.

Manning, Anita. 2005. "New Orleans' Health Care Might Never Be the Same." *USA Today,* September 19. Online at www.usatoday.com. Accessed on 9/19/2005.

Mellor, J. M., and J. Milyo. 2001. "Reexamining the Evidence of an Ecological Association Between Income Inequality and Health." *Journal of Health Politics, Policy and Law* 26, no. 3 (June): 487–522.

Mitchell, Peter. 1997. "US Health Care Continues to Fail the Poor and the Non-White Races." *Lancet* 350, no. 9075 (August 9): 420.

Morin, Richard, and Lisa Rein. 2005. "Some of the Uprooted Won't Go Home Again." *Washington Post,* September 16. Online at www.washingtonpost.com. Accessed on 9/16/2005.

Mourey, Risa L.; William C. Richardson; Robert K. Ross; and John W. Rowe. 2005. "Foreword: A Tale of Two Cities." *Health Affairs* 24, no. 2 (March–April): 313–15.

Murray, Mark. 2005. "Bush Approval at Lowest Level of His Presidency." NBC News, September 14. Online at www.msnbc.msn.com. Accessed on 9/19/2005.

National Congress of American Indians. n.d. "Community Development, Economic Development." Online at www.ncai.org. Accessed on 9/29/2005.

Nazroo, James V. 2003. "The Structuring of Ethnic Inequalities in Health: Economic Position, Racial Discrimination, and Racism." *American Journal of Public Health* 93, no. 2 (February): 277–284.

Nemecek, Sasha. 1999. "Unequal Health." *Scientific American* 280, no. 1 (January): 40–41.

O'Neil, John. 2005. "Disparities: A Small Step for Women's Hearts." *New York Times,* February 22.

Ozols, Jennifer B. 2005. "How Race Affects Your Health." *Newsweek,* web exclusive, February 3. Online at www.msnbc.msn.com/id/6907115/site/newsweek/. Accessed on 9/30/2005.

Page, Benjamin I., and Robert Y. Shapiro. 1992. *The Rational Public: Fifty Years of Trends in Americans' Policy Preferences.* Chicago: University of Chicago Press.

Page, Susan, and Maria Puente. 2005. "Polls Shows Racial Divide on Storm Response." *USA Today,* September 12.

Pappas, Gregory; Susan Queen; Wilbur Hadden; and Gail Fisher. 1993. "The Increasing Disparity in Mortality between Socioeconomic Groups in the United States, 1960 and 1986." *New England Journal of Medicine* 329, 2 (July 8): 103–9.

Patel, Kant, and Mark Rushefsky. 1998. *Politics, Power & Policy Making: The Case of Health Care Reform in the 1990s.* Armonk, NY: M.E. Sharpe.

Patel, Kant, and Mark Rushefsky. 2005. *The Politics of Public Health in the United States.* Armonk, NY: M.E. Sharpe.

Payne, January W. 2005. "At Risk Before the Storm: Prior Disparities Due to Race, Poverty Multiply Death, Disease." *Washington Post,* September 13. Online at www.washington post.com. Accessed on 9/14/2005.

Petersen, L.A.; S.M. Wright; and E.D. Peterson. 2002. "Impact of Race on Cardiac Care and Outcomes in Veterans with Acute Myocardial Infarction." *Medical Care* 40, no. 1 (Supplement):186–96.

Poker, Anna; Heddy Hubbard; and Beth A. Collins. 2004. "The First National Reports on United States Healthcare Quality and Disparities." *Journal of Nursing Care Quality* 19, no. 4 (October–December): 316–21.

"QuickStats: Percentage of Adults Aged > 18 Years Who Assessed Their Health as Excellent or Very Good, by Race—United States, 1999–2003." 2005. *Morbidity and Mortality Weekly Report* 54, no. 29 (July): 725.

Rhoades, Jeffrey A. 2005a. *The Uninsured in America, 2004: Estimates for the U.S. Civilian Noninstitutionalized Population Under Age 65.* Medical Expenditure Panel Survey, Statistical Brief # 83. Washington, D.C.: Agency for Health Care Research and Quality, Rockville, MD. Online at www.meps.ahrq.gov/papers/st83/stat83.pdf. Accessed on 8/22/2005.

Rhoades, Jeffrey A. 2005b. *Health Insurance Status of Children in America, 1996–2004: Estimates for the U.S. Civilian Noninstitutionalized Population Under Age 18.* Medical Expenditure Panel Survey, Statistical Brief # 85. Agency for Healthcare Research and Quality, Rockville, MD. Online at www.meps.ahrq.gov/papers/st85/stat85.pdf. Accessed on 8/22/2005.

Salganicoff, Alina, and Roberta Wyn. 2005. *Women and Health Care: A National Profile.* Washington, D.C.: Kaiser Family Foundation.

Schneider, Eric C.; Alan M. Zaslavsky; and Arnold M. Epstein. 2002. "Racial Disparities in the Quality of Care for Enrollees in Medicare Managed Care." *Journal of American Medical Association* 287, no. 10 (March 13): 1288–94.

Schwartz, Barry. 1996, "Rereading the Gettysburg Address: Social Change and Colllective Memory." *Qualitative Sociology* 19, no. 3: 395–422.

Sherman, A. 1997. *Rescuing the American Dream: Halting the Economic Freefall of Today's Young Families with Children.* Washington, D.C.: Children's Defense Fund.

Sieber, Sam D. 2005. *Second-Rate Nation: From the American Dream to the American Myth.* Boulder, CO: Paradigm.

Skocpol, Theda. 2004. "Voices of Inequality: The Transformation of American Civic Democracy." *Perspectives on Politics* 2, no. 1 (March): 3–20.

Smedley, Brian D.; Adrienne T. Stith; and Alan R. Nelson. Eds. 2002. *Unequal Treatment: Confronting Racial/Ethnic Disparities in Healthcare.* Washington, D.C.: National Academy Press.

Sochen, June. 1974. *Her Story: A Woman's View of American History.* New York: Alfred Publishing Company.

Starfield, Barbara. 2004. "Promoting Equity in Health Through Research and Understanding." *Developing World Bioethics* 4, no. 1 (May): 76–95.

Starr, Paul. 1993. "The Politics of Health Care Inequality." In David E. Rogers and Eli Ginzberg, eds., *Medical Care and the Health of the Poor,* 21–32. Boulder, CO: Westview.

Szabo, Liz. 2005. "Lawmakers Call for an End to Gaps in Health Care." *USA Today,* March 10.

Thomas, Kadesha M. 2005. "'Navigator' Guides Patients of Color." *Boston Globe,* August 22. Online at www.Boston.com. Accessed on 8/23/2005.

Tocqueville, Alexis de. 1961. *Democracy in America.* Volume 1. New York: Schocken Books.

Trivedi, Amal N.; Alan M. Zaslavsky; Erick C. Schneider; and John Z. Ayanian. 2005. "Trends in the Quality of Care and Racial Disparities in Medicare Managed Care." *New England Journal of Medicine* 353, no. 7 (August 18): 692–99.

"Uninsured Working Adults Face Barriers to Health Care." 2005. *Nation's Health* 35, no. 5 (June–July): 6.

U.S. Department of Health and Human Services. 1985. *Task Force on Black and Minority Health*. 8 vols. Washington, D.C.: U.S. Government Printing Office.

U.S. Department of Health and Human Services. 2000. *Healthy People 2010: Understanding and Improving Health*. 2nd ed. Washington, D.C.: U.S. Government Printing Office.

U.S. Department of Health and Human Services. 2004. "The Initiative to Eliminate Racial and Ethnic Disparities in Health: HHS Fact Sheet." Online at raceandhealth.hhs.gov. Accessed on 2/25/2005.

"US Health Care: A State Lottery?" 2004. Editorial. *Lancet* 364, no. 9448 (November 20): 1829–30.

Vaccarino, Viola; Saif S. Rathore; Nanette K. Wenger; Paul D. Frederick; Jerome L. Abramson; Hal V. Barron; Ajay Manhapra; Susmita Malik; and Harlan M. Krumholz. 2005. "Sex and Racial Differences in the Management of Acute Myocardial Infarction, 1994 through 2002." *New England Journal of Medicine* 353, no. 7 (August 18): 671–82.

Waldmann, Robert J. 1992. "Income Distribution and Infant Mortality." *Quarterly Journal of Economics* 107, no. 4 (November): 1283–1302.

Watson, Sidney D. 2001. "Race, Ethnicity and Quality of Care: Inequalities and Incentives." *American Journal of Law and Medicine* 26, no. 2/3: 203–24.

White, Ronald C., Jr. 2002. *Lincoln's Greatest Speech: The Second Inaugural*. New York: Simon and Schuster.

Whiteis, David G. 2000. "Poverty, Public Policy, and Pathogenesis: Economic Justice and Public Health in the US." *Critical Public Health* 10, no. 2 (June): 257–71.

Wild, Sarah, and Paul McKeigue. 1998. "Cross Sectional Analysis of Mortality by Country of Birth in England and Wales." *British Medical Journal* 314, no. 7082 (March 8): 705–10.

Wilkinson, Richard G. 1992. "Income Distribution and Life Expectancy." *British Medical Journal* 304, no. 6820 (January 18): 165–68.

Wilkinson, Richard G. 1996. *Unhealthy Societies: The Afflictions of Inequality*. New York: Routledge.

Williams, David R. 2001. "Race and Health: Trends and Policy Implications." In James A. Auerbach and Barbara K. Krimgold, eds., *Income, Socioeconomic Status and Health: Exploring the Relationship*, 67–85. Washington, D.C.: National Policy Association.

Williams, David R., and Pamela B. Jackson. 2005. "Social Sources of Racial Disparities in Health." *Health Affairs* 24, no. 2 (March–April): 325–34.

Zwillich, Todd. 2005. "New Fight for Racial Equality in Health Care." Online at my.webmd.com/content/article/100/105506.htm. Accessed on 6/23/2005.

2

African Americans and Health Care

Over the last twenty years a significant amount of literature has pointed to the health care inequality suffered by African Americans. African Americans comprise around 13 percent of the U.S. population but, as a group, their health status continues to lag behind that of whites (Kaiser Commission 2000). Despite some of the progress made in ensuring political equality for African Americans through post–Civil War amendments and the civil rights movement, African Americans have not shared equally in the progress made on the economic and health care fronts in American society. The gap in income between African Americans and the rest of the population has essentially remained the same since the 1960s, and 30 percent of African Americans lived below the poverty level in 1990 (Quaye 1994). This has led to the argument that the health care status of African Americans is a function of their marginal position in the U.S. health care system and a direct result of poverty and discrimination (Quaye 1994).

The idea that poor health status of African Americans is a direct result of poverty is often referred to as "culture of poverty" perspective. It argues that the state of African American health is the direct result of the disorganized nature of families that live isolated socially, politically, and economically from mainstream patterns and norms of behavior. Large numbers of African Americans live in communities populated by poor people and are characterized by long-term unemployment and long spells of endemic poverty (Wilson 1987). However, *The Healthy People 2000* report by the U.S. Department of Health and Human Services (1990) concluded that even if socioeconomic effects were set aside, disparities experienced by African Americans will still remain because the differences in survival and health between African Americans and whites are not solely explained by poverty but also by rather unique experiences and cultural orientations of African Americans. Still others have argued that regardless of which factors help explain existing disparities, the fact remains that disparity in access and health status experienced by African Americans is unfair and that the problems of African Americans are American society's problems as well (Dula and Goering 1994).

The former surgeon general David Satcher has called the poor state of African American health "a matter of life and death" (Valentine 2004). The National Association for the Advancement of Colored People (NAACP) as well as members of the Congressional Black Caucus have increasingly turned their attention to eliminating disparities and making sure that all Americans have access to care. Many people have come to view the fight for quality health care as today's civil rights battle (Valentine 2004). In recognition of this problem, Senators Orrin Hatch (R-UT) and Joe Lieberman (D-CT) in October 2005 introduced a bill, called FairCare, aimed at addressing shortcomings in health care for racial and ethnic minorities. The proposed bill would also have standardized data collection to make it easier to identify disparities in health care quality, offer incentives to health care providers to improve standards for all patients, and establish a system of grants to reduce health disparities ("Hatch, Lieberman Promote Minority Health Care" 2005). However, the Congress thus far has failed to act on the bill.

In this chapter we examine the problem of health care inequality suffered by African Americans. We first look at the disparity in health status/outcome, in access to health care, and quality of care for African Americans. Next, we examine explanatory factors that have been advanced to explain the current disparities. Finally, we provide some preliminary assessment of progress in reducing disparities.

Health Status/Outcomes

In 1999, the Congress of the United States requested the Institute of Medicine (IOM) to assess the extent of racial and ethnic disparities in health care. The IOM study committee reviewed more than one hundred studies that assessed the quality of health care for various racial and ethnic groups while holding constant variations in insurance status, patient income, and other access related factors. The IOM's report, *Unequal Treatment: Confronting Racial and Ethnic Disparities in Healthcare* (Smedley, Stith, and Nelson 2002), helped draw public attention to the existence of racial and ethnic disparities in health care.

According to former surgeon general David Satcher, almost 84,000 African Americans die each year because of unequal treatment (Limtanakool 2005). African Americans on average have higher mortality rates than whites. Between 1991 and 2000, age-adjusted mortality rates for white males and females were an average of 29 percent and 24 percent lower, respectively, than those for African Americans. As of 2000, the mortality rates for African American infants and adults aged twenty-five to fifty-four years was more than double that of whites ("Closing the Gap" 2005; Woolf et al. 2004). Despite the fact that significant reductions in death rates occurred between 1960 and 2000, the disparity between the higher mortality rates of blacks and lower mortality rates among whites has not changed appreciably (Satcher et al. 2005). A multilevel statistical analysis of Massachusetts' all-cause mortality rate from 1989 through 1991 found a significant neighborhood variation. Neighborhood variation in mortality was much greater for the black population than for the white population and was related to census tracts level variation in poverty rates (Subramanian et al. 2005).

For many health conditions, such as disease, injury, disability and death, African Americans bear a disproportionate burden (Centers for Disease Control and Prevention 2005). Infectious diseases, a major cause of mortality, morbidity, and disability in the United States, affect racial minorities disproportionately. An analysis of 2002 data from the Nationally Notifiable Diseases Surveillance System (NNDSS) revealed that for three of the six infectious deceases (chlamydia, gonorrhea, salmonellosis, Lyme disease, shigellosis, and giardiasis) and for eight of the forty-two nationally notifiable diseases, the incidence rates for blacks were at least twice as high as the rates for whites (Adekoya and Hopkins 2005). An analysis of National Health Interview Survey (NHIS) data from 2000–2001 showed that the prevalence of strokes was 2.3 percent among whites and 2.7 percent among blacks, and black stroke survivors had greater activity limitations than white stroke survivors (McGruder et al. 2005).

African Americans suffer higher rates of cancer, stroke, heart disease, HIV, and mental illness compared to whites, and racial disparities are also found in the utilization of specialists, care, preventive services, and a variety of surgical procedures (Ibrahim, Thomas, and Fine 2003). A study of 5,302 adult African Americans found that study participants had a high prevalence of diabetes, hypertension, obesity, and related disorders (Taylor et al. 2005). Black families are being destroyed by an epidemic of heart disease, diabetes, and HIV/AIDS, and African Americans admitted to hospitals receive less medical care than whites of the same age, gender, and sickness (Davis 2003). The top five leading causes of death for all African Americans are heart disease, cancer, cerebrovascular diseases (CVD), accidents, and diabetes. Among African Americans ages twenty-five to forty-four, the top five leading causes of death are HIV/AIDS, heart disease, accidents, cancer, and homicide (*Key Facts* 2003). A wide disparity exists between blacks and whites for three causes of death—homicide, heart disease, and cancer. The homicide rate for African Americans in 2000 was about six times higher than it was for whites.

In 2000, death rates from coronary heart disease for blacks were 30 percent higher than for whites (Williams and Jackson 2005). Racial disparities also persist in the treatment of heart disease. The chance of African Americans undergoing angioplasty and coronary bypass surgery for treatment of heart disease is about half that of whites (*Key Facts* 1999). A study of the management of acute myocardial infarction from 1994 to 2002 found that rates of reperfusion therapy, coronary angiography, and in-hospital death after myocardial infarction also varied by race and gender (Vaccarino et al. 2005). According to another study, an analysis of more than one million Medicare patients who were hospitalized for a heart attack between 1997 and 2001 revealed that death rate following a heart attack is increased significantly at hospitals that disproportionately serve black patients (Skinner et al. 2005). The study included 4,289 hospitals that were rated from one to ten based on the extent to which they treated black patients. Category 1 hospitals treated no black heart patients during the study period whereas in category 10 hospitals about one-third of all heart attack patients were black. The study found that the percentage of patients who die within ninety days after suffering a heart attack was significantly higher in category 10 hospitals compared to category 1 hospitals—23.7 percent versus 20.1 percent. The study further concluded that differences in mortality between category 1 and category 10 hospitals could not be explained by income, hospital ownership status, the volume of heart attacks treated at the hospitals, census region, or urban status (Skinner et al. 2005).

In 1950, blacks had lower cancer rates than whites but by the year 2000 the cancer rate for blacks was 30 percent higher than for whites (Williams and Jackson 2005). As a group, African American men have the highest proportion of current smokers and the lowest proportion of subjects who had never smoked. Among cigarette smokers, African Americans are more susceptible to lung cancer than whites, Japanese Americans, and Latinos (Haiman et al. 2006). Studies have also demonstrated racial disparities in advice given to patients from health care providers. For example, one study found that African Americans receive smoking counseling less frequently than whites (Houston et al. 2005). Another study that examined disparities in smoking cessation rates between African Americans and whites from 1990 through 2000 found that whites were significantly more likely than African Americans to be former smokers and the disparity in quit ratios persisted throughout the study period (King et al. 2004).

In 1992, rates of receipt of nine major high-cost surgical procedures for men and women enrolled in Medicare were higher for whites than blacks. A recent study examined data for the same nine surgical procedures (abdominal aortic aneurysm repair, back surgery, coronary-artery bypass grafting [CABG], percutaneous transluminal coronary angioplasty, cardiac valve replacement, carotid valve replacement, total hip replacement, total knee replacement, and appendectomy) for Medicare patients between 1992 and 2001 found that the difference between the rates among whites and blacks increased for five of the nine procedures, remained the same for three procedures, and narrowed significantly for one procedure. The major conclusion of the study was that for the decade of the 1990s there was no evidence, nationally or locally, that efforts to eliminate racial disparities in the use of high-cost surgical procedures were successful (Jha et al. 2005).

African Americans are almost twice as likely to be uninsured as whites. In 1999, 23 percent of African Americans compared to 14 percent of whites had no health insurance. In 2001, 20 percent of African Americans had no health insurance compared to 12 percent of whites. As a result, government programs such as Medicaid and Medicare have become an important source of health coverage for African Americans. In 1999, 39 percent of low-income (income below 200 percent of federal poverty level) African Americans had Medicaid coverage. By 2001, 41 percent of low income African Americans had Medicaid coverage. Similarly, African Americans are far more likely than whites to rely solely on the traditional Medicare program for insurance protection. For example, in 1999, 23 percent of

African American Medicare beneficiaries had no supplemental insurance coverage compared to only 10 percent of whites.

More African Americans than whites are likely to report problems in getting needed medical care and access to specialized care (*Key Facts* 1999; *Key Facts* 2003). More than half of the minority Medicare population is African American. Two-thirds of all white beneficiaries have Medigap or employer-sponsored retiree benefits compared to only a third of African Americans ("Medicare and Minority Americans" n.d.)

Another growing phenomenon in the United States since the late 1970s is the number of young African Americans who self-destruct. For example, among blacks between the ages of fifteen to nineteen, the rate of suicide had more than doubled since the 1980s. The rate of suicide increased from 3.6 in 1980 to 8.1 deaths per 100,000 in 1996. The suicide rate among black males increased from 7.9 per 100,000 in 1970 to 10.9 per 100,000 in 1997. The suicide rate for all blacks increased from 5.1 in 1970 to 6.2 in 1997 (Poussaint and Alexander 2000).

Ethnic and racial minorities live in a social and economic environment of inequality that includes greater exposure to racism, discrimination, violence, and poverty. People in the lowest strata of income, education, and occupation are more likely than those in the highest strata to experience mental illness. The legacy of slavery, racism, and discrimination significantly influences the social and economic standing of African Americans in particular. African Americans are over-represented in vulnerable, high-need populations. For example, the safety net providers furnish a disproportionate share of mental health care to African Americans. Yet, African Americans have less access to mental health services partly due to lack of health insurance. African Americans as a result are less likely than whites to receive treatment. For some disorders such as schizophrenia and mood disorders, errors in diagnosis are made more often for African Americans than for whites (U.S. Department of Health and Human Services 2001). According to another study, major depression and factors associated with depression are more frequent among members of minorities such as African Americans and Hispanics than among whites. Higher depression rates among minorities are typically associated with a greater health burden and lack of health insurance (Dunlop et al. 2003).

Diabetes, the sixth leading cause of death in the United States, is a major health problem for African Americans. Diabetes is also a major cause of amputations, blindness, and kidney disease in adults. It is also a major risk factor for heart disease and stroke (Yancey et al. 2005). Complications and death rates from diabetes are higher for African Americans than for whites. Individuals with diabetes are more susceptible to episodes of influenza. An analysis of data of 1,906 individuals with diabetes from the 1998 National Health Interview Survey (NHIS) revealed that whites had higher vaccination rates than did African Americans, and the disparity was independent of access to care, health care coverage, or socioeconomic status (SES) (Egede and Zheng 2003). Another study found prevalence of racial disparities for glucose control among patients with diabetes (Trivedi et al. 2005). Being overweight and/or obese and a lack of regular physical activity and a balanced diet (not eating fruits, vegetabless and whole grain foods) are linked to increased risk of developing diabetes. On average, African American adults and adolescents have higher rates of being overweight and lower rates of meeting physical activity and nutritional requirements (Yancey et al. 2005).

In the last twenty years, deaths due to HIV-AIDS have increased dramatically among African Americans(*Key Facts* 1999). HIV is the third leading cause of death for African Americans between the ages of twenty-five and forty-four ("HIV/AIDS Policy Fact Sheet: African Americans" 2006). The AIDS case rate per 10,000 population was 10.2 times greater for African American adults/adolescents than whites in 2004 ("HIV/AIDS Policy Fact Sheet: African Americans" 2006). African Americans accounted for 40 percent of all AIDS cases since the beginning of the epidemic and 49 percent of cases diagnosed in 2004 alone ("HIV/AIDS Policy Fact Sheet: African Americans" 2006). African Americans have the highest AIDS case rate of any racial/ethnic group and survival after an AIDS diagnosis is lower among African Americans than any other racial/ethnic group ("HIV/AIDS Policy Fact Sheet: The HIV/AIDS Epidemic" 2005). Among both males and females, African Americans represent the largest percentage of HIV/AIDS diagnoses in every age group (Prejean and Satcher 2006).

Thus, not surprisingly, 35 percent of African Americans view HIV/AIDS as the most urgent public health problem facing the country compared to only 13 percent of whites. Similarly, 55 percent of African Americans compared to 25 percent of whites indicate that they are personally concerned about becoming infected ("HIV/AIDS Policy Fact Sheet: African Americans" 2003). In a national poll, 56 percent of African Americans compared to 33 percent of whites indicated that the United States is losing ground when it comes to the problem of HIV/AIDS. In the same poll, 64 percent of African Americans indicated that they personally knew someone who had AIDS or had died of AIDS compared to 42 percent of whites ("New Survey" 2004). A study comparing national administrative data on survival rates among HIV-positive U.S. veterans also found that African American HIV-positive veterans experience poorer survival rates than white veterans (McGinnis et al. 2003).

In 2002, non-Hispanic blacks trailed non-Hispanic whites in at least four positive health indicators: persons aged younger than sixty-five years with health insurance (81 percent versus 87 percent); adults aged older than sixty-five years vaccinated against influenza (50 percent versus 69 percent) and pneumococcal disease (37 versus 60 percent); women receiving prenatal care (75 percent versus 89 percent); and persons aged older than eighteen years who participated in regular, moderate physical activity (25 percent versus 35 percent). Blacks also had a significantly higher proportion of negative health indicators compared to whites in the following four areas: new cases of gonorrhea (742 versus 31 per 100,000 population); deaths from homicide (21 percent versus 2.8 percent); persons aged six through nineteen who were overweight or obese (22 percent versus 12 percent); and adults who were obese (40 percent versus 29 percent) (Centers for Disease Control and Prevention 2005).

Research has also shown that transplant medicine has a race problem. Black patients face longer delays in getting referred, spend longer times on waiting lists, and have worse survival rates after receiving an organ transplant. According to the agency that administers the organ allocation system, the United Network for Organ Sharing (UNOS), ethnic populations make up 50 percent of the people on the waiting list but white patients receive 63 percent of the organs. For kidney transplants, minorities make up 60 percent on the waiting list, but less than 45 percent of transplants (Whitford 2005). Financial status could not explain this difference since Medicare funding should provide a level playing field. Some have argued that subconscious bias or overt racism may account for this disparity while others point to an imbalance in supply and demand of suitable organs for minorities and argue that minority patients, especially African Americans, are more genetically diverse, making it hard for them to find tissue matches (Whitford 2005).

The Healthcare Research and Quality Act (HRQA) of 1999 directed the Agency for Healthcare Research and Quality (AHRQ) to prepare two annual reports: a national health care quality report and a national health care disparities report dealing with priority populations.[1] The Agency for Healthcare Research and Quality (2003) issued its first *2003 National Healthcare Disparities Report*. The report found racial, ethnic, and socioeconomic differences with respect to quality of care and access to needed medical services. Many of the findings were consistent with other research findings. The report found that certain minorities and poor people are less likely to be insured. Blacks and people of lower socioeconomic status (SES) have higher death rates for all cancers combined. Some minorities and people of low SES receive fewer preventive services such as cancer screening, blood pressure and cholesterol screening, immunization, and dental care. They have difficulty obtaining referrals to specialists and are more likely to have difficulty communicating with their physicians. The report also found that gaps in national data often exist and currently collected data are often not sufficient for examining racial, ethnic, and socioeconomic differences in health care. The national data also often do not collect certain types of demographic information and do not differentiate between patient responsibility and health care system responsibility. The report concluded that greater improvement was possible.

The *2004 National Healthcare Disparities Report* by the Agency for Healthcare Research and Quality (2005a) identified three key themes for policy makers and healthcare providers: health care disparities are pervasive, gaps in information exist, and improvement is possible. The report found that disparities existed across all dimensions of quality of health care, access to care, and many clinical conditions.

Access to Health Care

The *2004 National Healthcare Disparities Report* defines access to health care as "the timely use of personal health services to achieve the best health outcome" (Agency for Healthcare Research and Quality 2005a, 59). The report argues that attaining good access to care requires: (1) getting into the health care system—getting entry into the system; (2) getting care within the health care system—getting to a specific site/location to receive specific services that are needed; and (3) finding providers who meet individual patient needs—finding specific providers with whom one can develop a relationship based on communication and trust. The report further suggests that health care access can be measured using (1) structural indicators (for example, presence or absence of specific resources, such as health insurance, that enable one to receive health care); (2) patient assessment measures, such as patients' perceptions of how well providers interact with them; and (3) health care utilization, that is, the successful receipt of needed services.

As mentioned above, according to the Institute of Medicine report *Unequal Treatment* (Smedley, Stith, and Nelson 2002) minorities have greater difficulty accessing needed health services and minorities are less likely than whites to receive needed services, including clinically necessary procedures. Furthermore, minority communities often lack quality health care services and providers. Even when it comes to government programs such as Medicare, African American beneficiaries are likely to encounter more problems getting needed care than their white counterparts ("Medicare and Minority Americans" 2005). Lack of financial resources, geographic location, cultural and language difficulties, and discrimination may account for some of the lack of access and resulting health care disparities ("Closing the Gap" 2005). The issue of health care disparities and geographic location is discussed in Chapter 8.

A significant amount of research has documented difficulties African Americans experience in accessing health care services. For example, a study found that black adolescents made fewer doctors visits than their white peers in 1992 and were more likely to lack usual sources of routine and acute care as well as continuity in care. The racial differences persisted even after adjusting for family income, health insurance, needs, and other factors (Lieu, Newacheck, and McManus 1993). Another study found that fewer blacks than whites received health care in physicians' offices, outpatient clinics, and emergency departments (Bliss et al. 2004). Research also indicates that African Americans receive less pain medication than whites and that race and ethnicity are associated with barriers to hospice care ("IV: Race, Ethnicity, and Culture" 2003). Blacks also receive less curative surgery for early stage lung, colon, and breast cancer than do whites (Ervin 2004). The presence of significant variation within the African American population in the number of office visits, outpatient clinic visits, hospital discharges, and days hospitalized itself has been found to be significantly related to age, gender, poverty, rural residence, and presence or absence of health insurance (Rust et al. 2004).

Disparity in access to mental health services has continued to persist across racial and ethnic groups in the United States. According to the U.S. Department of Health and Human Services (2001) racial and ethnic minorities have less access to mental health services than do non-Hispanic whites. Some of the important barriers to mental health services, according to the research literature, include factors such as location of services, cultural insensitivities of mental health personnel (Swartz et al. 1998), lack of or inadequate health insurance (Snowden and Thomas 2000), a societal stigma attached to mental health (U.S. Department of Health and Human Services 2001), and disjointed services (Smedley, Stith, and Nelson 2002). Another study that examined the barriers to use of mental health care services among low income African Americans identified three types of barriers to access—individual, environmental, and institutional. Individual barriers include things such as denial, avoidance, fear, mistrust, disability, lack of knowledge, and financial obstacles, among others. Environmental barriers included factors such as lack of resources, difficulty in finding options for mental health services, and factors that adversely affect health seeking. Institutional barriers included time limitations, mental health professionals' attitudes about access to services, and rules that inhibited access to services (Hines-Martin et al. 2003).

Environment also plays a role in access to and support for a healthy lifestyle associated with lower risks for diseases in poorer communities with a high proportion of African Americans. A study that examined the availability and food options at restaurants in less affluent and more affluent areas of Los Angeles County found that in less affluent areas it is difficult for residents to eat healthy food away from home and fewer healthy options are available in food selection as well as food preparation and that restaurants in such neighborhoods heavily promote unhealthy food options for residents (Blair-Lewis et al. 2005).

One of the most important barriers in getting access to health care services is lack of health insurance. According to the 2000 report *Racial and Ethnic Disparities in Access to Health Insurance and Health Care* (Brown et al. 2000), African Americans' access to health care services is compromised by an uninsurance rate that is one and one-half times the rates for whites. In addition, 53 percent of African Americans compared to 70 percent of whites had job-based insurance. As a result, Medicaid serves as an important safety net for African Americans, and cuts in the Medicaid program invariably have a negative impact on African Americans (Brown et al. 2000). The mid-1990s saw a sizable decline, from 27 percent in 1994 to 21 percent in 1997, in Medicaid and other public coverage. In addition, welfare reform also resulted in many African Americans moving into low-wage entry-level jobs where health benefits are less likely to be offered (Kaiser Commission 2000). Thus, many factors, such as less education, lower pay, and discrimination, disadvantage African Americans in the workplace. This is reflected in the fact that about 18 percent of African American adults with jobs are uninsured compared to 11 percent of adult whites with jobs ("Study: Millions of Black Americans Have No Insurance Coverage" 2004).

Between 2000 and 2004, the overall number of uninsured Americans increased by six million largely due to a decline in employer-based insurance. Most of the increases occurred among adults because the drop in employer-sponsored insurance was not offset by an increase in public coverage (Holahan and Cook 2005). Children fared much better because the decline in their private coverage was offset by increased public coverage under the State Children's Health Insurance

Program (SCHIP) and the Medicaid program ("The Uninsured and Their Access to Health Care" 2005). Fifty-five percent of the increase in uninsured during the 2000–2004 period occurred among whites because whites had the largest increase in the number falling below 200 percent of the federal poverty level. Yet, the rate of uninsured among whites in 2004 was 13.2 percent compared to 21.2 percent for blacks (Holahan and Cook 2005). Thus, it is clear that minorities are more likely than whites to lack health insurance and thus they are more likely to face barriers in accessing health care services (Rhoades 2005).

A majority of African Americans on Medicare tend to be poor and a sizable number of them face access problems due to lack of prescription drug coverage. African Americans on Medicare tend to be in poorer health than their white counterparts. In 2002, 65 percent of African Americans on Medicare had incomes of less than 150 percent of the federal poverty level. Also, in 2002, 43 percent of African Americans on Medicare lacked prescription drug coverage for either part of the year or the full year, and 36 percent relied on Medicaid for prescription drug coverage (Elam and Strollo 2005).

Overall, it is clear that adults who lack health insurance are more likely to go without needed medical care, receive fewer cancer screenings, are less likely to have a personal doctor or a health care provider, receive less dental care, receive fewer flu shots, and are more likely to report poor or fair health than those who have insurance coverage (Robert Wood Johnson Foundation 2004). Between 2001 and 2004, 4.6 million more Americans became uninsured, leaving a total of 45.8 million without insurance coverage. Federal spending on the health care safety net has not kept pace with the growth in the number of uninsured. State and local governments have been unable to maintain, let alone increase, their level of support for the health safety net (Hadley and Holahan 2005). As more Americans go without health insurance and access to affordable health care decreases, many more holes in America's health safety net are left (Hoffman and Sered 2005). A review of studies that were specifically designed to quantify the contribution of health insurance to racial/ethnic disparities in access provides evidence that a sizable share of the differences in whether a person has a regular source of care could be reduced if African Americans and other minorities were insured at the same level as that of whites (Lillie-Blanton and Hoffman 2005). Thus it appears that improving access to and utilization of quality health services are two of the major challenges in trying to eliminate health care disparities (Copeland 2005).

According to the *2004 National Healthcare Disparities Report*, African Americans have worse access to health care than do whites. In fact, of the thirty-one measures of access tracked between 2000 and 2001, the report concluded that blacks had worse access to care than whites for about 40 percent of measures in both 2000 and 2001 (Agency for Healthcare Research and Quality 2005a). According to the *2005 National Healthcare Disparities Report* (Agency for Healthcare Research and Quality 2005b), blacks had worse access to health care than whites for half (50 percent) of core access measures.

Quality of Health Care

The IOM's 2002 report *Unequal Treatment: Confronting Racial and Ethnic Disparities in Healthcare* (Smedley, Stith, and Nelson 2002) argued that African Americans receive lower quality care across a range of disease areas and they are more likely than whites to receive less desirable services such as an amputation of all or part of a limb. The *2004 National Healthcare Disparities Report* by the Agency for Healthcare Research and Quality (2005a) argued that quality health care that is effective, safe, timely, patient centered, equitable, and efficient and health care quality can be measured using clinical performance measures, patient assessment, and outcome of care.

Several studies have demonstrated lower quality of care received by African Americans for specific health care services or procedures. For example a study (Wenneker and Epstein 1989) that examined all admissions for circulatory diseases or chest pain to Massachusetts hospitals in 1985 found that whites underwent significantly more angiography and coronary artery bypass grafting procedures than blacks. Whites also underwent more angioplasty procedures, but the difference was not statistically significant. The study concluded that substantial racial inequality existed in the use of procedures for patients hospitalized with coronary heart disease.

A significant amount of research in the 1990s documented the differences in quality of care received by Medicare beneficiaries based on race. One study examined the differences in the rates of coronary artery bypass grafting (CABG) between white and black Medicare patients using data from all Medicare patients in the United States in 1986 and found that nationally the CABG rate was 27.1 per 10,000 for white patients but only 7.6 for blacks (Goldberg et al. 1992). Another study (Kahn et al. 1994) of 9,932 Medicare patients sixty-five years or older, from 297 acute care hospitals in thirty areas within five states, found that within rural, urban non-teaching and teaching hospitals, patients who are black or are from poor neighborhoods had worse processes of care and greater instability at discharge than other patients. Still another study (Gornick et al. 1996) that examined 1,993 Medicare administrative data for 26.3 million Medicare beneficiaries sixty-five years or older found that race and income had significant effects on mortality and use of services. For mortality, the black-white ratios were 1.19 for men and 1.16 for women. For every 100 women, there were 26.0 mammograms among whites compared to 17.1 among blacks. For every 1,000 beneficiaries, there were 515 influenza immunizations among whites compared to 313 among blacks. Thus, Medicare coverage alone does not promote effective patterns of use by all beneficiaries. Black Medicare patients are more likely than whites to live in areas where medical procedure rates and quality of care are low (Williams and Jackson 2005).

Among adults with diabetes, not only do whites have higher influenza and pneumococcal vaccination rates than do African Americans, the differential in vaccination rates is independent of age, access to care, health care coverage, and socioeconomic status (Egede and Zheng 2003).

Research has also documented differences in quality of care received by whites and blacks with respect to foster care, orphanage, and mental health services. For example, an examination of New York's foster care system following the end of the Great Depression of the 1930s showed that segregation of foster care and orphanage services by race had negative consequences for the children who were being served. Racial segregation negatively affected the quality of care received by African American children because they were often "warehoused" for long periods of time in facilities that were ill-prepared for them while white children were seen as in need of mental health services in outpatient and private clinics and offices (Rosner 1997). African Americans are also less likely than whites to receive mental health counseling and psychotherapy but more likely to receive pharmacotherapy (Richardson et al. 2003).

Blacks also receive poorer quality emergency room care than whites and racial differences in the quality of care and intensity of treatment persist even after taking into consideration factors such as socioeconomic status, patient preference, severity of disease, and coexisting medical conditions (Williams and Jackson 2005).

A National Kidney Foundation survey in 2000 reported that 33 percent of African Americans were offered the option of transplantation compared to 44 percent of Caucasians. African Americans are not only less likely to be referred by their dialysis center for renal transplant evaluation but, even after they are referred to a transplant center, are less likely than whites to be accepted as suitable candidates for a transplant. Also, the population-based mortality rate from congestive heart failure is 1.8 times higher for African Americans than Caucasian men and 2.4 times higher for African American women than Caucasian women (Flattery and Baker 2004).

The United States has always had difficulty in attracting sufficient health care providers to rural areas and the impoverished inner city urban areas where many African Americans live. Given the high cost of medical and other health professional education, caring for the poor ethnic/racial minority population is not seen by many health care professionals as compatible with paying off a large educational debt. Also, the fact that minorities such as African Americans, Hispanics, and American Indians and Alaska Natives are heavily underrepresented in a health profession also impinges on not only the availability but also the quality of care received by minorities (Trevino 1999). Quality of health care for minorities is also related to issues of resources and priorities. Clinics that operate in low-income minority communities are often understaffed and operate under limited financial resources and thus provide lower quality of care ("Closing the Gap" 2005).

In contrast to all previous studies that have documented significant racial/ethnic disparities and quality of care received by African Americans, a recent study of the quality of primary care in the United States concluded that blacks and Hispanics tend to receive slightly better day-to-day medical care than whites when they see a doctor (Asch et al. 2006). The conclusions of this study startled many researchers and have sparked a new debate about the impact of race on health care in America.

According to the study, all patients are getting only about half of recommended care regardless of race/ethnicity, place of residence, and insurance status. The study found no significant differences among patients from different ethnic groups or incomes in quality of care received once they get to see a doctor. However, the study did stress that other disparities in health care exist. For example the poor and minorities are less likely to see a doctor in the first place and they receive far less expensive care. The study utilized medical records and telephone interviews of a random sample of people living in twelve communities who had made at least one visit to the doctor in the previous two years. The critics suggest that the findings of the study may be skewed because the study may have missed the poorest people who do not have telephones or never see a doctor. The data in this study are certainly not consistent with lots of available national data.

The *2004 National Healthcare Disparities Report* (Agency for Healthcare Research and Quality 2005a) found that of the thirty-eight measures of quality tracked between 2000 and 2001, African Americans received poorer quality of care than whites for about two-thirds of quality measures. For example, the report found that compared to whites, the rates of late stage colorectal cancer were higher among blacks, the proportion of adults with diabetes who receive all five recommended diabetics services was lower among blacks, blacks received less adequate dialysis, and the influenza vaccination rate was lower among blacks. According to the *2005 National Healthcare Disparities Report* (Agency for Healthcare Research and Quality 2005b), blacks received poorer quality of care than whites for about 40 percent of core quality of care measures, indicating some closing of the gap between blacks and whites on quality of care measures. According to the *2006 National Heathcare Disparities Report* (Agency for Healthcare Research and Quality 2006), blacks received poorer quality of care compared to whites on 51 percent of the core quality of care measures. Thus, the disparity in quality of care received by whites and blacks seems to have increased again after some decline.

Perceptions of the Health Care System

Public opinion data show that ethnic/racial minorities and white Americans have very different views regarding their own health status, their personal experiences with health care providers, and how they view the American health care system. In 1994, in the National Comparative Survey of Minority Health Care of a sample of 3,789 adults sponsored by the Commonwealth Fund, a sizable portion of ethnic/racial minority individuals who consulted a physician reported negative experiences with the American health care system, with 15 percent believing that they would have received better care if they had been members of a different race (Trevino 1999; Johnson et al. 2004). The Commonwealth Fund's 2001 Healthcare Quality Survey of a total of 6,299 adults again reaffirmed earlier findings that African Americans remained more likely to believe that they would have received better medical care if they belonged to a different race/ethnic group and that the medical staff judged them unfairly or treated them with disrespect based on race/ethnicity (Johnson et al. 2004).

More specifically, poll data show fundamental differences in opinions of African Americans and whites when it comes to their views about America's health care system. Compared to whites, African Americans are less likely to be satisfied with the qualitative ways in which physicians treat them when they are ill and more dissatisfied with the care they receive when hospitalized (Blendon et al. 1989). In a 1995 Detroit area study, black adults reported significantly worse self-rated health compared to whites with similar levels of self-reported morbidity (Broadman 2004).

The 1999 Henry J. Kaiser Family Foundation (1999a) *Survey of Race, Ethnicity and Medical Care: Public Perceptions and Experiences* showed that when asked how big a problem racism is in health care, only 16 percent of whites compared to 35 percent of African Americans stated that it was a major problem. Similarly only 23 percent of whites stated that African Americans receive lower quality of care while 64 percent of African Americans expressed the belief that they receive lower quality of care. Sixty-one percent of whites believed that African Americans with heart disease are just as likely as whites who have heart disease to get specialized medical procedures and surgery while only 41 percent of African Americans expressed the same belief. Sixty-four percent of African Americans agreed with the statement that whites with HIV or AIDS are more likely than African Americans with HIV or AIDS to get the newest medicines and treatment compared to only 43 percent of whites who believed that to be the case. Finally, with respect to personal experience with the American health care system, only 1 percent of whites compared to 12 percent of African Americans stated that they have felt that a doctor or health care provider judged them unfairly or treated them with disrespect because of their race or ethnic background.

African Americans' self-rating of their own health care is related to race of the health care provider. An analysis of data gathered by the 1999 Kaiser Family Foundation Survey mentioned above also showed that among African Americans, stronger belief about racial discrimination in health care is associated with preferring an African American physician. Those who preferred and had an African American physician were more likely to rate their physician as excellent (57 percent) than did African Americans who preferred an African American physician but had a non–African American physician (20 percent). In other words, African Americans who perceive racism in health care are more likely to prefer a physician of their own race or ethnicity. However, it is important to emphasize that only 22 percent of African American respondents preferred an African American physician (Chen et al. 2005). It should also be noted that African Americans are heavily underrepresented in the health care profession despite some successful efforts by some individuals, groups of African Americans, and philanthropists to establish African Americans in the medical profession (Watson 1999). In 2004, one out of every eight Americans was African American but fewer than one of every twenty dentists and physicians in the country were African American (Mangan 2004). In fact, *Missing Persons:*

Minorities in the Health Professions, a report issued by the Sullivan Commission on Diversity in the Healthcare Workforce (2004), has argued that lack of minority health professionals is compounding the nation's racial and ethnic health disparities. The report argues that diversity is a key to excellence in health care, and glaring disparities in quality of care has led to thousands of premature deaths each year and caused unnecessary pain and suffering.

A focus group study commissioned by the Henry J. Kaiser Family Foundation (1999b) showed that African Americans experienced difficulties in receiving quality care even when they had insurance coverage. African American patients also reported that they did not trust medical professionals to accurately diagnose their problems. Another focus group study of a predominantly African American community to obtain a comprehensive view of the community's health-related attitudes and behaviors found that participants in the focus group expressed the view that health care providers discriminated against the uninsured, that long wait times in the physicians office were a hindrance to receiving quality care, and that the best physician's were reserved for patients with private insurance. They also expressed lack of trust in their health care providers to deliver high-quality care (Miller, Seib, and Dennie 2001). An in-depth interview (Becker and Newsom 2003) of sixty African Americans who had one or more chronic illnesses found that low-income respondents expressed more dissatisfaction with health care than did middle-income respondents. Low-income respondents reported spending more time dealing with health care bureaucracy, gaining access to the system, and being turned away, and felt that physicians were inattentive to their health problems.

Despite a growing emphasis on providing health care consumers with more information about quality care, in a random telephone survey in the state of New York conducted in September 2002 and March 2003, African American respondents were the least likely to recall receiving or being exposed to quality-related information (Boscarino and Adams 2004).

Possible Explanations for Health Care Disparities

As the discussion thus far has demonstrated, not only is there significant health care inequality between African Americans and whites with respect to health status/outcome, access to care, and quality of care, but both races also have very divergent perceptions and hold different views about their own health and the American health care system. What factors help explain the existence of health care inequality between African Americans and whites? Obviously, no one single factor explains such disparity. For example, racial discrimination by itself cannot explain the current disparities. Rather, a multitude of factors combined together might help explain such disparity. Nor is it easy to establish a clear cause–effect relationship. In the remainder of the chapter we discuss a variety of factors that research suggests are related to health care disparity between African Americans and whites. However, we make no claim of causality.

Racism, Bias, and Discrimination

The IOM's 2002 report *Unequal Treatment: Confronting Racial and Ethnic Dispari-ties in Healthcare* (Smedley, Stith, and Nelson 2002) concluded that bias, prejudice, and stereotyping on the part of health care providers was one of the sources that contributed to disparities in health care. The report defined prejudice as unjusti-fied negative attitudes based on a person's group membership and suggested that prejudice may not be always recognized or deliberate. Sometimes prejudice results from stereotypes and biases that may affect clinical encounters.

Racial disparities in health care can result from bias, discrimination, and ste-reotypes on the part of the individual health care provider or it can result from institutional racism in which different forms of racism are embedded in the health care institutions themselves. Sometimes, racial health care disparities may result from structural racism, which is normalization and legitimation of historical, cultural, institutional, and interpersonal forces that give advantages to whites and produce adverse outcomes for persons of color. Most determinants of health may lie outside of the health care system and structural racism may contribute to social and economic inequalities that in turn may be responsible for most of the health care disparities ("Closing the Gap" 2005). Some have argued that for African Americans, a critical factor affecting their health status is the continuing influence of structural inequality in American society shaped by conditions of enslavement, racial op-pression, and economic exploitation (Semmes 1996). A culture of oppression has taken a significant toll on the minds and bodies of African Americans as reflected in problems of suicide, mental health, and others (Poussaint and Alexander 2000).

It has been argued that to understand the current health care crisis in the African American population, one must understand the legacy of the experience of slavery and the role of racism in health care delivery and public health planning (Hollar 2001). It is an undeniable fact that the historical experience of African Americans in the United States has been shaped by the institution of slavery, segregation, and racism. Former Senator Bill Bradley once observed that slavery was America's original sin and race remains its unresolved dilemma (Geiger 1997). African Americans' experience in America is distinctly different from that of any other group of immigrants or refugees because of the extended period of slavery, segregation, and discrimination. In con-trast to immigrants, African Americans came to America chained together as human cargo and treated as property rather than persons and characterized as a subhuman species who lacked intelligence, feelings, and character. Millions of slaves died of disease, suicide, or murder on slave ships (Watts 2003). During the years of slavery, particularly in the South, African American health care can best be described as a history of neglect (Savitt 1978; Beardsley 1987).

Byrd and Clayton (2000; 2002) in tracing the medical history of African Ameri-cans, the problem of race, and health care in the United States in two volumes argue that today's health care crisis in the African American community grew out of the antebellum roots of the old slave health deficit and from society's historic acceptance of poor health status for blacks. They argue that sordid health care and poor nutrition given to slaves during the Middle Passage and upon arrival in America established the model health care for slaves and diminished expectations for black health. Scientifically defended theories of racial inferiority created a milieu in which African Americans were exploited for social experimentation. This in turn led to eugenics theories and shocking medical experiments on African Americans well into the twentieth century. During the early twentieth century, eugenics and public health battled over whether heredity played a significant role in infectious disease, but they also shared some common goals and methods with respect to control of infectious and hereditary diseases (Pernick 1997).

African Americans' skepticism and distrust of medical and mental health care communities have deep roots in American history due to medical experiments conducted on them and harmful myths and stereotypes perpetuated about African Americans through history (Poussaint and Alexander 2000). African Americans were medically exploited during the nineteenth and early twentieth centuries. For example, slaves were subjected to brutal experiments to test remedies for heatstroke and other diseases. African Americans continued to be used as unwilling subjects in medical experiments even after emancipation. Grave robbing was a common practice, particularly in the South, where grave robbers sent bodies of southern blacks to northern medical schools for use as anatomy cadavers. African American patients were also often used as guinea pigs by white physicians, placed in inferior hospitals wards, and given poor experimental care. Thus, African Americans' distrust of the medical profession goes further back than the public revelations about the Tuskegee Syphilis Study that has been often cited as the most attention-getting example of medical racism (Gamble 1997).

The Tuskegee Syphilis Study was a forty-year government experiment conducted from 1932 to 1972. In the study, 399 African American men from Macon County, Alabama, were deliberately denied effective treatment for syphilis in order to document the natural history of the disease. The Tuskegee story continues to reverberate through the African American community (Watts 2003). Historian Susan Reverby (1999) has called the Tuskegee Syphilis Study as an example of not just medical arrogance but of unethical behavior and racism. It is important to emphasize that while most attention has focused on the Tuskegee experiment, it was only one event among many other medical experiments African Americans were subjected to in American medicine over several hundred years. The Tuskegee experiment is a reflection of the racism and discrimination in American medicine experienced by African Americans (Geiger 1997). When former President Bill Clinton, in 1997, offered an apology to the eight surviving subjects of the Tuskegee experiment, he called the experiment racist (Weiss 2005).

The perception of the medical community is that the Tuskegee experiment accounts for most of the distrust of the health care system and clinical trials in particular among African Americans (Carlos and Chamberlain 2004). Thus, there is a widespread belief that minorities in the United States are less willing to participate than non-minorities in health research. However, a recent study has helped debunk this notion. This study claims that given the chance to participate, minorities, including African Americans, volunteer at least as often as whites do. While it is true that minorities are often underrepresented in health research, the reason is that doctors and scientists reach out to them less (Wendler et al. 2006). Nevertheless, public opinion surveys and other research have clearly demonstrated that African Americans demonstrate high levels of distrust of the medical community. Furthermore, the distrust of the American health care system extends beyond the Tuskegee experiment and is based not only on historical injustices but continued structural racism in American society and has spawned many conspiracy theories (Carlos and Chamberlain 2004). For example, in a survey released in February 2005, about half of African American respondents believed that a cure for AIDS exists but is being withheld from the poor, and one in six indicated that they believed that the government created AIDS as a means of controlling black population growth (Weiss 2005).

In a 1990 report, the Council of Ethical and Judicial Affairs of the American Medical Association concluded that the American health care system had not fully eradicated racial prejudice (Spital, Callender, and Miles 2004). A former secretary of Health and Human Services stated in 1991 that there was clear, demonstrable evidence of discrimination and racism in the America health care system (Sullivan 1991).

More recent research has demonstrated the conscious or subconscious racism and discrimination in contemporary American medicine and the role it has played in existing health care disparities. For example, *Mental Health: Culture, Race, and Ethnicity,* a report by the U.S. Department of Health and Human Services (2001), concluded that racial/ethnic minorities are treated differently than whites because of either cultural misunderstanding or racial bias. For example, an African American person is more likely to be diagnosed as schizophrenic while a white person is more likely to be diagnosed as having a less severe affective disorder, even though both present the same symptoms. African Americans are also more likely to be treated with higher doses of psychotropic medications. In another study, which explored the wait-list decisions among African Americans and white men and women, African American patients reported more racial discrimination and concluded that lifetime experiences of and response to discrimination may contribute to racial differences in access to care (Klassen et al. 2002). In a study that analyzed 150,391 visits by black and white Medicare beneficiaries to primary care physicians, physicians treating black patients reported experiencing greater difficulties in obtaining access for their patients to high-quality subspecialties, high-quality diagnostic imaging, and nonemergency hospital admissions (Bach et al. 2004).

Research has also demonstrated that managed care organizations shortchange minority Medicaid patients (Malveaux 2002). One study that examined 49,327 adults enrolled in Medicaid managed care plans in fourteen states from 1999 to 2000 found that even when enrolled in the same Medicaid managed care organizations (MCOs), African Americans and other minorities faced barriers and received lower quality of care and that African Americans and other minorities were more likely than white English speakers to be clustered in worse plans as rated by consumers (Weech-Maldonado et al. 2004).

A study by the St. Louis Health Department in Missouri in 2004 found that black residents in three ZIP codes received the poorest medical care and had the worst health in St. Louis. All three ZIP codes—63106, 63107, and 63113—are in the northern part of the city and are heavily African American. Dr. James Kimmey, president and chairman of the Missouri Foundation for Health, partly blamed racism for blacks' relatively poor health in St. Louis and suggested that the built-in racism and discrimination in the health care system leads to some people being viewed as less deserving of quality care ("Doctor: Racism Plays Role in Poor Health" 2005).

Research has also demonstrated that physicians' perceptions of the patient are often influenced by the patient's race/ethnicity and socioeconomic background. A study that analyzed 618 patient encounters found that physicians' perceptions of patients were influenced by patients' sociodemographic characteristics. Physicians tended to view African Americans and members of low and middle socioeconomic status (SES) groups more negatively on a number of different dimensions than they did whites and upper SES patients. The researchers found an association between race and physicians' assessment of patients' intelligence, feeling of affiliation toward the patient, and beliefs about patients' risk behavior and adherence with medical advice (van Ryn and Burke 2000).

Thus, a considerable amount of scholarly literature has made a claim that some of the disparities in health care are attributable to racism and discrimination in the American health care system. However, it is important to point out that other research has challenged this claim. Weisfeld and Perlman (2005) argue that there is little evidence that either covert or unconscious discrimination on the part of the physician is an important cause of racial disparities in health. Satel and Klick (2005) are critical of the claim made in IOM's report *Unequal Treatment: Confronting Racial and Ethnic Disparities in Health Care* (Smedley, Stith, and Nelson 2002) that medical studies document a systematic causal relationship between race and disparities in health care inputs and outcomes and argue that a majority of studies are not powerful enough to establish a causal link since many of these studies do not control for differences among patients that happen to correlate with race. Furthermore they argue that the relationship between care and health is weak in some cases. Epstein (2005) further argues that IOM's 2002 report is flawed because of an imprecise definition of discrimination that fails to distinguish between differences in treatment due to a breakdown in communication and differences in treatment populations that are prompted by racist motives of health care providers.

Socioeconomic Status (SES)

Another explanation offered for the racial health disparities is the low socioeconomic status (SES) of racial minorities compared to the whites. According to some, socioeconomic status, whether measured by income, education, or occupation, is a strong predictor of variations in health. They argue that Americans with low SES have more illness than people with high SES; that in American society, all the indicators of SES are strongly patterned by race; and, finally, that racial differences in SES contribute to racial differences in health (Williams and Jackson 2005). The *Health, United States, 2004* report argues that disparity in health and health care exists by race, ethnicity, and socioeconomic status (National Center for Health Statistics 2004). Persons living in poverty are more likely to be in poor health. For example, in 2002, the percentage of people reporting their health as fair or poor was more than three times as high for persons living below the poverty level as for those with a family income more than twice the poverty level (National Center for Health Statistics 2004). Inequality in distribution of income is strongly associated with self-rated health and an adverse impact on health (Kennedy et al. 1998). Poor people also receive poorer quality of care ("Disparities Remain a Major Public Health Challenge" 2005). Poor communities of color are exposed to greater health hazards and experience a high incidence of many chronic and acute health conditions but have access to relatively few health services (Lado 2001).

Race and social class significantly influence the health status, access to health care, and the scope and quality of health care of minority and poor populations (Geiger 1996). Health is unevenly distributed across socioeconomic status and persons of lower income, education, or occupational status experience worse health and die earlier than do their well-off counterparts. Furthermore, health disparities based on socioeconomic status persist across the life cycle beginning in fetal health and ending with health disparities among the elderly (Williams 2004). Thus, some have argued that SES is an important determinant of health and socioeconomic disparities in turn are major determinants of the racial disparities in health (Weisfeld and Perlman 2005).

As can be observed from the data presented in Table 2.1, African Americans experience considerably lower socioeconomic status than do whites. With respect to economic disparities, the per capita income of African Americans in 2003 was only $15,775 compared to $24,626 for whites. The median income of white households in 2003 was $45,631 compared to $29,645 of African American households. Considerably more African Americans live in poverty than whites. Twenty-four percent of African Americans lived below the poverty level in 2003 compared to only 10.5 percent of whites. During the same year, 22.3 percent of African American families lived below the poverty level compared to only 8.1 percent for white families. African American children experience significantly more poverty than do white children. Thirty-three percent of African Americans children compared to 13.9 percent of white children lived below the poverty line in 2003. Thus, it is not surprising that a much higher proportion of African Americans (24.4 percent) than whites (10.3) are on Medicaid programs.

Significant disparities also are found between whites and African Americans with respect to educational attainment. High school graduation rate among whites

Table 2.1

Socioeconomic Status of African Americans and Whites

	Whites	African Americans
Population (2004) in millions	236,058	37,502
Percent of U.S. population (2004)	80.3	12.8
Per capita income (in constant dollars, 2003)	$24,626	$15,775
Median income of households (in constant dollars 2003)	$45,631	$29,645
Percent of people below poverty level (2003)	10.5	24.4
Percent of families below poverty level (2003)	8.1	22.3
Percent of children below poverty level (2003)	13.9	33.6
Percent high school dropouts (2003)	3.7	4.5
Percent high school graduate or more (2004)	85.8	80.6
Percent college graduate or more (2004)	28.2	17.6
Percent without health insurance (2003)	14.6	19.6
Percent covered by Medicaid (2003)	10.3	24.4
Percent employed in managerial/professional occupation (civilian noninstitutionalized population 25 years old or older, 2004)	39.0	28.9
Percent unemployment rate (2004)	3.9	8.1
16 to 19 years old	15.0	31.7
20 to 24 years old	7.9	18.4

Source: U.S. Census Bureau, *Statistical Abstracts of the United States, 2006.* Washington, D.C.: Government Printing Office.

is almost 86 percent compared to about 81 percent for African Americans. The differences are even more striking with respect to college education. Twenty-eight percent of whites have a college degree or more compared to only 17.6 percent of African Americans. African Americans also have higher high school dropout rates than do whites. In inner cities across the country, more than half of all black men do not finish high school (Orfield 2006).

Finally, with respect to occupation, among the noninstitutionalized civilian employed population twenty-five years or older, 39 percent of whites are employed in managerial/professional occupations compared to about 28.9 percent of African Americans. The unemployment rate for African Americans is double that of whites. The unemployment rate among youth is much higher among African Americans than whites. Even though the 1990s were characterized as having the best labor market in thirty years, it was the worst decade for young black men (Edelman, Holzer, and Offner 2006). By 2004, 50 percent of black men in their twenties who lacked a college education and 72 percent of high school dropouts were jobless (Western 2006). A large pool of poorly educated black men has become disconnected from the mainstream of American society and has been left behind (Mincy 2006).

Research has also documented a strong association between the health and labor market outcomes for African Americans, Native Americans, and whites, with

African Americans having worse labor market outcomes and health and lower educational attainment than their white counterparts (Bound et al. 2003). Thus, some have argued that the health status of African Americans is the direct result of their marginal position within the U.S. economy because health status differences between African Americans and whites are affected by life opportunities and socioeconomic conditions (Quaye 1994). Income level has been characterized as one of the strongest predictors of mortality (McDonough et al. 1997).

Since most Americans receive health insurance coverage through their place of employment, it also follows that a much higher percentage of African Americans (19.6 percent) compared to whites (14.6 percent) were without any health insurance in 2003. Different sources of health insurance coverage influence access to medical care, and for people with Medicaid or no coverage at all, access to basic care is in fact worsening as a result of service cutbacks (Hurley, Pham, and Claxton 2005). As we have discussed earlier in the chapter, individuals without health insurance experience more health problems, face more barriers gaining access to care, and often receive lower quality care. For example, major depression and factors associated with depression are more frequent among members of minority groups than among whites. Furthermore, elevated depression rates among minority individuals are largely associated with a lack of health insurance and greater health burdens faced by minorities (Dunlop et al. 2003).

The lower SES confers many disadvantages on African Americans when it comes to the American health care system (Flattery and Baker 2004). A considerable amount of research has documented a strong relationship between SES and health disparities experienced by African Americans in many aspects of health care since the 1990s.

Research has demonstrated a relationship between SES and physician recommendations for mammography. In a study that investigated the relationship between physician recommendations for mammography and race/ethnicity, SES, and other factors in a rural population, 55 percent of white women reported that their physician had recommended a mammography compared to 45 percent of black women. The study found that SES, age, and other characteristics, but not race or ethnicity were related to reports of physician recommendations (O'Malley et al. 2001). Another study that examined the relationship between SES, limited access to health care, and racial inequalities in the incidence of end-stage renal disease (ESRD) found that low SES and limited access to health care were strong risk factors for kidney failure (Perneger, Whelton, and Klag 1995). Patients of lower SES who have asthma also have worse health outcomes post–hospital discharge (Haas et al. 1994).

Research has also documented that ethnic minority status, lower education, and poorer health status are significantly associated with lower rates of advice to quit smoking and that the smoking counseling differences between African Americans and whites were greater among those with lower income and those without health insurance (Houston et al. 2005). African American–white differences in smoking cessation are reduced considerably when statistical adjustments are made for sociodemographic factors. Thus, disparities in smoking cessation among racially classified social groups (RCSG) are strongly influenced by socioeconomic status (King et al. 2004).

Much scholarship has demonstrated a strong relationship between SES and a variety of health outcomes such as mortality or morbidity. Some of the literature suggests a causal linkage between the two, that is, lower SES causes health disparities. However, considerable debate persists among several disciplines about the direction of the causation. Economists in particular have suggested an alternative pathway—poor health contributes to lack of economic resources, that is, poor health may restrict a family's capacity to earn income or accumulate assets by limiting work (Smith 1999).

Despite the strong association demonstrated by research between SES and racial health disparities, it is important to emphasize that SES alone cannot explain all the differences in health between African Americans and whites. For example, the elevated mortality risk among the socioeconomically disadvantaged may be largely due to the higher prevalence of health risk behaviors among those with lower levels of education and income (Lantz et al. 1998). Similarly, a study that evaluated the influence of socioeconomic and cultural factors on the racial differences in breast cancer stage at diagnosis concluded that socioeconomic factors alone were not sufficient to explain the dramatic effect of race on breast cancer stages. However, socioeconomic variables combined with cultural beliefs and attitudes explained most of the observed effects (Lannin et al. 1998). While SES accounts for much of the observed racial disparities in health, racial differences often persist even at equivalent levels of SES (Williams 1999).

Culture

Another explanation offered by scholars for the racial health disparities between the whites and African Americans in American society is the African American population's cultural values, beliefs, and attitudes that influence their views of health, health practices, access to care, dietary habits, and lifestyle choices. While there are varied definitions of culture offered by scholars, in general, culture can be defined as the sum total of a population's customs, experiences, habits, beliefs, and values. Scholars have offered different explanations regarding factors that have shaped African American culture. Anthropological perspective suggests that African Americans' beliefs and practices have mostly been influenced by their African heritage. The sociological perspective has tended to view African Americans' beliefs and practices largely shaped by the institution of slavery, which destroyed the African heritage and led to the destruction of black family life and family structure. The historical perspective views black culture as a synthesis of the slaves' African heritage and white culture. The social science perspective has tended to view more recent social forces such as blacks' difficult transition from the rural South to destructive conditions of northern urban life as largely responsible for changing African Americans' family structure and culture (Franklin 1997).

It has been argued that African Americans' cultural beliefs and health practices have a major influence on their well-being regardless of their income and educational levels because they influence African Americans' lifestyle practices on health promotion, disease prevention, and health care maintenance (Russell and Jewell 1992). Three common threads running through the African American culture are religious orientation, social support network, and informal health care systems (Russell and Jewell 1992). Along the same line, Karanja (2003) has argued that African Americans have retained African roots in three important ways. One is the belief, derived from African American metaphysics, that human beings as part of the whole cycle of existence do not dominate nature. Human beings are part of nature. Second, is the strong belief in relationships and human networks, which was strengthened by the experience of slavery. Third, has to do with who possesses knowledge and how knowledge is acquired. In African epistemology, a supreme being is all-knowing and ancestors and the elders are next in hierarchy. How do such cultural values and beliefs influence African Americans' health practices?

Religious Values and Health Beliefs

It is fair to say that African Americans' religious orientation and beliefs are linked to their health beliefs and health practices. For example, since God is seen as protecting individual health, and health is seen as a gift from God, illness is perceived as alleviated through strong faith in God and the power of prayer. Thus, African American adults are more likely to use prayer as a means of coping with worries and ill health more than white adults (Russell and Jewell 1992). African Americans' perception of what is "healthy" includes a relatively high tolerance of discomfort from symptoms and as a result African Americans often ignore minor discomforts and they do not seek health care from mainstream health care facilities until such discomforts reach such proportions that they interfere with the business of living (Bailey 1991). In fact, many African Americans believe that one must endure suffering as a part of spiritual commitment and as a test of faith ("IV: Race, Ethnicity, and Culture" 2003). Spirituality and religious beliefs are often cited as an explanation for the preferences of African Americans for end-of-life treatment. Since God is responsible for physical and spiritual health, only God has the power to decide issues of life and death, and thus African Americans tend to oppose physician-assisted death or life-sustaining treatments. This also creates cultural barriers to use of hospice and palliative care, resulting in unequal access to such services (Johnson, Elbert-Avila, and Tulsky 2005; Ervin 2004; Reese et al. 1999).

Some surveys and studies tend to lend further credence to the idea of a strong relationship between religious beliefs and health beliefs and practices within the African American community. In a survey of African American churches in two communities in Kansas and Alabama, 30 percent of respondents indicated that their health was dependent on fate or destiny (Lewis and Green 2000). Another survey assessed the extent to which a belief in faith and destiny might explain certain health behaviors among African Americans. In this survey of 1,253 African Americans conducted in Alabama churches, 51 percent of the sample indicated that they believed in fate or destiny. The surprising finding in the study was that people with more education (college or postgraduate) believed in fate and destiny more than high school dropouts and high school graduates. Similarly, respondents who made more in annual income were more likely to believe in fate and destiny than people who made less. The study also showed that belief in fate or destiny also influenced respondents' health decisions. For example, women who reported never having a breast exam were more likely to believe in fate and destiny than women who did not have a belief in fate or destiny (Green and Lewis 2004). Still another study found that physicians' acceptance of the role of spirituality and of family were important cultural factors affecting nonwhite patients' quality of medical encounters (Napoles-Springer et al. 2005). A study of undergraduate students of African descent recruited from a historical black university found a positive relationship between cultural variables and health promoting behaviors (Bowen-Reid and Smalls 2004).

Strong belief in a social support network also leads African Americans to rely heavily on the nuclear and extended family rather than on outside traditional health and community service agencies during times of crisis and stress. Middle-aged and older black adults are more likely to rely on multiple family members for support than are their white counterparts (Russell and Jewell 1992). African American culture places a strong value on collective or community values as opposed to individualism. Thus, for example, caring for the sick and dying at home is a tradition in the African American community ("IV: Race, Ethnicity, and Culture" 2003).

In addition, African Americans' belief in the use of an informal health care system also affects health practices (Russell and Jewell 1992). In a national study, 87 percent of black Americans reported using an informal social network in dealing with a personal health problem (Neighbors 1985). A study of 185 low income inner-city pregnant women of whom 78 percent were black found that respondents received a median of twenty pieces of advice related to pregnancy health from a median of five members of their social network (St. Claire and Anderson 1989). According to Bailey (1991) primary reasons why African Americans extensively utilize informal social networks for health care problems include beliefs that the reciprocal give-and-take relationship between an individual and friends and neighbors: (1) can act as a buffer between an individual and a stressful situation; (2) can help alleviate stress by helping a person better cope with the situation; and (3) can give everyone an opportunity to be involved in the healing process. African Americans are also more likely to consult an alternative health practitioner not only for economic reasons but also because of their belief that alternative health practitioners have some control over the forces that cause anomalies and that Western medical practitioners cannot heal certain illnesses (Bailey 1991).

Cultural Values and Diet

As discussed earlier in this chapter, African Americans suffer higher rates of cancer, stroke, heart disease, HIV, and mental illness compared to whites (*Key Facts*

2003). Cancer, obesity, and diabetes are also some of the major health concerns for many African Americans and risk factors for obesity include lack of physical activity and a diet high in calories. More than 60 percent of adults in the United States are overweight or obese, and African Americans are disproportionately affected ("Major Diseases Have Racial Disparities" 2005). Some have argued that dietary differences may account for much of the racial and ethnic disparities in cardiovascular risk status between African Americans and whites. Research has demonstrated differences in adherence to healthy diet parameters by race and ethnicity (Diaz et al. 2005).

African Americans and children of the African diaspora fare worse in many health measures of diet, nutrition, morbidity, and mortality. Many African Americans suffer from the unfortunate consequences of calorie excess and diets high in fat and animal products (Okonkwo 2002; Luke et al. 2001). Semmes (1996) has suggested that the traditional African American dietary habits grew out of slave culture that relied on limited availability of different food sources and that slavery introduced new substances into African American consumption and new modes of thinking that have been detrimental to African American life. He cites examples of recreational consumption of alcohol and tobacco as palliative and consumption of coffee, refined sugar, syrups, and fatty meats combined with limited use of vegetables and fruits as examples of maladaptive dietary practices rooted in slave culture. Thus, he argues that leading causes of death and major risk factors that disproportionately affect African Americans such as heart disease, stroke, cancer, diabetes, obesity, infant mortality, and alcohol and tobacco consumption are strongly tied to social and historical factors, including inequality, that influence how African Americans live and consume. Studies of food consumption of African Americans during the early periods in American history have documented a diet high in carbohydrates, fats, proteins, and energy (Dirks and Duran 2001). Other studies have also found an association between acculturation and health-related behaviors in African Americans. African Americans have a lower intake of fruits/vegetables and higher intakes of fats, meats, and nuts (Ard et al. 2005).

Others have argued that to combat high mortality from diet-related diseases among African Americans would require changes to diets low in total fat, saturated fat, and salt, and high in fiber. However, such changes are likely to be contrary to some traditional African American cultural practices (Airhihenbuwa et al. 1996). For example, a focus group interview among low and middle income African Americans from an urban community in Pennsylvania revealed that to participants in the focus group, cultural attitudes about where and with whom food is eaten were as important as attitudes about specific foods (Airhihenbuwa et al. 1996). Similarly, in another focus group study of African Americans and Latino patients, participants agreed that certain foods and food additives play an important role in the cause and treatment of hypertension but they indicated that they found clinicians' recommended diets difficult to follow in the context of their family life, social situation, and culture (Horowitz 2004). Another focus group study that explored the relationship between culture and community impact on the nutrition attitudes, food choices, and dietary intake of a select group of African Americans in north-central Florida found that there was a general perception among participants that eating healthfully meant giving up part of their cultural heritage and conforming to the dominant culture (James 2004).

Culture, Family Structure, and Health Risk Behavior

In March 1965, Daniel Patrick Moynihan, a sociologist, in collaboration with two members of his staff in the Office of Policy Planning and Research for the Department of Labor (1965), issued a report titled *The Negro Family: The Case for National Action* also known as the *Moynihan Report,* which argued that there was a significant deterioration in the Negro family as reflected in nearly a quarter of urban Negro marriages ending in a dissolution, a quarter of Negro children born out of wedlock, and a quarter of Negro families headed by females. The report argued that this breakdown in African American family structure had led to an increase in welfare dependency. The report concluded that the root of the problem was slavery and the effects of Reconstruction on the family and specifically African American males. The socioeconomic system had produced an unstable family system. This report is consistent with the sociological approach that blames slavery for disrupting black family life and relies on the matriarchal argument to describe the black family structure. Critics argued that the *Moynihan Report* did not include enough comparison with whites to control for economic and educational variables. This raises the issue whether poverty is the result of "situation," that is, socioeconomic conditions, or "culture," that is, values and beliefs.

Franklin (1997) has argued that compared to white women, African American women are more likely to bear children as teenagers, less likely to marry, more likely to experience marital instability, and more likely to become parents outside of marriage. Thus, a much higher percentage of African American women are likely to live in poverty. African Americans are also more likely to engage in certain types of risky health behaviors.

Empirical evidence also tends to indicate the prevalence of certain risky health behavior among African Americans. An investigation of a sample of 502 African American men found a prevalence of high-risk sexual practices and a high percentage of respondents reported a history of sexually transmitted diseases (STDs) (Myers et al. 1997). Another study that examined the relationship between partner violence and sexual risk behavior in a sample of predominantly African American and Latina women who sought medical care from a New York city hospital emergency department found that nearly half of the 143 respondents reported that they had experienced physical, sexual, or life-threatening abuse by a boyfriend or spouse in the past. Abused women were also more likely than non-abused women to report having had an STD, having engaged in sex with a risky partner, having more than one sexual partner, and being tested for HIV (El-Bassel et al. 1998).

Recent empirical research has attempted to discover the relationship between socioeconomic conditions, culture, family structure, and risky health behaviors. One study (Blum et al. 2000) examined the unique and combined contribution of race/ethnicity, income, and family structure to adolescent cigarette smoking, alcohol use, involvement with violence, suicidal thoughts or attempts, and sexual intercourse based on a nationally representative sample of seventh through twelfth graders. The study concluded that white adolescents were more likely to smoke cigarettes, drink alcohol, and attempt suicide in younger years than blacks. Black youths were more likely to have had sexual intercourse and more likely to engage in violence than white teens. Interestingly, controlling for gender, race/ethnicity, income, and family structure together explained no more than 10 percent of the variation in each of the five risk behaviors among younger adolescents and no more than 7 percent among older youths. Thus, the findings suggested that race/ethnicity, income, and family structure taken together provided only limited understanding of adolescent risk behavior.

Three cross-sectional surveys conducted of African American respondents aged nine to seventeen from low income urban areas revealed that low levels of perceived parental monitoring were associated with participation in several health risk behaviors such as sexual behavior, substance/drug use and trafficking, school truancy, and violent behavior (Li, Feigelman, and Stanton 2000). Another study by the same authors (Li, Stanton, and Feigelman 2000), which examined the stability of parental monitoring over time and its long-term effect on health risk behavior among low-income, urban African American children and adolescents regarding unprotected sex, drug use, and drug trafficking, found that parental monitoring was inversely correlated with all three targeted risk behaviors cross-sectionally.

African American Political Participation, Representation, and Health

Research has tended to suggest that the electoral participation of lower class voters influences public policy. It further suggests political participation matters and that aggregate voter turnout is a predictor of welfare benefit levels in American states (Verba et al. 1993; Crotty 1991; Verba and Nie 1972). In other words, electoral participation of the lower class affects state redistributive policies (Hill, Leighley, and Hinton-Andersson 1995). Furthermore, it has also been suggested that lower degrees of representation of the lower class in American states is related to lower levels of welfare benefits (Hill and Leighley 1992). While it is difficult to prove whether political participation affects legislative decision making, it is reasonable to suggest that policy makers are more likely to pay attention to constituents who are politically active, more likely to vote, and are more vocal in their demands (Brodie 1996). For example, the failure of Congress to adopt health care reform during 1993–94 may be explained by the fact that those who were politically most active in the health care reform debate were more likely to self-identify themselves as conservative and more likely to prefer the status quo over major reform (Brodie 1996).

Table 2.2

Voter Registration, Voter Turnout, and Political Representation: African Americans and Whites

	Non-Hispanic white	African American
Voter registration and turnout in 2004 Presidential election		
Registered (%)	75.1	68.7
Voted (%)	67.2	60.0
Voter registration and turnout in 2002 Congressional elections		
Registered (%)	69.4	62.4
Voted (%)	49.1	42.3

	African American
House seats, 108th Congress (2003)	39*
109th Congress (2005)	42*
110th Congress (2007)	42*
Senate seats, 108th Congress (2003)	0
109th Congress (2005)	0
110th Congress (2007)	1

Sources: U.S. Census Bureau, November 2004. "Current Population Survey" and earlier reports and "Current Population Reports." Internet release date, May 26, 2005, , www.census. gov. Congressional data: www.house.gov and www.senate.gov.

*Total includes two non-voting delegates—from the District of Columbia and the U.S. Virgin Islands.

Electoral Participation

Recent research also has demonstrated that disparities in political participation across socioeconomic status affect health. More specifically, research has documented an association between voting inequality at the state level with individual self-rated health. Individuals living in states with the highest voting inequality tend to rate their own health as only fair to poor compared to individuals living in states with lower voting inequality (Blakely, Kennedy, and Kawachi 2001).

Perhaps one additional explanation for the racial health disparities between whites and African Americans is the lower level of political participation, especially with regard to voting, among African Americans compared to whites. African Americans also have less representation in policy-making institutions such as the Congress of the United States compared to whites. The lower level of participation and representation often translates to lack of political power to influence public policy.

As the data in Table 2.2 demonstrate, voter registration and voter turnout among African Americans tend to be lower than among whites when it comes to presidential and congressional elections. Voter participation has been historically higher among whites than blacks (Donovan 1992). The roots of the lower levels of electoral participation among African Americans can be traced to the Jim Crow era, from about 1890 to the 1960s, which was characterized by electoral disfranchisement, economic exploitation, legal segregation, and violence (Gavins 2004; Litwack 2004). However, it is important to point out that the voter turnout gap has somewhat narrowed between the two groups due to increased registration and turnout among blacks in recent years. What is interesting is that among blacks political cynicism and distrust seem to increase the propensity of blacks to vote, in direct contrast to the behavior of whites. Thus, attitudinal factors may play a role in voter registration and turnout (Southwell and Pirch 2003). Since the 1960s, due to the removal of many legal barriers through the civil rights and voting rights legislation passed by Congress, opportunities for African Americans to participate in politics have increased considerably.

Research also shows that church attendance plays a major role in facilitating political mobilization and participation among African Americans, and blacks who attend church belong to more politically relevant organizations, have more positive political attitudes, and vote at higher rates. However, among inner-city black residents, the negative influence of neighborhood poverty, social isolation, and never-married-parent households tends to indirectly undermine voting participation (Alex-Assensoh and Assensoh 2001).

Despite the increase in voter turnout among African Americans since the 1960s, their electoral turnout continues to lag behind that of whites. A variety of explanations have been offered by scholars for the persistent gap in the electoral participation of African Americans and whites. Danigelis (1977) has argued that the type of political climate is directly related to level of political activity among blacks. He argues that political climate is made up of formal and informal white rules governing black political behavior and attitudes of whites and blacks toward those rules. He also argues that a supportive political climate produces high levels of political activity while an intolerant political climate produces low levels of political activity among blacks. Levels of political activity among blacks tend to be similar to whites when the political climate is neutral or ambiguous.

Another explanation for political participation is provided by the SES model, which posits that people in high SES are more likely to participate in the political process than the members of lower SES across all racial and demographic groups. Since more blacks are in lower SES, they participate less. Still another explanation is the role of attitudinal factors in political participation. This is referred to as a social-psychological model that includes things such as sense of party identification, efficacy, political resources, and cultural variables such as distrust of the political system. The argument here is that the political orientations of African Americans differ significantly from those of whites in their attitudes about a host of values and issues, which in turn explains the variations in political participation and voter turnout. Hackey (1992) has argued that the most important factors influencing African American turnout in presidential elections are SES and the strength of partisanship.

Political Representation

African Americans constitute nearly 12 percent of the population but they hold less than 10 percent of the seats in the U.S. House of Representatives. In November 2005 Barack Obama became only the third African American to be elected to the U.S. Senate since Reconstruction (see Table 2.2). Most significant gains in representation among African Americans have occurred at local and state levels of government. In January 2001 there were 9,101 black elected officials (BEOs) in the country. In 1970, there were 1,469 BEOs. Most of these increases have been at county and state levels. There has been an increase in the number of female BEOs (Bositis 2001). Yet, overall, the number of elected black officials remains relatively small.

A considerable amount of debate has taken place in the country about the most effective way to promote political representation of African Americans. One strategy to increase African American representation has been the creation of majority-minority districts to ensure the election of African Americans. However, this strategy has been controversial. Two different views regarding majority-minority districts have emerged (Hutchings and Valentino 2004). One side has argued that the creation of majority-minority districts has led to diminished electoral security of white Democrats because African Americans who tend to vote overwhelmingly for Democrats are systematically removed from white Democratic districts in order to create such districts. In fact, this side argues that the creation of a record number of majority-minority districts following the 1990 redistricting contributed to Republican congressional successes in 1992 and 1994 (Hill 1995; Lublin 1997). However, the other side argues that this claim is overstated because Democratic-controlled state legislatures created most of these districts so that African American voters would be drawn away from largely Republican districts (Petrocik and Desposato 1998; Overby and Cosgrove 1996).

Does increased African American representation translate into better representation of African American interests on public policy issues? Evidence from research does tend to support the idea that African American legislators are far more likely than white Democrats to reflect the interests of African American constituencies in their roll call votes. They are also more likely to propose legislation consistent with African American policy preferences. Finally, African Americans who live in districts that have African American legislators are also more likely to participate in politics at a higher rate (Hutchings and Valentino 2004).

Does African American political empowerment positively impact African American health? Most sociological research on health has tended to examine the relationship between SES and health. However, most analysis has tended to ignore the relationship between political representation/political power and health. A significant amount of research has observed a link between SES and mortality and morbidity, as we discussed earlier in the section on socioeconomic status. The idea that political and community empowerment can lead to improved health status of the empowered group has received attention from health social scientists only since the 1990s. Given the increase in number of BEOs, this question has become more salient. If racial differences in mortality are a reflection of underlying powerlessness, has an increase in black political empowerment led to lowering of black mortality rates?

LaVeist (1992) tests this question using central cities as the unit of analysis. In his analysis, he included all U.S. central cities in 1980 that had a population of at least 50,000, and at least 10 percent of whom were black. He measured black political power using two methods. Absolute black political power was measured as a percentage of city council members who were black. Relative black political power was measured as the proportion of blacks on the city council divided by the proportion of blacks in the voting age population. He also included several correlates of infant and post-neonatal mortality in his analysis. The analysis found that a higher level of black political power relative to the black voting age population was associated with lower black post-neonatal mortality rates. However, he found that absolute black political power was not statistically related to black post-neonatal mortality. Furthermore, he also found that high black empowerment cities had higher expenditures for sewers, social welfare, health, hospitals, and other protective services, suggesting a relationship between black political representation and budgetary allocations to improve the general quality of life of black constituents.

Given the paucity of scholarship examining the relationship between African American political empowerment and African American health status, it is difficult to derive any definitive conclusions. However, early research does lend some credence to the argument that African American political participation and representation can lead to improvement in African American health and quality of life. Thus, not only SES factors but political organization, representation, and empowerment may have important consequences for health, and increased political empowerment of African Americans may help reduce some of the racial health disparities between African Americans and whites.

Reducing Health Care Disparities

In response to documentation of pervasive racial health care disparities in the American health care system by scholarly research, both the public and the private sectors have launched many initiatives to address this problem. The Department of Heath and Human Services (DHHS) has led many initiatives aimed at reducing health care disparities and improving quality of care. Some of these initiatives include programs such as: the National Breast and Cervical Cancer Early Detection Program funded by the Centers for Disease Control and Prevention (CDC); the Hospital, Nursing Home, Home Health, and End Stage Renal Disease Quality Initiatives undertaken by the Centers for Medicare and Medicaid (CMS); and many other activities coordinated by DHHS's Disparities Council and Office of Minority Health. Many private organizations, such as the National Business Group on Health, America's Health Insurance Plans, and the Ambulatory Care Quality Alliance, have also worked hard to improve care and reduce health care disparities (Agency for Healthcare Research and Quality 2005b). Have such efforts led to progress in reducing racial health care disparities?

The *2005 National Healthcare Disparities Report* (Agency for Healthcare

Research and Quality 2005b) finds that disparities related to race, ethnicity, and socioeconomic status still pervade America's health care system and disparities are still found in almost all aspects of health care including health status, all dimensions of access to care and quality of care, levels and types of care, and health care settings. The report concluded that in more cases racial disparities in quality of care had become smaller and in fewer cases racial disparities had become larger (Agency for Healthcare Research and Quality 2005b).

The *2006 National Healthcare Disparities Report* (Agency for Healthcare Research and Quality 2006) concluded that health disparities were still prevalent. The report also concluded that some disparities had diminished while others had increased. The *2007 National Healthcare Disparities Report* (Agency for Healthcare Research and Quality 2008) concluded that overall disparities in health care quality and access are not getting smaller. Some progress has been made but many of the biggest gaps in quality and access have not decreased and the problem of lack of health insurance continues to be a major barrier to reducing health disparities. The report used forty-two core measures of quality and six core measures of access. According to the report, disparity between blacks and whites lessened in only about one-third of the measures of quality of care for blacks while in over 60 percent of the measures of quality of care, disparity did not get smaller. Also, for blacks, 60 percent of core access measures have not changed or have gotten worse.

Conclusions

Scholarly literature has documented many health care disparities between African Americans and whites with respect to health status, access to care, and quality of care received. African American adults and children have higher mortality rates compared to whites; they suffer higher rates of cancer, strokes, heart disease, HIV, and mental illness; they are almost twice as likely to be uninsured as whites; they suffer disproportionately from diabetes; and in the last twenty years, they have suffered disproportionately from HIV-AIDS.

African Americans have worse access to health care than do whites. Research has documented the difficulties African Americans experience in accessing health care services. Research has also documented differences in quality of care received by whites and blacks with respect to foster care, orphanages, and mental health services. Blacks also receive poorer quality emergency room care than whites.

Given the health care disparities with respect to health status, access to care, and quality of care, it is perhaps not too surprising that public opinion data show that ethnic/racial minorities and white Americans have very different views regarding their own health status, their personal experiences of health care providers, and how they view the American health care system. More specifically, poll data show fundamental differences in opinions of African Americans and whites when it comes to their views about the American health care system.

Many explanations have been advanced to explain the persistence of health care disparities between African Americans and whites. These include racial discrimination, lower socioeconomic status of African Americans in American society, cultural values and belief systems of African Americans, and lack of political power. While no one single factor can explain all of the racial health care disparities, many of these factors combined together perhaps provide a prism through which existence of racial health care disparities in American society can be explained. While it is difficult to empirically demonstrate a direct causal linkage between these factors and racial health care disparities, these factors do help illuminate the problem and possible pathways for addressing the problem.

While the American health care system has a long way to go in eliminating or even dramatically reducing health care disparities found between African Americans and whites, the *2005 National Healthcare Disparities Report* (Agency for Healthcare Research and Quality 2005b) provides some hope that progress can be made.

Note

1. The Healthcare Research and Quality Act of 1999 defined priority population to include women, children, elderly, racial and ethnic minority groups, low income groups, residents of rural areas, and persons with special health care needs—specifically children with special needs, the disabled, people in need of long-term care, and people requiring end-of-life care.

References

Adekoya, N., and R.S. Hopkins. 2005. "Racial Disparities in Nationally Notifiable Diseases—United States, 2002." *Morbidity and Mortality Weekly Report* 54, no. 1 (January 14): 9–11.

Agency for Healthcare Research and Quality. 2003. *2003 National Healthcare Disparities Report.* Rockville, MD: U.S. Department of Health and Human Services. AHRQ Publication No. 04-RG004.

Agency for Healthcare Research and Quality. 2005a (March). *2004 National Healthcare Disparities Report.* Rockville, MD: U.S. Department of Health and Human Services. AHRQ Publication No. 04-RG004.

Agency for Healthcare Research and Quality. 2005b (December). *2005 National Healthcare Disparities Report.* Rockville, MD: U.S. Department of Health and Human Services. AHRQ Publication No. 06–0017.

Agency for Healthcare Research and Quality. 2006 (December). *2006 National Healthcare Disparities Report.* Rockville, MD: U.S. Department of Health and Human Services. AHRQ Publication No. 07–0012.

Agency for Healthcare Research and Quality. 2008. *2007 National Healthcare Disparities Report.* Rockville, MD: U.S. Department of Health and Human Services. AHRQ Publication No. 08–00041.

Airhihenbuwa, C.O.; S. Kumanyika; T.D. Agurs; A. Lowe; D. Saunders; and C.B. Morssink. 1996. "Cultural Aspect of African American Eating Patterns." *Ethnic Health* 1, no. 3 (September): 245–60.

Alex-Assensoh, Yvette, and A.B. Assensoh. 2001. "Inner-City Contexts, Church Attendance, and African-American Political Participation." *Journal of Politics* 63, no. 3 (August): 886–901.

Ard, Jamy; Celette Skinner; Chuhe Chen; Mike Aickin; and Laura Svetkey. 2005. "Informing Cancer Prevention Strategy for African Americans: The Relationship of African American Acculturation to Fruit, Vegetables, and Fat Intake." *Journal of Behavioral Medicine* 28, no. 3 (June): 239–47.

Asch, Steven M.; Eve A. Kerr; Joan Keesey; John L. Adams; Claude M. Setodji; Shaista Malik; and Elizabeth A. McGlynn. 2006. "Who Is at Greater Risk for Receiving Poor-Quality Health Care?" *New England Journal of Medicine* 354, no. 11 (March 16): 1147–56.

Bach, Peter B.; Hoangmai H. Pham; Deborah Schrag; Ramsey C. Tate; and Lee Hargraves. 2004. "Primary Care Physicians Who Treat Blacks and Whites." *New England Journal of Medicine* 351, no. 6 (August 5): 575–84.

Bailey, Eric J. 1991. *Urban African American Health Care.* New York: University Press of America.

Beardsley, Edward H. 1987. *A History of Neglect: Health Care for Blacks and Mill Workers in the Twentieth Century South.* Knoxville: University of Tennessee Press.

Becker, Gary, and Edwina Newsom. 2003. "Socioeconomic Status and Dissatisfaction with Health Care among Chronically Ill African Americans." *American Journal of Public Health* 93, no. 5 (May): 742–48.

Blair-Lewis, Lavonna; David C. Sloane; Lori M. Nascimento; Allison L. Diamant; Joyce J. Guinyard; Antronette K. Yancey; and Gwendolyn Flynn. 2005. "African American Access to Health Food Options in South Los Angeles Restaurants." *American Journal of Public Health* 95, no. 4 (April): 668–73.

Blakely, Tony A.; Bruce P. Kennedy; and Ichiro Kawachi. 2001. "Socioeconomic Inequality in Voting Participation and Self-Rated Health." *American Journal of Public Health* 91, no. 1 (January): 99–104.

Blendon, R.J.; L.H. Ailken; H.E. Freeman; and C.R. Corey. 1989. "Access to Medical Care for Black and White Americans: A Matter of Continuing Concern." *Journal of American Medical Association* 261, no. 2 (January 13): 278–81.

Bliss, Erica B.; David S. Meyers; Robert L. Phillips, Jr; George E. Fryer; Susan M. Dovey; and Larry A. Green. 2004. "Variation in Participation in Health Care Settings Associated with Race and Ethnicity." *Journal of General Internal Medicine* 19, no. 9 (September): 931–36.

Blum, R.W.; T. Beuhring; M.L. Shew; L.H. Bearinger; R.E. Sieving; and M.D. Resnick. 2000. "The Effects of Race/Ethnicity, Income, and Family Structure on Adolescent Risk Behavior." *American Journal of Public Health* 90, no. 12: 1879–1994.

Boscarino, Joseph A., and Richard E. Adams. 2004. "Public Perceptions of Quality Care and Provider Profiling in New York: Implications for Improving Quality Care and Public Health." *Journal of Public Health Management and Practice* 10, no. 3 (May–June): 241–50.

Bositis, David A. 2001. *Black Elected Officials: A Statistical Summary.* Washington D.C.: Joint Center for Political and Economic Studies. www.jointcenter.org. Accessed on 9/12/2005.

Bound, John; Timothy Waidmann; Michael Schoenbaum; and Jeffrey Bingenheimer. 2003. "The Labor Market Consequences of Race Differences in Health." *Milbank Quarterly* 81, no. 3 (September): 441–73.

Bowen-Reid, Terra L., and Ciara Smalls. 2004. "Stress, Spirituality and Health Promoting Behaviors among African American College Students." *Western Journal of Black Studies* 28, no. 1 (Spring): 283–81.

Broadman, Jason D. 2004. "Health Pessimism among Black and White Adults: The Role of Interpersonal and Institutional Maltreatment." *Social Science and Medicine* 59, no. 12 (December): 2523–33.

Brodie, Mollyann. 1996. "Americans' Political Participation in the 1993–94 National Health Care Reform Debate." *Journal of Health, Politics, Policy and Law* 21, no. 1 (Spring): 99–128.

Brown, E. Richard; Victoria D. Ojeda; Roberta Wyn; and Rebecka Levan. 2000. *Racial and Ethnic Disparities in Access to Health Insurance and Health Care.* Los Angeles: UCLA Center for Health Policy Research, and Washington, D.C.: Henry J. Kaiser Family Foundation. Copy of the report is available on the Kaiser Family Foundation website at www.kff.org and UCLA's Center for Health Policy Research at www.healthpolicy.ucla. edu. Accessed on 5/21/2005.

Byrd, Michael W., and Linda A. Clayton. 2000. *An American Health Dilemma: A Medical History of African Americans and the Problem of Race, Beginning to 1900.* New York: Routledge.

Byrd, Michael W., and Linda A. Clayton. 2002. *An American Health Dilemma: Race, Medicine, and Health Care in the United States, 1900–2000.* New York: Routledge.

Carlos, Elizabeth D., and Robert M. Chamberlain. 2004. "The Black-White Perception Gap and Health Disparities Research." *Public Health Nursing* 21, no. 4 (July–August): 372–79.

Centers for Disease Control and Prevention, Office of Minority Health. 2005. "Health Disparities Experienced by Black or African Americans—United States." *Morbidity and Mortality Weekly Report* 54, no. 1 (January 14): 1–31.

Chen, Frederick M.; George E. Fryer, Jr; Robert L. Phillips, Jr; Elisabeth Wilson; and Donald E. Pathman. 2005. "Patients' Beliefs about Racism, Preferences for Physician Race, and Satisfaction with Care." *Annals of Family Medicine* 3, no. 2 (March–April): 138–43.

"Closing the Gap: Solutions to Race-Based Health Disparities." 2005. Applied Research Center (Oakland, CA) & Northwest Federation of Community Organizations (Seattle, WA). Online at www.arc.org. Accessed on 8/25/2005.

Copeland, Valire C. 2005. "African Americans: Disparities in Health Care Access and Utilization." *Health & Social Work* 30, no. 3 (August): 265–70.

Crotty, William. 1991. "Political Participation: Mapping the Terrain." In William Crotty, ed., *Political Participation and American Democracy,* 1–22. New York: Greenwood Press.

Danigelis, Nicholas L. 1977. "A Theory of Black Political Participation in the United States." *Social Forces* 56, no. 1 (September): 31–47.

Davis, Dave. 2003. "Reporting on America's Widening Racial Health Gap." *Nieman Reports* 57, no. 1 (Spring): 18–19.

Diaz, Vanessa A.; Arch G. Mainous; Richelle J. Koopman; Peter J. Carek; and Mark E. Geesey. 2005. "Race and Diet in the Overweight: Association with Cardiovascular Risk in a Nationally Representative Sample." *Nutrition* 21, no. 6 (June): 718–25.

Dirks, Robert T., and Nac Duran. 2001. "Africa American Dietary Patterns at the Beginning of the 20th Century." *Journal of Nutrition* 131: 1881–89.

"Disparities Remain a Major Public Health Challenge." 2005. *Nation's Health* 35, no. 3 (April): 6.

"Doctor: Racism Plays Role in Poor Health." 2005. *News-Leader* (Springfield, MO), October 31.

Donovan, B. 1992. "New 'Majority Minority' Districts May Mean Lower Black Turnout." *Congressional Quarterly Weekly Report* 50, no. 10 (March 7): 563–64.

Dula, Annette, and Sara Goering. Eds. 1994. *It Just Ain't Fair: The Ethics of Health Care for African Americans.* Westport, CT: Praeger.

Dunlop, Dorothy D.; Jing Song; Larry M. Manheim; John S. Lyons; and Rowland W. Chang. 2003. "Racial/Ethnic Differences in Rates of Depression among Preretirement Adults." *American Journal of Public Health* 93, no. 11 (November): 1945–53.

Edelman, Peter; Harry J. Holzer; and Paul Offner. 2006. *Reconnecting Disadvantaged Young Men.* Washington, D.C.: Urban Institute Press.

Egede, Leonard E., and Deyi Zheng. 2003. "Racial/Ethnic Differences in Adult Vaccination among Individuals with Diabetes." *American Journal of Public Health* 93, no. 2 (February): 324–29.

Elam, Linda, and Michelle K. Strollo. 2005. "Implications of the Medicare Prescription Drug Benefit for African Americans." Presentation for African American Medical Briefing on November 14, 2005. Washington, D.C.: Henry J. Kaiser Family Foundation. Online at www.kff.org. Accessed on 12/1/2005.

El-Bassel, N.; L. Gilbert; S. Hrishnan; R. Schilling; T. Gaeta; S. Purpura; and S.S. Witte. 1998. "Partner Violence and Sexual HIV-Risk Behavior among Women in an Inner-City Emergency Department." *Violence and Victims* 13, no. 4 (Winter): 377–93.

Epstein, Richard A. 2005. "Disparities and Discrimination in Health Care Coverage: A Critique of the Institute of Medicine Study." *Perspectives in Biology and Medicine* 48, no. 1 supplement (Winter): S26–S41.

Ervin, Michelle G. 2004. "Unequal Access to Hospice and Palliative Care." *Journal of Palliative Medicine* 7, no. 2 (April): 301–2.

Flattery, Maureen P., and Kathy M. Baker. 2004. "Evidence for Racial Disparity in Cardiac Transplantation Survival Rate." *Journal of Cultural Diversity* 11, no. 1 (Spring): 25–30.

"IV: Race, Ethnicity, and Culture." 2003. *Hastings Center Report,* Supplement (March–April): 39–43.

Franklin, Donna L. 1997. *Ensuring Inequality: The Structural Transformation of the African-American Family.* New York: Oxford University Press.

Gamble, Vanessa N. 1997. "Under the Shadow of Tuskegee: African Americans and Health Care." *American Journal of Public Health* 87, no. 11 (November): 1773–78.

Gavins, Raymond. 2004. "Literature on Jim Crow." *OAH Magazine of History* 18, no. 2 (January): 13–16.

Geiger, Jack. 1996. "Race and Health Care—An American Dilemma?" Editorial. *New England Journal of Medicine* 335, no. 11 (September 12): 815–16.

Geiger, Jack H. 1997. "Annotation: Racism Resurgent—Building a Bridge to the 19th Century." *American Journal of Public Health* 87, no. 11 (November): 1765–66.

Goldberg, K.C.; A.J. Hartz; S.J. Jacobsen; and A.A. Rimm. 1992. "Racial and Community Factors Influencing Coronary Artery Bypass Graft Surgery Rates for All 1986 Medicare Patients." *Journal of American Medical Association* 267, no. 11 (March 18): 1473–77.

Gornick, Marian E.; Paul W. Eggers; Thomas W. Reilly; Renee M. Mentnech; Leslye K. Fitterman; Lawrence E. Kucken; and Bruce C. Vladeck. 1996. "Effects of Race and Income on Mortality and the Use of Services among Medicare Beneficiaries." *New England Journal of Medicine* 335, no. 11 (September 12): 791–99.

Green, Lee B., and Rhonda K. Lewis. 2004. "Powerlessness, Destiny, and Control: The Influence on Health Behavior of African Americans." *Journal of Community Health* 29, no. 1 (February): 15–27.

Haas, J.S.; P.D. Cleary; E. Guadagnoli; C. Fanta; and A.M. Epstein. 1994. "The Impact of Socioeconomic Status on the Intensity of Ambulatory Treatment and Health Outcomes after Hospital Discharge for Adults with Asthma." *Journal of General Internal Medicine* 9, no. 3 (March): 121–26.

Hackey, Robert B. 1992. "Competing Explanations of Voter Turnout among American Blacks." *Social Science Quarterly* 73, no. 1 (March): 71–89.

Hadley, Jack, and John Holahan. 2005. "Federal Spending on the Health Care Safety Net from 2001–2004: Has Spending Kept Pace with the Growth in the Uninsured?" Report no. 7425. November. Washington D.C.: Henry J. Kaiser Family Foundation. Online at www.kff.org. Accessed on 12/1/2005.

Haiman, Christopher A.; Daniel O. Stram; Lynne Wilkens; P.H. Malcolm; Laurence N. Kolonel; Brian E. Henderson; and Loic Le Marchand. 2006. "Ethnic and Racial Differences in the Smoking-Related Risk of Lung Cancer." *New England Journal of Medicine* 354, no. 4 (January 26): 333–42.

"Hatch, Lieberman Promote Minority Health Care." 2005. *Salt Lake Tribune,* November 1.

Henry J. Kaiser Family Foundation. 1999a. *Survey of Race, Ethnicity and Medical Care: Public Perceptions and Experiences.* Report No. 1528. Washington, D.C. Online at www.kff/org. Accessed on 10/18/2004.

Henry J. Kaiser Family Foundation. 1999b. *Perceptions of How Race and Ethnic Background Affect Medical Care: Highlights from Focus Groups.* Report No. 1524. Study conducted by Frederick Schneiders Research. Washington, D.C. Online at www.kff.org. Accessed on 12/2/2005.

Hill, Kevin A. 1995. "Does the Creation of Majority Black Districts Aid Republicans? An Analysis of the 1992 Congressional Elections in Eight Southern States." *Journal of Politics* 57, no. 2 (May): 388–401.

Hill, Kim Q., and Jan E. Leighley. 1992. "The Policy Consequences of Class Bias in State Electorates." *American Journal of Political Science* 36, no. 2 (May): 351–65.

Hill, Kim Q.; Jan E. Leighley; and Agela Hinton-Andersson. 1995. "Lower-Class Mobilization and Policy Linkage in the U.S. States." *American Journal of Political Science* 39, no. 1 (February): 75–86.

Hines-Martin, Vicki; Mary Malone; Sanggil Kim; and Ada Brown-Piper. 2003. "Barriers to Mental Health Care Access in an African American Population." *Issues in Mental Health Nursing* 24, no. 3 (April): 237–56.

"HIV/AIDS Policy Fact Sheet: African Americans & HIV/AIDS." 2002. Washington, D.C.: Henry J. Kaiser Family Foundation. August. Online at www.kff.org. Accessed on 10/15/2005.

"HIV/AIDS Policy Fact Sheet: African Americans and HIV/AIDS." 2003. Washington, D.C.: Henry J. Kaiser Family Foundation. August. Online at www.kff.org. Accessed on 10/15/2005.

"HIV/AIDS Policy Fact Sheet: African Americans and HIV/AIDS." 2005. Washington, D.C.: Henry J. Kaiser Family Foundation. August. Online at www.kff.org. Accessed on 10/15/2005.

"HIV/AIDS Policy Fact Sheet: African Americans and HIV/AIDS." 2006. Washington, D.C.: Henry J. Kaiser Family Foundation. August. Online at www.kff.org. Accessed on 9/5/2006.

"HIV/AIDS Policy Fact Sheet: The HIV/AIDS Epidemic in the United States." 2005. Washington, D.C.: Henry J. Kaiser Family Foundation. August. Online at www.kff.org. Accessed on 11/28/2005.

Hoffman, Catherine, and Susan S. Sered. 2005. *Threadbare: Holes in America's Health Care Safety Net.* Report No. 7245. November. Kaiser Commission on Medicaid and the Uninsured. Washington, D.C.: Henry J. Kaiser Family Foundation. Online at www.kff.org. Accessed on 11/20/2005.

Holahan, John, and Allison Cook. 2005. "Changes in Economic Conditions and Health Insurance Coverage, 2000–2004." *Health Affairs* Web Exclusive, W5–498. November 1.

Hollar, Milton C. 2001. "The Impact of Racism on the Delivery of Health Care and Mental Health Services." *Psychiatric Quarterly* 72, no. 4 (December): 337–45.

Horowitz, Carol R. 2004. "How Do Urban African Americans and Latinos View the Influence of Diet on Hypertension?" *Journal of Health Care for the Poor and Underserved* 15, no. 4 (November): 631–44.

Houston, Thomas K.; Isabel C. Scarinci; Sharina D. Person; and Paul G. Greene. 2005.

"Patient Smoking Cessation Advice by Health Care Providers: The Role of Ethnicity, Socioeconomic Status, and Health." *American Journal of Public Health* 95, no. 6 (June): 1056–61.

Hurley, Robert E.; Hoangmai Pham; and Gary Claxton. 2005. "A Widening Rift in Access and Quality: Growing Evidence of Economic Disparities." *Health Affairs,* Web Exclusive W-5 (December 6): 566–76.

Hutchings, Vincent L., and Nicholas A. Valentino. 2004. "The Centrality of Race in American Politics." *Annual Review of Political Science* 7, no. 1: 383–408.

Ibrahim, Said A.; Stephen B. Thomas; and Michael J. Fine. 2003. "Achieving Health Equity: An Incremental Journey." *American Journal of Public Health* 93, no. 10 (October): 1619–21.

James, Delores C. 2004. "Factors Influencing Food Choices, Dietary Intake and Nutrition-Related Attitudes among African Americans: Application of a Culturally Sensitive Model." *Ethnicity & Health* 9, no. 4 (November): 349–67.

Jha, Ashish K.; Elliott S. Fisher; Zhonghe Li; E. John Orav; and Arnold M. Epstein. 2005. "Racial Trends in the Use of Major Procedures among Elderly." *New England Journal of Medicine* 353, no. 7 (August 18): 683–91.

Johnson, Kimberly; Katja Elbert-Avila; and James A. Tulsky. 2005. "The Influence of Spiritual Beliefs and Practices on the Treatment Preferences of African Americans: A Review of the Literature." *Journal of the American Geriatric Society* 53, no. 4 (April): 711–19.

Johnson, Rachel L.; Samantha Saha; Jose J. Arbelaez; Mary K. Beach; and Lisa A. Cooper. 2004. "Racial and Ethnic Differences in Patient Perceptions of Bias and Cultural Competence in Health Care." *Journal of General Internal Medicine* 19, no. 2 (February): 101–10.

Kahn, K.L; M.L.; Pearson; E.R. Harrison; K.A. Desmond; W.H. Rogers; L.V. Rubenstein; R.H. Brook; and E.B. Keeler. 1994. "Health Care for Black and Poor Hospitalized Medicare Patients." *Journal of American Medical Association* 271, no. 15 (April 20): 1169–74.

Kaiser Commission on Medicaid and the Uninsured. 2000. "Key Facts: Health Insurance Coverage and Access to Care among African Americans." Washington, D.C.: Henry J. Kaiser Family Foundation. June. Online at www.kkf.org. Accessed on 10/15/2005.

Karanja, Njeri. 2003. "Cultural Competence in the Prevention and Treatment of Obesity: African Americans." *Permanente Journal* 7, no. 2 (Spring): 46–48.

Kennedy, Bruce P.; Ichiro Kawachi; Roberta Glass; and Deborah Prothrow-Stith. 1998. "Income Distribution, Socioeconomic Status, and Self-Rated Health in the United States: Multilevel Analysis." *British Medical Journal* 317, no. 7163 (October 3): 917–21.

Key Facts: Race, Ethnicity & Medical Care. 1999. Washington, D.C.: Henry J. Kaiser Family Foundation. Report no. 1523. Online at www.kff.org. Accessed on 9/12/2005.

Key Facts: Race, Ethnicity & Medical Care Update. 2003. Washington, D.C.: Henry J. Kaiser Family Foundation. Report no. 6069. Online at www.kff.org. Accessed on 5/7/2005.

King, Gary; Anthony Polednak; Robert B. Bendel; My C. Vilsaint; and Sunny B. Nahata. 2004. "Disparities in Smoking Cessation between African Americans and Whites: 1990–2000." *American Journal of Public Health* 94, No. 11 (November): 1965–71.

Klassen, Ann C.; Allyson G. Hall; Barbara Curbow; and David K. Klassen. 2002. "Relationship between Patients' Perception of Disadvantage and Discrimination and Listing for Kidney Transplants." *American Journal of Public Health* 92, no. 5 (May): 811–16.

Lado, Marianne E. 2001. "Unfinished Agenda: The Need for Civil Rights Litigation to Address Race Discrimination and Inequalities in Health Care Delivery." *Texas Journal of Civil Liberties and Civil Rights* 6, no. 1 (Summer): 45.

Lannin, Donald R.; Holly F. Mathews; Jim Mitchell; Melvin S. Swanson; Frances H. Swanson; and Maxine S. Edwards. 1998. "Influence of Socioeconomic and Cultural Factors on Racial Differences in Late-Stage Presentation of Breast Cancer." *Journal of American Medical Association* 279, no. 22 (June 10): 1801–7.

Lantz, Paula M.; James S. House; James M. Lepkowski; David R. Williams; Richard P. Mero; and Jieming Chen. 1998. "Socioeconomic Factors, Health Behaviors, and Mortality." *Journal of American Medical Association* 279, no. 21 (June 3): 1703–8.

LaVeist, Thomas A. 1992. "The Political Empowerment and Health Status of African-Americans: Mapping a New Territory." *American Journal of Sociology* 97, no. 4 (January): 1080–95.

Lewis, Rhonda K., and Lee B. Green. 2000. "Assessing the Health Attitudes, Beliefs, and Behaviors of African Americans Attending Church: A Comparison from Two Communities." *Journal of Community Health* 25, no. 3 (June): 211–24.

Li, X.; S. Feigelman; and B. Stanton. 2000. "Perceived Parental Monitoring and Health Risk Behavior among Urban, African American Children and Adolescents." *Journal of Adolescent Health* 27, no. 1 (July): 43–48.

Li, X.; B. Stanton; and S. Feigelman. 2000. "Impact of Perceived Parental Monitoring on Adolescent Risk Behavior over 4 Years." *Journal of Adolescent Health* 27, no. 1 (July): 49–56.

Lieu, Tracy A.; Paul W. Newacheck; and Margaret A. McManus. 1993. "Race, Ethnicity, and Access to Ambulatory Care among US Adolescents." *American Journal of Public Health* 83, no. 7 (July): 960–65.

Lillie-Blanton, Marsha, and Catherine Hoffman. 2005. "The Role of Health Insurance Coverage in Reducing Racial/Ethnic Disparities in Health Care." *Health Affairs* 24, no. 2 (March–April): 398–408.

Limtanakool, Tiffany H. 2005. "Unequal Treatment Linked to Thousands of Minority Deaths." *Nation's Health* 35, no. 4 (May): 6.

Litwack, Leon F. 2004. "Jim Crow Blues." *OAH Magazine of History* 18, no. 2 (January): 7–11, 58.

Lublin, D. 1997. *The Paradox of Representation.* Princeton, NJ: Princeton University Press.

Luke, A.; R.S. Cooper; T.E. Prewitt; A.A. Adeyemo; and T.E. Forrester. 2001. "Nutritional Consequences of the African Diaspora." *Annual Review of Nutrition* 21, no. 1: 47–71.

"Major Diseases Have Racial Disparities." 2005. *New York Amsterdam News,* October 24.

Malveaux, Julianne. 2002. "Blacks Suffer Most from Managed Care." *USA Today,* October 29.

Mangan, Katherine S. 2004. "Health Care Needs Diversity, Report Says." *Chronicle of Higher Education* 50, no. 24 (February 20): A11.

McDonough, Peggy; Greg J. Duncan; David Williams; and James House. 1997. "Income Dynamics and Adult Mortality in the United States, 1972 through 1989." *American Journal of Public Health* 87, no. 9 (September): 1476–83.

McGinnis, Kathleen A.; Michael J. Fine; Ravi K. Sharma; Melissa Skanderson; Joseph H. Wagner; Marie C. Rodrigeuz-Baradas; Linda Rebeneck; and Amy C. Justice. 2003. "Understanding Racial Disparities in HIV Using Data from the Veterans Aging Cohort 3-Site Study and VA Administrative Data." *American Journal of Public Health* 93, no. 10 (October): 1728–33.

McGruder, H.F.; K.J. Greenlud; J.B. Croft; and J.Z. Zheng. 2005. "Differences in Disability among Blacks and White Stroke Survivors—United States, 2000–2001." *Morbidity and Mortality Weekly Report* 54, no. 1 (January 14): 3–6.

"Medicare and Minority Americans." n.d. Washington, D.C.: Henry J. Kaiser Family Foundation. Online at www.kff.org. Accessed on 10/15/2005.

Miller, Stephanie T.; Hope M. Sieb; and Sheila P. Dennie. 2001. "African American Perspectives on Health Care: The Voice of the Community." *Journal of Ambulatory Care Management* 24, no. 3 (July): 37–44.

Mincy, Ronald B. 2006. *Black Males Left Behind.* Washington, D.C.: Urban Institute Press.

Myers, F.; P. Satz; B.E. Miller; E.G. Bing; G. Evans; M.A. Richardson; D. Forney; H. Morgenstern; E. Saxton; L. D'Elia; D. Longshore; and I. Mena. 1997. "The African-American Health Project (AAHP): Study Overview and Select Findings on High Risk Behaviors and Psychiatric Disorders in African American Men." *Ethnic Health* 2, no. 3 (August): 183–96.

Napoles-Springer, Anna M.; Jasmine Santoyo; Kathryn Houston; Eliseo Perez-Stable; and Anita L. Stewart. 2005. "Patients' Perceptions of Cultural Factors Affecting the Quality of Their Medical Encounters." *Health Expectations* 8, no. 1 (March): 4–17.

National Center for Health Statistics. 2004. *Health, United States, 2004: With Chartbook on Trends in the Health of Americans.* Washington, D.C.: Government Printing Office.

Neighbors, H.W. 1985. "Seeking Professional Help for Personal Problems: Black Americans' Use of Health and Mental Health Services." *Community Mental Health Journal* 21, no. 3 (Fall): 156–66.

"New Survey Finds Majority of African Americans Say U.S. Is Losing Ground on HIV/ AIDS." 2004. Washington, D.C.: Henry J. Kaiser Family Foundation. Online at www. kff.org. Accessed on 10/15/2005.

Office of Policy Planning and Research. Department of Labor. 1965. *The Negro Family: The Case for National Action.* Washington, D.C.: Government Printing Office.

Okonkwo, Sharon K. 2002. "Consequences of the African Diaspora on Nutrition." *Nutrition Noteworthy* 5, no. 1. Online at http://repositories.cdlib.org/uclabiolchem/ nutritionnoteworthy. Accessed on 9/15/2005.

O'Malley, M.S.; J.A. Earp; S.T. Hawley; M.J. Schell; H.F. Mathews; and J. Mitchell. 2001. "The Association of Race/Ethnicity, Socioeconomic Status, and Physician Recommendations for Mammography: Who Gets the Message about Breast Cancer Screening?" *American Journal of Public Health* 91, no. 1: 49–54.

Orfield, Gary. Ed. 2006. *Dropouts in America: Confronting the Graduation Rate Crisis.* Boston: Harvard Education Press.

Overby, Marvin L., and Kenneth M. Cosgrove. 1996. "Unintended Consequences: Racial Redistricting and the Representation of Minority Interests." *Journal of Politics* 58, no. 2 (May): 540–50.

Perneger, T.V.; P.K. Whelton; and M.J. Klag. 1995. "Race and End-Stage Renal Disease: Socioeconomic Status and Access to Health Care as Medicating Factors." *Archives of Internal Medicine* 155, no. 11 (June 12): 1201–8.

Pernick, Martin S. 1997. "Eugenics and Public Health in American History." *American Journal of Public Health* 87, no. 11 (November): 1767–72.

Petrocik, John. R., and Scott W. Desposato. 1998. "The Partisan Consequences of Majority-Minority Redistricting in the South, 1992 and 1994." *Journal of Politics* 60, no. 3 (August): 613–33.

Poussaint, Alvin, and Amy Alexander. 2000. *Lay My Burden Down: Unraveling Suicide and Mental Health Crisis among African-Americans.* Boston: Beacon Press.

Prejean, J., and A.J. Satcher. 2006. "Racial/Ethnic Disparities in Diagnoses of HIV/ AIDS–33 States, 2001–2004." *Morbidity and Mortality Weekly* 55, no. 5 (February 10): 121–25.

Quaye, Randolph. 1994. "The Health Care Status of African Americans." *Black Scholar* 24, no. 2 (Spring): 12–18.

Reese, D.J.; R.E. Ahern; S. Nair; J.D. O'Faire; and C. Warren. 1999. "Hospice Access and Use by African Americans: Addressing Cultural and Institutional Barriers through Participatory Action Research." *Social Work* 44, no. 6 (November): 549–59.

Reverby, Susan M. 1999. "Rethinking the Tuskegee Syphilis Study: Nurse Rivers, Silence, and the Meaning of Treatment." *Nursing History Review* 7: 3–28.

Rhoades, Jeffrey A. 2005. "The Uninsured in America, 2004: Estimates for the U.S. Civilian Noninstitutionalized Population under Age 65." Medical Expenditure Panel Survey. Rockville, MD: Agency for Healthcare Research and Quality, U.S. Department of Health and Human Services. Statistical Brief No. 83. Online at www.meps.ahrq.gov. Accessed on 11/26/2005.

Richardson, Jerome; Tanya Anderson; Joseph Flaherty; and Carl Bell. 2003. "The Quality of Mental Health Care for African Americans." *Culture, Medicine, and Psychiatry* 27, no. 4 (December): 487–98.

Robert Wood Johnson Foundation. 2004. *Characteristics of the Uninsured: A View from the States.* May. Prepared by the States Health Access Data Assistance Center, University of Minnesota. Online at www.rwjf.org. Accessed on 12/1/2005.

Rosner, David. 1997. "Race, Foster Care, and the Politics of Abandonment in New York City." *American Journal of Public Health* 87, no. 11 (November): 1144–49.

Russell, Kathleen, and Nancy Jewell. 1992. "Cultural Impact of Health-Care Access: Challenges for Improving the Health of African Americans." *Journal of Community Health Nursing* 9, no. 3: 161–69.

Rust, George; George E. Fryer, Jr; Robert L. Phillips Jr; Elvan Daniels; Harry Strothers; and David Satcher. 2004. "Modifiable Determinants of Healthcare Utilization within the African-American Population." *Journal of National Medical Association* 96, no. 9 (September): 1169–77.

Satcher, David; George E. Fryer, Jr; Jessica McCann; Adewale Troutman; Steven H. Woolf; and George Rust. 2005. "What If We Were Equal? A Comparison of the Black-White Mortality Gap in 1960 and 2000." *Health Affairs* 24, no. 2 (March/April): 459–64.

Satel, Sally, and Jonathan Click. 2005. "The Institute of Medicine Report: Too Quick to Diagnose Bias." *Perspectives in Biology and Medicine* 48, no. 1 supplement (Winter): S15–S25.

Savitt, Todd L. 1978. *Medicine and Slavery: The Diseases and Health Care of Blacks in Antebellum Virginia.* Chicago: University of Illinois Press.

Semmes, Clovis E. 1996. *Racism, Health, and Post-Industrialism: A Theory of African American Health.* Westport, CT: Praeger.

Skinner, Jonathan; Amitabh Chandra; Douglas Staiger; Julie Lee; and Mark McClellan. 2005. "Mortality After Acute Myocardial Infarction in Hospitals That Disproportionately Treat Black Patients." *Circulation* 112, no. 17 (October 25): 2634–41.

Smedley, Brian D.; Adrienne Y. Stith; and Alan R. Nelson. Eds. 2002. *Unequal Treatment: Confronting Racial and Ethnic Disparities in Healthcare.* Washington, D.C.: National Academies Press.

Smith, James P. 1999. "Healthy Bodies and Thick Wallets: The Dual Relationship between Health and Economic Status." *Journal of Economic Perspectives* 13, no. 2 (Spring): 145–66.

Snowden, L., and K. Thomas. 2000. "Medicaid and African American Outpatient Mental Health Treatment." *Mental Health Services Research,* 2, no. 2 (June): 115–20.

Southwell, Priscilla L., and Kevin D. Pirch. 2003. "Political Cynicism and the Mobilization of Black Voters." *Social Science Quarterly* 84, no. 4 (December): 906–17.

Spital, Aaron; Clive O. Callender; and Patrice V. Miles. 2004. "Institutionalized Racism and End-Stage Renal Disease: Is Its Impact Real or Illusionary." *Seminars in Dialysis* 17, no. 3 (May–June): 177–80.

St. Claire, P.A., and N.A. Anderson. 1989. "Social Network Advice during Pregnancy: Myths, Misinformation, and Sound Counsel." *Birth* 16, no. 3 (September): 103–8.

"Study: Millions of Black Americans Have No Insurance Coverage." 2004. *New York Amsterdam News* 95, no. 20 (May 13): 34.

Subramanian, S.V.; Jarvis T. Chen; David H. Rehkopf; Pamela D. Waterman; and Nancy Krieger. 2005. "Racial Disparities in Context: A Multilevel Analysis of Neighborhood Variation in Poverty and Excess Mortality among Black Populations in Massachusetts." *American Journal of Public Health* 95, no. 2 (February): 260–65.

Sullivan Commission on Diversity in the Healthcare Workforce. 2004. *Missing Persons: Minorities in the Health Professions.* Project administered by Duke University School of Medicine and Funded by W. K. Kellogg Foundation. Report is available online at www. sullivancommission.org. Accessed on 9/20/2005.

Sullivan, L.W. 1991. "From the Secretary of Health and Human Services: Effects of Discrimination and Racism on Access to Health Care." *Journal of American Medical Association* 266, no. 19 (November 20): 2674–76.

Swartz, M.S.; H.R. Wagner; J.W. Swanson; B.J. Burns; L.K. George; and D.K. Padgett. 1998. "Administrative Update: Utilization of Services. I. Comparing Use of Public and Private Mental Health Services: The Enduring Barriers of Race and Age." *Community Mental Health Journal* 34, no. 2 (April): 133–44.

Taylor, Herman A.; James G. Wilson; Daniel W. Jones; Daniel F. Sarpong; Asoka Srinivasan; Robert J. Garrison; Cheryl Nelson; and Sharon B. Wyatt. 2005. "Toward Resolution of Cardiovascular Health Disparities in African Americans: Design and Methods of the Jackson Heart Study." *Ethnicity & Disease* 15, no. 4 (Autumn): S6-4–S6-17.

Trevino, Fernando M. 1999. "Quality of Health Care for Ethnic/Racial Minority Population." *Ethnicity & Health* 4, no. 3 (August): 153–64.

Trivedi, Amal N.; Alan M. Zaslavski; Eric C. Schneider; and John J. Ayanian. 2005. "Trends in the Quality of Care and Racial Disparities in Medicare Managed Care." *New England Journal of Medicine* 353, No. 7 (August 18): 692–99.

"The Uninsured and Their Access to Health Care." 2005. Washington, D.C.: Henry J. Kaiser Family Foundation. Online at www.kff.org. Accessed on 12/1/2005.

U.S. Department of Health and Human Services. 1990. *Healthy People 2000.* Washington, D.C.: Government Printing Office.

U.S. Department of Health and Human Services. 2001. *Mental Health: Culture, Race, and Ethnicity. A Supplement to Mental Health: A Report of the Surgeon General.* Rockville, MD: U.S. Public Health Service, Substance Abuse and Mental Health Services Administration, Center for Mental Health Services.

Vaccarino, Viola; Saif S. Rathore; Nanette K. Wenger; Paul D. Freferick; Jerome L. Abramson; Hal V. Barron; Ajay Manhapra; Susmita Mallik; and Harlan M. Krumholz. 2005. "Sex and Racial Differences in the Management of Acute Myocardial Infarctions, 1994 through 2002." *New England Journal of Medicine* 353, no. 7 (August 18): 671–82.

Valentine, Victoria L. 2004. "The New Civil Rights Battle." *Crisis* 111, no. 6 (November–December): 2.

Van Ryn, M., and J. Burke. 2000. "The Effects of Patient Race and Socio-Economic Status on Physicians' Perception of Patients." *Social Science Medicine* 50, no. 6 (March): 813–28.

Verba, Sidney, and Norman H. Nie. 1972. *Political Participation in America.* New York: Harper and Row.

Verba, Sidney; Kay L. Scholzman; Henry Brady; and Norman H. Nie. 1993. "Citizen Activity: Who Participates? What Do They Say?" *American Political Science Review* 87, no. 2 (June): 303–18.

Watson, Wilbur H. 1999. *Blacks in the Profession of Medicine in the United States: Against the Odds.* New Brunswick, NJ: Transaction Publishers.

Watts, Rosalyn J. 2003. "Race Consciousness and the Health of African Americans." *Online Journal of Issues in Nursing* 8, no. 1: 130–41.

Weech-Maldonado, R.; M.N. Elliot; L.S. Morales; K. Spritzer; and R.D. Hays. 2004. "Health Plan Effects on Patient Assessments of Medicaid Managed Care among Racial/Ethnic Minorities." *Journal of General Internal Medicine* 19, no. 2 (February): 136–45.

Weisfeld, Alix, and Robert L. Perlman. 2005. "Disparities and Discrimination in Health Care: An Introduction." *Perspectives Biology and Medicine* 48, no. 1 supplement (Winter): S1–S9.

Weiss, Rick. 2005. "Study Debunks That Blacks Are Wary of Medical Research: Minorities Are Willing to Volunteer But Often Are Not Asked." *Washington Post,* December 6.

Wendler, David; Raynard Kington; Jennifer Madans; Gretchen van Wye; Heidi Christ-Schmidt; Laura A. Pratt; Otis W. Brawley; Cary P. Gross; and Ezekiel Emanuel. 2006. "Are Racial and Ethnic Minorities Less Willing to Participate in Health Research?" *PloS Medicine* 3, no. 2 (February): 1–10. Online at www.plosmedicine.org.

Wenneker, M.B., and A.M. Epstein. 1989. "Racial Inequalities in the Use of Procedures for Patients with Ischemic Heart Disease in Massachusetts." *Journal of American Medical Association* 261, no. 2 (January 13): 253–57.

Western, Bruce. 2006. *Punishment and Inequality in America.* New York: Russell Sage Foundation Press.

Whitford, Ben. 2005. "Who Gets the Organs? Experts Say Transplant Medicine Has a Race Problem." *Newsweek,* September 20.

Williams, David R. 1999. "Race, Socioeconomic Status, and Health: The Added Affects of Racism and Discrimination." *Annals of the New York Academy of Sciences* 896, no. 1: 173–88.

Williams, David R., and Pamela B. Jackson. 2005. "Social Sources of Racial Disparities in Health." *Health Affairs* 24, no. 2 (March–April): 325–34.

Williams, Fiscella K. 2004. "Health Disparities Based on Socioeconomic Inequities: Implications for Urban Health Care." *Academic Medicine* 79, no. 12 (December): 1139–47.

Wilson, Julius. 1987. *The Truly Disadvantaged: The Inner City, the Underclass, and Public Policy.* Chicago: University of Chicago Press.

Woolf, Steven H.; Robert E. Johnson; George E. Fryer, Jr.; George Rust; and David Satcher. 2004. "The Health Impact of Resolving Racial Disparities: An Analysis of US Mortality Data." *American Journal of Public Health* 94, no. 12 (December): 2078–80.

Yancey, Antronette; Melissa Gatchell; E. Richard Brown; William McCarthy; and Allison Diamant. 2005. "Diabetes Is Major Health Problem for African Americans." Health Policy Fact Sheet, UCLA Center for Health Policy Research. Online at www.healthpolicy.ucla.edu. Accessed on 10/15/2005.

3

Hispanics and Health Care

In the 2000 U.S. census, 35.5 million persons (12.5 percent of the U.S. population) identified themselves as Hispanic ("Health Disparities Experienced by Hispanics" 2004). In 2005, Hispanics made up 14 percent (41.3 million) of the U.S. population and had become the largest minority group, surpassing African Americans ("Inside America's Largest Minority" 2005). Hispanics are also the fastest-growing minority in the United States. Between 1990 and 2000, Hispanics experienced a 58 percent growth compared to 13 percent growth for the total population (Marotta and Garcia 2003). Hispanics are projected to account for 46 percent of all U.S. population growth over the next twenty years ("Inside America's Largest Minority" 2005). It is estimated that by 2020, Hispanics will constitute 15 percent of the total U.S. population (Marotta and Garcia 2003). By 2050, the Hispanic population is projected to be 81 million, about one-fifth of the projected American population (U.S. Bureau of the Census 1986). Large-scale immigration (especially unauthorized immigration) from Latin America, especially Mexico, accounted for most of the growth in the Hispanic population during the 1990s. However, births to Hispanic immigrants rather than immigration itself is projected to be the key source of growth in the Hispanic population in the future (Pew Hispanic Center 2005).

Nearly 80 percent of the Hispanic population is concentrated in the states of California, Texas, Florida, New York, Illinois, Arizona, New Jersey, New Mexico, and Colorado. However, the Hispanic population is becoming more dispersed, with states such as Oregon, Washington, Nevada, Georgia, North Carolina, Virginia, and Massachusetts experiencing significant growth (Pew Hispanic Center 2005). Ninety-one percent of Hispanics live in urban areas (Marotta and Garcia 2003).

It is important to emphasize that the Hispanic population is not an easily identifiable racial or ethnic group. Rather, it is made up of a mix of individuals and groups who often do not share a common language or culture. For example, some Hispanics speak only English, while others speak only Spanish and some are bilingual. Some trace their origins to countries in South and Central America. One overall trait that all Hispanics share in common is connection by ancestry to Latin America

(Pew Hispanic Center 2005). Thus, often the term Hispanics and Latinos are used interchangeably. The U.S. Census uses the term Hispanic. Hispanics are divided into five major subgroups: Mexican Americans, Puerto Ricans, Cuban Americans, Central or South Americans, and "other" Hispanics ("Hispanic Health in the United States" 1991). According to the 2000 U.S. Census, Mexicans represent the largest group of Hispanics (about 63 percent), followed by "other" (14 percent), Puerto Ricans (10 percent), South Americans (5 percent), Central Americans (4 percent), and Cuban Americans (4 percent) (Campo-Flores and Fineman 2005). The "other" category includes individuals from El Salvador, and Dominican Republic and other Caribbean countries. It is also important to remember that Hispanics can be of any race since the U.S. Census defines race as a social construct and not a scientific phenomenon. Furthermore, census data are based on self-identification which can be very subjective (Marotta and Garcia 2003).

Hispanics as a group have not shared equally in the economic wealth and health of the U.S. population. For example, 22 percent of Hispanics live in poverty compared to 8 percent of whites (Alter 2005). Compared to whites, Hispanics are more likely to be unemployed or underemployed (Marotta and Garcia 2003; "Hispanic Health in the United States" 1991). Of all workers in the U.S. labor force, Hispanics earn the least. Foreign-born Hispanics earn about $200 per week less than whites. The median earnings of native-born Hispanics are roughly $125 per week less than the earnings of whites (Pew Hispanic Center 2005).

Hispanics also experience disparities in health care. Hispanics are at an increased risk for certain medical conditions such as diabetes, hypertension, violent deaths, alcoholism, tuberculosis, and human immunodeficiency virus (HIV) infections ("Hispanic Health in the United States" 1991). They suffer a disproportionate share of disease, injury, disability, and death compared to non-Hispanic whites ("Health Disparities Experienced by Hispanics" 2004). During 2003–4, on average, 33 percent of Hispanics lacked health insurance compared to 20 percent of blacks and 11 percent of whites (Alter 2005). Hispanics are generally more obese and less physically active; have less access to health care services and lower rates of use; are less likely to have a regular source of care; and tend to underuse preventive services compared to non-Hispanic whites (Wray 1992).

However, it is important to note that on certain specific health indicators Hispanics fare better than non-Hispanic whites. For example, for the past twenty years, Hispanics as a group have experienced lower mortality outcomes than non-Hispanic whites regardless of their low socioeconomic position and access to care (Borrell 2005). Hispanics living in the Southwestern United States have lower age-adjusted mortality from heart disease and malignant neoplasm than do non-Hispanic whites (Wray 1992). This has been often referred to as the "Hispanic paradox." However, a closer examination reveals considerable variation in health status within the Hispanic population by age, gender, acculturation, country of birth, and Hispanic subgroups. While it is not clear what precisely explains the Hispanic paradox, it has been suggested that factors such as possible under-reporting of Hispanic deaths, healthy immigrant effect, and risk profile may contribute to the Hispanic paradox (Franzini, Ribble, and Keddie 2001). Recent studies have suggested that the so-called Hispanic health advantage or Hispanic paradox is misleading because it does not apply to all Hispanic subgroups and is relevant only to recent foreign-born Mexican immigrants (Borrell 2005). We discuss the notion of the Hispanic paradox in more detail in the next section.

It has also been suggested that part of the problem may be that discussions of health issues often treat Hispanic Americans as a monolithic group. However, recent studies have demonstrated significant variations in health status and health care utilization among different subgroups within the Hispanic community. For example, Mexicans and Cubans are less likely while Puerto Ricans more likely to have any emergency department visits than non-Hispanic whites (Weinick et al. 2004). Hispanic blacks have a higher prevalence of self-reported hypertension than white Hispanics, and Hispanic blacks have higher odds of having hypertension than non-Hispanic blacks and Hispanic whites (Borrell 2006).

Even the effect of social determinants of health is contingent upon ethnicity. For example, worse health is associated with higher levels of socioeconomic status (SES) and acculturation among Mexicans, but with lower levels of SES and ac-culturation among Latinos whose origins are from the Caribbean islands (Zsembik and Fennell 2005). This has led some to advocate collecting both race and ethnic-specific data by Hispanic subgroups (Zambrana and Carter-Pokras 2001). Others have argued for avoiding analyzing and reporting findings of health disparities using the broad category of "Hispanic" and to discuss and report research finding about health disparities by specific Hispanic subgroups (Paniagua 2005). Still others have advocated a need for improvement in federal health statistics for racial and ethnic groups that rely on scientific principles for the validation and definitions of catego-ries such as "race" and "ethnicity" and less on self-identification (Hahn 1992).

For the purpose of this chapter the following things should be kept in mind. One, we use the terms Hispanics and Latinos interchangeably. In reporting and discussing different research findings, we use the term the researchers have used. In all other cases we use the term Hispanic. Second, most of our discussion of health care disparities refers to Hispanics as a group since most available health dispar-ity data report on Hispanics as a group. When health disparity data are available by Hispanic subgroups, we have made an effort to report the data by subgroups. Third, the focus of this chapter is the discussion of health care disparities between Hispanics and non-Hispanic whites and not of health care disparities between His-panic subgroups and among other racial/ethnic minorities. The terms whites and non-Hispanic whites are used interchangeably. In reporting on research findings we use the term the researchers have used.

What follows is a discussion of health care disparities experienced by Hispanics in the American health care system with respect to health status/outcome, health care access, and quality of care. This is followed by a brief discussion of white and Hispanic public opinion related to self-reported health status and perceptions of the

American health care system. Next, we discuss a variety of factors that may help explain these health care disparities. Finally, the chapter ends with a discussion of unauthorized immigrants and health care.

Health Status/Outcomes

A comparison of the leading causes of death for whites and Hispanics in 1996 and 2003 helps us understand some of the differences in health status and outcomes as well as the changes that have occurred in the health status of the two groups (see Table 3.1).

The top two causes of death for both whites and Hispanics are heart disease and malignant neoplasms and have remained so from 1996 to 2003. Some of the differences between the two groups are in the areas of unintentional injuries, HIV, diabetes, homicide, suicide, and Alzheimer's disease. Unintentional injuries ranked as the third leading cause of death for Hispanics in both 1996 and 2003, while for whites it was the fifth leading cause of death. Diabetes also ranks higher for Hispanics than for whites as a leading cause of death. Homicide ranks as the seventh leading cause of death for Hispanics while it is not among the top ten causes of death for whites. Chronic liver disease ranked as the sixth leading cause of death for Hispanics in 2003 but it does not rank among the top ten for whites. Suicide and Alzheimer's emerge among the top ten causes of death for whites but not for Hispanics. Also for Hispanics certain conditions originating in the perinatal period rank as the tenth leading cause of death but not for whites. Some of the differences with respect to Alzheimer's and unintentional injuries may be related to differences in age categories. For example, the Hispanic population, which is much younger, may be more susceptible to injuries while the white population, which is much older, is likely to be more susceptible to Alzheimer's (Marotta and Garcia 2003).

There have also been some changes in leading causes of deaths for Hispanics from 1996 to 2003. In 1996, HIV ranked as the fifth leading cause of death among Hispanics. By 2003, HIV had dropped out of the top ten leading causes of death. Diabetes had moved up from the sixth leading cause of death in 1996 to the fifth in 2003. Similarly, chronic liver disease had also moved up from ninth in 1996 to sixth in 2003. Perinatal conditions were not among the top ten leading causes of death in 1996 but had emerged as the tenth leading cause of death for Hispanics in 2003.

On some health care indicators Hispanics fare better than whites. For example, with respect to tobacco use and exposure to secondhand smoke, low birth-weight, and infant mortality, Hispanics do better than whites ("Health Disparities Experienced by Hispanics" 2004). The Center for Disease Control and Prevention (CDC) analyzed self-reported data about adults' smoking habits from the 2004 National Health Interview Survey. The analysis indicated that overall smoking by adult Americans had declined from 22.5 percent of the population who smoked in 2002 to 20.9 percent in 2003. However, the prevalence of smoking varied significantly

Table 3.1

Leading Causes of Death among Whites and Hispanics, 1996 and 2003

1996		2003	
Whites	Hispanics	Whites	Hispanics
Diseases of the heart	Diseases of the heart	Diseases of the heart	Diseases of the heart
Malignant neoplasms	Malignant neoplasms	Malignant neoplasms	Malignant neoplasms
Cerebrovascular diseases	Unintentional injuries	Cerebrovascular diseases	Unintentional injuries
Chronic pulmonary diseases	Cerebrovascular diseases	Chronic lower respiratory disease	Cerebrovascular diseases
Unintentional injuries	HIV	Unintentional injuries	Diabetes mellitus
Pneumonia and influenza	Diabetes mellitus	Alzheimer's disease	Chronic liver disease
Diabetes mellitus	Homicide	Diabetes mellitus	Homicide
Suicide	Pneumonia and influenza	Pneumonia and influenza	Chronic lower respiratory disease
Chronic liver disease	Chronic liver disease	Nephritis, nephrotic syndrome, and nephrosis	Pneumonia and influenza
Alzheimer's disease	Chronic pulmonary diseases	Suicide	Certain perinatal conditions

Sources: National Center for Health Statistics. 1998. *Health, United States, 1998 with Socioeconomic Status and Health Chartbook.* Hyattsville, MD: U.S. Government Printing Office; National Center for Health Statistics. 2005. *Health United States, 2005 with Chartbook of Trends in the Health of Americans.* Hyattsville, MD: U.S. Government Printing Office.

across population subgroups. Among Asians (11 percent) and Hispanics (15 percent), smoking was much lower compared to American Indians/Alaska Natives (33.4 percent), non-Hispanic whites (22.2 percent), and non-Hispanic blacks (20.2 percent) ("Cigarette Smoking among Adults" 2004).

In 2003, the rate for low-birthweight (less than 2,500 grams) live births was 6.69 percent for Hispanics compared to 7.04 for non-Hispanic whites. Among Hispanic subgroups, Puerto Ricans had the highest low-birthweight rate (10.01 percent) and Mexicans had the lowest rate (6.28 percent) (National Center for Health Statistics 2005).

In 1997, the infant mortality rate (per 1,000 live births) for Latinos was 6.0 compared to 7.5 for non-Latinos (Giachello 2003). Between 1995 and 2003 infant mortality rates declined for all racial/ethnic population groups. Throughout this period Hispanics enjoyed a lower infant mortality rate compared to all other racial/ethnic groups with the exception of Asians/Pacific Islanders. In 1995 the infant mortality rate for Hispanics was 6.27 compared to 14.65 for non-Hispanic blacks, 9.04 for American Indian/Alaska Natives, 6.28 for non-Hispanic whites, and 5.27 for Asians/Pacific Islanders. In 2003 the infant mortality rates for Hispanics had dropped to 5.64 compared to 13.62 for non-Hispanic blacks, 8.73 for American Indian/Alaska Natives, 5.70 for non-Hispanic whites, and 4.83 for Asians/Pacific Islanders ("QuickStats" 2006; "Racial/Ethnic Disparities in Infant Mortality" 2005). Among Hispanic subgroups in 2002, Puerto Ricans had the highest infant mortality rate (8.2) and Cubans had the lowest rate (3.7) (National Center for Health Statistics 2005).

Despite the fact that Hispanics fare better on some health indicators as mentioned above, on a variety of other health indicators they do not do as well as whites. For example, in 2001, Hispanics experienced more age-adjusted years of potential life lost before age seventy-five per 100,000 population than non-Hispanic whites for certain causes of deaths such as strokes (18 percent more), chronic liver disease and cirrhosis (62 percent), diabetes (41 percent), HIV (168 percent), and homicide (128 percent). In 2000, Hispanics also had 168 percent higher age-adjusted incidence for cancer of the cervix ("Health Disparities Experienced by Hispanics" 2004). Hispanics also trailed non-Hispanic whites on a variety of other health measures. For example, in 2002, among persons under the age of sixty-five, only 66 percent of Hispanics had health insurance compared to 87 percent for non-Hispanic whites. Also in 2002, only 77 percent of Hispanics had a regular source of health care compared to 90 percent for non-Hispanic whites, and only 49 percent of Hispanics adults age sixty-five or under were vaccinated against influenza compared to 69 percent for non-Hispanic whites during the preceding twelve months ("Health Disparities Experienced by Hispanics" 2004).

Cardiovascular disease is primarily manifested by coronary heart disease (CHD) and cerebrovascular disease (CVD), commonly called strokes. The major risk factors for heart disease and strokes are high blood pressure, high cholesterol, diabetes, smoking, physical inactivity, and obesity ("Racial/Ethnic and Socioeconomic Disparities in Multiple Risk Factors" 2005). Studies of cardiovascular mortality by race/ethnicity in the United States have shown an overall lower rate for both Latino men and women compared to rates for both whites and African Americans (Liao et al. 2003; Perez-Stable, Juarbe, and Moreno-John 2001). In 1992, the percentage and rate of coronary deaths occurring outside of the hospital or in emergency rooms were lower in Hispanics than in non-Hispanic whites or blacks (Gillum 1997). Yet, surprisingly, research has documented a less favorable cardiovascular risk factor profile in Hispanics than non-Hispanic whites. For example, on average Hispanics have higher body mass indexes, more central obesity, and lower high density lipoprotein (HDL) and higher triglyceride levels compared to non-Hispanic whites (Liao et al. 2003). Similarly, in a national survey of the U.S. civilian population age eighteen and over, a higher percentage of Hispanic respondents (39.6 percent) reported that they suffered from multiple risk factors for heart disease and stroke compared to 35.5 percent non-Hispanic whites ("Racial/Ethnic and Socioeconomic Disparities in Multiple Risk Factors" 2005).

This has led some to question the accuracy of the mortality data for Hispanics on the grounds of misclassification of ethnicity and/or undercounting of Hispanic deaths. The lower than expected mortality rates for Hispanics for CHD despite their low socioeconomic status (SES) is called the "Hispanic paradox." Several explanations have been offered for this apparent paradox. One is called the "healthy migrant" effect explanation. This explanation suggests that Hispanic immigrants have a better diet, consisting of more fruits and vegetables, before leaving their country of birth and that, combined with health-preserving cultural and psychological effects, this creates less chronic disease risk exposure in the Hispanic population (Liao et al. 2003; Perez-Stable, Juarbe, and Moreno-John 2001). Another possible explanation is the "salmon" hypothesis, which states that Latinos, especially Mexican Americans, return to their birthplace to die and thus are missed in U.S. statistics (Perez-Stable, Juarbe, and Moreno-John 2001).

For the past twenty years, research has presented evidence of a Hispanic paradox in the United States in which most Hispanics are characterized by low socioeconomic status, but fare better than expected on certain health and mortality outcomes (Franzini, Ribble, and Keddie 2001). However, the notion of a Hispanic paradox has come under increased scrutiny and reexamination by researchers in recent years.

For example, Palloni and Arias (2004) tested several competing hypotheses regarding the adult Hispanic mortality paradox, data artifacts (errors), healthy migration effect, the "salmon-bias effect," and cultural or social buffering effect. According to the authors, the healthy-migrant effect posits that the migrants who come to United Sates tend to be more healthy and this accounts for the paradox. The "salmon-bias" effect is the propensity of non-U.S.-born Hispanic subgroups to return to their country of origin following a period of temporary unemployment and/or illness. The authors also found that the Hispanic mortality advantage holds true only among foreign-born Mexicans and foreign-born Hispanics other than Cubans or Puerto Ricans. They attribute the foreign-born Mexican advantage to return migration or the "salmon-bias." Markides and Eschbach (2005) also attribute the mortality advantage among Mexican Americans to selective return migration or the "salmon-bias."

Other researchers have argued that systematic data errors have created the appearance of a mortality advantage. They argue that evidence for a Hispanic mortality advantage comes from two types of evidence—mortality rates calculated by linking vital registration death data to census population counts and mortality rates calculated from cohort studies—and both data systems are subject to error (Patel et al. 2004). They conclude that the high proportion of under-ascertained deaths of foreign-born persons is consistent with the "salmon-bias" hypothesis. Similarly, Smith and Bradshaw (2006) argue that the Hispanic paradox does not exist and the Hispanic paradox described in past research derives from inconsistencies in counts of Hispanic-origin deaths and populations.

It is also important to emphasize that in 1997 Latino women experienced higher maternal mortality deaths than did white women. The age-adjusted rate of maternal mortality for Latino women was 7.6 per 100,000 compared to a rate of only 4.4 for white women. The rate of Latino mortality is related to complications of pregnancy and childbirth (Giachello 2003). The pregnancy-related mortality ratio is much higher among Hispanic women than non-Hispanic white women (Centers for Disease Control and Prevention 2001). Hispanic women are also at much higher risk for the adjusted odds of premature births than non-Hispanic white women (Frisbie, Forbes, and Hummer 1998). This in turn is related to fewer Latino mothers receiving prenatal care in the first three months of pregnancy. For example, in 1998, 74.3 percent of Latino mothers who gave birth began prenatal care in their first three months of pregnancy compared to 97.9 percent for white mothers (Giachello 2003). A California study that compared the use of family planning services by Hispanic and white adolescent females found that the adolescent birthrate among Hispanics was three times higher than among whites, and Hispanic adolescents were more likely to come from poorer families, have a poorer health status, and were less likely to have a regular source of health care (Solorio et al. 2004). Also, compared to non-Hispanic white women, Hispanic women were less likely to receive services that the woman initiates (Gavin et al. 2004).

Available data show that Latinos experience lower overall cancer rates than the non-Latino population. The incidence rates for prostrate, breast, lung, colon, and rectum cancer are lower among Latinos than whites. However, rates of incidences for cervical, stomach, primary liver, and gallbladder cancer are much higher among Latinos than whites (Ramirez and Suarez 2001).

National surveys have demonstrated a lower use of Pap smear screening among Latino women than white women (Boucher 2002). Latino women also tend to seek health care services less often than women in other ethnic groups. As a result Latino women are much less likely to participate in mammography screenings for early detection of breast cancer (Ramirez and Suarez 2001). Despite increased screening among all women over the years, Hispanic women still remain at the greatest risk of not being screened (Zambrana et al. 2003). Low income, uninsured status, and language barriers are often associated with lower use of preventive services among Hispanics (Asamoa et al. 2004).

Even Latinos enrolled in prepaid health plans and thus facing fewer financial barriers to care are less likely than whites to obtain recommended cancer-screening tests. A study of the attitudes of Latino patients toward cancer screening tests in California concluded that fatalism, machismo, and other attitudinal barriers may explain lower rates of testing for cancer among the Latino population. The study found that Latino respondents were more likely to cite attitudinal and personal factors such as feeling well, forgetfulness, carelessness, fear, and embarrassment for not obtaining cancer screening tests rather than structural factors such as cost and transportation problems ("California Study" 1995).

It is important to emphasize that there are some limitations associated with cancer data regarding the Latino population. Lack of adequate and accurate data can be attributed to insufficient research, inconsistency in data collection methods, and difficulty in interpreting available surveillance information (Ramirez and Suarez 2001).

Mental health is important to overall health and productivity as well as for successful contributions to family, community, and society. Research has documented the existence of racial/ethnic disparities in this area. In general, minorities have less access to mental health services, are less likely to receive needed mental health services, and often receive a poorer quality of mental health care (U.S. Department of Health and Human Services 2001). Hispanic Americans have overall rates of mental illness similar to those for whites. However, one finds significant variation within the Hispanic community. For example, U.S.-born Hispanic adults are more likely to experience symptoms of serious psychological distress compared to their immigrant counterparts. Also, U.S.-born Hispanic adults are more likely to experience serious psychological distress (4.4 percent) compared to white adults (2.7 percent). Among immigrants, Hispanic adults are more likely to experience serious psychological distress (3.6 percent) than whites (2.9 percent) (Dey and Lucas 2006). One of the explanations offered is that the "ethnic" protective effect is directly attributable to the superior health and mental health status of immigrants. This explanation suggests that Latinos such as Mexicans, Cubans, and Puerto Ricans generally immigrate or migrate with superior mental health status compared to that of the population of the United States as a whole and that over time Latino immigrants have increased risk of mental health problems as they become more acculturated to U.S. culture and as the effect of "ethnic" cultural protective factors diminishes. Thus, for example, the rates of divorce for Latino immigrants are much lower than among U.S.-born Latinos. Increasing exposure to American society and culture corresponds with the erosion of social support and traditional Latin American cultural values (Vega and Alegria 2001).

Hispanic mothers are at much higher risk for reporting postpartum depressive symptoms (43.9 percent) than white women (31.3 percent) (Howell et al. 2005). Hispanic adults and children are less likely than whites to receive needed mental health care. Hispanic Americans also have limited access to ethnically or linguistically similar health care providers. Furthermore, Hispanic youths are at significantly higher risk for poor mental health than white youths (U.S. Department of Health and Human Services 2001). According to the 2005 youth risk behavior survey conducted by the Centers of Disease Control and Prevention (CDC), Hispanic high school students attempted suicide at much higher rates than their black or white classmates. More than 11 percent of all Latino students and 15 percent of Latino girls stated they had attempted suicide compared to 7.6 percent of blacks and 7.3 percent of whites (Eaton et al. 2006). Stigma, language barriers, and cultural insensitivity are some of the problems Hispanics encounter when trying to access mental health services (Kidd 2005).

Another major health concern for the Hispanic community is diabetes, which disproportionately affects Hispanics. The prevalence of diabetes among Hispanics (9.8 percent) is almost twice that of non-Hispanic whites (5.0 percent). Diabetes also affects Hispanics at a younger age than non-Hispanic whites. For example, among people aged eighteen to forty-four years, 3.2 percent of Hispanics had diagnosed diabetes compared to 1.3 percent of non-Hispanic whites (Centers for Disease Control and Prevention 2005). The lifetime estimate for developing diabetes is much higher for Hispanic men and women than for whites. For example, Hispanic women born in 2000 have a 52.5 percent risk and Hispanic men have a 45.4 percent risk of developing diabetes in their lifetime compared to 31.2 percent risk for non-Hispanic white females and 26.7 percent risk for non-Hispanic white males (Centers for Disease Control and Prevention 2005). Among Hispanics, type 2 diabetes is the fifth leading cause of death (Smith and Barnett 2005; Luchsinger 2001). Hispanics also have a higher rate of complications related to diabetes and it is the leading cause of heart disease, strokes, kidney disease, blindness, and amputations (Centers for Disease Control and Prevention 2005; D'Arrigo and Keegan 2000). The prevalence of hypertension is much higher among Hispanics than whites and it is a major health threat to the Hispanic community. Furthermore, only about half of Hispanic Americans who suffer from hypertension are aware that they have high blood pressure and only about one-fourth of them have their blood pressure under control (Cangiano 1994). Mexican Americans are also less likely to have their blood cholesterol checked than whites (Fan et al. 2005).

Again, it is important to note that diabetes-related mortality differs significantly among Hispanic subgroups over thirty-five years of age. For example, the diabetes-related mortality rate is highest among Mexican Americans (251 deaths per 100,000) while lowest among Cuban Americans (101 deaths per 100,000). The Puerto Rican diabetes-related mortality rate falls between these two groups at 204 deaths per 100,000 (Smith and Barnett 2005). It is also important to emphasize that much of the data reported here are estimates based on the Behavioral Risk Factor Surveillance System (BRFSS) surveys conducted by the CDC and thus have several limitations. Estimates of prevalence of diabetes obtained from telephone surveys are likely to be lower than the actual prevalence since prevalence of diabetes is likely to be higher among persons without telephones and because some persons have undiagnosed diabetes. Also, the CDC analysis includes data from only six states and Puerto Rico and therefore may not be fully representative of all Hispanics in the United States ("Health Disparities Experienced by Hispanics" 2004).

HIV-AIDS disproportionately affects minorities in the United States. In 2004, Latinos constituted approximately 14 percent of the U.S. population but accounted for 19 percent of AIDS cases diagnosed since the start of the epidemic in 1981. HIV was the sixth leading cause of death for Latinos ages twenty-five to thirty-four in 2002 (Henry J. Kaiser Family Foundation 2006). Hispanics accounted for more than 8,000, or 20 percent, of the more than 42,000 new cases diagnosed in the United States in 2002 (Centers for Disease Control and Prevention 2006a). For the years between 1999 and 2003, HIV data reported by thirty-two states and the District of Columbia indicated that the HIV/AIDS diagnosis rate per 100,000 persons in 2003 was 74 for blacks, 25 for Hispanics, 11 for American Indians/Alaska Native, 9 for whites, and 7 for Asians/Pacific Islanders (Dean et al. 2005). In 2004, the estimated HIV/AIDS case rates per 100,000 were 76.3 for blacks, 29.5 for Hispanics, and 9.0 for whites. The rates for blacks and Hispanics were 8.5 and 3.3 times higher, respectively, than for whites (Centers for Disease Control and Prevention 2006b). There are also significant differences in survival rate in Hispanics compared to whites suffering from AIDS (Murrain 1996). Part of the reason may be because Hispanics tend to have HIV infections diagnosed late in the course of their disease and are less likely to have health insurance ("Health Disparities Experienced by Hispanics" 2004). A survey of the U.S. Latino population in 1998 revealed that Latinos demonstrate knowledge about how AIDS is transmitted. However, they continue to hold misconceptions such as availability of a vaccine and the existence of a cure for AIDS (Amaro, Vega, and Valencia 2001).

As the above discussion indicates, despite the "Hispanic paradox" on certain health status indicators, Hispanics experience disparities in health status/outcome on a variety of other health measures compared to whites.

Access to Health Care

Access to health care involves physical access (proximity to health care sites, transportation), financial access (health insurance, personal resources), and other factors such as ability to take time off from work to address health care needs and ability to navigate the complex health care system (U.S. General Accounting Office 2003). Numerous research findings have consistently demonstrated that two of the largest racial/ethnic minorities, Hispanics and African Americans, face greater barriers in access to medical care compared with the non-Hispanic white population (Castro, Coe, and Harmon 1996). Research also suggests that Hispanics are less likely to seek and receive health care services and that a significant gap exists in access to health care and preventive services among Hispanics versus non-Hispanics ("Access to Health-Care and Preventive Services" 2004). Compared to whites, Hispanics are more likely to be without a usual source of medical care, more likely to have gone without a health care visit in the past year, and at least twice as likely to receive late or no prenatal care (Henry J. Kaiser Family Foundation 2003). For example, in 2003–4, 30.9 percent of Hispanics between the ages of eighteen and sixty-four had no usual source of health care compared to only 14.8 percent of whites. Similarly, in 2004, 27 percent of Hispanics compared to only 14 percent of whites had no health care visits in the last twelve months. Also in 2004, the percentage of live births to mothers who received late or no prenatal care was 5.4 percent for Hispanics compared to 2.2 percent for whites (Henry J. Kaiser Family Foundation 2007).

Among Hispanic subgroups, Mexican Americans, other Hispanics, and Hispanics of unknown origin are more likely to receive either late or no perinatal care compared to Puerto Rican and Cuban women (Henry J. Kaiser Family Foundation 2007). The reasons Latino women confront problems in accessing the health care system for preventive and maintenance health care include the high cost of care and the lower levels of satisfaction Latino women experience when receiving such care (Giachello 2001).

The disparity in access to health care for Hispanics cuts across many diseases and health conditions. Research conducted at both the national and state levels has demonstrated the existence of disparities experienced by Hispanics in accessing health care services. For example, research has demonstrated the existence of a disparity in health care access and utilization between Hispanics and non-Hispanic adults with type 2 diabetes (Harris 2001), and with respect to access to infectious disease specialists as a regular source of care (Heslin et al. 2005). Other research has found that among individuals suffering from diabetes, whites have much higher vaccination rates than Hispanics (Egede and Zheng 2003); among people suffering from osteoarthritis, whites are twice as likely as Hispanics to undergo total knee replacement surgery despite the efficacy and cost-effectiveness of such a procedure (Suarez-Almazor et al. 2005); Hispanics are also less likely than whites to use mental health services and less likely to use a prescription drug for specific mental illness (Han and Liu 2005; Ruiz 1993). Hispanics are also less likely than non-Hispanics to be screened for blood cholesterol, for breast, cervical, and colorectal cancers, and to receive pneumococcal and influenza vaccinations ("Access to Health-Care and Preventive Services" 2004).

Hispanic women are less likely to use preventive services than non-Hispanic white women. Hispanic women in the U.S. under-use cancer screening tests and face important barriers to screening (Gorin and Heck 2005; Coughlin and Uhler 2002). A study of use of preventive services by Hispanic women in Atlanta, Georgia, and Miami, Florida, found that Hispanic women compared to non-Hispanic white women are less likely to have had Pap screening and less likely to use contraceptives (Asamoa et al. 2004). Lack of access to health care is more prevalent among Hispanic women who are poor or near poverty status, and who have less than a high school diploma or are foreign-born (Freeman and Lethbridge-Cejku 2006).

Since almost one-third of the country's Hispanics live in California, several studies have examined the issue of Hispanic access to health care services in California. Almost all of these studies have demonstrated significant problems faced by Hispanics in accessing health care services. For example, one study concluded that Hispanic adolescent females are less likely to use family planning services than white adolescent females (Solorio et al. 2004). Another study concluded that Latinos in California have less access to health care than other residents and when Latinos do get care, it is more often from hospital emergency rooms or community or public clinics (Shinkman 1997). Fifty-five percent of new Hispanic mothers surveyed in California reported that they had experienced problems or fears when applying for health care coverage under the state's Medicaid or children's health insurance program ("California Hispanics Face Barriers to Health Care" 2003). Mexican immigrants in California, who are in better overall health according to several health indicators than U.S.-born Latinos of Mexican ancestry, have trouble accessing heath care services when they need health care (Wallace, Gutierrez, and Brown 2003). Ethnic conflicts and partisan politics may contribute to deny or discourage access to health care to Hispanic women and children (Leichter 2004).

While racial/ethnic disparities in health care among adults have received considerable scholarly attention, few studies have focused on disparities among children. These studies have demonstrated the existence of disparities among children by race/ethnicity. An analysis of data for 2,608 children, ages four to thirty-five months, from the 2000 National Survey of Early Childhood Health, showed that Hispanic children were significantly less likely than whites to be in excellent or very good health. Furthermore, health care providers referred Hispanic children to specialists less often than they did the white children (Flores, Olson, and Tomany-Korman 2005). Compared to white children, Hispanic children are less likely to have a regular source of medical care, health professional or doctor visits, and dental visits in the previous year (Shi and Stevens 2005). There are also baseline racial and ethnic disparities among new enrollees in the State Children's Health Insurance Program (SCHIP), with Hispanic children faring worse than white children on many health system measures (Shone et al. 2003). Finally, another study found that among three groups of children—Mexican American children, non-Hispanic black children, and non-Hispanic white children—Mexican American children had the least health care access and utilization. The fact that in this study first-generation Mexican American children fared substantially worse than second- or third-generation children underscores the importance of generational status (Burgos et al. 2005). Barriers to access to health care services and utilization often include language problems, cultural differences, poverty, lack of health insurance, transportation difficulties, and long waiting lines (Flores et al. 1998).

What factors act as a barrier to Hispanics trying to access health care services? One of the primary factors is lack of health insurance coverage. Uninsured and under-insured individuals in the United States have only limited access to health, including mental health, services. They often receive health care via hospital emergency rooms, public hospitals, or community clinics. This is even more pronounced among racial/ethnic minorities because disproportionately more of them are uninsured (Ruiz 1993). The uninsured are up to three times more likely than those with insurance to report problems getting needed health care. The uninsured are less likely to have regular outpatient care and to receive timely preventive care, and more likely to be hospitalized for avoidable health problems. In addition, many uninsured fail to follow recommended treatment because of anticipated high medical bills (Kaiser Commission on Medicaid and the Uninsured 2006). When it comes to lack of health insurance among racial/ethnic minorities, Hispanics are worse off than non-Hispanic whites, African Americans, and American Indians and Alaska Natives.

Latinos are more than three times as likely as non-Latino whites to be uninsured. Hispanics have the largest percentage of uninsured and the lowest percentage of people with employer coverage. For example, in 2005 among the non-elderly population, 34 percent of Hispanics lacked health insurance coverage compared to 13 percent of whites, 21 percent of African Americans, and 32 percent of American Indians/Alaskan Natives. During the same year, among the non-elderly population, 69 percent of non-Hispanic whites received health insurance through their employer compared to 52 percent of African Americans, 47 percent of American Indians/ Alaska Natives, and 42 percent of Hispanics (Henry J. Kaiser Family Foundation 2007). Other studies have revealed that among adult rural residents, Hispanics are more likely to be uninsured compared to African Americans or whites (Blewett, Davern, and Rodin 2005; Glover et al. 2004). Among subgroups of Hispanic women, Mexican and Central or South American women are more likely than Puerto Rican or Cuban women to lack health insurance coverage (Freeman and Lethbridge-Cejku 2006).

In 2005, among children, 22 percent of Hispanic, 8 percent of non-Hispanic white, 13 percent of African Americans, and 28 percent of American Indians/ Alaska Natives were uninsured (Henry J. Kaiser Family Foundation 2007). Also in 2005, of the 35 million non-elderly Medicaid beneficiaries, Hispanics (25 percent) and non-Hispanic African Americans (23 percent) were disproportionately represented among Medicaid beneficiaries compared to non-Hispanic whites (45 percent), reflecting the relatively lower income of minority subgroups. Forty-four percent of African American children and 39 percent of Hispanic children received Medicaid coverage compared to 18 percent of white children (Henry J. Kaiser Family Foundation 2007).

Not only are racial/ethnic minorities disadvantaged when it comes to health insurance coverage, studies have also demonstrated that even among the uninsured, Hispanics and African Americans fare worse than uninsured whites in obtaining access to care. Thus, people of color, when uninsured, are doubly disadvantaged in the American health care system (Lillie-Blanton and Hoffman 2005).

The American health care system is built around the premise that most working-age Americans and their dependents receive health insurance coverage through their place of employment, that is, their employer. However, racial/ethnic minorities have lower rates of health insurance than whites because they are less likely to have employer-sponsored health insurance coverage. This is especially true of Hispanics because they are often are clustered in jobs that are low paying, less stable, more hazardous, and less likely to offer fringe benefits such as health insurance coverage (Del Pinal and Singer 1997). Thus, a major reason why so many Hispanics lack health insurance coverage is because their employers often do not offer such coverage. Many Hispanics work in agriculture, mining, service, and construction industries, which are less likely to offer health insurance coverage than other industries. Hispanics also tend to have greater employment in small firms, which are also less likely to offer health insurance coverage than large firms (Carrillo et al. 2001).

There are other secondary and tertiary barriers that further limit Hispanics' access to health care services. One of these is the degree to which the country's health care professions reflect the racial/ethnic composition of the general population. In 1990 Latinos made up only 2 percent of the U.S. health care workforce while they constitute 14 percent of the country's population. Hispanic Americans often seek medical care from Hispanic physicians because of personal preference and language and not solely due to geographic accessibility (Saha et al. 2000). Thus, a case can be made for producing a culturally diverse health care workforce in the United States (Cohen, Gabriel, and Terrell 2002).

Many Hispanic patients face the double burden of lack of health insurance and limited English proficiency. Thus, problems in gaining access to health care are often exacerbated for Hispanics who are less proficient in English (Doty 2003). Language barriers and lack of interpreters can seriously compromise doctor-patient communication. Poor communication between doctor and patient can lead to poor compliance with doctors' directives, increased patient dissatisfaction, and further limited access to health care services (Carrillo et al. 2001). In addition, organizational factors such as difficulty in getting appointments, lack of access to after-hours care, lack of transportation, and long waiting times for referrals to specialists can act as barriers to health care services (Carrillo et al. 2001).

Despite efforts to increase access to health care services for minorities, results thus far have been disappointing, especially for the Hispanic population. Between 1977 and 1996, overall racial/ethnic health care disparities actually increased, particularly for Hispanics (Weinick, Zuvekas, and Cohen 2000). According to the *2004 National Healthcare Disparities Report* (Agency for Healthcare Research and Quality 2004), of the thirty-one measures of access, with comparable data for 2000 and 2001, Hispanics had worse access to care than whites for about 90 percent of measures in both 2000 and 2001. Between 2000 and 2001, none of the thirty-one measures showed significant improvement among Hispanics. To facilitate comparison across racial/ethnic groups, subsequent reports have focused on fewer core access measures. According to the *2005 National Healthcare Disparities Report* (Agency for Healthcare Research and Quality 2005), Hispanics had worse access to health care than non-Hispanic whites for 88 percent (seven out of eight) of core access measures. The *2006 National Healthcare Disparities Report* (Agency Healthcare Research and Quality 2007) concluded that Hispanics had worse access than non-Hispanic whites for 83 percent (five out of six) of core access measures. According to the *2007 National Healthcare Disparities Report*, of the six core measures of access, 80 percent of core access measures either remained unchanged or had gotten worse for Hispanics (Agency for Healthcare Research and Quality 2008). Thus, no significant gains have been recorded in increasing Hispanic access to health care.

Even providing insurance coverage to the uninsured may not necessarily guarantee equal access to medical services. Gornick (2000) has demonstrated that when health care needs of racial minorities and the disadvantaged are taken into account, disparities still persist for those covered by Medicare.

Of course, even if one has access to health care services, it does not guarantee quality care. How do Hispanics fare with respect to quality of care compared to whites?

Quality of Health Care

A report issued by the Institute of Medicine (IOM) (2002) is credited with drawing the nation's attention to the disparities in health care experienced by racial/ethnic minorities in the United States. The IOM's study committee reviewed over one hundred studies that assessed the quality of health care for various racial/ethnic minorities. The study committee was struck by the consistency of research findings that indicated that minorities are less likely to receive needed services across a wide range of diseases. The report concluded that minorities and non-English-speaking patients not only had greater difficulty in accessing health services but also tended to receive lower quality of health care than whites even when they had the same types of health insurance. Furthermore, the report argued that Hispanics in particular tend to receive a lower quality of health care across a range of disease areas including cancer, cardiovascular disease, HIV-AIDS, diabetes, mental illness, and other chronic and infectious diseases and clinical services (Institute of Medicine 2002).

Many other studies have documented the lower quality of care received by Hispanics compared to non-Hispanic whites. One study conducted an analysis of 11,296 cardiac artery bypass graft (CABG) surgeries performed in New York State in 1996. The study relied on regression technique to identify significant associations between patients' race, HMO enrollment, and the quality of the surgeon performing the surgery measured by the surgeon's risk-adjusted mortality rate (RAMR). The results of the analysis indicated that non-whites were more likely than whites to have access to surgeons of higher RAMR. The study concluded that even when racial minorities do gain access to CABG services, they are more likely than whites to receive care from lower-quality providers (Mukamel, Murthy, and

Weimer 2000). Other studies have also documented that Latinos are less likely than whites to undergo angiography and bypass graft surgery (Carlisle, Leake, and Shapiro 1995, 1997). Another study in 1996 found disparities in the use of diagnostic and therapeutic procedures in hospital settings for cerebrovascular disease. For example, compared to non-Hispanic whites, Hispanics had higher rates of non-invasive diagnostic procedures while the odds of using invasive diagnostic testing and therapeutic procedures were lower for Hispanics (Elixhauser et al. 2002). Patients' experiences with hospital care also differ by race and ethnicity, with Latinos and blacks reporting more problems with respect to their preferences compared to whites (LeRoi et al. 2005).

Research has also demonstrated racial/ethnic differences in care and management of diabetes, one of the important health issues confronting the Hispanic population. Latinos have lower rates of self-monitoring blood glucose and worse glycemic control than do whites (Brown et al. 2003). As a result, Hispanics have an increased risk of retinopathy and end-stage renal disease. Also, immediate outcomes of care are inclined to be worse for Hispanics (Lanting et al. 2005). However, the quality of care given to Latinos and whites with diabetes tends to be similar (Brown et al. 2003).

One study examined whether the magnitude of racial/ethnic and language-based differences in patients' evaluation of the quality of primary care varies by capitation and gatekeeping. It concluded that English-speaking Hispanics' perception of the quality of primary care was different from whites' when capitation or gatekeeping is used in managed care as opposed to when these policies are not used (Stepanikova and Cook 2004). Another study has documented that Medicare managed care providers fail to provide equal treatment for mental illness across different races. According to this study, compared to whites, minorities receive substantially less follow-up after hospitalization for mental illness. The thirty days follow-up rate for whites was 60.2 percent compared to 52.6 percent for Hispanics. The rate of optimal practitioner contact for whites was 12.5 percent compared to 10.6 percent for Hispanics (Virnig et al. 2004). Another study also found that compared to whites, Hispanics were more likely to receive less care than needed or were likely to receive delayed care. Also, among those with need, whites were more likely than Hispanics to receive active alcoholism, drug abuse, or mental health treatment (Wells et al. 2001).

Research has also documented differences in quality of care provided to Hispanics and whites in other areas. For example, young Hispanic children admitted to hospital for asthma exacerbation were less likely to receive maximally effective preventive therapy compared to white children. The study also identified marked differences in the quality of care planned after hospital discharge for Hispanic patients compared with white patients (Finkelstein et al. 1995). Hispanic men are much less likely to receive colorectal cancer screening, cardiovascular risk factor screening and management, and vaccinations. Thus, Hispanic men are more likely to receive a poorer quality of health care than white men (Felix-Aaron et al. 2005).

Communication is one of the key factors in patient-doctor relationships. Patients with low English-speaking proficiency present a challenge to physician-patient communication (Richardson, Babcook, and Tamayo-Sarver 2003). Language barriers can limit access to health care, can adversely affect quality of care, and can act as a risk factor for adverse outcomes (Timmins 2002). Lack of language proficiency can also influence the quality of patient-physician interaction, patients' perception of the care they receive, and their level of satisfaction (Saha, Arbelaez, and Cooper 2003). Quality of care is compromised when patients with limited English proficiency do not receive the services of an interpreter (Flores 2005).

Despite increased access to medical services provided by the Medicaid program, racial/ethnic minorities and persons with limited English proficiency enrolled in the program tended to report worse care than did whites (Weech-Maldonado et al. 2003). Hispanic mothers who received prenatal care were more likely to experience language or communication problems than non-Hispanic women. Language barriers limited Hispanic mothers' ability to ask questions about their prenatal care and to understand information given to them during prenatal visits, and lessen their desire to return for subsequent appointments. Hispanic mothers are also less likely than non-Hispanic mothers to perceive that doctors, nurses, and office staff treated them with respect during their prenatal care visit (Tandon, Parillo, and Keefer 2005). Spanish-speaking Latinos are at increased risk of receiving lower quality of care and adverse health outcomes (Morales et al. 1999).

Hispanics with Hispanic physicians are more likely than those with non-Hispanic physicians to be satisfied with their health care overall (Saha et al. 1999). Patients who are members of minority groups are more likely than others to consult physicians of the same race or ethnic group. Unfortunately, communities with a high proportion of Hispanic or black residents were four times as likely as others to have a shortage of physicians, regardless of community income (Komaromy et al. 1996). Overall, across a wide range of diseases, Hispanic Americans tend to receive less and lower quality health care than whites (Sullivan Commission 2004).

According to the *2004 National Healthcare Disparities Report* (Agency for Healthcare Research and Quality 2004), of the thirty-eight measures of quality with comparable data for 2000 and 2001, information for Hispanics was available for only thirty-six measures. Of these thirty-six measures, Hispanics received poorer quality of care than non-Hispanic whites for half (50 percent) of the measures in both 2000 and 2001. Between 2000 and 2001, five of the measures demonstrated significant improvement while one demonstrated significant deterioration. To facilitate comparison across racial/ethnic groups, subsequent reports have often focused on a smaller number of core measures of quality of care. According to the *2005 National Healthcare Disparities Report* (Agency for Healthcare Research and Quality 2005), Hispanics received poorer quality of care than non-Hispanic whites for over half (about 53 percent) of core quality measures (twenty-one out of thirty-eight) and better quality of care for 16 percent (six out of thirty-eight) of measures. According to the *2006 National Healthcare Disparities Report* (Agency for Healthcare Research and Quality 2007), Hispanics received poorer quality of care than non-Hispanic whites for 77 percent of core measures (seventeen out of twenty-two) and better quality of care for 18 percent (four out of twenty-two) of core quality measures. Thus, it appears that the quality of care received by Hispanics has gotten worse over the last few years. The *2007 National Healthcare Disparities Report* focused on sixteen of the forty-two core measures of quality of care. According to this report, for Hispanics, seven core measures (43.7 percent) showed improvement, six measures (37.5 percent) remained the same, and three measures (18.7 percent) showed deterioration. Thus, the progress in decreasing the disparities in quality of care received by Hispanics and non-Hispanic whites has been uneven at best (Agency for Healthcare Research and Quality 2008).

Perceptions of the Health Care System

Public opinion polls have consistently revealed a significant racial divide between whites' and Hispanics' views of American society and health care system. The racial divide is perhaps not as wide as the one between African Americans and whites discussed in Chapter 2. A survey conducted in 1991, almost twenty-five years since the height of the civil rights movement, revealed that Archie Bunker is alive and well in America. The survey asked individuals in 300 communities in the United States to rate blacks, Hispanics, Jews, Asians, and whites on several characteristics. The results showed how difficult it is to get rid of stereotypes. Civil rights efforts reformed public policies but did not reshape the public's attitudes. For example, a majority of the respondents in the poll believed that blacks are more likely to be lazy, violence prone, less intelligent, and less patriotic. Hispanics were viewed just as negatively ("Archie Bunker, Alive and Well" 1991).

Another study in 1996 based on a national sample focused on stereotypes and social distance attitudes pertaining to blacks, Hispanics, Asians, and Jews. The results of this study indicated that, in general, cohorts born after World War II tended to be less prejudiced than prewar cohorts toward each of the minorities (Wilson 1996). The notion that younger cohorts of adults are less prejudiced is based on the notion of generational effect, that is, each succeeding generation is more tolerant and less prejudiced. However, this same study also found that most recent postwar cohorts of Americans (born between 1961 and 1972) showed no tendency to be less prejudiced than their immediate predecessors born since World War II. More interestingly, most recent cohorts residing outside of the South actually tended to be more prejudiced than their elders (Wilson 1996). What explains this? The author speculates that the civil rights movement and other events taking place in the 1950s, 1960s, and 1970s may have promoted a favorable racial attitude among cohorts coming of age during that period and the subsequent conservative shift associated with the Reagan presidency may have had the opposite effect on people coming of age in the 1980s. The study found that unfavorable stereotypes were strongest for blacks and Hispanics and somewhat less strong for Asians. Thus, the liberalizing of attitudes toward minorities occurring in successive generations may have slowed or may have even halted entirely (Wilson 1996).

Gallup's Annual Rights and Relations poll conducted in 2004 revealed that African Americans (83 percent) and Hispanics (60 percent) were less satisfied than whites (47 percent) with the way things were going in the United States (Mazzuca 2004). The 2006 Gallup's Annual Rights and Relations poll (Carroll 2006) also underscored the different economic realities faced by whites and minorities in American society. For example, 53 percent of whites believed that whites and minorities have equal job opportunities while only 34 percent of Hispanics and 17 percent of blacks thought that to be the case. What is interesting to note is that 67 percent of African Americans agreed with the notion that American society is divided into the "haves" and "have-nots" while 42 percent of whites and only 31 percent of Hispanics felt that way. When respondents were asked which group they belonged to, 62 percent of whites stated that they belong to the "have" group while only 41 percent of Hispanic and African American respondents put themselves in the "have" group (Carroll 2006). When respondents were asked how different groups are treated in American society, Hispanics and blacks rated the treatment of their own group more negatively than other groups. Only 40 percent of Hispanics were satisfied with the way Hispanics were treated compared with 45 percent of blacks and 62 percent of whites (Jones 2006). However, Hispanics rated white–Hispanic relations more positively (68 percent) compared to 55 percent of blacks and 61 percent of whites (Jones 2006). It seems that at least for Hispanics, the American dream is still alive. According to a CBS News/*New York Times* poll ("Hispanic Views" 2003), 60 percent of Hispanics agreed with the statement that it is still possible to start out poor in this country, work hard, and become rich.

These divergent perceptions and opinions of whites and Hispanics regarding race relations and equal opportunities in American society are also reflected in views about health care in America. When asked to self-report their own health status, Hispanics are more likely to report poor health than whites (Ren and Amick 1996a; Henry J. Kaiser Family Foundation 2007). A Kaiser Family Foundation survey conducted in 1999 found that a majority of Americans were uninformed about health care disparities. Furthermore, most minority Americans perceive that they get a lower quality of care than whites, but most whites think otherwise (Blizzard 2003; Lillie-Blanton et al. 2000). An analysis of cross-section data from a health care satisfaction module added to the 2000 Behavior Risk Factor Surveillance System (BRFSS) surveys found that Hispanics, compared to whites, were significantly more likely to be dissatisfied with overall health care and how their doctors and health providers listen, explain, show respect, and spend enough time with them (Merrill and Allen 2003).

In a nationwide survey of Latinos conducted in 2002 by the Pew Hispanic Center and the Kaiser Family Foundation (2004), one in seven (15 percent) Latinos said that they or another member of their household needed medical care but did not get it during the past year; one in five (22 percent) Latinos reported that they had trouble paying their medical bills in the past year; and three in ten (30 percent) stated that they had problems communicating with health providers over the past year. In 2004, Hispanics (44 percent) were twice as likely to report trouble paying for health care compared to whites (23 percent) (McMurray 2004). In 2005, 46 percent of Hispanics compared to only 24 percent of non-Hispanic whites reported that they did not have enough money to pay for medical care (Blizzard 2005).

The analysis of combined survey results from March 2007 and June 2007 by the Kaiser Family Foundation (2007) indicated that 64 percent of Hispanics compared to only 29 percent of non-Hispanic whites reported being worried about their own health care security. Similarly, a study conducted by the AARP found that of the roughly 73 percent of Hispanics who had purchased prescription drugs in a previous year, 41 percent of Hispanics had a problem paying for prescription medications. The result was that Hispanics who had difficulty paying for prescription drugs (about 33 percent) took at least one measure potentially harmful to their health such as delaying getting a prescription, skipping a dosage, or taking less medication than recommended by the health care provider. Thus affordability of prescription drugs is also an important issue for the Hispanic community (American Association of Retired Persons 2007).

The above discussion illustrates the racial divide that exists between whites and Hispanics with respect to perceptions and views about American society in general and the American health care system in particular. It is clear that disparities exist between whites and Hispanics with respect to health status/outcome, access to health care, and the quality of care received. On some health indicators Hispanics are better-off than whites (thus, the Hispanic paradox), but in most other areas they do not fare as well as their white counterparts. Within the Hispanic community itself, some subgroups are doing better than others. What factors help explain the existence of health care disparities between Hispanics and whites?

Possible Explanations for Health Care Disparities

Socioeconomic Status (SES)

Socioeconomic status (SES) is used frequently as a proxy for class to explain variations in health care status/outcome, access, and quality of care. SES is often measured by stratification in income, education, and occupation. Research has consistently demonstrated that SES remains a persistent and persuasive predictor of variation in health care disparities. Some studies have argued that each higher level of SES is associated with better health status while other studies have argued that at a certain threshold (usually around the median income) there is a weakening of the association between SES and health (Williams and Collins 1995).

Furthermore, research also shows that race is strongly correlated with SES, that is, certain racial/ethnic minorities occupy a much lower socioeconomic status in American society compared to whites. Thus, it has been argued that socioeconomic differences between racial groups are largely (thought not entirely) responsible for the observed disparities in health care. Therefore the argument is made that reducing differences in SES between different racial/ethnic groups will significantly reduce (but not eliminate) racial disparities in the American health care system.

According to research, one of the strongest and most consistent predictors of a person's morbidity and mortality experience is the person's SES. This finding persists, with few exceptions, across all diseases, continues throughout an entire life span and extends across any risk factors for disease. Some studies have suggested that certain dimensions of SES are more important than others. For example, Winkleby et al. (1992) found that those with the lowest educational attainment exhibited the highest prevalence of risk factors for cardiovascular disease (smoking, high blood pressure, and high total high-density lipoprotein cholesterol) while income and occupations were less consistent risk predictors. However, they acknowledge that using only one indicator of SES may yield misleading results. Another study, by Kington and Smith (1997), examined the relationship between wealth and income and selected racial and ethnic differences in health. This study concluded that SES plays a much greater role in explaining racial/ethnic differences in the ability to function once a person has a chronic illness and a moderate amount of difference in explaining disease prevalence.

Despite their low socioeconomic status, Hispanics as a group are often omitted from the health disparity discourse because of the so-called Hispanic paradox (Borrell 2005). It is also important to keep in mind that the Hispanic population is very heterogeneous in terms of culture, history, socioeconomic status, and health status. For example, health indicators for Puerto Ricans are significantly worse than for the other Hispanic-origin subgroups. The health indicators of Cuban persons are often better than those of other subgroups. Cuban persons generally have a higher SES while Puerto Ricans have low SES (Hajat, Lucas, and Kington 2000).

There is no denying that compared to whites, Hispanics enjoy a much lower socioeconomic status in American society. Table 3.2 provides some comparative data for Hispanics and whites with respect to income, education, and occupation to demonstrate the contrasting SES of the two groups. Hispanics lag behind whites in per capita income as well as median household income. In 2003, 10.5 percent of white persons and 8.1 of white families lived below the poverty level compared to 22.5 percent of Hispanics persons and 20.8 percent of Hispanic families. Similarly, in 2003, 13.9 percent of white children were below the poverty level compared to 29.5 percent of Hispanic children.

Hispanics also lag far behind whites with respect to education. The high school dropout rate for Hispanics (6.5 percent) was almost double that of whites (3.7 percent) in 2003. In 2004, the high school graduation rate for whites was 85.8 percent compared to only 58.4 percent for Hispanics. Similarly, 28.2 percent of whites were college graduates compared to only 12.1 percent of Hispanics.

Table 3.2

Socioeconomic Status of Hispanics and Whites

	Whites	Hispanics/ Latino
Population (2004)	236,058	41,322
Percent of U.S. population (2004)	80.3	14.0
Per capita income (in constant dollars, 2003)	$24,626	$13,492
Median income of households (in constant dollars 2003)	$45,631	$32,997
Percent of people below poverty level (2003)	10.5	22.5
Percent of families below poverty levels (2003)	8.1	20.8
Percent of children below poverty level (2003)	13.9	29.5
Percent high school dropouts (2003)	3.7	6.5
Percent high school graduate or more (2004)	85.8	58.4
Percent college graduate or more (2004)	28.2	12.1
Percent without health insurance (2003)	14.6	32.7
Percent covered by Medicaid (2003)	10.3	21.0
Percent employed in managerial/professional occupation (civilian noninstitutionalized population 25 years old or older, 2004)	39.0	19.1
Percent unemployment rate (2004)	3.9	5.7
16 to 19 years old	15.0	20.4
20 to 24 years old	7.9	9.3

Source: U.S. Census Bureau, *Statistical Abstracts of the United States, 2006.* Washington, D.C.: Government Printing Office.

In 2004, the unemployment rate for Hispanics was 5.7 percent compared to 3.9 percent for whites. Also, among all noninstitutionalized civilian employees twenty-five years and over, 39.0 percent of whites were employed in managerial/ professional occupations compared to only 19.1 percent for Hispanics.

Thus on all three measures—income, education, and occupation—generally used to measure SES, Hispanics rank much lower than whites. However, they rank slightly better than African Americans in comparison to whites (see Table 2.1 in Chapter 2). The lower SES of Hispanics is also reflected in the fact that in 2003, 21 percent of Hispanics were covered by Medicaid compared to only 10.3 percent of whites. Also, during the same year, 32.7 percent of Hispanics were without health insurance compared to 14.6 percent of whites.

How does lower SES influence health care disparities experienced by Hispanics? There is a considerable amount of research on this subject. One of the primary explanations for lack of access to health care by Hispanics is lack of health insurance. In 2005, 34 percent of Hispanics were uninsured. However, among low-income non-elderly Hispanics, 44 percent were uninsured. Among Hispanics overall, 13.3 percent rated their own health as fair or poor in 2004, compared to 20.2 percent of Hispanics who lived under 100 percent of the federal poverty level (Henry J. Kaiser Family Foundation 2007).

A lack of health insurance or having public insurance is also related to the likelihood of Latino adolescents being overweight (Haas et al. 2003). Compared to whites, Hispanics are more likely to assess their own health as poor and report having functional limitations in their daily activities. Socioeconomic factors play a different role in explaining these disparities. In respect to global health and functional limitations, education tended to play a significant role in explaining disparities between whites and Hispanics (Ren and Amick 1996b).

SES can also influence the use of and access to health care services. For example, a study that assessed the relative influence of psychological barriers, SES, and ethnic difference in mammography use found that use of mammography was strongly associated with SES among Hispanic women. Controlling for SES and ethnicity revealed that psychological barriers such as concern about cost remained an independent predictor of mammography use (Stein, Fox, and Murata 1991).

Another study that examined the racial/ethnic disparities in access to and use of mental health services among whites, blacks, and Hispanics concluded that neighborhood poverty is a key to understanding racial/ethnic disparities in the use of mental health services (Chow, Jaffee, and Snowden 2003). Low income, uninsured status, and language barriers are also strongly associated with low use of preventive health services by Hispanics (Asamoa et al. 2004). Hispanics (50 percent) also report receiving smoking counseling less frequently compared with whites (72 percent). Ethnic minority status, lower education, low income, and poor health status are strongly related to lower rates of advice to quit smoking (Houston et al. 2005).

Research has also found an inverse relationship between SES indicators and physiological and behavioral cardiovascular diseases (CVD) risk factors in Hispanics with low English proficiency (Elder et al. 1998). One of the biggest health problems facing Hispanics today is obesity leading to increased risks for hypertension, diabetes, coronary heart disease, osteoarthritis, and breast, prostrate, and colon cancer (Morales et al. 2002). A study examined the differences in individual measures of health-related physical fitness in a sample of African American, Hispanic, and white female high school students representing low, moderate, and high SES groups. The study found significant differences between socioeconomic groups with respect to percent fat, a body mass index (BMI), and physical activity level with individuals from low SES engaged in less physical activity than individuals from high SES (Falhman, Hall, and Lock 2006). Lack of regular physical activity and poor physical fitness during youth are factors shown to be associated with the health risk associated with adult obesity and increased morbidity and mortality as well as increased risk for cardiovascular disease later in life. Research has also shown that, among patient with diabetes and HIV, treatment adherence is much lower among individuals with low SES (Goldman and Smith 2002). Lower SES is also strongly associated with a significantly higher mean hemoglobin A1c (HbA1c). Hispanic youth with type 1 diabetes mellitus (DM) have poorer metabolic control than their white non-Hispanic counterparts (Gallegos-Macias et al. 2003). As discussed earlier, Hispanic households have disproportionately lower income compared to white households. Research shows that low SES is also associated with poor diet, food insufficiency, and poor child health Mazur, (Marquis, and Jensen 2003).

Finally, among Hispanics, lower SES is associated with unhealthy behaviors or lifestyles. Among Hispanic women, smoking cigarettes, being overweight, and being physically inactive are more common among persons with lower SES than those with high SES (Morales et al. 2002).

As the above discussion demonstrates, low SES is certainly one of the major factors that helps explain the health care disparities between Hispanics and whites. However, it is not the only factor. Another factor that plays a significant role in explaining health care disparities with respect to problems of access to and use of health care services, lower quality of care, and poorer health status/ outcome on certain health indicators is Hispanic cultural values and the Hispanic belief system.

Culture

One of the major challenges faced by the U.S. health care system is providing high quality health care to an increasingly diverse population. This problem is made serious due to shortages of ethnically and linguistically diverse physicians and other health care providers in the United States. Thus, there is an urgent need for creating a culturally competent health service. This starts with an understanding of how patients' culture affects health and risk behavior, the quality of medical encounters, and health outcomes.

According to a focus group study of African Americans, Latinos, and non-Latino white patients, definitions of culture common to all three ethnic groups included a system of shared norms, values, and beliefs, manifest customs such as food and music, self-identified ethnicity (including nationality or country of origin), and stereotypes about specific ethnic groups (Napoles-Springer et al. 2005). Some of the differences among the three ethnic groups about what constitutes culture included the following: The focus group consisting of white patients described culture as shared experiences that define a group such as drug or hip-hop culture. Nonwhite patients described culture as experiencing different treatment because of one's cultural background. Latino patients viewed language as a way to distinguish among cultural groups (Napoles-Springer et al. 2005).

All three groups cited complementary and alternative medicine; discrimination based on health insurance status, social class, and age; and ethnic concordance of the physician and patients as cultural factors that influence medical encounters. African Americans mentioned experience about physicians' acceptance of complementary and alternative medicine while Latino women emphasized prevention and attention to holistic mind-body connections. Spanish-speaking Latinos particularly emphasized the effect of language in the quality of their medical encounters (Napoles-Springer et al. 2005).

The above discussion highlights values and belief systems, customs, and language as important components of culture that can influence health care behavior, health outcomes, and health care encounters. For Hispanics who immigrated to the United States, another very important factor is the effect of acculturation on Hispanic health.

Acculturation

Acculturation is generally defined as the acquisition of the cultural elements of the host society—language, values, norms, attitudes, food, dress, music, sports— through which assimilation of immigrant groups in the host country happens. During acculturation individuals are thought to relinquish the behavioral norms of their culture of origin while adopting those of the host country's dominant culture (Morales et al. 2002). Gordon (1964) described the acculturation of European ethnic immigrants in the United States in the late nineteenth and early twentieth centuries as unidirectional and inevitable. He further argued that to become assimilated into the host society, immigrant ethnic groups had to make major accommodations and to adopt memories, sentiments, and attitudes of the middle class cultural patterns of largely white Protestant, Anglo-Saxon origin. The unidirectional view of acculturation is often referred to as a "zero-sum game" and assumes a linear continuum from total immersion in the culture of origin to total immersion in the dominant culture of the host country (Lara et al. 2005).

Bidirectional models of acculturation have questioned the validity of the assumption of the unidirectional model and have argued that acquiring elements of the dominant host culture is independent of the degree to which immigrants continue to value and adhere to the norms of the culture of their origin. Bidirectional acculturation models argue that different outcomes are possible including: (1) assimilation: lack of desire to stick to the culture of origin leading to complete acquisition of the dominant host culture; (2) separation: rejection and avoidance of the dominant host culture and maintenance of the culture of origin; (3) integration: embracing and valuing both cultures; and (4) marginalization: exclusion (voluntary or not) of both cultures (Lara et al. 2005).

However, as Marin (1992) has pointed out, individual immigrants may not have complete control over possible outcomes. For example, separation or marginalization can result from societal circumstances such as prejudice, institutional racism, segregation laws, and historical circumstances including territorial invasion or annexation.

Acculturation can have a positive, negative, or mixed impact. For example, in health care, a negative effect of acculturation would be reflected in worse health outcomes, behaviors, or perceptions. By the same token, a positive effect of acculturation could result in better health outcomes, behaviors, and perceptions. A mixed impact would be reflected in a positive effect on some health outcomes, behaviors, and perceptions and a negative effect on others (Lara et al. 2005). For example, if smoking were more frequent among men from another culture than among men in the United States, then the acculturation process could have a positive effect, that is., decreased smoking, on men from that culture and vice versa.

Among Hispanics, acculturation has been found to be significantly associated with health-related behavior. A review of research literature by Lara et al. (2005) on the effects of acculturation on Hispanic immigrants' health shows both negative and positive impacts. The effects of acculturation also vary between Hispanic men and women. Research points to an association between acculturation and several negative health-related risk behaviors and outcomes for Latinos in the areas of substance abuse and illicit drug use, alcohol abuse, smoking, birth outcomes, and nutrition and dietary behaviors. The negative effect of acculturation on the use of drugs such as marijuana, cocaine, and other illicit drugs is stronger in females than in males (Lara et al. 2005). The negative effect of acculturation on drinking is also clearer in Hispanic women than men. This may be due to the fact that Hispanic men start with a higher prevalence of alcohol consumption. Overall, acculturation is an important factor in growing rates of alcohol problems among Hispanics (Morales et al. 2002; Marks, Garcia, and Solis 1990).

The negative effect of acculturation on smoking is about equal between Hispanic men and women (Lara et al. 2005). However, the smoking rate varies among Hispanic subgroups, with Mexican men having a smoking rate equal to that of whites—29 percent—while the smoking rate among Puerto Ricans is lower (23 percent) (Morales et al. 2002).

With respect to health outcomes, research also provides evidence that higher acculturation is associated with worse birth and prenatal outcomes—prematurity, low birth weight, teen pregnancy, and neonatal mortality. The negative effect of acculturation is also reflected in prenatal and postnatal behaviors such as smoking and drug use during pregnancy. A study that examined the relationship between acculturation and contraceptive use among 291 low to moderately acculturated Latinas found that moderately acculturated women expressed lower intention to use contraceptives and lower social support for contraceptive use compared to women with low acculturation. Thus, social norms and low self-efficacy may place moderately acculturated women at high risk for unintended pregnancy and sexually transmitted diseases (Unger 2000).

Studies have also found evidence that less acculturated Latinos consume a healthier diet than their more acculturated counterparts (Lara et al. 2005; Morales et al. 2002). U.S. Latino adults have experienced an 80 percent increase in obesity in the last decade. A cross-section survey of a sample of eighteen- to sixty-four-year-old Latino women and men from an agricultural labor camp in Monterey County, California, found that higher acculturation based on generational status and years lived in the United States were strongly correlated with obesity, less exercise, and poorer diet in this community sample (Hubert, Snider, and Winkleby 2005). Latinos are at higher risk than non-Latino whites in the area of physical activity (Carvajal et al. 2002). A study of health-promoting lifestyle behavior of the Spanish-speaking (less acculturated) Hispanics found they scored lowest for physical activity and highest for spiritual growth (Hulme et al. 2003).

Research has also documented some positive effects of acculturation on Hispanic health. For example, more acculturated Latinos have higher rates of insurance coverage and access to health care. More acculturated Latinos also have fewer barriers to health care. Acculturation is also associated with higher use of certain preventive services such as screening for breast cancer and pap smears by Latino women (Lara et al. 2005; Marks, Garcia, and Solis 1990).

Values, Beliefs, Attitudes, and Perceptions

Values, belief systems, attitudes and perceptions may also contribute to barriers faced by Hispanics. For example, Hispanics view inclusion of family members in medical decision making as very important but it may be overlooked by physicians. Hispanics feel that it is important to seek the family's input prior to making medical decisions about surgery or the treatment of serious illness (Napoles-Springer et al. 2005). Also, Hispanic patients may mistakenly perceive impersonal professional behavior of physicians and other health care providers for lack of respect due to cross-cultural differences in Hispanic and American cultures (Morales et al. 2002). Patients who perceive or experience disrespect in their medical encounters are less likely to use health care services (Blanchard and Lurie 2004). For example, Hispanics tend to use hospice services to a lesser degree than whites or blacks because of cultural characteristics such as stoicism and familism, health care providers' lack of understanding of Hispanic culture, and limited English proficiency (Kemp 2001).

One of the strong and universal values in Hispanic community is familism or *familismo,* the valuing of family consideration over individual or community needs. It is more highly valued than patient autonomy. Family members and relatives participate in both the physical and spiritual care of the patient including traveling long distances to stay in the home of the patient to provide care (Kemp 2001). Thus, it is not too surprising to find that a majority of Hispanic elders elect to live with their spouse, alone, or with family members rather than electing for nursing homes or other forms of institutional care. Caring for "one's own" and caring for aging parents has a strong tradition in the Hispanic community (Magilvy et al. 2000). Similarly, because of the high value placed on stoicism, it is common for some patients to deny the presence of significant pain or other symptoms, especially in the presence of family members (Kemp 2001).

The value of patient submissiveness also influences physician-patient interaction in the Hispanic community. Latinos tend to view themselves as too submissive with physicians in complete control of the medical environment (Napoles-Springer 2005). Thus, it is uncommon for Hispanic patients to be aggressive or assertive in health care interactions. A typical response to a medical decision that the patient or family disagrees with is silence or noncompliance (Kemp 2001).

Since a great majority of Hispanics are Roman Catholics, spiritual and religious influences also play a major role in the areas of health and illness. Faith in God is closely associated with physical and mental health; healing, life's joys and suffering are viewed as an opportunity to serve God (Magilvy et al. 2000). God's help should be sought for minor health problems and physicians' help should be sought only for serious illnesses (Napoles-Springer et al. 2005; Larkey et al. 2001). Health and illnesses are attributed to fate and the will of God, which can be influenced through prayer and rituals. Hispanics are more likely to rely on prayer to relieve pain while whites are more likely to utilize self-care behavior (Hastie, Riley, and Fillingim 2005). Thus, it is possible that a sick Hispanic patient may simultaneously be using prayer, folk (folk healers) and/or herbal medicine, and prescription medications prescribed by a nurse practitioner or physician (Kemp 2001). In some Latino communities, folk medicine may substitute for Western biomedicine because of the barriers in accessing the formal health care system, and healing and healers are seen as essential to the experience of recovery from sickness and disease (Lopez 2005; Zapata and Shippee-Rice 1999).

Language and Communication

One of the reasons for health care disparities between Hispanics and whites is the problem of communication (Ross 1995). A significant number of Hispanic patients face a language barrier when they seek health care. Language is critical when Spanish-speaking patients interact with health care providers who do not speak Spanish and who do not have professional interpreters available (Morales et al. 2002). In a survey of minority Americans in 2001, 33 percent of Hispanics reported one or more of the following problems: their doctor did not listen to everything they said, they did not fully understand their doctor, and/or they had questions during the visit to a physician but they did not ask their physician. Hispanic respondents who did not speak English as their primary language reported having greater communication problems than those for whom English was their primary language (Collins et al. 2002).

Poor communication between patient and health care providers can have negative consequences for the quality of care as well as the outcome of care. Poor patient-provider communications can lead to inappropriate medical testing for diagnosis due to lack of sufficient understanding of the patients' medical history and lack of adherence or noncompliance with health care provider instructions for prescription medication (Morales et al. 2002). Lack of explanation of side effects of medication can correlate negatively with compliance (David and Rhee 1998).

Language concordance and clear communication between patient and health care providers can result in better health outcomes (Perez-Stable, Napoles-Springer, and Miramontes 1997). Studies have documented that Latino/Hispanic respondents are significantly more dissatisfied with provider communication than Latino/English and white respondents (Morales et al. 1999; David and Rhee 1998). Inability to communicate may encourage some individuals not to seek or access health services. As many as one in five Spanish-speaking Latinos do not seek medical care due to language barriers (Institute of Medicine 2002). Latino physicians who speak the language and share the culture of their patients may help bring marginalized patients into the health care system (De Chavez et al. 2003–2004). Spanish-speaking Latinos, who shy away from the health care system because of a language problem, may be at increased risk for a lower quality of care and poor health outcomes (Morales et al. 1999).

Racial Prejudice and Discrimination

Perceived or real racial prejudice and stereotyping of minority groups can have negative consequences by restricting access to the quantity and quality of health-related services. Racial prejudice and stereotyping may be intentional (overt and explicit) or unintentional (implicit and subconscious). White health care providers may not be overtly biased but may fail to recognize their own unconscious implicit negative attitudes and stereotypes (Institute of Medicine 2002). Stereotypes tend often to be biased and unfair (Institute of Medicine 2002).

Patients' experience with racial prejudice can also induce psychological stress that could adversely affect physical and mental health status. Research seems to support the notion that the experience of racial discrimination is negatively related to health outcomes (Williams and Collins 1995). Failure to recognize that the Latino population is characterized by considerable heterogeneity with respect to SES, distribution of disease, and risk factors for disease can prevent identification of the health needs of this specific group (Williams and Collins 1995).

In medical encounters, bias or racial prejudice and stereotypes held by providers about the behavior or health of a minority group can lead to clinical uncertainty when interacting with minority patients. Diagnostic and treatment decisions and feelings about patients can be influenced by a patient's race or ethnicity (Institute of Medicine 2002).

At times, patients may perceive the existence of (real or imagined) racial bias and prejudice, which can also have negative consequences for the health of minorities since it can lead to distrust between patients and providers. For example, Hispanics, along with African Americans and Asians, are more likely than whites to perceive (1) that there is a system-wide bias, (2) that they would have received better medical care if they belonged to a different race/ethnic group, and (3) that medical staff judged them unfairly and treated them with disrespect based on their race/ethnicity (Johnson et al. 2004).

A study of a large health maintenance organization (HMO) found significant differences by race and ethnicity with respect to patients' rating of quality of care. Latinos rated physicians' accessibility less favorably than did whites (Murray-Garcia et al. 2000). The Commonwealth Fund 2001 survey (Collins et al. 2002) found that compared with whites, Hispanics report less confidence in their doctor and are less satisfied overall with their health care. Nearly three-quarters of the whites (72 percent) stated that they had a great deal of confidence in their doctors compared to only 57 percent of Hispanics. Among Spanish-speaking Latinos, only

44 percent expressed confidence in their doctor. Hispanics and African Americans perceive more racial discrimination than whites in the American health care system (LaVeist, Rolley, and Diala 2003). In a 2001 nationwide survey, 57 percent of Hispanics believed that there was a lot of prejudice and discrimination against people living with HIV-AIDS compared to 49 percent of whites who believed such to be the case (Henry J. Kaiser Family Foundation 2001).

A focus group study of perspectives of black and Hispanic residents of the South Bronx revealed a deep and pervasive distrust of the health care system (Kaplan et al. 2006). Latinos with stronger beliefs about the existence of discrimination in health care are also more likely to prefer a Latino physician (Chen et al. 2005). However, as we have stated before, minorities are not well represented in the health care profession. Together African Americans, Hispanic Americans, and American Indians make up more than 25 percent of the U.S. population, but they are not represented in significant numbers in the makeup of the nations' physicians, nurses, and dentists (Sullivan Commission 2004). A shortage of minority health care professionals and their maldistribution, combined with self-isolation and suspicion of the health care system, adds to the difficulty Hispanics face in gaining access to health care services (Freire 2002).

Research has also documented prejudice and discrimination along racial and ethnic lines in the health/mental health care delivery system. A study of mental health care utilization among federal employees found that Hispanic employees received twenty-three annual mental health visits in comparison to thirty-one mental health visits for whites (Scheffler and Miller 1991).

Understandably, the vast majority of research on prejudice and discrimination has focused on African Americans. Few studies have systematically addressed how prejudice and discrimination affect other minority groups such as Hispanics. More empirical studies are needed to understand the effect of prejudice and discrimination on Hispanic health care (Cain and Kington 2002).

Political Power

Economic and political power is unevenly distributed in society. The amount of political power a group has and how successful the group is in using that power to influence public policies depend on two factors. One is their representation in policy-making institutions. The other is the size of the group and its rate of political participation. Large size and higher rates of political participation can be used to exercise political leverage in the electoral arena and policy-making process. A group with less influence is likely to be less competitive in policy making and thus experience inequities in a broad range of societal outcomes related to the lack of political power (Williams and Collins 1995).

As we discussed in an earlier section, Hispanics are characterized by low SES compared to whites in American society. This helps explain health care disparities. How do Hispanics as a group fare with respect to political power in American society?

Today, Hispanics are the largest and the fastest growing minority in American society. It is because of these two facts that many pundits have often referred to Hispanics as "the sleeping giant" that could be galvanized into a potent political force. In the 1980s pollsters predicted that Hispanics would soon become a "voting time bomb" (Griffin 1992). For example, Hispanics were expected to have a major impact on the 1988 presidential election. However, an analysis of the results of the 1988 election showed that Hispanics did not have any significant impact because of demographic and political factors (DeSipio and Rocha 1992). One of the factors often cited for lack of Hispanic political influence is the de jure exclusion of Hispanics from political incorporation and participation and the de facto marginalization of Hispanics (DeSipio 1996).

Hispanics register less and vote less compared to other groups in American society. As Table 3.3 shows, Hispanics registered and voted in much smaller numbers than whites in the presidential election of 2004. The same was the case for 2002 congressional elections. In the 2004 presidential election, 75.1 percent of non-Hispanic white citizens had registered to vote compared to 64 percent of Hispanic citizens. Sixty-seven percent of non-Hispanic whites compared to only 47.2 percent of Hispanics voted in the 2004 presidential election. What accounts for the low voter turnout among Hispanics?

Hispanic advocates often have argued that two forms of discrimination work against minorities' political empowerment. One involves the drawing of legislative district lines to reduce the effectiveness of Hispanic votes in a given jurisdiction. The other form of discrimination, according to Hispanic leaders is that the at-large electoral system is inherently biased against minority groups. To address the issue of political empowerment, Congress in 1975 extended the Voting Rights Act of 1965 to apply to Hispanics and mandated bilingual ballots in jurisdictions where more than 5 percent of the citizens of voting age were Spanish-speaking (Griffin 1992).

There are several other reasons why Hispanic voter registration and turnout tends to be very low compared to non-Hispanic whites or African Americans. One reason is that more than one-third of the Hispanic population are non-citizens (unauthorized immigrants or holders permanent resident status) and thus they cannot vote. Second, about one-third of the Hispanic population is under the age of eighteen, making them ineligible to vote (Masci 2003). For example, in 2003, the Hispanic population totaled 39.4 million but only 15.7 million (40 percent) were eligible to vote. In contrast 73 percent of the total non-Hispanic population was eligible to vote. Similarly, 34 percent of the Hispanic population is less than eighteen years old compared to 23 percent of the non-Hispanic white population. In addition, Hispanic U.S. citizens aged eighteen to twenty-nine (who are eligible to vote) are less likely to register and vote, just like all other young adults ("The Hispanic Electorate in 2004" n.d.). Because of these factors, as the data in Table 3.3 show, the registration and voter turnout rate in the total Hispanic population tends to be very low. Even among Hispanic U.S. citizens, registration and voter turnout tend to be lower than among non-Hispanic whites and African Americans (for data on African Americans, see Table 2.2 in Chapter 2). Thus, the Hispanic population

Table 3.3

Voter Registration, Voter Turnout, and Political Representation: Hispanics and Non-Hispanic Whites

	Non-Hispanic white citizens	Hispanic citizens	Total Hispanic population
Voter registration and turnout in 2004 Presidential election			
Registered (%)	75.1	64.0	34.9
Voted (%)	67.2	47.2	28.0
Voter registration and turnout in 2002 Congressional elections			
Registered (%)	69.4	52.5	32.8
Voted (%)	49.1	30.4	18.9

	Hispanic
House seats, 108th Congress	25*
(2003)	
109th Congress (2005)	24*
110th Congress (2007)	24*
Senate seats, 108th Congress	0
(2003)	
109th Congress (2005)	2
110th Congress (2007)	3

Sources: U.S. Census Bureau, November 2004. "Current Population Survey" and earlier reports and "Current Population Reports." Internet release date, May 26, 2005, www.census. gov. Congressional data: www.house.gov and www.senate.gov.
    *Total includes one non-voting delegate from Puerto Rico.

increase does not correspondingly translate into the same increase in Hispanic voters. For example, between 2000 and 2004 the Hispanic population increased by 5.7 million but it yielded only 2.1 million new eligible voters (Suro, Fry, and Passel 2005).

The election of Antonio Villaraigosa as the speaker of the General Assembly of California was seen as a sign that Hispanics were making their presence felt in the political process. Furthermore, Villaraigosa took the reins from Cruz Bustamonte, the first Hispanic ever to hold the office (Masci 1998). On the other hand, Cruz Bustamonte suffered a humiliating defeat at the hands of Arnold Schwartzenegger for the governorship of California in 2002. Bustamonte garnered 32 percent of the vote compared to 49 percent for Schwartzenegger (Masci 2003).

Many experts saw the defeat of Bustamonte as a sign that Latinos nationwide have yet to attain political power commensurate with their numbers (Masci 2003). Cecilia Munoz, vice president of legislative affairs for the National Council of La Raza, a Hispanic advocacy group, argues that the growing numbers of Hispanics in many midwestern and southern states such as Illinois, Missouri, Iowa, the Carolinas, Georgia, Arkansas, Tennessee, and Alabama will force both political parties to pay more attention to Spanish-speaking voters because they will become the swing votes in these states. However, others have noted that most Latinos moving to politically competitive states are non-citizen immigrants and hence unlikely to be a political force in the near future (Masci 2003).

However, there is no denying that Hispanics are the fastest growing segment in American society. Half the nation's population growth is happening among Hispanics due to immigration and a higher birth rate. There are 3.5 births per each Hispanic woman, compared to 2.7 among African Americans and 2.1 for the nation as a whole. According to the U.S. Census Bureau's prediction, a quarter of the nation will be Hispanic by 2050 (Masci 2003). As the population of Hispanic citizens grows, and if they register and vote in large numbers, they have the potential to become a major political force in American politics.

When it comes to representation of Hispanics in the Congress of the United States, they are underrepresented compared to their population. Hispanics constitute around 14 percent of the U.S. population, but hold less than 6 percent of the seats in the U.S. House of Representatives. Senate seats increased from zero in 2003 to three in 2007 (see Table 3.3). It is clear that a sustained growth of the Hispanic population is translating into representational gains in the U.S. Congress and in state legislatures (Fraga and Ramiacurez 2003–2004). Hispanics have also made important political gains at local levels in recent years. There are about 6,000 Hispanic elected officials nationwide. Hispanic political gains are also reflected in the election of Antonio Villaraigosa as the mayor of Los Angeles in November 2004—the first Hispanic to hold that office in 133 years (Campo-Flores and Fineman 2005).

Hispanics are also likely to gain political clout in states where they constitute a large percentage of the electorate. For example, in Florida, Hispanics make up 14 percent of the eligible voters. In Arizona, Hispanics constitute 16 percent of the eligible voters and in New Mexico they constitute 40 percent of eligible voters ("The Hispanic Electorate in 2004" n.d). However, optimism about the increased political influence of Latinos must be tempered with their vulnerability to marginalization and manipulation by competing electoral majorities (Fraga and Ramiacurez 2003–2004). Hispanics will also have to confront the prospect of increased misgivings on the part of African Americans to surging Hispanic political influence since African Americans have been accustomed to playing the dominant role in a multiracial coalition. Hispanics also may find it difficult to pursue a singularly Hispanic campaign strategy because of many differences between various Hispanic subgroups (Campo-Flores and Fineman 2005).

In summary, the low SES, discrimination, linguistic and cultural differences, and lack of political power combined together explain a great deal of health care disparities between Hispanics and non-Hispanic whites. Hispanics' health care needs are often ignored because it is easy to ignore the needs of economically and politically weak people. Lack of economic and political power make it difficult to make demands for health care or even to draw public attention to their needs (Freire 2002).

Unauthorized Immigrants and Health Care

According to the March 2005 Current Population Survey there were 11.1 million unauthorized migrants in the United States. The number had increased to 11.5 to 12 million by March of 2006. Since 2000, the growth in unauthorized immigrants has averaged about 500,000 per year. Unauthorized migrants accounted for 30 percent of the foreign-born population in 2005 (Passel 2006). Most unauthorized migrants come from Mexico. In 2005, there were 6.2 million unauthorized migrants from Mexico, accounting for 56 percent of the total. Another 2.5 million came from the rest of Latin America, mostly from Central America. Unauthorized migrants from Mexico and Latin America represented 78 percent of the unauthorized population (Passel 2006).

The term "unauthorized migrant" is defined as a person who resides in the United States but is not a U.S. citizen, has not been admitted as a permanent resident, and is not in an authorized temporary status permitting longer-term residence and work. On the other hand, immigrants who arrived before 2000 are presumed to be legal. So are immigrants who have obtained the status of permanent residence in the United States (Passel 2006).

Federal and state public policies have a major impact on the health care of unauthorized immigrants living in the United States. Under federal law, legal immigrants are prohibited from enrolling in Medicaid and the State Children's Health Insurance Program for the first five years they live in the United States. Unauthorized immigrants are not eligible for Medicaid and SCHIP regardless of how long they have lived in the United States. However, all immigrants are eligible for emergency Medicaid, which covers treatment for medical emergencies regardless of immigrants' legal status. Thus, for example, hospital emergency departments generally must screen and stabilize people with an emergency medical condition under the federal Emergency Treatment and Labor Act ("With Minimal Federal Help" 2006).

The Personal Responsibility and Work Opportunity Reconciliation Act (PRWO-RA) of 1996 and its amendments restricted federal and state health benefits available to non-citizen immigrants who are lawful permanent residents. By implication, unauthorized immigrants are excluded from receiving these benefits. States that wish to provide health benefits to unauthorized immigrants must pass a specific law to do so (Berk et al. 2000).

Non-citizen families have poor access to both ambulatory medical and emergency room care, despite the fact that even unauthorized immigrants receive emergency medical services. Non-citizens and their children are also less likely to be insured. Even insured non-citizens and their children have less access to medical care than insured foreign-born citizens. Non-citizen immigrants and their children have large gaps in their health insurance and access to care even when their children are U.S. citizens (Ku and Matani 2001). Immigrants in general are more likely to use a hospital emergency room for basic treatment than go to the doctor's office (Jacobson 2005).

Since most unauthorized immigrants lack health insurance, they rely primarily on the safety net providers for health care (Staiti, Hurley, and Katz 2006). As the number of unauthorized immigrants rises, hospitals bear a great deal of the cost of health care provided to unauthorized immigrants. For example, in a two-year span, Lee Memorial Hospital in Fort Myers, Florida, racked up more than $1.2 million in unreimbursed care for just six illegal Central American immigrants. Hospitals throughout the United States are seeing big dollar numbers for uncompensated care for uninsured non-citizens. A hospital in Arizona documented a 300 percent increase in uncompensated care for unauthorized immigrants. According to the chief financial officer of New York City's Hospital and Health Corporation, about 20 to 30 percent of annual uncompensated care—about $238 million—is related to care for immigrants (Bilchik 2001).

To help hospitals stuck with uncompensated care, the Medicare reform law of 2003 set aside $1 billion over five years to help compensate hospitals that treat unauthorized immigrants in their emergency departments. However, hospital administrators argue that it is not easy to demonstrate how many unauthorized immigrants they treat since the system does not collect immigration information. Hospitals do not routinely screen patients to determine their residency status (Tieman 2004).

The cost of health care for unauthorized immigrants has created a strong anti-immigration sentiment in the general population. This is despite the fact that considerable research has challenged the belief that immigrants are to blame for the rising cost of U.S. health care and that a large number of unauthorized immigrants come to the United States for jobs and not for health care or other social services benefits (Jacobson 2005; Berk et al. 2000).

Recent polls have found that nine out of ten Americans view immigration as a serious problem and three-fourths want more done to curb unauthorized immigrants ("Latest Immigration 'Crisis' Defies Simplistic Solutions" 2006). According to a Gallup poll conducted between June 8 and 25, 2006, Americans are more than twice as likely to believe that illegal immigrants cost taxpayers too much by using government services such as public education and health services rather than becoming productive citizens. The opinion is divided along racial/ethnic lines. Hispanics overwhelmingly (65 percent) say that illegal immigrants eventually become productive citizens rather than being a drain on the system. However, whites (74 percent) and blacks (56 percent) tend to view illegal immigrants as a burden on taxpayers (Jones 2006).

California voters in the November 1994 election passed a referendum called Proposition 187 making undocumented immigrants ineligible for public services including education, health care, and welfare benefits. The law also requires law enforcement officers, public school officials, and health care workers to report people they suspect of being illegal immigrants to the Attorney General of California and the U.S. Immigration and Naturalization Service (Colino 1995; Summer 1995).

In 2005, about eighty bills were introduced in twenty states to cut non-citizens' access to health care or other services or to require benefit agencies to tell authorities about applicants with immigration violations. Arizona voters approved such a requirement in 2004 with Proposition 200 (Bernstein 2006). Especially since the terrorist attack of September 11, 2001, the political climate in the United States has become increasingly hostile to immigrants. Politicians are falling over each other with promises to round up and deport unauthorized immigrants, erect massive walls along the U.S.-Mexican border, and to crack down on employers who hire unauthorized immigrants. President Bush's comprehensive immigration reform proposal, which provided a path to citizenship for unauthorized immigrants if they met certain conditions and paid a penalty, was defeated in Congress. Ironically, a strong majority of Democrats supported the reform proposal while Republicans strongly opposed it. Thus, the status quo is likely to continue at least until the presidential election of 2008. The issue of immigration reform may resurface again on the legislative agenda after the presidential election.

Conclusions

This chapter has documented significant disparities in health status/outcome, health care access, and quality of care between Hispanics and whites. Some of the differences between the two groups are in the areas of unintentional injuries, HIV, diabetes, homicide, suicide, and Alzheimer's disease. Hispanics fare worse than whites on these indicators of health status/outcomes. However, on some health care indicators Hispanics fare better than whites. For example, with respect to tobacco use, exposure to secondhand smoke, low birth-weight, and infant mortality, Hispanics do better than whites. The fact that Hispanics rank low on SES but still do better on some health indicators compared to whites is referred to as Hispanic paradox. Recent research findings have challenged the idea of Hispanic paradox.

Hispanics have greater difficulty accessing health care services including preventive services. Research shows that Hispanics are less likely to seek and receive health care services, and that a significant gap exists in access to health care and preventive services among Hispanics versus non-Hispanics. Compared to whites, Hispanics are more likely to be without a usual source of medical care, more likely to be without a health care visit in the past year, and at least twice as likely to receive late or no prenatal care. Hispanics are more likely to be uninsured compared to both whites and African Americans. Hispanics are clustered in jobs that are low paying, less stable, more hazardous, and unlikely to offer fringe benefits such as health insurance coverage. Many Hispanics work in agriculture, mining, service, and construction industries, which are less likely to offer health insurance coverage. Hispanics also tend to have greater employment in small firms, which are also less likely to offer health insurance coverage.

Hispanics tend to receive a lower quality of health care across a range of disease areas including cancer, cardiovascular disease, HIV-AIDS, diabetes, mental illness, and other chronic and infectious diseases and clinical services. Hispanics are less likely than whites to undergo angiography and bypass graft surgery. Hispanics also fail to receive equal treatment for mental illness and receive less follow-up after hospitalization for mental illness. According to several annual *National Healthcare Disparities Reports* the quality of care received by Hispanics has gotten worse over the last few years.

Public opinion polls show that whites often hold negative stereotypes about Hispanics. Given the health care disparities between whites and Hispanics, it is not too surprising that Hispanics show less trust and satisfaction with health care providers.

Many factors have contributed to the health care disparities between whites and Hispanics. These factors include SES, cultural values and beliefs, acculturation, language and communication problems, racial prejudice and discrimination, and lack of political power to shape public health policies. SES by itself does not explain all the disparities between whites and Hispanics. Rather, it is a combination of factors that helps account for the existing health care disparities.

For unauthorized immigrants, the situation has gotten worse because of the strong anti-immigration mood in the country since the 9/11 terrorist attack. The failure of Congress to pass an immigration reform package proposed by President Bush in 2007, which would have allowed temporary work permit visas and a path to citizenship for unauthorized immigrants who are already in the country, reflected this anti-immigration mood. Both the federal government and many states have adopted new laws making it more difficult for unauthorized immigrants to receive health and other social services. This has the potential to increase the health care disparities.

References

"Access to Health-Care and Preventive Services among Hispanics and Hon-Hispanics—United States, 2001–2002." 2004. *Morbidity and Mortality Weekly Report* 53, no. 40 (October): 937–41.

Agency for Healthcare Research and Quality. 2004. *2004 National Healthcare Disparities Report.* Rockville, MD: U.S. Department of Heath and Human Services. AHRQ Publication No. 05–0014.

Agency for Healthcare Research and Quality. 2005. *2005 National Healthcare Disparities Report.* Rockville, MD: U.S. Department of Health and Human Services. AHRQ Publication No. 06–0017.

Agency for Healthcare Research and Quality. 2007. *2006 National Healthcare Disparities Report.* Rockville, MD: U.S. Department of Health and Human Services. AHRQ Publication No. 07–0012.

Agency for Healthcare Research and Quality. 2008. *2007 National Healthcare Disparities Report.* Rockville, MD: U.S. Department of Health and Human Services. AHRQ Publication No. 08–0041.

Alter, Jonathan. 2005. " The Other America." *Newsweek,* September 10: 42–48.

Amaro, Hortensia; Rodolfo R. Vega; and Dellanira Valencia. 2001. "Gender, Context, and HIV Prevention among Latinos." In Marilyn Aguirre-Molina, Carlos W. Molina, and Ruth Enid Zambrana, eds., *Health Issues in the Latino Community,* 301–24. San Francisco: Jossey-Bass.

American Association of Retired Persons. 2007. *AARP 2006 Prescription Drug Study with Hispanics and African Americans.* Washington, D.C.: American Association of Retired Persons.

"Archie Bunker, Alive and Well." 1991. *Newsweek,* January 21.

Asamoa, Kwame; M. Rodriguez; Venus Gines; Rosa Varela; Ken Dominguez; Gerry C. Mills; Gerry Sotomayor; and Consuelo M. Beck-Sague. 2004. "Use of Preventive Health

Services by Hispanic/Latino Women in Two Urban Communities: Atlanta, Georgia and Miami, Florida." *Journal of Women's Health* 13, no. 6 (July): 654–61.

Berk, Marc L.; Claudia L. Schur; Leo R. Chavez; and Martin Franke. 2000. "Health Care Use among Undocumented Latino Immigrants." *Health Affairs* 19, no. 4 (July–August): 51–64.

Bernstein, Nina. 2006. "Resources Grown Slim for Immigrants Who Fall Ill." *New York Times,* March 3.

Bilchik, Gloria S. 2001. "No Easy Answer." *Hospitals and Health Networks* 75, no. 5 (May): 59–60.

Blanchard, Janice, and Nicole Lurie. 2004. "R-E-S-P-E-C-T: Patient Reports of Disrespect in Health Care Setting and Its Impact on Care." *Journal of Family Practice* 53, no. 9 (September): 721.

Blewett, L.A.; M. Davern; and H. Rodin. 2005. "Employment and Health Insurance Coverage for Rural Latino Populations." *Journal of Community Health* 30, no. 3 (June): 181–95.

Blizzard, Rick. 2003. "Minorities Last in Satisfaction with Health Status." *Gallup Poll Tuesday Briefing,* September 30. Washington, D.C.: Gallup Organization. Online at www.gallup.com. Accessed on 6/16/2007.

Blizzard, Rick. 2005. "Medical Costs Yet Another Hurdle for Hispanics." *Gallup Poll Tuesday Briefing,* August 9. Washington, D.C.: Gallup Organization. Available online at www. gallup.com. Accessed 6/16/2007.

Borrell, Luisa N. 2005. "Racial Identity among Hispanics: Implications for Health and Well-Being." Editorial. *American Journal of Public Health* 95, no. 3 (March): 379–81.

Borrell, Luisa N. 2006. "Self-Reported Hypertension and Race among Hispanics in the National Health Interview Survey." *Ethnicity & Disease* 16, no. 1 (Winter): 71–77.

Boucher, Schenker F. 2002. "Cervical Cancer among Hispanics: Assessing the Impact on Farmworkers." *Journal of Immigrant Health* 4, no. 3 (July): 159–65.

Brown, Arleen F; Robert B. Gerzoff; Andrew J. Karter; Edward Gregg; Monika Safford; Beth Waitzfelder; Gloria Beckles; Rebecca Brusuelas; and Carol M. Mangione. 2003. "Health Behaviors and Quality of Care among Latinos with Diabetes in Managed Care." *American Journal of Public Health* 93, no. 10 (October): 1694–98.

Burgos, A.E.; K.E. Schetzina; L.B. Dixon; and F.S. Mendoza. 2005. "Importance of Generational Status in Examining Access to and Utilization of Health Care Services by Mexican American Children." *Pediatrics* 115, no. 3 (March): e322–30.

Cain, Virginia S., and Raynard S. Kington. 2002. "Investigating the Role of Racial/Ethnic Bias in Health Outcomes." Editorial. *American Journal of Public Health* 93, no. 2 (February): 191–92.

"California Hispanics Face Barriers to Health Care." 2003. *Nations' Health* 33, no. 1 (February): 12.

"California Study Looks at Attitudes of Latino Patients towards Cancer Screening Tests." 1995. *Nation's Health* 25, no. 3 (March): 11.

Campo-Flores, Arian, and Howard Fineman. 2005. "A Latin Power Surge." *Newsweek,* May 30: 25–31.

Cangiano, J.L. 1994. "Hypertension in Hispanic Americans." *Cleveland Clinic Journal of Medicine* 61, no. 5 (September–October): 345–50.

Carlisle, David M.; Barbara D. Leake; and Martin M. Shapiro. 1995. "Racial and Ethnic Differences in the Use of Invasive Cardiac Procedures among Cardiac Patients in Los Angeles County, 1986 through 1988." *American Journal of Public Health* 85, no. 3 (March): 352–56.

Carlisle, David M.; Barbara D. Leake; and Martin M. Shapiro. 1997. "Racial and Ethnic Disparities in the Use of Cardiovascular Procedures: Association with Type of Health Insurance." *American Journal of Public Health* 87, no. 2 (February): 263–66.

Carrillo, Emilio J.; Fernando M. Trevino; Joseph R. Betancourt; and Alberto Coustasse. 2001. "Latino Access to Health Care: The Role of Insurance, Managed Care, and Institutional Reforms." In Marilyn Aguirre-Molina, Carlos W. Molina, and Ruth Enid Zambrana, eds., *Health Issues in the Latino Community,* 55–73. San Francisco: Jossey-Bass.

Carroll, Joseph. 2006. "Whites, Minorities Differ in Views of Economic Opportunities in U.S.: Most See Education System as Solution to Inequality." Gallup Poll Briefing, July 10. Online at www.gallup.com. Accessed on 6/16/2007.

Carvajal, S.C.; C.E. Hanson; A.J. Romero; and K.K. Coyle. 2002. "Behavioral Risk Factors and Protective Factors in Adolescents: A Comparison of Latinos and non-Latino Whites." *Ethnicity & Health* 7, no. 3 (August): 181–93.

Castro, Felipe G.; Kathryn Coe; and Mary Harmon. 1996. "The Effects of Ethnic/Racial Matches between Provider and Patient on the Use of Health Services by Hispanics and African Americans." In Marsha D. Lillie-Blanton, Wilhelmina A. Leigh, and Ana I. Alfaro-Correa, eds., *Achieving Equitable Access: Studies of Health Care Issues Affecting Hispanics and African Americans,* 7–26. Washington, D.C.: Joint Center for Political and Economic Studies.

Centers for Disease Control and Prevention. 2001. "Pregnancy-Related Deaths among Hispanics, Asian/Pacific Islander, and American Indian/Alaska Native Women—United States, 1991–1997." *Morbidity and Mortality Weekly Report* 50, no. 18 (May 11): 361–64.

Centers for Disease Control and Prevention. 2005. "Fact Sheet: Prevalence of Diabetes among Hispanics in Six U.S. Geographical Locations." Online at http://www.cdc.gov. Accessed on 6/14/2006.

Centers for Disease Control and Prevention. 2006a. "HIV/AIDS among Hispanics." Online at www.cdc.gov. Accessed on 6/14/2006.

Centers for Disease Control and Prevention. 2006b. "Epidemiology of HIV\AIDS—United States, 1981–2005." *Morbidity and Mortality Weekly* 55, no. 21 (June 2): 589–92.

Chen, F.M.; G.E. Fryer; R.L. Phillips; E. Wilson; and D.E. Pathman. 2005. "Patients' Beliefs about Racism, Preferences for Physician Race, and Satisfaction with Care." *Annals of Family Medicine* 3, no. 2 (April): 138–43.

Chow, Julian Chun-Chung; Kim Jaffee; and Lonnie Snowden. 2003. "Racial/Ethnic Disparities in the Use of Mental Health Services in Poverty Areas." *American Journal of Public Health* 93, no. 5 (May): 792–97.

"Cigarette Smoking among Adults—United States, 2004." 2005. *Morbidity and Mortality Weekly Report* 54, no. 44 (November 11): 1121–24.

Cohen, Jordan J.; Barbara A. Gabriel; and Charles Terrell. 2002. "The Case for Diversity in the Health Care Workforce." *Health Affairs* 21, no. 5 (September–October): 90–102.

Colino, Stacey. 1995. "The Fallout from Proposition 187." *Human Rights: Journal of the Section of Individual Rights and Responsibilities* 22, no. 1 (Winter): 16–17.

Collins, Karen S.; Dora L. Hughes; Michelle M. Doty; Brett L. Ives; Jennifer N. Edwards; and Katie Tenney. 2002. *Diverse Communities, Common Concerns: Assessing Health Care Quality for Minority Americans.* New York: Commonwealth Fund.

Coughlin, Steven S., and Robert J. Uhler. 2002. "Breast and Cervical Cancer Screening Practices among Hispanic Women in the United States and Puerto Rico, 1998–1999." *Preventive Medicine* 34, no. 2 (February): 242–51.

D'Arrigo, Terri, and Andrew Keegan. 2000. "Diabetes and Latinos: A Community at Risk." *Diabetes Forecast* 53, no. 6 (June): 42–46.

David, Rand A., and Michelle Rhee. 1998. "The Impact of Language as a Barrier to Effective Health Care in an Underserved Urban Hispanic Community." *Mt. Sinai Journal of Medicine* 65, no. 5 & 6 (October–November): 393–97.

Dean, H.D.; C.B. Steele; A.J. Satcher; and A.K. Nakashima. 2005. "HIV/AIDS among

Minority Races and Ethnicities in the United States, 1999–2003." *Journal of National Medical Association* 97, no. 7 supplement (July): 5S–12S.

De Chavez, Phillip M.; Anamaria Cobo; Amy Schlom; Sharmila Chaterjee; and Fan Jiang. 2003–2004. "Defense of Social Justice: Latino Physicians as a Means to Reduce Disparities." *Harvard Journal of Hispanic Health* 16: 111–14.

Del Pinal, Jorge, and Audrey Singer. 1997. "Generations of Diversity: Latinos in the United States." *Population Bulletin* 52, no. 3 (October): 1–48.

DeSipio, Louis. 1996. *Counting on the Latino Vote: Latinos as a New Electorate.* Charlottesville: University of Virginia Press.

DeSipio, Louis, and Gregory Rocha. 1992. "Latino Influence on National Elections: The Case of 1988." In Rodolfo O. De la Garza and Louis DeSipio, eds., *From Rhetoric to Reality: Latino Politics in the 1988 Elections,* 3–22. Boulder, CO: Westview.

Dey, Achintya N., and Jacqueline W. Lucas. 2006. *Physical and Mental Health Characteristics of U.S.- and Foreign-Born Adults: United States, 1998–2003.* Advance Data from Vital and Health Statistics, no. 369. Hyattsville, MD: National Center for Health Statistics.

Doty, Michelle M. 2003. *Hispanic Patients' Double Burden: Lack of Health Insurance and Limited English.* New York: Commonwealth Fund. Publication No. 592.

Eaton, Danice K.; Laura Kahn; Steve Kinchen; James Ross; Joseph Hawkins; William A. Harris; Richard Lowry; Tim McManus; David Chyen; Sari Shanklin; Connie Lim; Jo Anne Grunbaum; and Howell Wechsler. 2006. "Youth Risk Surveillance—United States, 2005." *Morbidity and Mortality Weekly Report* 55, no. SS05 (June 9): 1–108.

Egede, Leonard E., and Deyi Zheng. 2003. "Racial/Ethnic Differences in Adult Vaccination among Individuals with Diabetes." *American Journal of Public Health* 93, no. 2 (February): 324–29.

Elder, John P.; Susan I. Woodruff; Jeanette Candelaria; Amanda L. Golbeck; Jeffrey L. Alvarez; Michael H. Criqui; Craig D. Norquist; and Joan R. Rupp. 1998. "Socioeconomic Indicators Related to Cardiovascular Disease Risk Factors in Hispanics." *American Journal of Health Behavior* 22, no. 3 (May–June): 172–85.

Elixhauser, A.; R.M. Weinick; J.R. Betancouurt; and R.M. Andrew. 2002. "Difference between Hispanics and Non-Hispanic Whites in Use of Hospital Procedures for Cerebrovascular Disease." *Ethnicity & Disease* 12, no. 1 (Winter): 29–37.

Falhman, Mariane M.; Heather L. Hall; and Robyn Lock. 2006. "Ethnic and Socioeconomic Comparisons of Fitness, Activity Levels, and Barriers to Exercise in High School Females." *Journal of School Health* 76, no. 1 (January): 12–17.

Fan, A.Z.; K.J. Greenland; S. Dai; and J.B. Croft. 2005. "Disparities in Screening for and Awareness of High Blood Cholesterol—United States, 1999–2002." *Morbidity and Mortality Weekly Report* 54, no. 5 (February 11): 117–19.

Felix-Aaron, K.; E. Moy; M. Kang; M. Patel; F.D. Chesley; and C. Chesley. 2005. "Variations in Quality of Men's Health Care by Race/Ethnicity and Social Class." *Medical Care* 43, no. 3 supplement (March): 172–81.

Finkelstein, Jonathan A.; Randall W. Brown; Lynda Schneider; Scott T. Weiss; Jose M. Quintana; Donald A. Goldmann; and Charles J. Homer. 1995. "Quality of Care for Pre-School Children with Asthma: The Role of Social Factors and Practice Setting." *Pediatrics* 95, no. 3 (March): 389–94.

Flores, Glenn. 2005. "The Impact of Medical Interpreter Services on the Quality of Health Care: A Systematic Review." *Medical Care Research* 62, no. 3: 255–99.

Flores, Glenn; M. Abreu; M.A. Oliver; and B. Kastner. 1998. "Access Barriers to Health Care for Latino Children." *Archives of Pediatric & Adolescent Medicine* 152, no. 11 (November): 1119–25.

Flores, Glenn; Lynn Olson; and Sandra Tomany-Korman. 2005. "Racial and Ethnic Disparities in Early Childhood Health and Health Care." *Pediatrics* 115, no. 2 (February): 183–93.

Fraga, Luis R., and Ricardo Ramiacurez. 2003–2004. "Demography and Political Influence: Disentangling the Latino Vote." *Harvard Journal of Hispanic Policy* 16: 69–96.

Franzini, Luisa; John C. Ribble; and Arlene M. Keddie. 2001. "Understanding the Hispanic Paradox." *Ethnicity & Disease* 11, no. 3: 496–518.

Freeman, G., and M. Lethbridge-Cejku. 2006. "Access to Health Care among Hispanic or Latino Women: United States, 2000–2002." *Advance Data* 368 (April 20): 1–25.

Freire, Gloria M. 2002. "Hispanics and the Politics of Health Care." *Journal of Health and Social Policy* 14, no. 4: 21–35.

Frisbie, Parker W.; Douglas Forbes; and Robert A. Hummer. 1998. "Hispanic Pregnancy Outcomes: Additional Evidence." *Social Science Quarterly* 79, no. 1 (March): 149–69.

Gallegos-Macias, Angela R.; Santiago R. Macias; Ellen Kaufman; Betty Skipper; and Norton Kalishman. 2003. "Relationship between Glycemic Control, Ethnicity, and Socioeconomic Status in Hispanic and White Non-Hispanic Youths with Type 1 Diabetes Mellitus." *Pediatric Diabetes* 4, no. 1 (March): 19–23.

Gavin, Norma; Kathleen E. Adams; Katherine Hartman; Beth M. Benedict; and Monique Chireau. 2004. "Racial and Ethnic Disparities in the Use of Pregnancy-Related Health Care among Medicaid Pregnant Women." *Maternal & Child Health Journal* 8, no. 3 (September): 113–26.

Giachello, Aida L. 2001. "The Reproductive Years: The Health of Latinas." In Marilyn Aguirre-Molina, Carlos W. Molina, and Ruth E. Zambrana, eds., *Health Issues in the Latino Community,* 107–56. San Francisco: Jossey-Bass.

Giachello, Aida L. 2003. "The Reproductive Years: The Health of Latinas." In Marilyn Aguirre-Molina and Carlos W. Molina, eds., *Latina Health in the United States: A Public Health Reader,* 77–131. San Francisco: Jossey-Bass.

Gillum, Richard F. 1997. "Sudden Cardiac Death in Hispanic Americans and African Americans." *American Journal of Public Health* 87, no. 9 (September): 1461–66.

Glover, S.; C.G. Moore; M.E. Samuels; and J.C. Probst. 2004. "Disparities in Access to Care among Rural Working-Age Adults." *Journal of Rural Health* 20, no. 3 (Summer): 193–205.

Goldman, Data P., and James P. Smith. 2002. "Can Patient Self-Management Help Explain the SES Health Gradient?" *Proceedings of the National Academy of Science* 99, no. 16 (August): 10929–34.

Gordon, Milton M. 1964. *Assimilation in American Life: The Role of Race, Religion, and National Origins.* New York: Oxford University Press.

Gorin, S.S., and J.E. Heck. 2005. "Cancer Screening among Latino Subgroups in the United States." *Preventive Medicine* 40, no. 5 (May): 515–26.

Gornick, Mariam W. 2000. *Vulnerable Populations and Medicare Services.* New York: Century Foundation.

Griffin, Rodman D. 1992. "Hispanic Americans: Can They Find Economic Prosperity and Political Power?" *Congressional Quarterly Researcher* 2, no. 40 (October 30): 929–52.

Haas, J.S.; L.B. Lee; C.P. Kaplan; D. Sonneborn; K.A. Phillip; and S. Liang. 2003. "The Association of Race, Socioeconomic Status, and Health Insurance Status with the Prevalence of Overweight among Children and Adolescents." *American Journal of Public Health* 93, no. 12 (December): 2105–10.

Hahn, R.A. 1992. "The State of Federal Health Statistics on Racial and Ethnic Groups." *Journal of American Medical Association* 267, no. 2 (January 8): 268–71.

Hajat, Anjum; Jacqueline B. Lucas; and Raynard Kington. 2000. *Health Outcomes among Hispanic Subgroups: Data from the National Health Interview Survey, 1992–1995.* Advance Data from Vital and Health Statistics, no. 310. Hyattsville, MD: National Center for Health Statistics.

Han, E., and G. Liu. 2005. "Racial Disparities in Prescription Drug Use for Mental Illness among Population in U.S." *Journal of Mental Health Policy and Economics* 8, no. 3 (September): 131–43.

Harris, M.I. 2001. "Racial and Ethnic Differences in Health Care Access and Health Outcomes for Adults with Type 2 Diabetes." *Diabetes Care* 24, no. 3 (March): 454–59.

Hastie, Barbara A.; Joseph L. Riley; and Roger B. Fillingim. 2005. "Ethnic Differences and Responses to Pain in Healthy Young Adults." *Pain Medicine* 6, no. 1 (February): 61–71.

"Health Disparities Experienced by Hispanics—United States." 2004. *Morbidity and Mortality Weekly Report* 53, no. 40 (October 15): 935–37.

Henry J. Kaiser Family Foundation. 2001. *Latinos Views of HIV-AIDS Epidemic at 20 Years: Findings from a National Survey.* Washington, D.C.: Henry J. Kaiser Family Foundation.

Henry J. Kaiser Family Foundation. 2003. *Key Facts: Race, Ethnicity & Medical Care.* Washington, D.C.: Henry J. Kaiser Family Foundation.

Henry J. Kaiser Family Foundation. 2006. "HIV/AIDS Policy Fact Sheet: Latinos and HIV/AIDS." Online at www.kff.org. Accessed on 3/10/2006.

Henry J. Kaiser Family Foundation. 2007. *Key Facts: Race, Ethnicity & Medical Care.* Washington, D.C.: Henry J. Kaiser Family Foundation.

Heslin, K.C.; R.M. Anderson; S.L. Ettner; and W.E. Cunningham. 2005. "Racial and Ethnic Disparities in Access to Physicians with HIV-related Expertise." *Journal of General Internal Medicine* 20, no. 3 (March): 283–89.

"The Hispanic Electorate in 2004." n.d. Pew Hispanic Center. Henry J. Kaiser Family Foundation. Online at www.pewhispanic.org/files/factsheets/8.pdf. Accessed on 6/15/2007.

"Hispanic Health in the United States." 1991. *Journal of American Medical Association* 265, no. 2 (January 9): 248–52.

"Hispanic Views." 2003. *National Journal* 35, no. 35 (August 30): 26–35.

Houston, Thomas K.; Isabel. C. Scarinci; Sharina D. Person; and Paul. G. Greene. 2005. "Patient Smoking Cessation Advice by Health Care Providers: The Role of Ethnicity, Socioeconomic Status, and Health." *American Journal of Public Health* 95, no. 6 (June): 1056–61.

Howell, E.A.; P.A. Mora; C.R. Horowitz; and H. Leventhal. 2005. "Racial and Ethnic Differences in Factors Associated with Early Postpartum Depressive Symptoms." *Obstetric & Gynecology* 105, no. 6 (June): 1442–50.

Hubert, H.B.; J. Snider; and M.A. Winkleby. 2005. "Health Status, Health Behaviors, and Acculturation Factors Associated with Overweight and Obesity in Latinos from a Community and Agricultural Labor Camp Survey." *Preventive Medicine* 40, no. 6 (June): 642–51.

Hulme, P.A.; S.N. Walker; K.J. Effle; L. Jorgensen; G.M. McGowan; J.D. Nelson; and E.N. Pratt. 2003. "Health-Promoting Lifestyle Behaviors of Spanish-Speaking Hispanic Adults." *Journal of Transcultural Nursing* 14, no. 3 (July): 244–54.

"Inside America's Largest Minority." 2005. *Time,* August 22.

Institute of Medicine. 2002. *Unequal Treatment: Confronting Racial and Ethnic Disparities in Health Care.* Washington, D.C: National Academy Press.

Jacobson, Sherry. 2005. "Gap in Immigrant Health Care Noted." *Dallas Morning News,* July 26.

Johnson, Rachel L.; Somnath Saha; Jose J. Arbelaez; Mary C. Beach; and Lisa A. Cooper. 2004. "Racial and Ethnic Differences in Patient Perceptions of Bias and Cultural Competence in Health Care." *Journal of General Internal Medicine* 19, no. 2 (February): 101–10.

Jones, Jeffrey M. 2006. "Hispanics, Whites, Blacks Not in Complete Agreement on Illegal Immigration: Whites, Blacks Think Illegals Cost Taxpayers Too Much, Hispanics Disagree." *Gallup Poll Briefing,* July 10: 1–5.

Jones, Jeffrey M. 2007. "Whites, Blacks, Hispanics Disagree about Way Minority Groups Treated: Whites Diverge from Blacks, Hispanics in Their Views of Black-Hispanic Relations." Gallup Poll Briefing, July 11. Online at www.gallup.com. Accessed on 6/16/2007.

Kaiser Commission on Medicaid and the Uninsured. 2006. *The Uninsured: A Primer: Key Facts about Americas Without Health Insurance.* Washington, D.C.: Henry J. Kaiser Family Foundation.

Kaiser Family Foundation. 2007. "Kaiser Health Security Watch." June. Online at www. kff.org. Accessed on 6/29/2007.

Kaplan, S.A.; N.S. Calman; M. Golub; J.H. Davis; C. Ruddock; and J. Billings. 2006. "Racial and Ethnic Disparities in Health: A View from the South Bronx." *Journal of Healthcare for the Poor and Underserved* 17, no. 1 (February): 116–27.

Kemp, Carles. 2001. "Culture and End of Life: Hispanic Cultures (Focus on Mexican Americans)." *Journal of Hospice and Palliative Care* 3, no. 1 (January–March): 29–34.

Kidd, Lauren O. 2005. "Report: State Must Address Latino's Metal Health Needs." *Asbury Park Press,* September 21.

Kington, Raynard S., and James P. Smith. 1997. "Socioeconomic Status and Racial and Ethnic Differences in Functional Status Association with Chronic Diseases." *American Journal of Public Health* 87, no. 5 (May): 805–10.

Komaromy, Miriam; Kevin Grumbach; Michael Drake; Karen Vranizan; Nicole Lurie; Dennis Keane; and Andrew B. Bindman. 1996. "The Role of Black and Hispanic Physicians in Providing Health Care for Underserved Population." *New England Journal of Medicine* 334, no. 20 (May 16): 1305–10.

Ku, Leighton, and Sheetal Matani. 2001. "Left Out: Immigrants' Access to Health Care and Insurance." *Health Affairs* 20, no. 1 (January–February): 247–56.

Lanting, Loes C.; Inez M.A. Joung; Johan P. Mackenbach; Steven W.J. Lamberts; and Aart H. Bootsma. 2005. "Ethnic Differences in Mortality, End-Stage Complications, and Quality of Care among Diabetic Patients." *Diabetes Care* 28, no. 9 (September): 2280–88.

Lara, Marielena; Cristina Gamboa; Lya M. Kahramanian; Leo S. Morales; and David E. Bautista. 2005. "Acculturation and Latino Health in the United Sates: A Review of the Literature and Its Sociopolitical Context." *Annual Review of Public Health* 26, no. 1: 367–97.

Larkey, Linda K.; Michael L. Hecht; Katherine Miller; and Carlos Alatorre. 2001. "Hispanic Cultural Norms for Health-Seeking Behaviors in the Face of Symptoms." *Health Education and Behavior* 28, no. 1: 65–80.

"Latest Immigration 'Crisis' Defies Simplistic Solutions." 2006. *USA Today,* March 30.

LaVeist, T.A.; N.C. Rolley; and C. Diala. 2003. "Prevalence and Patterns of Discrimination among U.S. Health Care Consumers." *International Journal of Health Services* 33, no. 2: 331–44.

Leichter, Howard. 2004. "Ethnic Politics, Policy Fragmentation, and Dependent Health Care Access in California." *Journal of Health Politics, Policy, and Law* 29, no. 2 (April): 177–201.

LeRoi, Hicks S.; John E. Ayanian; John Oray; Jane Soukup; Michael McWilliams; Sharon S. Choi; and Paula A. Johnson. 2005. "Is Hospital Service Associated with Racial and Ethnic Disparities in Experiences with Hospital Care?" *American Journal of Medicine* 118, no. 5 (May): 529–35.

Liao, Youlian; Richard S. Cooper; Guichan Cao; Jay S. Kaufman; Andrew E. Long; and Daniel L. McGee. 2003. "Mortality from Coronary Heart Disease and Cardiovascular

Disease among Adult U.S. Hispanics." In Marilyn Aguirre-Molina and Carlos W. Molina, eds., *Latina Health in the United States: A Public Health Reader,* 175–87. San Francisco: Jossey-Bass.

Lillie-Blanton, Marsha; M. Brodie; D. Rowland; D. Altmam; and M. McIntosh. 2000. "Race, Ethnicity, and the Health Care System: Public Perception and Experiences." *Medical Care Research and Review* 57, no. 3 Supplement (November): 218–35.

Lillie-Blanton, Marsha, and Catherine Hoffman. 2005. "The Role of Health Insurance Coverage in Reducing Racial/Ethnic Disparities in Health Care." *Health Affairs* 24, no. 2 (March–April): 398–408.

Lopez, R.A. 2005. "Use of Alternative Folk Medicine by Mexican American Women." *Journal of Immigrant Health* 7, no. 1 (January): 23–31.

Luchsinger, Alejandro José. 2001. "Diabetes." In Marilyn Aguirre-Molina, Carlos W. Molina, and Ruth Enid Zambrana, eds., *Health Issues in the Latino Community,* 277–300. San Francisco: Jossey-Bass.

Magilvy, Joan K.; Joann Congdon; Ruby J. Martinez; Renel Davis; and Jennifer Averill. 2000. "Caring for Our Own: Health Care Experiences of Rural Hispanic Elders." *Journal of Aging Studies* 14, no. 2 (June): 171–90.

Marin, G. 1992. "Issues in the Measurement of Acculturation among Hispanics." In Kurt F. Geisinger, ed., *Psychological Testing of Hispanics,* 23–51. Washington, D.C.: American Psychological Association.

Markides, Kyriakos S., and Karl Eschbach. 2005. "Aging, Migration, and Mortality: Current Status of Research on the Hispanic Paradox." *Psychological Sciences and Social Sciences* 60, no.2: 68–75.

Marks, Gary; Melinda Garcia; and Julia M. Solis. 1990. "Health Risk Behavior of Hispanics in the United States: Findings from HHANES." *American Journal of Public Health* 80, no. 12 (December Supplement): 20–26.

Marotta, Sylvia A., and Jorge G. Garcia. 2003. "Latinos in the United States in 2000." *Hispanic Journal of Behavioral Sciences* 25, no. 1 (February): 13–34.

Masci, David. 1998. "Hispanic-Americans' New Clout: Will Hispanics Desert the Democratic Party?" *Congressional Quarterly Researcher* 8, no. 35 (September 15): 809–32.

Masci, David. 2003. "Latino's Future: When Will They Yield Greater Political Power?" *Congressional Quarterly Researcher* 13, no. 36 (October 30): 869–92.

Mazur, Robert E.; Grace Marquis; and Helen Jensen. 2003. "Diet and Food Insufficiency among Hispanic Youths: Acculturation and Socioeconomic Factors in the Third National Health and Nutrition Examination Survey." *American Journal of Clinical Nutrition* 78, no. 6 (December): 1120–27.

Mazzuca, Josephine. 2004. "Minorities Unhappy with the Way Things Are Going." *Gallup Poll Tuesday Briefing,* August 3. Washington, D.C.: Gallup Organization. Online at www.gallup.com. Accessed on 8/5/2005.

McMurray, Coleen. 2004. "U.S. Minorities Still Struggle to Pay for Healthcare." *Gallup Poll Tuesday Briefing,* July 27. Washington, D.C.: Gallup Organization. Online at www.gallup.com. Accessed on 8/5/2004.

Merrill, R.M., and E.W. Allen. 2003. "Race and Ethnic Disparities in Satisfaction with Doctors and Health Providers in the United States." *Ethnicity & Disease* 13, no. 4 (Fall): 492–98.

Morales, Leo S.; William E. Cunningham; Julie A. Brown; Honghu Liu; and Ron D. Hays. 1999. "Are Latinos Less Satisfied with Communication by Health Care Providers?" *Journal of General Internal Medicine* 14, no.7: 409–17.

Morales, Leo S.; Raynard S. Kington; Robert O. Valdez; and Jose J. Escarce. 2002. "Socioeconomic, Cultural, and Behavioral Factors Affecting Hispanic Health Outcomes." *Journal of Health Care for Poor and Underserved* 13, no. 4 (November): 477–503.

Mukamel, D.B.; A.S. Murthy; and D.L. Weimer. 2000. "Racial Differences in Access to High-Quality Cardiac Surgeons." *American Journal of Public Health* 90, no. 11 (November): 1774–77.

Murrain, Michelle. 1996. "Differential Survival in Blacks and Hispanics with AIDS." *Ethnicity & Health* 1, no. 4 (December): 373–82.

Murray-Garcia, Jann L.; Joe Selby; Julie Schmittdiel; Kevin Grumbach; and Charles P. Quesenberry. 2000. "Racial and Ethnic Differences in Patient Survey: Patients' Values, Ratings, and Reports Regarding Physician Primary Care Performance in a Large Health Maintenance Organization." *Medical Care* 38, no. 3 (March): 300–310.

Napoles-Springer, Anna M.; Jasmine Santoyo; Kathryn Houston; Eliseo J. Perez-Stable; and Anita L. Stewart. 2005. "Patient's Perceptions of Cultural Factors Affecting the Quality of Their Medical Encounters." *Health Expectations* 8: 4–17.

National Center for Health Statistics. 1998. *Health, United States, 1998 with Socioeconomic Status and Health Chartbook.* Hyattsville, MD: U.S. Government Printing Office.

National Center for Health Statistics. 2005. *Health, United States 2005 with Chartbook of Trends in the Health of Americans.* Hyattsville, M.D: U.S. Government Printing Office.

Palloni, Alberto, and Elizabeth Arias. 2004. "Paradox Lost: Explaining the Hispanic Adult Mortality Advantage." *Demography* 41, no. 3: 385–415.

Paniagua, Freddy A. 2005. "Implications of the United States Census 2000 in Analyzing and Reporting New Findings of Disparities in Health." *Psychological Reports* no. 1 (August): 29–32.

Passel, Jeffrey S. 2006. *The Size and Characteristics of the Unauthorized Migrant Population in the U.S.: Estimates Based on the March 2005 Current Population Survey.* Washington, D.C.: Pew Hispanic Center.

Patel, Kushang V.; Karl Eschbach; Laura A. Ray; and Kyriakos S. Markides. 2004. "Evaluation of Mortality Data for Older Mexican Americans: Implications for the Hispanic Paradox." *American Journal of Epidemiology* 159, no. 7: 707–15.

Pérez-Stable, Eliseo; Teresa Juarbe; and Gina Moreno-John. 2001. "Cardiovascular Disease." In Marilyn Aguirre-Molina, Carlos W. Molina, and Ruth Enid Zambrana, eds., *Health Issues in the Latino Community,* 245–76. San Francisco: Jossey-Bass.

Pérez-Stable, Eliseo; Anna Napoles-Springer; and Jose M. Miramontes. 1997. "The Effects of Ethnicity and Language on Medical Outcomes with Patients with Hypertension or Diabetes." *Medical Care* 35, no. 12 (December): 1212–19.

Pew Hispanic Center. 2005. *Hispanics: A People in Motion.* Washington, D.C.: Pew Research Center.

Pew Hispanic Center and Kaiser Family Foundation. 2004. "Health Care Experiences." *Survey Brief,* March. Washington, D.C. Online at www.pewhispanic.org. Accessed on 4/15/2006.

"QuickStats: Infant Mortality Rates, by Maternal Race/Ethnicity—United States, 1995 and 2003." 2006. *Morbidity and Mortality Weekly Report* 55, no. 24 (June 23): 683.

"Racial/Ethnic and Socioeconomic Disparities in Multiple Risk Factors for Heart Disease and Stroke—United States, 2003." 2005. *Morbidity and Mortality Weekly Report* 54, no. 5 (February 11): 113–17.

"Racial/Ethnic Disparities in Infant Mortality—United States, 1995–2002." 2005. *Morbidity and Mortality Weekly Report* 54, no. 22 (June 10): 553–56.

Ramirez, Amelie, and Lucina Suarez. 2001. "The Impact of Cancer on Latino Populations." In Marilyn Aguirre-Molina, Carlos W. Molina, and Ruth Enid Zambrana, eds., *Health Issues in the Latino Community,* 211–44. San Francisco: Jossey-Bass.

Ren, Xinhua S., and Benjamin C. Amick. 1996a. "Racial and Ethnic Disparities in Self-Assessed Health Status: Evidence from the National Survey." *Ethnicity and Health* 1, no. 3 (September): 293–303.

Ren, Xinhua S., and Benjamin C. Amick. 1996b. " Race and Self-Assessed Health Status: The Role of Socioeconomic Factors in the USA." *Journal of Epidemiology and Community Health* 50, no. 3 (June): 269–73.

Richardson, Lynne D.; Charlene Babcock; and Joshua H. Tamayo-Sarver. 2003. "Racial and Ethnic Disparities in the Clinical Practice of Emergency Medicine." *Academy of Emergency Medicine* 10, no. 11 (November): 1184–88.

Ross, Jon. 1995. "Hispanic Americans." *Hospitals and Health Network* 69, no. 19 (October 5): 65–67.

Ruiz, Pedro. 1993. "Access to Health Care for Uninsured Hispanics: Policy Recommendations." *Hospital and Community Psychiatry* 44, no. 10 (October): 958–62.

Ruiz, Pedro. 2002. "Hispanic Access to Health/Mental Services." *Psychiatric Quarterly* 73, no. 2 (Summer): 81–85.

Saha, Somnath; J.J. Arbelaez; and L.A. Cooper. 2003. "Patient-Physician Relationships and Racial Disparities in the Quality of Health Care." *American Journal of Public Health* 93, no. 10 (October): 1713–19.

Saha, Somnath; Miriam Komaromy; Thomas D. Koespell; and Andrew B. Bindman. 1999. "Patient-Physician Racial Concordance and the Perceived Quality and Use of Health Care." *Archives of Internal Medicine* 159, no. 9 (May 10): 997–1004.

Saha, Somnath; Sara H. Taggart; Miriam Komaromy; and Andrew B. Bindman. 2000. "Do Patients Choose Physicians of Their Own Race?" *Health Affairs* 19, no. 4 (July–August): 76–83.

Scheffler, R.M., and A.B. Miller. 1991. "Differences in Mental Health Service Utilization among Ethnic Subpopulations." *International Journal of Law and Psychiatry* 14: 363–76.

Shi, Leiyu, and Gregory D. Stevens. 2005. "Disparities in Access to Care and Satisfaction among U.S. Children: The Role of Race/Ethnicity and Poverty Status." *Public Health Reports* 120, no. 4 (July–August): 431–41.

Shinkman, Ron. 1997. "Studies: California Latinos behind in Access to Care." *Modern Healthcare* 27, no. 50 (December 15): 25.

Shone, L.P.; A.W. Dick; C. Brach; K.S. Kimminau; B.J. LaClare; E.A. Shenkman; J.F. Col; V.A. Schaffer; F. Mulvihill; P.G. Szilagyi; J.D. Klien; K. VanLandeghem; and J. Bronstein. 2003. "The Role of Race and Ethnicity in the State Children's Health Insurance Program (SCHIP) in Four States: Are There Baseline Disparities, and What Do They Mean for SCHIP?" *Pediatrics* Supplement 112, no. 6 (December): e521–32.

Smith, C.A., and E. Barnett. 2005. "Diabetes-Related Mortality among Mexican-Americans, Puerto Ricans, and Cuban Americans in the United States." *American Journal of Public Health* 18, no. 6 (December): 381–87.

Smith, David P., and Benjamin S. Bradshaw. 2006. "Rethinking the Hispanic Paradox: Death Rates and Life Expectancy for U.S. Non-Hispanic Whites and Hispanic Populations." *American Journal of Public Health* 96, no. 9 (September): 1686–92.

Solorio Rosa M.; Yu Hongjian; Richard E. Brown; Lida Becerra; and Lillian Gelberg. 1991. "A Comparison of Hispanic and White Adolescent Females" Use of Family Planning Services in California." *Perspectives on Sexual and Reproductive Health* 36, no. 4 (July/August 2004): 157–161.

Staiti, Andrea B.; Robert H. Hurley; and Aaron Katz. 2006. *Stretching the Safety Net to Serve Undocumented Immigrants: Community Responses to Health Needs.* Issue Brief no. 104. Washington, D.C.: Center for Studying Health System Change.

Stein, Judith A.; Sarah A. Fox; and Paul J. Murata. 1991. "The Influence of Ethnicity, Socioeconomic Status, and Psychological Barriers on Use of Mammography." *Journal of Health and Social Behavior* 32, no. 2 (June): 101–13.

Stepanikova, I., and K.S. Cook. 2004. "Insurance Policies and Perceived Quality of Care among Privately Insured Patients: Do Features of Managed Care Widen the Racial, Ethnic, and Language-Based Gaps?" *Medical Care* 42, no. 10 (October): 966–74.

Suarez-Almazor, Maria E.; Julianne Souchek; Adam P. Kelly; Kimberly O'Malley; Margaret Byrne; Marsha Richardson; and Chong Pak. 2005. "Ethnic Variation in Knee Replacement: Patient Preference or Uniformed Disparity?" *Archives of Internal Medicine* 165, no. 10 (May 23): 1117–24.

Sullivan Commission on Diversity in the Healthcare Workforce. 2004. *Missing Persons: Minorities in the Health Professions.* Project administered by Duke University School of Medicine and funded by W.K. Kellogg Foundation. Online at www.sullivancommission. org. Accessed on 9/20/2005.

Summer, David. 1995. "Proposition 187 and Health Care for Illegal Aliens." *Journal of Law, Medicine & Ethics* 23, no. 1 (Spring): 103–4.

Suro, Roberto; Richard Fry; and Jeffrey Passel. 2005. *Hispanics and the 2004 Election: Population, Electorate, and Voters.* Washington, D.C.: Pew Hispanic Center.

Tandon, S.D.; K.M. Parillo; and M. Keefer. 2005. "Hispanic Women's Perceptions of Patient-Centeredness during Prenatal Care: A Mixed-Method Study." *Birth* 32, no. 4 (December): 312–17.

Tieman, Jeff. 2004. "Immigrant Care Costs Hospitals." *Modern Healthcare* 34, no. 23 (June 6): 14–15.

Timmins, C.L. 2002. "The Impact of Language Barriers on the Health Care of Latinos in the United States: A Review of the Literature and Guidelines for Practice." *Journal of Midwifery Women's Health* 47, no. 2 (April): 80–96.

Unger, Jennifer B. 2000. "Acculturation and Attitudes about Contraceptive Use among Latina Women." *Health Care for Women International* 21, no. 3 (April–May): 235–49.

U.S. Bureau of the Census. 1986. *Projections of the Hispanic Population.* Current Population Reports, Series P-25, No. 995. Washington, D.C.: Government Printing Office.

U.S. Department of Health and Human Services. 2001. *Mental Health: Culture, Race, and Ethnicity. A Supplement to Mental Health: A Report of the Surgeon General.* Rockville, MD: U.S. Public Health Service, Substance Abuse and Mental Health Services Administration, Center for Mental Health Services.

U.S. General Accounting Office. 2003. *Health Care: Approaches to Address Racial and Ethic Disparities: Briefing for Congressional Staff of Senator Bill Frist, Majority Leader, United States Senate.* Washington, D.C.: U.S. General Accounting Office.

Vega, William A., and Margarita Alegria. 2001. "Latino Mental Health and Treatment in the United States." In Marilyn Aguirre-Molina, Carlos W. Molina, and Ruth Enid Zambrana, eds., *Health Issues in the Latino Community,* 179–208. San Francisco: Jossey-Bass.

Virnig, B.; Z. Huang; N. Lurie; D. Musgrave; A.M. McBean; and B. Dowd. 2004. "Does Medicare Managed Care Provide Equal Treatment for Mental Illness across Races?" *Archives of General Psychiatry* 61, no. 2 (February): 201–5.

Wallace, Steven P.; Veronica Gutierrez; and Richard Brown. 2003. "Mexican Immigrants Are Generally Healthier, But Have Less Access to Needed Health Care." *Health Policy Fact Sheet* (October, 12–19). Publication of the UCLA Center for Health Policy Research. Online at www.healthpolicy.ucla.edu/pubs/publication.asp?pubID=76. Accessed on 10/15/2005.

Weech-Maldondo, Robert; Leo S. Morales; Marc Elliot; Karen Spritzer; Grant Marshall; and Ron D. Hayes. 2003. "Race/Ethnicity, Language, and Patients' Assessment of Care in Medicaid-Managed Care." *Health Services Research* 38, no. 3 (June): 789–808.

Weinick, Robert M.; E.A. Jacobs; L.C. Stone; A.N. Ortega; and H. Burstin. 2004. "Hispanic Healthcare Disparities: Challenging the Myth of a Monolithic Hispanic Population." *Medical Care* 42, no. 4 (April): 313–20.

Weinick, Robert M.; Samuel H. Zuvekas; and Joel W. Cohen. 2000. "Racial and Ethnic Differences in Access to and Use of Health Care Services." *Medical Care Research and Review* 57, no. 3 (November): 36–55.

Wells, Kenneth; Ruth Klap; Alan Koike; and Cathy Sherbourne. 2001. "Ethnic Disparities in Unmet Need for Alcoholism, Drug Abuse, and Mental Health Care." *American Journal of Psychiatry* 158, no. 12 (December): 2027–32.

Williams, David R., and Chiquita Collins. 1995. "US Socioeconomic and Racial Differences in Health: Patterns and Explanations." *American Review of Sociology* 21: 349–86.

Wilson, Thomas C. 1996. "Cohort and Prejudice: Whites' Attitudes toward Blacks, Hispanics, Jews, and Asians." *Public Opinion Quarterly* 60, no. 2 (Summer): 253–74.

Winkleby, Marilyn A.; Darius E. Jatulis; Erica Frank; and Stephen P. Fortmann. 1992. "Socioeconomic Status and Health: How Education, Income, and Occupation Contribute to Risk Factors for Cardiovascular Disease." *American Journal of Public Health* 82, no. 6 (June): 816–20.

"With Minimal Federal Help, Community Safety Nets Are Straining to Care for Uninsured Immigrants." 2006. *Hospital and Health Networks* 80, no. 4 (April): 90.

Wray, L.A. 1992. "Health Policy and Ethnic Diversity in Older Americans, Dissonance or Harmony?" *Western Journal of Medicine* 157, no. 3 (September): 357–61.

Zambrana, Ruth E.; Nancy Breen; Sarah A. Fox; and Mary Lou Gutierrez-Mohamed. 2003. "Use of Cancer Screening Practices by Hispanic Women." In Marilyn Aguirre-Molina and Carlos W. Molina, eds., *Latina Health in the United States: A Public Health Reader,* 188–211. San Francisco: Jossey-Bass.

Zambrana, Ruth E., and O. Carter-Pokras. 2001. "Health Data Issues for Hispanics: Implications for Public Health Research." *Journal of Health Care for the Poor and Underserved* 12, no. 1 (February): 20–34.

Zapata, Jeiny, and Raelene Shippee-Rice. 1999. "The Use of Folk Healing and Healers by Six Latino Living in New England: A Preliminary Study." *Journal of Transcultural Nursing* 10, no. 2 (April): 136–42.

Zsembik, B.A., and D. Fennell. 2005. "Ethnic Variation in Health and the Determinants of Health among Latinos." *Social Science & Medicine* 61, no. 1 (July): 53–63.

4

American Indians, Alaska Natives, and Health Care

In comparison to African Americans and Hispanics, American Indians and Alaska Natives (AI/AN) constitute a very small minority in American society. In the 2000 census, 4.1 million people (1.5 percent) identified themselves as AI/AN or in combination with one or more races. Of this number, 2.5 million (0.9 percent) identified themselves as AI/AN only, while another 1.6 million (0.6 percent) identified themselves as AI/AN plus one or more other races. For the first time, the 2000 census asked separate questions on race and Hispanic origin. Hispanics who reported their race as AI/AN, either alone or in combination with one or more races, were included in the number of American Indians. Because of these changes, the 2000 census data on race are not directly compatible with the 1990 and earlier censuses (U.S. Bureau of the Census 2002). Thus, the term "American Indians and Alaska Natives" refers to people having origins in any of the original people of North and South America (including Central America), and who maintain tribal affiliation or community attachment (U.S. Bureau of the Census 2002). According to the 2000 census, 43 percent of the American Indian population lived in the West, 31 percent in the South, 17 percent in the Midwest, and 9 percent in the Northeast. The ten states with the largest American Indian population in 2000 were California, Oklahoma, Arizona, Texas, New Mexico, New York, Washington, North Carolina, Michigan, and Alaska (U.S. Bureau of the Census 2002). Most Alaska Natives live in villages spread throughout Alaska.

History of Health Care Policy for American Indians and Alaska Natives

Health care for members of American Indian tribes and Alaska natives is delivered from a system that is separate from that of mainstream America. This has evolved from the unique and complex history of interaction between the various tribes and the U. S. government (Shelton 2004).

The United States acquired Russia's rights to Alaska in 1867. The Treaty of Cession provided that Alaska Natives would be treated the same as aboriginal peoples in the rest of the United States. However, treaties were never negotiated with Alaska Natives and few reservations were created in Alaska. The federal government, through the Bureau of Indian Affairs, pursued its relationship with Alaska natives on a village-by-village basis. The Alaska Native Claims Settlement Act of 1971 (ANCSA) addressed the land claims of Alaska Natives. Native corporations were created to hold settlement funds and lands. In general, the regional Native nonprofit corporations provide health care to Alaska Native people (Shelton 2004).

Upon gaining independence, the United States assumed the role previously held by England with respect to American Indians. The commerce clause (Article I, section 8, clause 3) and the Treaty Clause (Article II, section 2, clause 2) of the U.S. Constitution grant the federal government exclusive authority to regulate commerce and to make treaties with Indian tribes on behalf of the United States. The four most basic principles of federal Indian law established early in the United States are: (1) Tribes retain all of their inherent sovereignty that the federal government has not encroached upon; (2) the federal government, and not states, is in charge of Indian affairs; (3) the federal government only deals with tribes it has recognized; and (4) the United States has assumed trust responsibility toward the Indian nations (Shelton 2004).

Bureau of Indian Affairs

The federal government has provided health care to American Indians since the early nineteenth century both as a treaty obligation and as a consequence of its role as a trustee. Until 1849, health care was provided by military doctors because the Bureau of Indian Affairs (BIA) was part of the War Department. In 1849, the BIA was transferred to the newly created Department of the Interior (Kunitz 1996), and thus Indian health care passed from military to civilian control. By 1880, seventy-seven physicians were serving the entire American Indian population in the United States (Cohen 1982). During the last half of the nineteenth century, the efforts of the U.S. government were directed at the eradication and removal of Indians from their land through treaties in an attempt to integrate them into American society. With the rise of "Indian Wars" in the last part of the nineteenth century, federal policy shifted from integration to vanquishing Indians in massacres (Shelton 2004).

In the early twentieth century the policy of assimilation—with the goal of bringing American Indians into mainstream American society—gained favor as the best way to deal with the federal government's "Indian problem." Allotments of reservation land and education of AI became the primary tools of assimilation. Many American Indian traditional health care activities were banned during the period of assimilation. Congress began formally appropriating funds for BIA health care services in 1910 (Shelton 2004). In 1921, Congress passed the Snyder Act, which provided explicit legislative authorization for federal provision of health care services to members of all federally recognized American Indians tribes and for the conservation of the health of Indian communities (Roubideaux 2002). The Merriam Report, published in 1928 by the nongovernmental Institute for Government at the request of the Secretary of the Interior, described the devastation caused by land allotment, the failure of Indian education, and the dreadful health status of American Indians. This set the stage for an era of reorganization (Shelton 2004).

In 1934, the Commissioner of Indian Affairs, a longtime Indian reform activist, issued a report calling for undoing the damage done by allotment and assimilation policies by encouraging the revival of tribalism and the preservation of Indian heritage. Congress passed the Johnson-O'Malley Act of 1934, which authorized the Secretary of the Interior to contract with states and territories for provision of services, including health services, for Indians. This allowed the BIA to contract for provision of Indian health services. The Indian Reorganization Act of 1934 encouraged economic development and provided for self-determination by Indian tribes (Shelton 2004).

By the early 1950s, an assimilation policy reemerged. The Hoover Commission's Task Force on Indian Policy advocated the integration of Indians into the larger U.S. population. The policy of assimilation became the formal federal Indian policy during the Eisenhower years. The policy involved terminating federal recognition of Indian tribes, encouraging the relocation of Indians from reservations to cities, and ultimately the weakening and dismantling the BIA (Kunitz 1996). This policy was promoted as a way to "free" Indians from supervision and control by the BIA. The result was a marked increase in the Indian population in cities across the country. In 1954, the Transfer Act moved responsibility for Indian health to the Public Health Service, which at that time was part of the Department of Health, Education, and Welfare (Shelton 2004). The Indian Health Service (IHS) was established as an agency under the Public Health Service in 1955. At present, the Indian Health Service (IHS) within the Public Health Service is part of the U.S. Department of Health and Human Services (DHHS). Thus, the IHS is the federal agency with primary responsibility for fulfilling the United States' trust obligation to provide health care for AI/AN people (Shelton 2004).

The American Indian Movement of the 1960s and 1970s brought about a shift from a policy of termination toward a policy of self-determination for American Indian tribes. President Nixon specifically rejected the policy of "forced termination" of the Eisenhower years in a message to Congress on the grounds that (1) federal responsibility was not simply an act of generosity toward a disadvantaged people but a solemn obligation, (2) the practical result of forced termination had been clearly harmful in instances where it has been tried, and (3) the fear of one extreme policy, forced termination, had produced the opposite extreme, excessive dependence on the federal government (Kunitz 1996). The Nixon administration's Indian policy was embodied in two major pieces of legislation passed by Congress: the Indian Self-Determination and Education Assistance Act of 1975 and the Indian Health Care Improvement Act of 1976.

The Indian Self-Determination and Education Assistance Act directed the Secretary of the Department of the Interior (DOI) and the Secretary of Health and Human Services, upon the request of any Indian tribe, to enter into self-determination contracts or compacts with tribal organizations for planning, conducting, and/or administering programs that are provided by the federal government for the benefit of Indians. The Indian Health Care Improvement Act of 1976 contained many provisions designed to increase the quantity and quality of Indian health services, and to improve the participation of Indians in planning and providing these services, with the national goal of providing the highest health status to Indians and providing existing Indian health services with all necessary resources to effect that policy. For the first time, the law authorized Medicare and Medicaid reimbursement for services performed at Indian health facilities. Although the Indian Health Care Improvement Act reauthorization expired in 2000, Congress has continued to appropriate funds for IHS each year (Shelton 2004).

President Clinton, in 1994, issued executive orders to facilitate tribal involvement in the administration of Indian programs. In 1998, Clinton issued an executive order that further defined the policy of requiring executive departments and agencies to consult with tribal governments. President George W. Bush has continued the policy of tribal consultation (Shelton 2004).

Today, under the broad authorization of the 1921 Snyder Act, Congress every year appropriates funds to the IHS to fulfill the federal government's trust responsibility to provide health services to AI/AN people.

Indian Health Service

IHS is primarily a rural health care delivery system. There are three major ways in which IHS delivers health services. First, IHS uses its own hospitals, outpatient health centers, and smaller health stations. Second, IHS contracts with tribes under the Indian Self-Determination and Education Act to operate its hospitals, health centers, and health stations. Third, IHS purchases services not available through its own facilities from non-tribal, private sector hospitals and health practitioners. IHS services are provided free of charge to eligible AI/AN people (Forquera 2001). However, IHS has a limited reach because eligibility for its services does not extend to all AI/AN for two reasons. First, IHS services are limited to members of federally recognized tribes. Thus, many AI/AN who are not members of federally recognized tribes are ineligible to receive IHS services (Katz 2004). Second, IHS services are provided to AI/AN living on or near reservations. However, today, a majority of AI/AN people live in urban areas. Data from the 2000 census indicated that about 2.7 million, or 66 percent, of the 4.1 million people who identified themselves solely or partially as AI/AN live in metropolitan areas. These two factors combined together to limit the IHS service population to only about 1.5 million (Forquera 2001).

It is important to keep in mind that historically the migration of AI/AN to urban areas was the direct result of the federal government's "relocation" policy in effect during the 1950s. Over 160,000 AI/AN were forcibly moved from their reservations into cities to promote their assimilation into American society. As a result, many Indians frequently lost access to health care and other benefits granted to them when they lived on reservations. Thus, many urban Indians who are members of federally recognized tribes do not have access to health services through IHS because they are not living on or near Indian reservations. Furthermore, many Indians are not enrolled members of federally recognized tribes and IHS generally does not consider these individuals eligible for services provided by its hospitals and clinics or those run by tribes under contract with IHS.

As the urban Indian population increased, in part, due to the government's relocation program, the need for health services for Indians living in urban areas also increased. Several cities, particularly those designated as relocation sites, independently developed health services for urban Indians. The Indian Health Care Improvement Act of 1976, in recognition of the plight of urban Indians who lacked of access to health services, provided for the creation of an urban Indian health program (Bergman et al. 1999). This was a major departure for the IHS because previously it had not included Indians living outside IHS service areas. The purpose was to make outpatient health services available to urban Indians directly or by referrals. The IHS administers a program of grants and contracts to nonprofit urban Indian health organizations (Forquera 2001).

Urban Indian health organizations (UIHOs) are generally independent, nonprofit clinics that provide outpatient health services and referrals to urban Indians on an income-based, sliding-scale fee schedule. Thus, this service is not free. The patients are asked to pay what they can afford. Most urban Indian health organizations receive their income from patient fees, public and private insurers, tribal funds, and a mix of public and private grants, including funding from IHS contracts. More than half of the UIHOs are certified as federally qualified health centers, making them eligible for additional federal funds (Renfrew 2006). The services at urban health programs are restricted to primary care, and referrals for inpatient hospital care, specialty services, diagnostics, and the like are at the clinics' expense (Forquera 2001).

Urban Indians, like other American citizens, are eligible for health coverage under Medicaid, Medicare, or the State Children's Health Insurance Program (SCHIP) if they meet the eligibility requirements of these programs. However, some Indians do not enroll in public programs because they believe the federal government is obligated by treaty and laws to pay for their health care and they should not have to enroll in health care programs for the general population. Despite this reluctance, many urban Indians are enrolled in public programs (Forquera 2001). Since UIHOs are recognized by law as federally qualified health centers, they have an opportunity to enroll eligible urban Indians in Medicaid. In their benefit package, state Medicaid programs are required to cover the services provided by federally qualified health centers and such centers are entitled to payments for these services at a specified rate under the law (Forquera 2001).

One of the major changes made by the Indian Heath Care Improvement Act of 1976 was a provision that allowed IHS to bill Medicaid for services provided to Medicaid-eligible patients. This was not the case prior to 1976. Since Medicaid is a joint federal-state program funded on a matching basis, this would have increased costs to the state government. To limit state resistance to this provision, Congress provided in the law a 100 percent federal medical assistance percentage (FMAP). This opened a new stream of federal funding for IHS. However, the Center for

Medicare and Medicaid Services (CMS) has narrowly interpreted this provision to provide 100 percent federal reimbursement only for care provided inside IHS facilities. State and tribal advocates have sought to apply this provision to health care services offered to AI/AN through IHS programs outside of IHS facilities. State governments have challenged CMS's narrow interpretation of this statutory provision in courts. Health care advocates for AI/AN have argued that the 100 percent federal medical assistance percentage provision should be interpreted broadly to provide full funding for transportation to and from IHS facilities, referrals from IHS facilities, and care provided in urban UIHOs with IHS contracts (Renfrew 2006; Schneider 2005).

Finally, critics have also argued that another shortcoming of IHS in providing health care services to AI/AN is that IHS is critically underfunded (Lillie-Blanton 2005). For example, the IHS budget for fiscal year 2002 was $2.8 billion. Tribal leadership estimates that a need-based budget for Indian health care should be closer to $18 billion. It is not surprising that in 2001, per capita expenditure for Indian health care was about one-third of that for the U.S. population in general (Roubideaux 2002). One of the consequences of this low level of expenditures is that IHS hospitals provide a more limited range of diagnostic and therapeutic services than community hospitals in general. The inadequacy of government appropriations has become increasingly clear (Kunitz 1996). President Bush's proposed budget for fiscal year 2008 has requested $4.1 billion to finance health services for AI/AN ("2008 Budget Fact Sheets" 2007). This is still a far cry from what is needed

To make matters worse, in his proposed fiscal year 2007 federal budget, President Bush recommended eliminating federal funding for the Urban Indian Health Program, which had started in 1976 with the passage of the Indian Health Care Improvement Act. The proposed budget would cut $33 million from the IHS budget, which funds thirty-four UIHOs. The Bush administration argued that this program duplicates other public programs and federal funding for expanding community health centers could fill the gap (Krisberg 2006). Congress failed to act on this proposal. However, President Bush's fiscal year 2008 budget request has again proposed to eliminate 32.7 million in funding for the Urban Indian Health programs ("NPAIHB Policy Brief" 2007). Many members of both the House and the Senate have called for restoration of this funding on the grounds that its elimination will leave 430,000 American Indians living in forty-one cities without direct access to health services. It remains to be seen what action, if any, Congress takes on this matter.

Despite these problems, there have been some improvements in the health status of AI/AN. Since the establishment of IHS, Indian mortality rates have declined and life expectancy has improved. There have been major improvements in infant and child mortality and declines in infectious diseases. This suggests that IHS has been effective in reducing preventable and treatable conditions such as infectious diseases but has not had much impact on certain chronic conditions such as diabetes and certain types of cancers (Kunitz 1996). Furthermore, despite some of the successes, it is clear that AI/AN still experience significant health care disparities when it comes to health status/outcome, access to health care, and quality of health care not only in comparison to whites but also the general U.S. population. In certain areas, AI/AN fare even worse than African Americans or Hispanics.

Before we discuss the health care disparities suffered by AI/AN, it is important to note that a comprehensive assessment of disparities faced by AI/AN is difficult because of the significant gaps in health data for AI/AN reported in the annual National Healthcare Disparities Report produced by the Agency for Health Care Research and Quality. The gaps in data for AI/AN are larger than the gaps for most other racial/ethnic groups (Moy et al. 2006). For example, only 42 percent of measures of health care quality and access indicators tracked in the 2004 annual report could be used to assess disparities among AI/AN. Patient safety data are especially limited for AI/AN. With respect to quality of care, data were available for blacks on all measures, for Hispanics on 95 percent of all measures, but for AN/AN on only 55 percent of quality measures. On measures of access, data were available for African Americans and Hispanics on all measures but only on 52 percent of access measures for AI/AN (Moy et al. 2006). Overall, AI/AN are underrepresented in national data sets. This is especially true of older AI/AN (Rhoades 2006). According to the National Committee on Vital and Health Statistics, data collection on AI/AN is seriously inadequate and improved efforts at data collection were needed (Rhoades 2006). Another data problem arises from misclassification of AI/AN on death certificates, which makes it difficult to measure and reduce health care disparities (Stehr-Green, Bettles, and Robertson 2002).

Health Status/Outcomes

When Columbus arrived in the Western hemisphere, he found American Indians to be clean, fit, and without illness. Today, American Indians have higher occurrences of diseases than other racial/ethnic minorities (Ambler 2003). For example, America Indians have a higher prevalence of disease risk factors such as obesity, hypertension, high cholesterol, and tobacco smoking than other racial/ethnic minorities (Liao, Tucker, and Giles 2003). According to a report issued by the U.S. Commission on Civil Rights (2004, 7–8), "Native Americans are 770 percent more likely to die from alcoholism, 650 percent more likely to die from tuberculosis, 420 percent more likely to die from diabetes, 280 percent more likely to die from accidents, and 52 percent more likely to die from pneumonia or influenza than the rest of the United States, including white and minority population." For all health behaviors and status measures, AI/AN elders report greater risk factors than white elders (Denny et al. 2005). Mortality data also show an excessive overall mortality among AI/AN as well as excesses for specific causes of death (Mahoney and Michalek 1998). Within AI/AN communities, males' death rates exceed those of females from every age up to seventy-five years and for six of the eight leading causes of death (Rhoades 2003).

Table 4.1 shows data about leading causes of death among AI/AN and whites for 1980 and 2004. It demonstrates not only some significant differences between AI/AN and whites but also some significant changes that have taken place in the leading causes of death especially within the AI/AN community. Diseases of the heart were the leading cause of death for both whites and AI/AN in 1980 and 2004. However, unintentional injury was the second leading cause of death among AI/AN in 1980 and the third leading cause of death in 2004. Among whites, unintentional injuries was the fourth leading cause of death in 1980 and it had dropped to fifth place in 2004. Suicide was ranked the tenth leading cause of death for both whites and AI/AN in 1980. In 2004, suicide remained the tenth leading cause of death among whites but it had climbed to the eighth rank among AI/AN. One of the most dramatic shifts in leading causes of death for AI/AN is for diabetes mellitus. It was the eighth leading cause of death among AI/AN in 1980 but jumped to fourth place by 2004.

Diabetes is one of the most serious health problems confronting AI/AN and is responsible for significant morbidity and mortality rates among AI/AN. Most AI/AN with diabetes have type 2 diabetes, also known as adult onset diabetes, which is characterized by high levels of blood glucose stemming from impaired insulin secretion and/or the body's resistance to the action of insulin. Native Americans have the highest prevalence of diabetes in the world. Furthermore, the rate of diabetes among AI/AN is increasing at almost epidemic proportions. In some AI/AN communities, more than half of the adult populations suffers from diabetes (U.S. Commission on Civil Rights 2004). For example, a cross-sectional study of men/women ages forty-five to seventy-four years in thirteen American Indian tribes or communities in Arizona, Oklahoma, and South and North Dakota found that Arizona had the highest age-adjusted rates of diabetes—65 percent in men and 72 percent in women. The study also found that in all the communities included in the study, diabetes was more prevalent in women than men. According to the study, diabetes rates were positively associated with age, amount of Indian ancestry, parental diabetes status, and level of obesity (Lee et al. 1995).

What is troubling is that the incidence of diabetes is increasing among AI/AN at an alarming rate. For example, the number of AI/AN aged younger than thirty-five with diabetes diagnosed through IHS more than doubled from 6,001 in 1994 to 12,313 in 2004. While the rates of diabetes increased among both males and females, the prevalence of diabetes was greater among females than males in all age groups ("Diagnosed Diabetes" 2006).

Diabetes is related to obesity and American Indians of all ages and both sexes have a high prevalence of obesity. Thus, obesity has also become a major health problem in American Indians in the past one to two generations. Obesity is believed to be associated with the relative abundance of high-fat foods and the rapid changes from an active to a more sedentary lifestyle (Story et al. 1999; Welty 1991).

The leading cause of mortality in the AI/AN community is heart disease and

Table 4.1

Leading Causes of Death among American Indians and Alaska Natives and Whites, 1980 and 2004

Rank	1980		2004	
	Whites	AI/AN	Whites	AI/AN
1.	Diseases of heart	Diseases of heart	Diseases of heart	Diseases of heart
2.	Malignant neoplasms	Unintentional injuries	Malignant neoplasms	Malignant neoplasms
3.	Cerebrovascular diseases	Malignant neoplasms	Cerebrovascular diseases	Unintentional injuries
4.	Unintentional injuries	Chronic liver disease and cirrhosis	Chronic lower respiratory diseases	Diabetes mellitus
5.	Chronic obstructive	Cerebrovascular pulmonary diseases	Unintentional injuries	Cerebrovascular diseases
6.	Pneumonia and influenza	Pneumonia and influenza	Alzheimer's disease	Chronic liver disease and cirrhosis
7.	Diabetes mellitus	Homicide	Diabetes mellitus	Chronic lower respiratory diseases
8.	Atherosclerosis	Diabetes mellitus	Diabetic mellitus	Suicide
9.	Chronic liver disease and cirrhosis	Certain conditions originating in the prenatal period	Nephritis, nephrotic syndrome, nephrosis	Influenza and pneumonia
10.	Suicide	Suicide	Suicide	Nephritis, nephrotic syndrome and nephrosis

Source: National Center for Health Statistics 2006. Health, United States, 2006. Washington, D.C.: U.S. Department of Health and Human Services.

the largest percentage of deaths from heart disease is caused by diabetes. Another startling fact is that in recent years type 2 diabetes has become a significant threat to Native American children. Type 2 diabetes in the past was largely confined to adults. IHS has documented a 54 percent increase since 1996 in the prevalence of diagnosed diabetes among Native American youth fifteen to nineteen years of age ("Diagnosed Diabetes" 2006; U.S. Commission on Civil Rights 2004; Fagot-Campagna, Pettitt, and Engelgan 2000). Perhaps related to the high rate of diabetes in the AI/AN population is also the fact that the AI/AN community also suffers from a higher prevalence of visual impairment and normal-tension glaucoma compared to other racial/ethnic groups (Mansberger et al. 2005).

The diabetes rate for AI/AN is more than twice that for whites. Native Americans are 2.6 times more likely to be diagnosed with diabetes than non-Hispanic whites of similar age. From 1994 through 1996, the IHS age-adjusted rates for diabetes were 350 percent greater than the rates for the rest of the U.S. population (U.S. Commission on Civil Rights 2004).

Cardiovascular disease is another major health problem confronting AI/AN communities. Available data suggest that cardiovascular disease has become the leading cause of death in AI/AN (Lee et al. 1990). In the past, heart disease and strokes were rare among AI/AN. However, today they have become the number one leading cause of death. While the general population has experienced a 50 percent decrease in heart disease, it has increased among AI/AN. This has helped widen health care disparities. For example, cardiovascular disease rates among AI/AN are twice that of the general population. The soaring rates of cardiovascular disease can be traced to the high rates of diabetes, high blood pressure, and the presence of other risk factors such as poor diet and a more sedentary lifestyle (U.S. Commission on Civil Rights 2004). While the death rates from strokes remains relatively lower for AI/AN (39.7 percent) than the national death rate (61.8 percent), the data point to future problems because at lower age brackets, the risk is two times higher for AI/AN (U.S. Commission on Civil Rights 2004).

AI/AN have the highest rates of smoking by adults among all ethnic groups (U.S. Department of Health and Humans Services 2000). According to a national telephone survey conducted by the Centers for Disease Control and Prevention (CDC), a sizable percentage of AI/AN suffered from specific risk factors such as high blood pressure (22 percent), high cholesterol (16 percent), and obesity (21.5 percent). In addition, 30.8 percent of AI/AN were smokers (Centers for Disease Control and Prevention 2000). Having more than one risk factor for heart disease is also more common among older AI/AN. For example, a study found that among Medicare enrollees, hospitalization for congestive heart failure is much higher among AI/AN, African Americans, and Hispanics than among whites (Mensah et al. 2005). Other studies have suggested that cardiovascular mortality among AI/AN is underestimated because of procedural and data errors such as misclassification of America Indian race on death certificates (Graber et al. 2005). According to another study, without accounting for misclassification, AI/AN initially had the lowest mortality rates from major cardiovascular disease compared to all races, including the white population. However, after adjustment for misclassification was made, the data showed a rapidly growing disparity between cardiovascular mortality rates among AI/AN compared with rates in all races and the white population. For example, between 1996 and 1998, the age- and misclassification-adjusted number of cardiovascular deaths per 100,000 among AI/AN was 195.9 compared with age-adjusted rates of 166.1 for all U.S. races and 159.1 for whites (Rhoades 2005).

Death and disabilities from unintentional injuries are another major concern for AI/AN. Unintentional injuries are the leading cause of death for AI/AN under the age of forty-four. The age-adjusted injury death rate for AI/AN is about 250 percent higher than that for the total U.S. population. The financial costs of treating these injuries are also very high (U.S. Commission on Civil Rights 2004). As Table 4.1 shows, overall unintentional injuries were the third leading cause of death for AI/AN in 2004. There are stark disparities in unintentional injury rates between AI/AN and whites. For example, between 1985 and 1996, the four major causes of unintentional injuries among children were motor vehicle crashes, pedestrian-related motor vehicle crashes, drowning, and fire-related injuries. The death rate for motor vehicle crashes among AI/AN children was twice that of white children. The death rate from pedestrian-related motor crashes among AI/AN children was three times greater than for white children. The death rate from drowning among AI/AN children were twice the rates for white children. The death rate from fire-related injuries was three times the rate for white children (U.S. Commission on Civil Rights 2004).

AI/AN are also at a much higher risk for mental health disorders than any other racial/ethnic group in American society. Among the high-need population in mental health services, AI/AN are consistently overrepresented. According to a report by the Surgeon General of the United States, this overrepresentation may be associated with high rates of homelessness, incarceration, alcohol and drug abuse, and stress and trauma (Satcher 2001). An examination of the prevalence of trauma in two large American Indian communities revealed that members of both tribes witnessed traumatic events, experienced trauma to loved ones, and were victims of physical attacks more often than in the overall U.S. population (Manson et al. 2005).

The most significant public health concerns in AI/AN communities are substance abuse, depression, anxiety, violence, and suicide. American Indians experience the highest rate of suicide of all racial/ethnic groups in the United States (Olson and Wahab 2006). The suicide rate for AI/AN continues to escalate and is now 190 percent of the rate of the general population. Between 1985 and 1996, AI/AN children committed suicide at a rate two and one-half times that of white children. The highest suicide rate for the general U.S. population is found among individuals seventy-four years old and older. In sharp contrast, among AI/AN the highest suicide rate is found within the fifteen to thirty-four age group (U.S. Commission on Civil Rights 2004). At the same time, research also shows that many suicidal young people avoid asking for help. For example, in a study of a sample of 101

American Indians between the ages of fifteen and twenty-one who had thought about or attempted suicide, 74 participants indicated that they had avoided seeking help for largely internal factors such as embarrassment, lack of problem recognition, or a belief that nobody could help. Participants rarely cited structural factors such as lack of money or service availability as reasons for not seeking help (Freedenthal and Stiffman 2007). Research also suggests that suicide attempts among AI/AN youths are associated with factors such as friends or family members having attempted or succeeded in committing suicide, somatic symptoms, physical or sexual abuse, substance abuse, gang involvement, and availability of guns (Borowsky et al. 1999).

Alcohol abuse is also a significant concern in AI/AN communities and contributes to mental health problems. Studies show that drinkers in the highest risk category for alcohol dependence are also more likely to report drug use disorders, mood/anxiety disorders, alcohol-related physical disorders, and a lower quality of life (Novins et al. 2006).

Overall, little is known about effective mental health care services among AI/AN because of the lack of culturally appropriate models of mental health in the AI/AN community (Johnson and Cameron 2001). What is clear is that despite a significant demand for mental health services, there are approximately only 101 mental health professionals available per 100,000 AI/AN compared with 173 per 100,000 whites (U.S. Commission on Civil Rights 2004).

Cancer is another growing concern among AI/AN. While AI/AN have lower cancer incidence and mortality rates than whites, cancer has become the leading cause of death for Alaska Native Americans and American Indian women. Also, the ratio of cancer deaths to new cancer cases is higher for AI/AN than the ratio for all other races (U.S. Commission on Civil Rights 2004). AI/AN have the poorest cancer survival rates among any racial group in American society. Furthermore, among AI/AN there has been a steady increase in cancer incidence and mortality. Despite this, malignant disease is not generally recognized as a leading cause of death among AI/AN (Clegg et al. 2002; Mahoney and Michalek 1999; Sugarman, Dennis, and White 1994).

The most common types of cancers among AI/AN are breast, colon and rectal, and lung. In eight of the nine IHS areas, death caused by lung cancer is the most common, and 87 percent of all lung cancer deaths can be linked to tobacco smoking (UCLA Center for Health Policy Research 2004). AI/AN have high rates of tobacco use, especially cigarette smoking, compared to the general population. Epidemiological data from a population-based, cross-sectional study of Southwestern and Northern Plains American Indians ages fifteen to fifty-four years found that 19 percent of Southwestern men, 10 percent of Southwestern women, 49 percent of Northern Plains men, and 51 percent Northern Plains women smoked regularly (Henderson, Jacobsen, and Beals 2005). It is important to point out that racial misclassification and undercounting are often major obstacles to obtaining accurate and informative data on the AI/AN populations (Swan et al. 2006). In reality, cancer rates among the AI/AN population are shown to be considerably higher when more accurate methods are used to estimate the incidence of cancer (Puukka, Stehr-Green, and Becker 2005).

Data also reveal a disparity in tuberculosis rates between AI/AN and non-Hispanic whites. For example, according to the American Lung Association, the incidence rate of tuberculosis among AI/AN in 1998 was 12.6 cases per 100,000 persons compared to 2.3 cases per 100,000 for non-Hispanic whites (U.S. Civil Rights Commission 2004). However, the good news is that the tuberculosis rate among AI/AN is declining; by 2002 the rate among AI/AN had dropped to 7 cases per 100,000 persons (U.S. Civil Rights Commission 2004). Between 1993 and 2002, the tuberculosis rates declined 40.4 percent in the AI/AN population. Nonetheless, tuberculosis continues to be a significant public health problem for the AI/AN population (Schneider 2005; Young 1997).

Finally, significant disparities also exist between American Indians and whites living in the same metropolitan areas with respect to pregnancy-related health services, with American Indian women receiving inadequate care compared to white women (Grossman et al. 2002).

Access to Health Care

Research has shown that a lack of health insurance negatively affects people's health because they are less likely to receive preventive care, are more likely to be hospitalized for avoidable health problems, and are more likely to be diagnosed in the late stages of disease. Those lacking health insurance coverage are more financially vulnerable to the high cost of care and end up paying more out-of-pocket costs for care. In contrast, having health insurance improves overall health and could reduce mortality rates of those currently uninsured by 10 to 15 percent (Kaiser Commission on Medicaid and the Uninsured 2006). Having health insurance coverage increases the chances of having a "medical home" and thus improves access to preventive screening, medical care for acute illness, and ongoing care for chronic medical conditions (Kaiser Commission of Medicaid and the Uninsured 2000).

In 1998 less than half of AI/AN had job-based health coverage compared to 72 percent of whites. Native Americans have fewer opportunities to get jobs that are likely to offer health benefits. Medicaid and other public programs are the primary source of coverage for almost a quarter of Native Americans (Kaiser Commission on Medicaid and the Uninsured 2000). High unemployment and low income are major reasons for the low rates of private insurance coverage among AI/AN. Indian Health Service–eligible persons residing in the most sparsely populated areas have the lowest rates of private health insurance coverage and more likely to rely exclusively on IHS coverage (Cunningham 1993). In 2004, 29.1 percent of the non-elderly AI/AN was uninsured compared to only 13.2 percent of non-Hispanic whites. The un-insurance rate among AI/AN was second worst, behind only the Hispanic non-elderly population (34.3 percent un-insurance rate) (Kaiser Commission on

Medicaid and the Uninsured 2006). More than a third (35 percent) of uninsured AI/AN report that they did not have a usual source of care. Over a quarter (29 percent) of uninsured AI/AN do not meet a minimal standard of routine physician care, that is, annual visits for children under age of six and adults in fair to poor health. Having insurance more than cuts that rate in half (Kaiser Commission on Medicaid and the Uninsured 2000).

Various studies have documented that AI/AN have less access to health services compared to whites. Using data from the 1997 and 1999 National Survey of America's Families to estimate odds ratios for several measures of access and utilization, a study by Zuckerman et al. (2004) found that AI/AN had less insurance coverage and worse access and utilization than whites. Availability of medical providers, place of residence and travel time, and financial factors were some of the major factors strongly associated with the use of health care services by AI/AN (Cunningham and Cornelius 1995). High rates of poverty, low rates of other health insurance coverage, and the lack of private providers in many areas inhabited by AI/AN also contributed to less access and utilization (Cunningham and Altman 1993). Other studies have documented that American Indian women have lower rates of preventive screening than other groups regardless of risk status (Wilcox and Mosher 1993), and American Indians, despite similar referral rates for renal transplantation, are less likely than whites to be placed on transplant waiting lists or receive a transplant (Sequist et al. 2004). All of the research suggest that AI/AN face significant barriers to care (Late 2005).

The U.S. Commission on Civil Rights (2004), in its report *Broken Promises: Evaluating the Native American Health Care System,* found that social and cultural factors such as a health care system that is insensitive to AI/AN peoples' unique culture, bias among health care workers, disproportionate poverty and low levels of education among AI/AN acted as significant barriers to Native Americans' access to health care and contribute to health care disparities. In addition, structural factors such as high staff turnover and loss of continuity of care, long distances to travel to receive even primary care, lengthy waiting lines upon arrival, and many outdated health facilities act as added barriers to access to health care.

The U.S. Government Accountability Office (2005) conducted a study of the availability of health services for AI/AN and whether they were accessible to AI/AN in the IHS facility area. The study included site visits in three IHS areas in October–November of 2004. The site visits included interviews with officials at thirteen IHS facilities—four hospitals, eight health centers, and one health station— eight of which were federally operated and five of which were operated by Indian tribes. The study found that the availability of primary care—medical, dental, and vision service—largely depended on the extent to which AI/AN were able to gain access to the services offered at the thirteen IHS-funded facilities. While IHS facilities generally offered primary care services, access to these services was not assured because of factors such as waiting times between the call to make an appointment and the delivery of service, and long travel distances to facilities or lack of transportation. Waiting times often ranged from two to six months for certain types of appointments, and some Native Americans were required to travel over ninety miles one way to obtain care.

The study further found that certain services were not always available to Native Americans because of gaps in services offered. Gaps in services were found in diagnosis and treatment of nonurgent conditions such as arthritis, knee injuries, and chronic pain. Gaps were also found in specialty dental and behavioral health care. Three factors were associated with variations in the availability of services: facility's structure, location, and funding from sources other than IHS. For example, hospitals offered a broader array of services than did health centers. Facility location had a great deal to do with the ability to recruit and retain staff and control the costs of providing health services. For example, geographically remote facilities faced difficulty in recruiting and retaining staff and more transportation costs. Whether a facility's funding came from reimbursement from private health insurance and federal health insurance programs for on-site services or from tribal contributions also affected the extent to which facilities were able to offer services. The amount of funding from these two sources varied among facilities (U.S. Government Accountability Office 2005).

Finally, urban Indian communities are intertribal and represent over half of the Native American population, yet they lack access to sufficient health services because the clinics are highly underfunded (Burhansstipanov 2000). American Indians living in urban areas are not eligible for federally mandated health care provided by the IHS (Kramer 1992b). Furthermore, resource limitations compel some eligible persons to go outside of the IHS to receive health care (Cunningham 1993).

Health care access data for AI/AN are not as extensive as for other minorities such as African Americans and Hispanics. For example, according to the *2004 National Healthcare Disparities Report* (Agency for Healthcare Research and Quality 2004), of the thirty-one measures of access with comparable data from 2000 and 2001, information on AI/AN was available for only sixteen of the measures. Of these sixteen measures of access, AI/AN had worse access to care than whites for about half of measures in 2000 and 2001. According to the *2005 National Healthcare Disparities Report* (Agency for Healthcare Research and Quality 2005), AI/AN had worse access than whites for about half of the access measures. The *2006 National Healthcare Disparities Report* (Agency for Healthcare Research and Quality 2006) showed only slight improvement. AI/AN had worse access than whites on 40 percent of measures of access. According to the *2007 National Healthcare Disparities Report,* 60 percent (three out of five) of core measures for access that can be tracked showed improvement for AI/AN (Agency for Healthcare Research and Quality 2008).

Quality of Health Care

According to the Institute of Medicine (2001b) report, the two core dimensions of health care quality are the components of health care and consumer perspective on health care needs.The components of health care quality include safety, effective-ness, patient centeredness, and timeliness. The health care needs reflect consumers' need for different types of health care across the life cycle. Equity represents a key parameter that cuts across both dimensions. The Institute of Medicine (2003) documented the existence of racial and ethnic disparities in quality of care and called for the development of population-specific quality measures that could allow for targeted quality improvement interventions.

While progress has been made in the provision of quality health care over the past decade, it is also clear that health care quality is not equitably distributed throughout the general population in the United States. Health care consumers who are members of certain groups, such as racial and ethnic minorities, low-income persons, children, women, the elderly, rural and urban residents, and the like, of-ten do not receive the same quality of care as the general population (Agency for Healthcare Research and Quality 2003). Compared to whites, AI/AN have higher reported morbidity and mortality for pneumonia/influenza, liver disease, obesity, bronchiolitis, diabetes, sudden infant death syndrome, and diabetic kidney failure. AI/AN have lower rates of mammography, poorer blood pressure control, and appear to receive suboptimal care (Agency for Healthcare Research and Quality 2003).

Unfortunately, there is a limited amount of data available regarding quality of care for AI/AN. Some of the data on the quality of care received by AI/AN comes from local- and state-level studies that have highlighted deficiencies in receipt of health care services among specific AI/AN populations. However, the findings of these studies vary based on the age of the population included, the frequency of testing considered appropriate, and the urban/rural clinical practice setting (Sequist 2005). For example, receipt of an inadequate pattern of prenatal care has been found to be significantly higher for rural than urban mothers of AI/AN infants (Baldwin et al. 2002). Another study found that rural American Indians who seek alcohol, drug, or mental health treatments confront a variety of obstacles that include quality of care, privacy issues, and problems of communication and trust (Duran et al. 2005).

Although poor health status of AI/AN can be attributed to a variety of factors such as poverty, related environmental factors, and lack of access to health care, a significant contribution is also made by racial and ethnic disparities in the quality of medical care, specifically by differences in the diagnostic work-up and treatment of minority patients in the American health care system. Scholarly research in the United States has provided strong evidence that racial/ethnic minorities, including AI/AN, are less likely to receive coronary artery angioplasty or bypass surgery, ad-vanced cancer treatment, renal transplantation, or surgery for lung cancer compared with whites with similar insurance status, income, education, severity of disease, comorbidity, age, hospital type, and other possible confounders (Geiger 2001).

The amount of funding for health care also affects the quality of health services. The IHS has been underfunded over the years and increases in funding would go a long way toward improving the quality of health services provided to AI/AN. Underfunding also affects the ability to recruit and retain competent health care providers, which in turn has a direct bearing on the quality of care. Overworked staff develop burnout, resulting in high turnover rates, which also negatively affects the quality of care provided. It has been well documented that historically IHS has experienced shortages of doctors, dentists, pharmacists, and nurses. IHS also faces problems in recruiting and retaining health care providers because of the remoteness of some of the heath clinics. It is difficult to recruit and retain health care providers who are willing to live and work in remote tribal communities (U.S. Commission on Civil Rights 2004). The problem is further compounded by factors such as a lack of parity in pay, insufficient or inadequate housing, a lack of jobs for spouses, insufficient opportunities for continuing education, and the like. It is clear that a shortage of health care providers negatively affects the quality of care for AI/AN (U.S. Commission of Civil Rights 2004).

Another problem caused by high provider turnover rates is that AI/AN patients do not receive consistent care from the same provider. This, combined with a lack of resources and the remoteness of health care facilities, often leads to misdiagnosis or late diagnosis of diseases. This can negatively affect health outcomes. For example, early detection of cancer can increase the patient's chance of survival while late diagnosis decreases chance of survival. Unfortunately, in AI/AN communities, misdiagnosis of a disease is too common (U.S. Commission on Civil Rights 2004).

Donabedian (1983, 1985, 1987, 1988, 1999) has provided a conceptual framework for measuring quality of care that includes three dimensions of quality—structure, process, and outcomes. Structure of care involves determining whether important resources are in place to provide quality care. Process of care includes measuring the clinical performance of the health care system and its providers, including technical aspects of care such as accuracy and timely diagnosis, appropriateness of therapy, and over-, under-, or misuse of care. Outcomes of care involve determining the effects of therapy, relief of symptoms, patient satisfaction with care, and other medical outcomes. Roubideaux (2004) reviewed the literature and existing data on all three dimensions of quality for AI/AN. She found that most of the information available on AI/AN health care deals with process data or clinical performance in IHS but very few studies have addressed the issue of outcomes of care.

With respect to structure of care, Roubideaux (2004) found that IHS has implemented a variety of initiatives to monitor and assess the quality of care delivered within its system. A structure is also in place for measuring the quality of care for AI/AN who use IHS. However, the monitoring of the quality of care has become more problematic due to recent changes in the IHS, such as more contracted services by tribes or tribes managing the health programs in their communities under the Indian Self-Determination and Educational Assistance Act. Thus, the Indian Health System is now made up of programs managed by IHS, tribes, and urban Indian health organizations. This has led to the reduction in the administrative infrastructure at IHS headquarters and area offices. This decentralization in turn has raised concerns about how IHS would maintain its core function of public health surveillance. Thus, for example, no studies have compared the quality of care in tribal versus IHS health programs. The situation for urban Indian health programs is even less clear since services provided by the IHS-funded thirty-four urban Indian health organizations operating in twenty states vary significantly. Not all programs provide direct medical services and some provide only referrals. Given this diversity of urban Indian health programs, measuring the quality of health care for urban Indians is very difficult.

Roubideaux (2004) also found that most of the available data on health care quality with respect to AI/AN focuses on processes of care, especially on access and clinical performance. Earlier in this chapter we discussed the significant disparities in access and utilization of health services by AI/AN. Even though the IHS serves as a valuable resource for the health care needs of the AI/AN, disparities in access and utilization persist, especially for those who live in urban areas. The IHS routinely gathers data on clinical performance indicators using the Resource and Patient Management System. The IHS has documented improvements each year since 1997 in diabetes care, blood pressure control, cancer screening, well-child visits, alcohol and substance abuse treatment, access to dental services, and prevention indicators such as vaccination and injury rates. However, the results for most indicators still fall below national targets. Roubideaux (2004) concludes that overall, in terms of process of care, both the IHS and non-IHS sources of data have documented some improvements. Yet, significant disparities in access and clinical performance of care continue for AI/AN for a variety of health conditions and care settings. Efforts to measure quality of care for AI/AN nationally outside of the IHS are limited by the difficulty of gathering representative data due to varying sources and types of care.

The IHS publication *Trends in Indian Health,* which provides information on general outcomes of care, suggests that in general mortality rates for AI/AN have improved but significant disparities persist. Other national sources of data on the health status of AI/AN include the health status indicators of the Healthy People 2000 initiative. Between 1990 and 1998, out of seventeen indicators, six showed no improvement for AI/AN. These indicators included the percent of low-birth-weight infants, total age-adjusted death rate, and age-adjusted death rates for stroke, lung cancer, female breast cancer, and suicide (Keppel, Pearcy, and Wagener 2002). In summary, indicators of general outcomes of care, including health status, reveal significant and persistent disparities for AI/AN.

After reviewing the literature on the quality of health care for AI/AN, Roubideaux (2004) concludes that significant disparities in the quality of care for AI/AN exist in all dimensions of quality—structure, process, and outcomes. According to an Institute of Medicine (2001a) report, *Crossing the Chasm: A New Health System for the 21st Century,* improvements in the quality of health care are needed in six areas—safety, effectiveness, patient-centeredness, timeliness, efficiency, and equity. Unfortunately, data on safety, timeliness, efficiency, and equity, are meager for

AI/AN. There is a strong need for quality measures specific to populations suffering from disparities for two reasons—equity and relevance. Quality measures help insure that health care is equitably distributed. Use of population-specific measures makes it possible to target quality improvement interventions that can help eliminate disparities. The second reason for developing quality measures for a specific population is that quality measures developed for a general population may not be relevant to populations suffering from disparities. The prevalence and impact of various health conditions and types of health care needed to treat these conditions may differ between groups due to differences in race/ethnicity, age, gender, income, geographic location, and the like (Agency for Healthcare Research and Quality 2003).

The *2007 National Healthcare Disparities Report* (Agency for Healthcare Research and Quality 2008) measured disparities between AI/AN and whites for sixteen core quality measures. The report concluded that over 60 percent of disparities in quality of care had not gotten smaller. Thus, the disparities in quality of care between AI/AN and whites continue to remain a major concern.

Possible Explanations for Health Care Disparities

Socioeconomic Status (SES)

As we have discussed in previous chapters, compared to whites, African Americans and Hispanics enjoy a lower socioeconomic status (as defined by income, education, and occupation). The same is the case with AI/AN. The data on income, education, and occupation for AI/AN are not easy to find and many government reports, such as *Statistical Abstracts of the United States,* do not even include AI/AN as a separate category when discussing socioeconomic factors by race. Nonetheless, the compilation of data for AI/AN on socioeconomic factors from a variety of sources, as reported in Table 4.2, clearly demonstrates the low SES of AI/AN in American society.

As the data in Table 4.2 show, the median income of AI/AN households in 1999 was only $30,599, compared to $44,687 for whites. Similarly, in 2000, per capita income of AI/AN was $21,587 compared to $23,582 for whites. Only about 9.1 percent of whites lived below the poverty level in 1999 in comparison to 25.7 percent of AI/AN who lived below the poverty level. In 2005, 34 percent of AI/AN lived below 100 percent of the federal poverty level compared to only 12 percent of whites.

With respect to educational attainment, in 2000, 84.9 percent of whites had graduated from high school and had some college education compared to only 52.6 percent of AI/AN. During the same year, 26.6 percent of whites had graduated from college and had some graduate course work, compared to only 7.6 percent of AI/AN.

With respect to occupation, in 2004 of all whites who were employed, 39 percent

Table 4.2

Socioeconomic Status of American Indians/Alaska Natives (AI/AN) and Whites

	Whites	AI/AN only
Population (2005)[a]	198.4 (million)	2.2 (million)
Percent of U.S. population (2005)[a]	67.0	1.0
Median income of households (in constant dollars 1999)[b]	$44,687	$30,599
Per capita income (2000)[b]	$23,582	$21,587
Percent of people below poverty level (1999)[b]	9.1	25.7
Percent of poor people with <100% of FPL (2005)[a]	12.0	34.0
Percent high school graduate or more (2000)[b, c] (25 years plus)	84.9	52.6
Percent college graduate or more (2000)[b, c] (25 years plus)	26.6	7.6
Percent managerial, professional-related occupation (2000)[b, c]	39.0	24.3
Percent private health insurance coverage (2004) (persons <65 years of age)[d]	71.4	44.7
Percent without health insurance (2004) (persons <65 years of age)[d]	16.1	34.6
Percent Medicaid coverage (2004) (persons <65 years of age)[d]	10.4	18.4

Sources:
 [a] *Key Facts: Race, Ethnicity & Medical Care*, January 2007. Washington, D.C.: Henry J. Kaiser Family Foundation. Online at www.kff.org.
 [b] U.S. Census Bureau, *Statistical Abstracts of the United States, 2004–2005*. Washington, D.C.: Government Printing Office.
 [c] U.S. Census Bureau. *Statistical Abstract of the United States, 2006*. Washington, D.C.: Government Printing Office.
 [d] National Center for Health Statistics. *Health, United States, 2006*. Washington, D.C.: U.S. Department of Health and Human Services.

worked in managerial and other professional-related occupations. Out of all AI/AN who were employed in 2000, only 24.3 percent worked in managerial, professional, and related occupations.

The relatively low SES status of AI/AN is also reflected in the fact that in 2004 only 44.7 percent of them had private health insurance compared to 71.4 percent of whites. During the same year, 34.6 percent of AI/AN were without health insurance compared to only 16.1 percent of whites. Also in 2004, only 10.4 percent of whites were covered by Medicaid compared to 18.4 percent of AI/AN.

One of the explanations for health care disparities experienced by AI/AN is their relatively low SES in American society. Part of the disparity exists because of disproportionate poverty, poor education, and the absence of adequate health service delivery in most AI/AN communities (Ambler 2003). Poor health correlates with poverty rates nationwide and AI/AN are the poorest of the poor. They are more likely to be unemployed. In fact, in some tribal college communities, the unemployment rate is as high as 60 or 70 percent (Ambler 2003).

Many studies have documented a relationship between the socioeconomic conditions of AI/AN and health care disparities. In a study of the relationship between self-reported health status and mortality among many racial/ethnic minorities including AI/AN between 1986 and 1994, McGee et al. (1999) found a strong association between self-reported health status and both socioeconomic status and subsequent mortality. According to the authors, people with low SES were more likely to report poor health status and a self-report of poor health status was associated with at least a twofold increased risk of mortality for all racial/ethnic groups.

Another study, involving personal interviews of 410 adult residents of a Rocky Mountain state American Indian reservation, found that residents without telephones generally were less educated, had lower income, and were more likely to be unemployed (Pearson et al. 1994). Furthermore, the study found that the prevalence of unhealthful lifestyle practices/factors was consistently higher for residents without telephones. The study also demonstrated the problems of developing estimates of sociodemographic, health, and lifestyle characteristics of a Native American reservation using a telephone survey.

As we have discussed in this chapter, the incidence of certain diseases such as obesity and diabetes, cancer, coronary heart disease, liver disease, and tuberculosis is much higher in AI/AN communities compared to other groups in American society. Several studies have demonstrated the relationship between such diseases and SES. For example, using data from the 1994–96 Continuing Survey of Food Intake by Individuals, conducted by the U.S. Department of Agriculture, Paeratakul et al. (2002) found that there was a graded increase in diabetes, hypertension, and high serum cholesterol with increased body weight in nearly all gender, racial, and socioeconomic groups. While the nature of obesity-related health risks is similar in all populations, the specific level of risk associated with a given level of obesity may be different depending on gender, race, and socioeconomic condition. According to a recent study by Wang and Beydoun (2007) of the Johns Hopkins Bloomberg School of Public Health, minorities and low socioeconomic status groups are disproportionately affected by obesity. Furthermore, according to the authors, people purchase food based on their income level and perception of a food's health benefits; furthermore, cost and ethnicity, gender, and environmental factors also influence people's choice of food.

Among both men and women, five-year survival rates for all cancers combined is 10 percent lower among persons who live in poorer than in more affluent census tracts. Even when census tract poverty rate is accounted for, AI/AN and African Americans have lower five-year survival rates than non-Hispanic whites (Ward et al. 2004). Another study (Singh and Hoyert 2000) examined the trends and ethnic and socioeconomic differentials in chronic liver disease and cirrhosis mortality in the United States. For both men and women aged twenty-five years and older, the authors found significant mortality differentials by age, race/ethnicity, marital status, family income, and employment status. The authors argue that given the substantial ethnic and socioeconomic differences in cirrhosis mortality, there is a need for social and public health policies and interventions that target such high-risk groups as American Indians, Hispanic Americans, the socially isolated, and the poor.

Tuberculosis (TB) case rates are higher among racial and ethnic minorities than among whites in the United States. Cantwell et al. (1998) tried to determine what proportion of this risk is attributable to SES. Values of six SES indicators—crowding, income, education, unemployment, poverty, and public assistance—were assigned to U.S. TB cases reported from 1987 to 1993 by ZIP code and demographic-specific matching to 1990 U.S. census data. They found that the relative risk for TB increased with lower SES quartile for all six indicators on univariate analysis. They concluded that SES accounts for much of the increased risk of TB previously associated with race/ethnicity.

Finally, a study of childhood mortality from 1950 to 1993 found that American Indian, black, Hawaiian, and Puerto Rican children and those in the lower socioeconomic strata were at an increased risk of death. Thus, reducing socioeconomic disparities and improving access to health care may bring about a decline in overall and injury-related childhood mortality (Singh and Yu 1996).

Available evidence does suggest that some of the health care disparities experienced by AI/AN are attributable to their lower SES in American society. However, SES alone cannot explain all the health care disparities between AI/AN and whites.

Culture

Culture is another variable that can help explain at least part of the health care disparities in American society, especially as it relates to racial/ethnic minorities. Racial/ethnic minorities often have cultural values that may differ from the mainstream cultural values. In Chapters 2 and 3 we discussed how cultural values unique to African Americans and Hispanics influence perceptions about health and illness, healing, and treatment, and can affect nutrition and lifestyle behaviors. The same is the case with AI/AN communities. The cultural values shared by AI/AN certainly influence their lifestyle and risk and health behaviors.

O'Nell and Mitchell (1996, 566) define culture as the "framework, beliefs, expressive symbols, and values in terms of which individuals define their world, express their feelings, and make judgments. . . . It is the fabric of meaning in terms of which human beings interpret their existence and guide their actions." Some of the constructs related to culture include: acculturation, ethnic identity, enculturation, cultural orientation, biculturalism, and ethnic identification (Herman-Stahl, Spencer, and Duncan 2003). Acculturation refers to the process of assimilation into the majority culture. Ethnic identity refers to part of an individual's social identity stemming from attachment to a cultural group. Enculturation refers to the process by which an individual identifies with his/her own minority culture. Cultural orientation refers to the independent identification with both minority and majority culture. Biculturalism refers to the extent to which individuals are oriented toward both their own and the majority culture. Finally, ethnic identification is the action of associating oneself with an ethnic or cultural group and the degree of satisfaction one feels with this group (Herman-Stahl, Spencer, and Duncan 2003).

The issue of cultural orientation is complex for American Indians for many reasons. Some ethnic groups voluntarily immigrated to the United States. In the case of American Indians, the majority culture forced its beliefs, values, and practices on them and removed them from their ancestral lands. In addition, many American Indians reside on geographically remote reservations isolated from mainstream culture. American Indians also suffered from forced institutionalized policies that demeaned their culture. American Indians also live under the unique conditions of having politically sovereign land yet being largely dependent on the U.S. federal government (Herman-Stahl, Spencer, and Duncan 2003).

Perhaps more than any other ethnic group in American society, traditional Native American Indians have consistently resisted acculturation into mainstream society. Many traditional American Indian cultural values are in sharp contrast to the mainstream European-American values. Native American Indians' traditional values consist of sharing, cooperation, being, importance of group, extended family, harmony and balance with nature, deep respect for elders, a time orientation toward living in the present, and preference for explanations of natural phenomena according to the supernatural. This stands in sharp contrast to mainstream American cultural values that emphasize domination over nature, competition and aggression, winning, individualism, nuclear family, a time orientation toward living in the future, a preference for scientific explanations of everything, and reverence for youth (Garrett and Garrett 1994).

Needless to say, native American Indians differ greatly in their commitment to traditional values and customs. Traditional American Indians speak and think in native language and practice only traditional values and beliefs. Transitional American Indians are those who generally speak both a native language and English but they do not fully accept the cultural heritage of their tribal group nor identify completely with the mainstream culture. Bicultural American Indians are those who are generally accepted by the dominant culture and simultaneously accept and practice traditional and mainstream values. Assimilated American Indians are those who are accepted by the dominant culture and who embrace only the mainstream culture (Garrett and Garrett 1994).

Traditional American Indians often encounter difficulties when dealing with Western medicine and practices. Transitional and bicultural American Indians often may find themselves facing cultural value conflicts when dealing with the mainstream health care system. For example, American Indians' emphasis on a nonverbal communication style, avoiding direct eye contact, respect for authority figures, speaking slowly and softly, and the like, may be misinterpreted by mainstream health care providers as slow, lazy, uncooperative, passive, withdrawn, and non-assertive. This creates communication barriers and room for misunderstanding between health care providers and patients (Garrett and Garrett 1994).

Most American Indians who live on tribal reservations tend to be very traditional and are provided health care by the IHS. American Indians living in urban areas again present a more complex problem. As a result of the massive migration of American Indians to urban settings from the 1920s to the 1950s, a majority of the American Indian population today lives off the reservation. More than half of the entire American Indian population also lives in the Western states (Kramer 1992b). Attitudes of American Indians living in urban areas toward Western medicine can range from indifference by traditionalists to acceptance by bicultural and assimilated individuals. However, American Indians in general do perceive various barriers to obtaining social and health services based on a mutual misinterpretation of cultural norms and etiquette. Some American Indian patients may perceive Western health care providers as rude by getting right down to business, addressing strangers in a loud tone, and by frequently interrupting speakers (Kramer 1992a). Older American Indians express fear of non-Indian health professionals, do not expect to be treated fairly, and anticipate adverse contact experiences (Kramer 1992a).

Another area where we can see the influence of culture is in substance abuse. Research suggests that one-quarter to one-third of American Indians have a problem of substance abuse in a given year. Three-quarters of males and over one-third of females experience a substance abuse disorder some time during their lives. American Indian drinkers are more likely to drink large quantities, suffer blackouts, and suffer alcohol-related problems than the general population (Herman-Stahl, Spencer, and Duncan 2003).

For centuries, many indigenous cultures in America have used non-pharmacologic methods such as sleep deprivation, drumming, pain, and fasting to achieve altered mind states. Prior to contact with the Europeans, mind-altered states were viewed as a social good in cultures of the Plains Indians associated with a quest for enlightenment, powers of healing, and facilitation of war-making. In more contemporary times, it is common to see the use of alcohol in an Iroquois vision quest as well as the use of non-alcoholic psychotropic substances such as jimsonweed, peyote, and tobacco. The use of such substances and the states they induced occurred under the umbrella of religious and social sanctions (Frank 2000).

Some scholars have traced the roots of the epidemic of alcohol-related problems among AI/AN to a cultural response to European arrival and the use of alcohol in frontier society. It has been suggested that Native Americans' responses to alcohol were heavily influenced by the example of white frontiersmen who drank a lot and engaged in unacceptable behavior while drunk. Whites also deliberately pressed alcohol upon the natives because it was a very profitable trade good. Alcohol was used as a tool of "diplomacy" in official dealings between authorities and natives. Alcohol was also used as a bargaining chip in the appropriation of traditional land holdings (Frank 2000).

A study was conducted to examine the relationship between cultural orientation and substance abuse behavior among American Indians. The study was based on a sample of 2,449 American Indian adults, aged eighteen years or older, living on reservations in South Dakota. The study found that cultural orientation did have relevance for American Indian substance use behavior. Even when age, gender, education, and employment were controlled for, cultural orientation was found to be a significant correlate of past heavy drinking and alcohol abuse and dependence. Bicultural American Indians were almost three times as likely to drink heavily and 2.3 times as likely to have an alcohol use disorder as compared to American Indians with a traditional cultural orientation. American Indians with a low orientation toward traditional culture were more than 4.4 times as likely to be heavy drinkers compared to Americans Indians with a traditional cultural orientation (Herman-Stahl, Spencer, and Duncan 2003).

Another area where cultural values play a role among AI/AN is in the use of traditional practices such as the use of healers. A study that relied on semistructured interviews with a sample of 150 adult patients at an urban Indian Health Service clinic in Milwaukee, Wisconsin, found that 38 percent of the patients sought the help of a healer. Furthermore, of those who did not see a healer, 86 percent indicated that they would consider seeing a healer in the future. The most frequently visited healers were herbalists, spiritual healers, and medicine men. The respondents reported that they sought the help of a healer for spiritual reasons (Marbella et al. 1998). What was even more interesting was that more than a third of the patients seeing healers received different advice from their physicians, and healers and the patients rated their healer's advice higher than their physician's advice over 60 percent of the time. Also, only about 15 percent of the patients who were seeing healers had told their physician about their use (Marbella et al. 1998).

Another study found that 70 percent of urban AI/AN patients in primary care used traditional health practices. The use of traditional health practices was strongly associated with cultural affiliation, i.e., living a native way of life (Buchwald, Beals, and Manson 2000). Still another study found that among American Indian veterans, use of traditional ceremonies and indigenous healing options was much greater in the Southwest than in the Northern Plains (Gurley et al. 2001).

Behavioral Risk Factors

Another factor that can account for health care disparities between AI/AN and the rest of the population is the high prevalence of certain risky behavior among AI/AN. Despite some improvement, the health status of AI/AN has continued to lag behind other Americans. Even though few data exist on health risk behaviors among AI/AN, survey and face-to-face interviews have often been used to estimate the prevalence of certain risk behaviors among AI/AN. A face-to-face interview of American Indians ages fifteen to forty-nine years in two Montana locations on the Blackfeet Reservation and in Great Falls found that the prevalence of certain health risk behavior was higher in these populations than in adult Montana residents in general (Goldberg et al. 1991). For example, the prevalence of tobacco use was much higher among AI/AN than the general population. The same was the case with the use of smokeless tobacco. Other high risk behavior included acute heavy drinking, being overweight, living a sedentary lifestyle, and non-use of seatbelts (Goldberg et al. 1991).

Another study, of 13,454 seventh through twelfth grade AI/AN youths from non-urban schools from eight Indian Health Service areas, found a strong correlation between those who reported poor physical health and social risk factors of physical and sexual abuse, suicide attempts, substance abuse, and nutritional inadequacies. In general, AI/AN adolescents reported high rates of health-compromising behaviors and risk factors related to unintentional injury, substance abuse, emotional distress, and suicide (Blum et al. 1992). According to a study by Cheadle et al. (1994), the high prevalence of risk-taking behavior among America Indians and their poor self-reported health status remained after adjustment for socioeconomic status. In fact, among American Indians, higher levels of income and education were not associated with improved self-reported health and lower prevalence of tobacco use as was the case with the comparison groups (Cheadle et al. 1994).

More recent studies have reaffirmed these findings. A study that explored the covariation of risk behaviors in a national sample of America Indian reservation-based youth found that three risk behavior factors were fairly stable across sex and age—the use of alcohol, tobacco, and other drugs; risky sexual behavior; and suicidal behaviors. The use of tobacco, alcohol, and other drugs was frequently related to other risk behavior factors (Potthoff et al. 1998). Similarly, suicide rates among American Indian youth are found to be associated with using alcohol, marijuana and other drugs, emotional problems, gang involvement, physical or sexual abuse, availability of guns, and friends or family members attempting or completing suicide (Borowsky et al. 1999). Finally, aside from high incidences of tobacco and alcohol use, AI/AN are more likely than respondents of other racial/ethnic groups to report obesity and no leisure-time physical activity (Denny, Holtzman, and Cobb 2003). Nutritional factors contribute to at least four of the top ten leading causes of deaths among AI/AN—heart disease, cancer, cirrhosis, and diabetes—and to the prevalence of overweight, obesity, and hypertension (Basiotis, Lino, and Anand 1999; Story et al. 1998).

Racial Discrimination and Stereotyping

According to a great deal of literature, SES accounts for much of the observed racial/ethnic disparities in health. However, research has also found that racial difference often continues to persist even at "equivalent" levels of SES. Racial discrimination and stereotyping of minority groups by the dominant group may contribute to the persistence of health care disparities. Individual as well as institutional discrimination combined with the stigma of inferiority can adversely affect health (Williams 1999). Although the poor health status of African Americans, people of Hispanic origin, and AI/AN can largely be attributed to low SES and other cultural, social, political, physical, and biological factors. Racial discrimination and stereotyping cannot be discounted as an additional contributing factor. Research in the United States has provided strong evidence that African Americans, Hispanics, and AI/AN are less likely to receive coronary artery angioplasty or bypass surgery, advance cancer treatment, renal transplantation, and surgery for lung cancer compared with white patients matched for insurance status, income or education, severity of disease, comorbidty, age, hospital type, and other possible confounders (Geiger 2001). Similar differences have been found in basic clinical care such as the adequacy of physical examination, history-taking, and laboratory tests (Geiger 2001).

It is clear that more attention needs to be given to how racial discrimination can negatively affect the health status of minority groups. The concept of SES often overlaps with race but is not equivalent to race. More data and better quality data are needed on how racial discrimination/stereotyping can affect individual health (Williams, Lavizzo-Mourey, and Warren 1994). Often the failure to consider past and present *de jure* and *de facto* discrimination can lead to incomplete understanding of the health of minority populations (Krieger 2001).

Research on the effects of racial discrimination on the health status of AI/AN in the United States is rather limited. However, some of the research does point to a relationship between racial discrimination (perceived or otherwise) and some negative heath consequences. For example, a study (Whitebeck et al. 2001) of 195 American Indians grades five through eight from three reservations in the upper Midwest examined internalizing and externalizing symptoms as potential mediators of the relationship between perceived discrimination and early substance abuse. The findings indicated that perceived discrimination contributed significantly to internalizing symptoms among the adolescents. However, internalizing symptoms were unrelated to early substance abuse. The effects of perceived discrimination on early substance abuse were mediated by adolescent anger and delinquent behavior. Similarly, another study (Walters and Simoni 2002) concluded that the health problems of Native American women are not simply an artifact of native genetics, culture, or lifestyle but are products of racism, discrimination, poverty and geography that undermine their physical and mental health outcomes. Among women of color, perceptions of racism or gender-based discrimination have been related to increased stress, depression and psychological distress, hypertension, higher blood pressure levels, and decreased satisfaction with medical care (Walters and Simoni 2002).

American Indian adults experience significant depressive symptoms at rates several times higher than adults in the general population. Many researchers have argued that depressive symptoms are associated with conflicts between American Indian traditional cultural values, practices, and beliefs and those of the majority culture. A study (Whitebeck et al. 2002) of 287 American Indian adults from the upper Midwest took into account two cultural effects—perceived discrimination as an indicator of cultural conflict, and traditional practices as a measure of cultural identification. The results indicated that perceived discrimination was strongly associated with depressive symptoms among American Indian adults while engaging in traditional practices was negatively related to depressive symptoms. Engaging in traditional practices tended to buffer the negative effects of discrimination among those who regularly participated in them.

Political Power

American Indians are generally a forgotten minority in any discussion of American politics due to their concentration on remote reservations in some of the Western states and their general lack of participation in the American political process. However, their concentration in a few states, such as Alaska, Arizona, Colorado, Montana, New Mexico, Oklahoma, and South Dakota, also gives them the potential to exert political power at state and local levels (Peterson and Duncan n.d.).

Political Activism

The period of 1960 to 1990 witnessed the emergence of the American Indian movement and the rise of Red Power. During this period, the number of Americans identifying themselves as "American Indian" in the U.S. census tripled. This sizable increase cannot be attributed solely to population growth. According to Nagel (1995), this increase was due to "ethnic switching" whereby individuals who previously had identified themselves as non-Indian changed their race to "Indian" in a later census. This switching was made possible by the U.S. Census Bureau when, in 1960, it moved away from a system in which enumerators assigned each person a race to a system that allowed individual racial self-identification. Nagel (1995) argues that this ethnic renewal was made possible by three factors—federal Indian policy, American ethnic politics, and American Indian political activism.

First, the post–World War II program of job training and urban relocation policy for American Indians led to the creation of many American Indian organizations that acted as an intertribal network and informal communication system and helped the development of a supertribal level of Indian identity (Nagel 1995).

Second, Lyndon Johnson's War on Poverty program and the civil rights movement of the 1960s helped create increasingly cosmopolitan and politically sophisticated American Indians who lobbied successfully for federal War on Poverty dollars directed toward impoverished urban and reservation communities. Also, large-scale mobilization of urban Indians also marked the rapid growth of political organizations, newspapers, and community programs. This gave American Indian minorities a chance to cast off their negative stereotypes, reinvent ethnic pride and supertribal identification, and political activism. American Indians were able to successfully navigate the changing current of ethnic politics and increase their financial resources. The settlement of land claims by the Indian Claims Commission and the U.S. federal court system during the 1970s and 1980s provided additional sources of funds (Nagel 1995).

Third, the 1960s and 1970s also spawned many American Indian activist organizations, such as the American Indian Movement (AIM) and the National Indian Youth Council (NIYC), that produced a number of important protest actions such as the nineteen-month occupation of Alcatraz Island in 1969; the Trail of Broken Treaties, which culminated in the week-long occupation of the Bureau of Indian Affairs in Washington, D.C., in 1972; the seventy-one-day siege at Wounded Knee in South Dakota in 1973; and the 1975 shootout on the Pine Ridge Reservation in South Dakota. This Red Power played an important symbolic role in American Indian ethnic renewal (Nagel 1995).

Thus, it was not a surprise that the Nixon administration advocated a policy of self-determination without termination for American Indians. The Nixon administration's policy was embodied in two major laws passed by Congress during this time—the Indian Self-Determination and Education Assistance Act of 1975 and the Indian Health Care Improvement Act of 1976 (Kunitz 1996).

Political Participation

The official U.S. government policy for American Indians has been assimilation and acculturation into the majority culture. Failure of this policy often led to a policy of eradication and relocation. For example, the Indian Removal Act of 1830 led to the "Trail of Tears" in which the Five Civilized Tribes were forced to relocate to Oklahoma. This was followed by the signing of several treaties with Indian tribes that were ignored by the federal government. However, these treaties did extend citizenship to American Indians. Thus, by 1917, almost two-thirds of all American Indians were citizens of the United States. The passage of the Snyder Act in 1924 granted suffrage to all American Indians, although it did not necessarily guarantee the right to vote (Peterson and Duncan n.d.). Just like the freed slaves, American Indians suffered from the Jim Crow laws that denied them access to the voting booth. Since the repeal of many of these disenfranchising laws in the 1950s and 1960s, American Indians have been allowed to vote in tribal, local, state, and national elections. American Indians have been able to exercise the power of the ballot box more successfully in the local (city and county) elections, particularly in those few Western states where they constitute a sizable minority. Often, Indian reservations are as large as a county and some cover several counties. However, American Indians have participated in very low numbers in national elections. Given their small numbers nationally, their impact on the ballot box at the national level is very limited (Peterson and Duncan n.d.).

Representation in Government

For many reasons measurement is one of the major barriers to the study of American Indian representation in government. For many decades the U.S. census did not differentiate between American Indians and Asians, lumping them together in the "other" category. Even the *Current Population Survey* conducted by the U.S. Department of Labor did not recognize American Indians as a separate category until 1990. It is also not easy to define who is American Indian and who is not due to multiple origins that can produce overlapping categories, for example, native American Indians as opposed to American Indians of Hispanic origins. American Indians are also less likely to participate in government measurement efforts due to the understandable lack of trust in the federal government. Finally, some American Indians deny their heritage for the purpose of gaining access to white society. The same kinds of problems are evident in trying to figure out American Indian representation in elected offices at different levels of government.

At the national level, AI/AN have achieved relatively little representation. Very few AI/AN have served in the cabinet or the upper levels of the federal judiciary. In the 108th Congress (2003), most unusually, there were two American Indian members of the House of Representatives and one in the Senate; these numbers subsequently declined to one House member.

American Indians have achieved greater success in state and local governments because of the localization of the AI/AN population. Thus, not surprisingly, states that have the highest percentage of AI/AN population also have the highest percentage of AI/AN in state and local government (Peterson and Duncan n.d.).

AI/AN are engaged in more grassroots movements designed to help elect more AI/AN public offices. For example, the Indigenous Democratic Network is a grassroots political organization devoted to recruiting and electing Native American candidates by mobilizing voters throughout the country. Of the twenty-six AI/AN candidates endorsed by the group, twenty won statewide offices in the 2006 elections. Between 2002 and 2005, electoral participation among American Indians increased 130 percent (Free 2006).

In summary, it is reasonable to conclude that given the low level of political participation by AI/AN and their low representation in government at the national level, AI/AN lack the political power to influence health policy.

Conclusions

In comparison to African Americans and Hispanics, American Indians and Alaska Natives (AI/AN) constitute a very small minority in American society, but they experience some of the worst health care disparities. Health care for members of American Indian tribes and Alaska natives is delivered from a system that is separate from that of mainstream America. This separate health care delivery system for AI/AN people has evolved from the unique and complex history of interaction between the various tribes and the U.S. government. The Indian Health Service (IHS) is primarily responsible for delivering health services to AI/AN populations. Critics have argued that one of the reasons for the health care disparity is that IHS is critically underfunded.

The disparity experienced by AI/AN with respect to health status and outcome is well documented. American Indians have higher occurrence of diseases than other racial/ethnic minorities. For example, America Indians have a higher prevalence of diabetes and cardiovascular diseases and also higher prevalence of disease risk factors such as obesity, hypertension, high cholesterol, and tobacco smoking than other racial/ethnic minorities. Mortality data also show an excessive overall mortality among AI/AN as well as excesses for specific causes of death. Diabetes is one of the most serious health problems confronting AI/AN and is responsible for significant morbidity and mortality rates among AI/AN. Additionally, the rate of diabetes is increasing among AI/AN at an alarming rate. Cardiovascular disease is another major health problem confronting AI/AN communities. AI/AN have the highest rates of smoking in adults among all ethnic groups. Death and disabilities from unintentional injuries are another major concern for AI/AN. AI/AN are also at a much higher risk for mental health disorders than any other racial/ethnic group in American society. Finally, other major public health concerns in AI/AN communities are substance abuse, depression, anxiety, violence, and suicide.

Many factors have contributed to making health care access more difficult for AI/AN. Lack of insurance is one such factor. Various studies have documented that AI/AN have less access to health services compared to whites. Even access to primary care services is not assured because of factors such as a long waiting time between the call to make an appointment and the delivery of service, long travel distances to facilities, or lack of transportation. Finally, urban Indian communities represent over half of the Native American population, yet they lack access to sufficient health services because urban Indian clinics are highly underfunded.

There is a limited amount of data available regarding quality of care for AI/AN. Some data on the quality of care received by AI/AN come from local- and state-level studies that have highlighted deficiencies in receipt of health care services among specific AI/AN populations. However, research suggests that significant disparities in the quality of care for AI/AN exist in all dimensions of quality—structure, process, and outcomes.

Some of the possible explanations for the health care disparities between AI/AN and whites include SES, culture, behavioral risk factors, racial discrimination, and lack of political power. American Indian communities experience some of the worst rates of poverty and unemployment. AI/AN per capita income as well as median family income is much lower than that of whites. The incongruity between values and beliefs of AI/AN communities and the majority culture also contributes to health care disparities. AI/AN culture plays a role in issues related to substance abuse such as alcohol and tobacco, and use of healers and Western health care services. AI/AN also engage in high risk behavior such as heavy smoking, acute heavy drinking, being overweight, living a sedentary lifestyle, and non-use of seatbelts. Research has also demonstrated a link between perceived racial discrimination and substance abuse and depression. Finally, lack of political power also translates to inability to influence health policy decisions at the national level.

References

Agency for Healthcare Research and Quality. 2003. *Assessing Health Care Quality for Minority and Other Disparity Populations.* Washington, D.C.: U.S. Department of Health and Human Services.

Agency for Healthcare Research and Quality. 2004. *2004 National Healthcare Disparities Report.* Rockville, MD: U.S. Department of Health and Human Services.

Agency for Healthcare Research and Quality. 2005. *2005 National Healthcare Disparities Report.* Rockville, MD: U.S. Department of Health and Human Services.

Agency for Healthcare Research and Quality. 2006. *2006 National Healthcare Disparities Report.* Rockville, MD: U.S. Department of Health and Human Services.

Agency for Healthcare Research and Quality. 2008. *2007 National Healthcare Disparities Report.* Rockville, MD: U.S. Department of Health and Humans Services.

Ambler, Marjane. 2003. "Reclaiming Native Health." *Tribal College Journal* 15, no. 2 (Winter): 8–9.

Baldwin, Laura-Mae; David C. Grossman; Susan Casey; Walter Hollow; Jonathan R. Sugarman; William L. Freeman; and L. Gary Hart. 2002. "Perinatal and Infant Health among Rural and Urban American Indians/Alaska Natives." *American Journal of Public Health* 92, no. 9 (September): 1491–97.

Basiotis, Peter P.; Mark Lino; and Rajen Anand. 1999. "The Diet Quality of American Indians: Evidence from the Continuing Survey of Food Intake by Individuals." *Family Economics & Nutrition Review* 12, no. 2: 44–46.

Bergman, Abraham B.; David C. Rossman; Angela M. Erdrich; John G. Todd; and Ralph Forquera. 1999. "A Political History of Indian Health Service." *Milbank Quarterly* 77, no. 4: 571–604.

Blum, R.W.; B. Harmon; L. Harris; L. Bergeisen; M.D. Resnick. 1992. "American Indian–Alaska Native Youth Health." *Journal of American Medical Association* 267, no. 12 (March 25): 1634–44.

Borowsky, Iris W.; Michael D. Resnick; Marjorie Ireland; and Robert W. Blum. 1999. "Suicide Attempt among American Indians and Alaska Native Youths." *Archives of Pediatric and Adolescent Medicine* 153, no. 6 (June): 573–80.

Buchwald, Dedra; Janette Beals; and Spero M. Manson. 2000. "Use of Traditional Health Practices among Native Americans in a Primary Care Setting." *Medical Care* 38, no. 12 (December): 1191–99.

Burhansstipanov, Linda. 2000. "Urban Native American Health Issues." *Cancer* 88, no. 55: 1207–13.

Cantwell, Michael F.; Matthew T. McKenna; Eugene McCray; and Ida M. Onorato. 1998. "Tuberculosis and Race/Ethnicity in the United States." *American Journal of Respiratory and Critical Care Medicine* 157, no. 4 (April): 1016–20.

Centers for Disease Control and Prevention. 2000. *Facts about Heart Disease and Stroke among American Indians and Alaska Natives.* Online at www.cdc.gov. Accessed on 6/12/2003.

Cheadle, Allen; David Pearson; Edward Wagner; Bruce M. Psaty; Paula Diehr; and Thomas Koepsell. 1994. "Relationship between Socioeconomic Status, Health Status, and Lifestyle Practices of American Indians: Evidence from a Plains Reservation Population." *Public Health Reports* 109, no. 3 (May–June): 405–13.

Clegg, Limin X.; Frederick P. Li; Benjamin F. Hankey; Kenneth Chu; and Brenda K. Edwards. 2002. "Cancer Survival among US Whites and Minorities." *Archives of Internal Medicine* 162, no. 17: 1985–93.

Cohen, Felix S. 1982. *Handbook of Federal Indian Law.* Charlottesville, VA: Michie Bobbs-Merrill.

Cunningham, Peter J. 1993. "Data Watch: Access to Care in the Indian Health Service." *Health Affairs* 12, no. 3 (Fall): 224–33.

Cunningham, Peter J., and Barbara M. Altman. 1993. "The Use of Ambulatory Health Care Services by American Indians with Disabilities." *Medical Care* 31, no. 7 (July): 600–616.

Cunningham, Peter. J., and L.J. Cornelius. 1995. "Access to Ambulatory Care for American Indians and Alaska Natives: The Relative Importance of Personal and Community Resources." *Social Science & Medicine* 40, no. 3 (February): 393–407.

Denny, Clark H.; Deborah Holtzman; and N. Cobb. 2003. "Surveillance for Health Behaviors of American Indians and Alaska Natives: Findings from the Behavioral Risk Factor Surveillance System, 1997–2000." *Morbidity and Mortality Weekly Report* 52, no. 7 (August 1): 1–13.

Denny, Clark H.; Deborah Holtzman; Turner Goins; and Janet B. Croft. 2005. "Disparities in Chronic Disease Risk Factors and Health Status between American Indian/Alaska Native and White Elders: Findings from a Telephone Survey, 2001 and 2002." *American Journal of Public Health* 95, no. 5 (May): 825–27.

"Diagnosed Diabetes among American Indians and Alaska Natives Aged <35 Years—United States, 1994–2004." 2006. *Morbidity & Mortality Weekly* 55, no. 44 (November 10): 1201–3.

Donabedian, Avedis. 1983. "Quality Assessment and Monitoring: Retrospect and Prospect." *Evaluation & Health Professions* 6, no. 3 (September): 363–75.

Donabedian, Avedis. 1985. "Twenty Years of Research on the Quality of Medical Care." *Evaluation & Health Professions* 8, no. 3 (September): 243–65.

Donabedian, Avedis. 1987. "Commentary on Some Studies on the Quality of Care." *Health Care Financing Review* (December): 75–85.

Donabedian, Avedis. 1988. "The Assessment of Technology and Quality: A Comparative Study of Certainties and Ambiguities." *International Journal of Technological Assessment of Health Care* 4, no. 4: 487–96.

Donabedian, Avedis. 1999. "Measuring the Quality of Health Care." A Statement by the National Roundtable on Health Care Quality, Division of Health Care Services, Institute of Medicine, Washington, D.C.: National Academic Press.

Duran, Bonnie; John Oetzel; Julie Lucero; Jiang Yizhou; Douglas K. Novins; Spero Manson; and Janette Beals. 2005. "Obstacles for Rural American Indians Seeking Alcohol, Drug, or Mental Health Treatment." *Journal of Consulting & Clinical Psychology* 73, no. 5 (October): 819–29.

Fagot-Campagna, A.; D.J. Pettitt; and M.M. Engelgan. 2000. "Type 2 Diabetes among North American Children and Adolescents: An Epidemiologic Review and a Public Health Perspective." *Journal of Pediatric* 136, no. 5 (May): 664–72.

Forquera, Ralph. 2001. *Urban Indian Health.* Washington, D.C.: Henry J. Kaiser Family Foundation.

Frank, John W. 2000. "Historical and Cultural Roots of Drinking Problems among American Indians." *American Journal of Public Health* 90, No 3 (March): 344–51.

Free, Kalyn. 2006. "Tribes Plan for Increased Representation." Indigenous Democratic Network. Tulsa, Oklahoma. Online at http://indnslist.org/node/356. Accessed on 11/6/07.

Freedenthal, Stacey, and Arlene R. Stiffman. 2007. "They Might Think I Was Crazy: Young American Indians' Reasons for Not Seeking Help When Suicidal." *Journal of Adolescent Research* 22, no. 1 (January): 58–77.

Garrett, J.T., and M.W. Garrett. 1994. "The Path of Good Medicine: Understanding and Counseling Native American Indians." *Journal of Multicultural Counseling and Development* 22, no. 3 (July): 134–44.

Geiger, Jack. 2001. "Racial Stereotyping and Medicine: The Need for Cultural Competence." *Canadian Medical Association Journal* 164, no. 12 (June 12): 1699–1700.

Goldberg, H.I.; C.W. Warren; L.L. Oge; S.D. Helgerson; D.D. Pepion; E. LaMere; and J.S. Friedman. 1991. "Prevalence of Behavioral Risk Factors in Two American Indian Populations in Montana." *American Journal of Preventive Medicine* 7, no. 3 (May–June): 155–60.

Graber, Judith M.; Brenda E. Corkum; Nancy Sonnenfeld; and Paul L. Kuehnert. 2005. "Underestimation of Cardiovascular Disease Mortality among Maine American Indians: The Role of Procedural and Data Errors." *American Journal of Public Health* 95, no. 5 (May): 827–30.

Grossman, David C.; Laura-Mae Baldwin; Susan Casey; Brigitte Nixon; Walter Hollow; and Gary L. Hart. 2002. "Disparities in Infant Health among American Indians and Alaska Natives in US Metropolitan Areas." *Pediatrics* 109, no. 4 (April): 627–33.

Gurley, Diana; Douglas K. Novins; Monica C. Jones; Janette Beals; James H. Shore; and Spero M. Manson. 2001. "Comparative Use of Biomedical Services and Traditional Healing Options by American Indian Veterans." *Psychiatric Services* 52, no. 1 (January): 68–74.

Henderson, Patricia N.; Clemma Jacobsen; and Janette Beals. 2005. "Correlates of Cigarette Smoking among Selected Southwest and Northern Plains Tribal Groups: The AL-SUPERRFP Sud." *American Journal of Public Health* 95, no. 5 (May): 867–72.

Herman-Stahl, Mindy; Donna L. Spencer; and Jessica E. Duncan. 2003. "The Implications of Cultural Orientation for Substance Use among American Indians." *American Indian & Alaska Native Mental Health Research* 11, no. 1: 46–66.

Institute of Medicine. 2001a. *Crossing the Quality Chasm: A New Health System for the 21st Century.* Washington, D.C.: National Academy Press.

Institute of Medicine. 2001b. *Envisioning the National Health Care Quality Report.* Washington, D.C.: National Academy Press.

Institute of Medicine. 2003. *Unequal Treatment: Confronting Racial and Ethnic Disparities in Health Care.* Washington, D.C.: National Academy Press.

Johnson, Jeannette L., and Mark C. Cameron. 2001. "Barriers to Providing Effective Mental Health Services to American Indians." *Mental Health Services Research* 3, no. 4 (December): 215–23.

Kaiser Commission on Medicaid and the Uninsured. 2000. *Key Facts: Health Insurance Coverage and Access to Care among American Indians and Alaska Natives.* Washington, D.C.: Henry J. Kaiser Family Foundation.

Kaiser Commission on Medicaid and the Uninsured. 2006. *The Uninsured: A Primer. Key Facts about Americans without Health Insurance.* Washington, D.C.: Henry J. Kaiser Family Foundation.

Katz, Ruth J. 2004. "Addressing the Health Care Needs of American Indians and Alaska Natives." *American Journal of Public Health* 94, no. 1 (January): 13–14.

Keppel, K.G.; J.N. Pearcy; and D.K. Wagener. 2002. *Trends in Racial and Ethnic-Specific Rates for the Health Status Indicators: United States, 1990–1998.* Healthy People Statistical Notes, no. 23. Hyattsville, MD: National Center for Health Statistics.

Kramer, Josea B. 1992a. "Cross-Cultural Medicine: A Decade Later." *Western Journal of Medicine* 157, no. 3: 281–85.

Kramer, Josea B. 1992b. "Health and Aging of Urban American Indians." *Western Journal of Medicine* 157, no. 3 (September): 281–85.

Krieger, Nancy. 2001b. "The Ostrich, the Albatross, and Public Health: An Ecosocial Perspective—Or Why an Explicit Focus on Health Consequences of Discrimination and Deprivation Is Vital for Good Science and Public Heath Practice." *Public Health Reports* 116, no. 5 (September–October): 419–23.

Krisberg, Kim. 2006. "Budget Cuts for Urban Indian Programs a Danger to Health." *Nation's Health* 36, no. 5 (June–July): 1, 18.

Kunitz, Stephen J. 1996. "The History and Politics of US Health Care Policy for American Indians and Alaskan Natives." *American Journal of Public Health* 96, no. 10 (October): 1464–73.

Late, Michele. 2005. "Health Status of American Indians, Alaska Natives Still Lagging." *Nation's Health* 35, no. 5 (June–July): 8.

Lee, Elisa T.; Barbara. V. Howard; Peter. J. Savage; Linda. D. Cowan; Richard. R. Eabsitz; Arvo J. Oopik; J. Yeh; O. Go; D.C. Robbins; and Y.K. Welty. 1995. "Diabetes and Impaired Glucose Tolerance in Three American Indian Populations Aged 45–74 Years: The Strong Heart Study." *Diabetes Care* 18, no. 5 (May): 599–610.

Lee, Elisa T.; Thomas K. Welty; Richard Fabsitz; Linda D. Cowan; Ngoc-Anh Le; Arvo J. Oopik; Rew J. Cucchiara; Peter J. Savage; and Barbara V. Howard. 1990. "The Strong Heart Study: A Study of Cardiovascular Disease in American Indians—Designs and Methods." *American Journal of Epidemiology* 132, no. 6: 1141–55.

Liao, Y.; P. Tucker; and W.H. Giles. 2003. "Health Status of American Indians Compared with Other Racial/Ethnic Minority Population." *Morbidity & Mortality Weekly Report* 52, no. 47: 1148–52.

Lillie-Blanton, Marsha. 2005. "Understanding and Addressing the Health Care Needs of American Indians and Alaska Natives." *American Journal of Public Health* 95, no. 5 (May): 759–61.

Mahoney, Martin C., and Arthur M. Michalek. 1998. "Health Status of American Indians/ Alaska Natives: General Patterns of Mortality." *Family Medicine* 30, no. 3: 190–95.

Mahoney, Martin C., and Arthur M. Michalek. 1999. "The Health Status of American Indians and Alaska Natives: 2. Lessons for Cancer Educators." *Journal of Cancer Education* 14, no. 1 (Spring): 23–27.

Mansberger, Steven L.; Francine C. Romero; Nicole H. Smith; Chris A. Johnson; George A. Cioffi; Beth Edmunds; Choi Dongseok; and Thomas M. Becker. 2005. "Causes of Visual Impairment and Common Eye Problems in Northwest American Indian and Alaska Natives." *American Journal of Public Health* 95, no. 5 (May): 881–86.

Manson, Spero M.; Janette Beals; Suzell A. Klein; and Calvin D. Croy. 2005. "Social Epidemiology of Trauma among 2 American Indian Reservation Populations." *American Journal of Public Health* 95, no. 5 (May): 851–59.

Marbella, Anne M.; Mickey C. Harris; Sabina Diehr; Gerald Ignace; and Georginna Ignace. 1998. "Use of Native American Healers among Native American Patients in an Urban Native American Health Center." *Archives of Family Medicine* 7, no. 2 (March–April): 182–85.

McGee, Daniel L.; Youlian Liao; Guichan Cao; and Richard S. Cooper. 1999. "Self-Reported Heath Status and Mortality in a Multiethnic US Cohort." *American Journal of Epidemiology* 149, no. 1 (January 1): 41–46.

Mensah, George A.; Ali H. Mokdad; Earl S. Ford; Kurt J. Greenlund; and Janet B. Croft. 2005. "State of Disparities in Cardiovascular Health in the United States." *Circulation* 111, no. 10 (March 15): 1233–41.

Moy, Ernest; Colleen R. Smith; Patrick Johansson; and Roxanne Andrews. 2006. "Gaps in Data for American Indians and Alaska Natives in the National Healthcare Disparities Report." *American Indian & Alaska Native Mental Health Research* 13, no. 1: 52–59.

Nagel, Joane. 1995. "American Indian Ethnic Renewal: Politics and the Resurgence of Identity." *American Sociological Review* 60, no. 6 (December): 947–65.

Novins, Douglas K.; Janette Beals; Calvin Croy; Anna E. Baron; Paul Spicer; and Dedra Buchwald. 2006. "The Relationship between Patterns of Alcohol Abuse and Mental and Physical Health Disorders in Two American Indian Populations." *Addiction* 101, no. 1 (January): 69–83.

"NPAIHB Policy Brief: President's 2008 IHS Budget Request." 2007. Northwest Portland Area Indian Health Board. Online at www.npaihb.org. Accessed on 3/29/08.

Olson, Lenora M., and Stephanie Wahab. 2006. "American Indians and Suicide: A Neglected Area of Research." *Trauma, Violence & Abuse* 7, no. 1 (January): 19–33.

O'Nell, T.D., and C.M. Mitchell. 1996. "Alcohol Use among American Indian Adolescents: The Role of Culture in Pathological Drinking." *Social Science and Medicine* 42, no. 4: 565–78.

Paeratakul, S.; J.C. Lovejoy; D.H. Ryan; and G.A. Bray. 2002. "The Relation of Gender, Race, and Socioeconomic Status to Obesity and Obesity Comorbidities in a Sample of US Adults." *International Journal of Obesity* 26, no. 9 (September): 1205–10.

Pearson, D.; A. Cheadle; E. Wagner; R. Tonsberg; and B.M. Psaty. 1994. "Differences in Sociodemographics, Health Status, and Lifestyle Characteristics among American Indians by Telephone Coverage." *Preventive Medicine* 23, no. 4 (July): 461–64.

Peterson, Geoff, and Robert Duncan. n.d. "American Indian Representation in the 20th and 21st Centuries." Unpublished paper. Eau Claire, University of Wisconsin. Online at www. uwec.edu/petersgd/research/Ichapter.pdf. Accessed on 11/6/2007.

Potthoff, Sandra J.; Linda H. Bearinger; Carol L. Skay; Nadav Cassuto; Robert W. Blum; and Michael D. Resnick. 1998. "Dimensions of Risk Behaviors among American Indian Youth." *Archives of Pediatrics and Adolescent Medicine* 152, no. 2 (February): 157–63.

Puukka, Emily; Paul Stehr-Green; and Thomas M. Becker. 2005. "Measuring the Health Gap for American Indians/Alaska Natives: Getting Closer to the Truth." *American Journal of Public Health* 95, no. 5 (May): 838–43.

Renfrew, Megan J. 2006. "The 100% Federal Medical Assistance Percentage: A Tool for Increasing Federal Funding for Health Care for American Indians and Alaska Natives." *Columbia Journal of Law and Social Problems* 40, no. 2 (Winter): 173–224.

Rhoades, Dorothy A. 2005. "Racial Misclassification and Disparities in Cardiovascular Disease among American Indians and Alaska Natives." *Circulation* 111, no. 10 (March 15): 1250–56.

Rhoades, Dorothy A. 2006. "Disparities in Data for American Indians and Alaska Natives." *American Indians and Alaska Native Mental Health Research* 13, no. 1: 70–74.

Rhoades, Everett R. 2003. "Health Status of American Indians and Alaska Native Males." *American Journal of Public Health* 93, no. 5 (May): 774–78.

Roubideaux, Yvette. 2002. "Perspectives on American Indian Health." *American Journal of Public Health* 92, no. 9 (September): 1401–6.

Roubideaux, Yvette. 2004. *A Review of the Quality of Health Care for American Indians and Alaska Natives.* New York: Commonwealth Fund.

Satcher, David. 2001. *Mental Health: Culture, Race, and Ethnicity—A Supplement to Mental Health: A Report of the Surgeon General.* Washington, D.C.: U.S. Department of Health and Human Services.

Schneider, Andy. 2005. "Reforming American Indian/Alaska Native Health Care Financing: The Role of Medicaid." *American Journal of Public Health* 95, no. 5 (May): 766–68.

Schneider, Eileen. 2005. "Tuberculosis among American Indians and Alaska Natives in the United States, 1993–2002." *American Journal of Public Health* 95, no. 5 (May): 873–80.

Sequist, Thomas D. 2005. "Information Technology as a Tool to Improve the Quality of American Indian Health Care." *American Journal of Public Health* 95, no. 12 (December): 2173–79.

Sequist, Thomas D.; A.S. Narva; S.K. Stiles; S.K. Karp; A. Cass; and J.Z. Ayanian. 2004. "Access to Renal Transplantation among American Indians and Hispanics." *American Journal of Kidney Disease* 44, no. 2 (August): 344–52.

Shelton, Brett L. 2004. *Legal and Historical Roots of Health Care for American Indians and Alaska Natives in the United States.* Washington, D.C.: Henry J. Kaiser Family Foundation.

Singh, G.K., and D.L. Hoyert. 2000. "Social Epidemiology of Chronic Liver Disease and Cirrhosis Mortality in the United States, 1935–1997: Trends and Differentials by Ethnicity, Socioeconomic Status, and Alcohol Consumption." *Human Biology* 72, no. 5 (October): 801–20.

Singh, D.K., and S.M. Yu. 1996. "US Childhood Mortality, 1950 through 1993: Trends and Socioeconomic Differentials." *American Journal of Public Health* 86, no. 4: 505–12.

Stehr-Green, Paul; James Bettles; and L. Dee Robertson. 2002. "Effects of Racial/Ethic Misclassification of American Indians and Alaska Natives on Washington State Death Certificates, 1989–1997." *American Journal of Public Health* 92, no. 3 (March): 443–44.

Story, Mary; Marguerite Evans; Richard R. Fabsitz; Theresa E. Clay; Bonnie Holy Rock; and Brenda Broussard. 1999. "The Epidemic of Obesity in American Indian Communities and the Need for Childhood Obesity-Prevention Programs." *American Journal of Clinical Nutrition* 69, no. 4 (April): 747–54.

Story, Mary; K.F. Strauss; E. Zephier; and B.A. Broussard. 1998. "Nutritional Concerns in American India and Alaska Native Children: Transition and Future Direction." *Journal of American Dietetic Association* 98, no. 2 (February): 170–76.

Sugarman, Jonathan R.; Leslie K. Dennis; and Emily White. 1994. "Cancer Survival among American Indians in Western Washington State (United States)." *Cancer Causes and Control* 5, no. 5 (September): 440–48.

Swan, Judith; Nancy Breen; Linda Burhansstipanov; Delight E. Satter; William W. Davis; Timothy McNeel; and Matthew C. Snipp. 2006. "Cancer Screening and Risk Factor Rates among American Indians." *American Journal of Public Health* 96, no. 2 (February): 340–50.

"2008 Budget Fact Sheets." 2007 (February). Online at www.whitehouse.gov/infocus/budget/BudgetFY2008.pdf. Accessed on 3/29/08.

UCLA Center for Health Policy Research. 2004. "American Indian and Alaska Native Cancer Fact Sheet." Los Angeles, CA. Online at www.healthpolicy.ucla.edu. Accessed on 10/15/2005.

U.S. Bureau of the Census. 2002. *The American Indian and Alaska Native Population: 2000.* Washington, D.C.: U.S. Department of Commerce, Economic and Statistics Administration.

U.S. Commission on Civil Rights. 2004. *Broken Promises: Evaluating the Native American Health Care System.* Washington, D.C.: U.S. Commission on Civil Rights.

U.S. Department of Health and Human Services. 2000. *Healthy People 2010: Understanding and Improving Health.* Washington, D.C.: Government Printing Office.

U.S. Government Accountability Office. 2005. *Indian Health Service: Health Care Services Are Not Always Available to Native Americans.* Report to the Committee on Indian Affairs, U.S. Senate. Washington, D.C.: U.S. General Accountability Office.

Walters, Karina, and Jane M. Simoni. 2002. "Reconceptualizing Native Women's Health: An 'Indigenist' Stress-Coping Model." *American Journal of Public Health* 92, no. 4 (April): 520–24.

Wang, Youfa, and Mary A. Beydoun. 2007. "Obesity Rates Continue to Climb in the United States." Public Health News Center, John Hopkins Bloomberg School of Public Health. Online at www.jhsph.edu/publichealthnews/press_releases/2007/wang_adult_obesity.html. Accessed on 10/29/2007.

Ward, Elizabeth; Jemal Ahmedin; Vilma Cokkkinides; Gopal K. Singh; Cheryll Cardinez; Asma Ghafoor; and Michael Thun. 2004. "Cancer Disparities by Race/Ethnicity and Socioeconomic Status." *CA Cancer Journal for Clinicians* 54, no. 2: 78–93.

Welty, T.K. 1991. "Health Implications of Obesity in American Indians and Alaska Natives." *American Journal of Clinical Nutrition* 53, no. 6 Supplement (June): 1616–20.

Whitebeck, Les B.; Dan R. Hoyt; Barbara J. McMorris; X. Chen; and Jerry D. Stubben. 2001. "Perceived Discrimination and Early Substance Abuse among the American Indian Children." *Journal of Health and Social Behavior* 42, no. 4 (December): 405–24.

Whitebeck, Les B.; Barbara J. McMorris; Dan R. Hoyt; Jerry D. Stubben; and Teresa Lafromboise. 2002. "Perceived Discrimination: Traditional Practices, and Depressive Symptoms among American Indians in the Upper Midwest." *Journal of Health and Social Behavior* 43, no. 4 (December): 400–418.

Wilcox, L.S., and W.D. Mosher. 1993. "Factors Associated with Obtaining Screening among Women of Reproductive Age." *Public Health Reports* 108, no. 1 (January–February): 76–86.

Williams, David R. 1999. "Race, Socioeconomic Status, and Health: The Added Effects of Racism and Discrimination." *Annals of the American Academy of Sciences* 896, no. 1: 173–88.

Williams, David R.; R. Lavizzo-Mourey; and R.C. Warren. 1994. "The Concept of Race and Health Status in America." *Public Health Reports* 109, no. 1 (January–February): 26–41.

Young, T. Kue. 1997. "Recent Health Trends in American Indian Population." *Population Research and Policy Review* 16, no. 1–2 (April): 147–67.

Zuckerman, Stephen; Jennifer Haley; Yvette Roubideaux; and Marsha Lillie-Blanton. 2004. "Health Service Access, Use, and Insurance Coverage among American Indians/Alaska Natives and Whites: What Role Does the Indian Health Service Play?" *American Journal of Public Health* 94, no. 1 (January): 53–59.

—— 5 ——

Gender and Health Care

Historically, women were for the most part relegated to a second-class status, often seen as no more than property, subject to the will of their fathers and then their husbands. The desire for equality on the part of women had an early expression in 1776.

The Second Continental Congress was meeting in Philadelphia to consider the question of whether the thirteen colonies should break away from their colonial ruler, England. One of the major agitators for independence was the Massachusetts lawyer and farmer John Adams. While he was attending the Philadelphia deliberations, his wife, Abigail, was at home taking care of the children and running the family farm in Braintree. During this time, they communicated by letter. Recall from history and our discussion in Chapter 1 the famous phrase from the Declaration of Independence that the Philadelphia convention adopted. It stated that: "We hold these truths to be self evident, that all men are created equal." In one of her letters to John, Abigail reminded her husband that the word "men" had a narrow connotation:

> and by the way in the new Code of Laws which I suppose it will be necessary for you to make I desire you would Remember the Ladies, and be more generous and favourable to them than your ancestors. Do not put such unlimited power into the hands of the Husbands. Remember all Men would be tyrants if they could. If perticuliar care and attention is not paid to the Ladies we are determined to foment a Rebelion, and will not hold ourselves bound by any Laws in which we have no voice, or Representation.
>
> That your Sex are Naturally Tyrannical is a Truth so thoroughly established as to admit of no dispute, but such of you as wish to be happy willingly give up the harsh title of Master for the more tender and endearing one of Friend. Why then, not put it out of the power of the vicious and the Lawless to use us with cruelty and indignity with impunity. Men of Sense in all Ages abhor those customs which treat us only as the vassals of your Sex. Regard us then as Beings placed by providence under your protection and in immitation of the Supreem Being make use of that power only for our happiness. (Adams 1776)

Women's struggle for equality in the United States has taken many forms. Further, women's health and equality issues are affected by other factors that we have discussed, such as race, ethnicity, and class. One of the first efforts in the United States to achieve a more politically and socially equal society began as a reaction to the abolitionist (anti-slavery movement) (Barbour and Wright 2001). In 1848, delegates met at Seneca Falls, New York, to consider women's rights. They adopted "The Declaration of Sentiments" written by Elizabeth Cady Stanton. The declaration was deliberately modeled after the Declaration of Independence. It states: "We hold these truths to be self-evident: that all men and women are created equal; that they are endowed by their Creator with certain inalienable rights" (Declaration of Sentiments 1848). It then lists a series of grievances against the treatment of women by men, followed by a set of resolutions that, if fulfilled, would result in equality between the sexes.

The three Civil War amendments, the Thirteenth through the Fifteenth, addressed the rights of the former slaves, but did not touch upon women's rights. The Fifteenth Amendment gave the former slaves the right to vote (in theory, if not in practice) but did not mention women. The failure to obtain the right to vote led to the women's suffrage movement, under the direction of Stanton and Susan B. Anthony. The goal was a constitutional amendment giving women the right to vote. The belief was that if women could vote, then the other things desired would be forthcoming. While states in the western United States did allow women to vote, there was no federal right. The suffrage movement succeeded with the passage of the Nineteenth Amendment in 1920. That did not, however, lead to the equality and rights that activists hoped for.

An interesting development in the women's movement occurred during World War II. Because of the manpower required to fight the war, women were recruited into many of the jobs that men had left behind. They showed themselves more than capable of doing the work; "Rosie the Riveter" was the icon of the workingwoman. We should note that one of the authors came across a t-shirt with the "Rosie the Riveter" picture on the front, only "Rosie's" face had been replaced with that of Senator Hillary Rodham Clinton (D-NY), a candidate for president of the United States in 2008.

The modern women's movement had its inspiration with the publication of *The Feminine Mystique* (Friedan 1963). Betty Friedan argued that women, particularly middle-class women, were trapped in a very narrowly defined role (stay-at-home motherhood) and were very dissatisfied with that role. The assertion was that women were more than mothers and housewives (a phrase that could be interpreted as being married to the house). The typical stereotypes were the 1950s television shows *Ozzie and Harriet* and *Leave It to Beaver.* Also in 1963, Congress passed the Equal Pay Act, which prohibition pay discrimination on the basis of sex or gender. Friedan would later, in 1967, found the major women's rights organization, the National Organization of Women (NOW).

The following year the Civil Rights Act of 1964 was passed. The legislation was enacted in response to the civil rights movement and demonstrations in the South that were met with violence. An ironic part of the history of the bill was the role of Representative Howard Smith (D-VA.). Smith was the chair of the House Rules Committee, often the graveyard of civil rights legislation, and opposed to the civil rights movement. There was concern among activist women that, as with the Fifteenth Amendment, the Civil Rights Act would not include protections for women against discrimination. Smith added the word "sex" to the phrase listing the categories of protected people. He hoped that this would lead to the defeat of the legislation. However, the bill passed with the added provision (Barbour and Wright 2001). In 1965, President Lyndon Johnson, via executive order, created affirmative action programs that sought to help women (and minorities) gain an equal chance at jobs and education as white men. Those programs were expanded by President Johnson and then by President Nixon. They also became controversial as opponents argued that they discriminated against white males.

Despite the 1964 Civil Rights Act and other legislation and court decisions, women still perceived themselves as in a second-class status. Discrimination on the basis of race has been considered automatically suspect by the U.S. Supreme Court because of the Civil War amendments. The rights of women did not have a similar constitutional status. Therefore, the Equal Rights Amendment (ERA) was proposed in 1972. Congress gave the proposed amendment a ten-year period in which to be ratified by state legislatures. When by 1982 it failed to get the required number, it became a dead letter.

However, another important piece of legislation was passed in 1972. This was Title IX of the Education Amendments. It stated that schools receiving federal funding could not discriminate against women. The major role of Title IX has been in providing greater funding and participation for women in collegiate sports (Barbour and Wright 2001). Other legislation passed in the 1970s prohibited discriminating against women in obtaining credit and provided protection for working women who were pregnant. In 1986 the Supreme Court, in *Meritor Savings Bank v. Vinson* (477 US 57), ruled that sexual harassment was a form of job discrimination.

Despite all these pro-woman civil rights actions, women in many ways remain the unequal majority, including within the health care system. We can see this through statistics.

Women are a little over 51 percent of the population (Health Resources and Services Administration 2005). Seventeen percent of women are sixty-five years of age and older, 13 percent are fifty-five to sixty-four, 19 percent are forty-five to fifty-four, 38 percent are twenty-five to thirty-four, and 12 percent are eighteen to twenty-four. Just over seventy percent of women are white, while blacks and Hispanic women each account for about 12 percent of the female population. There are differences by age. Whereas white women make up about 82 percent of the sixty-five and older population among women, they make up only 62 percent of the twenty-five to thirty-four group. Women make up almost 58 percent of those sixty-five and older, so women are a majority of the elderly (Health Resources and

Services Administration 2005). Fifty-five percent are married, another 25 percent are widowed, divorced, or separated, 7 percent are living with a partner, and 14 percent have never married. As a comparison, about 45 percent of men are married and about 8 percent are widowed, divorced, or separated. Thirty-eight percent of women are parents or guardians of children under eighteen, 62 percent are not (U.S. Bureau of the Census 2007; Salganicoff, Ranji, and Wyn 2005).

Thirty-one percent of women are low income, defined as having an income less than 200 percent of the poverty line. For a family of three, the federal poverty line in 2004 was $15,066 (U.S. Bureau of the Census n.d.). Therefore, low income women are defined as in families with an income less than $30,132 for a family of three. The poverty rate for women (2003 data) was 12.4 percent. The poverty rate for female-headed families was 24.4 percent (Health Resources and Services Administration 2005). Fifteen percent of women never completed high school. Thirty-three percent completed high school, and 24 percent completed college. Forty-one percent of women are working full-time, 13 percent are working part-time, 21 percent are not employed, and 19 percent are retired (Salganicoff, Ranji, and Wyn 2005).

Men in general come out better in these measures than women. Overall, the poverty rate for men in 2004 was 11.5 percent. The poverty rate for women was higher than for men in all racial and ethnic groups. Now consider poverty status by head of household. The poverty rate for families with a married couple as head was 5.5 percent in 2004. For families with only a male head of household, the poverty rate was 13.5 percent. The corresponding figure for female-only head of households was 28.4 percent, more than five times that of married heads of household and more than two times that of male-only heads of household (U.S. Bureau of the Census 2006).

History of Women's Health Care

The history of women and health care in the United States can be divided into five periods. Weisman (1998) refers to five megamovements. She notes that they tended to occur at the same time as the larger women's rights movements discussed above.

The first period may be called the Popular Health Movement (Weisman 1998). This began in the 1830s and 1840s. At that time, new ideas of gender roles were being formed. Related to the beginnings of industrialization, men's roles were outside the home as workers and providers. Women's roles were to take care of the home, and have children and raise them. Indeed, much of the history of women and health care is focused on reproductive issues and in these early years reproductive issues defined women (Solinger 2005). Weisman (1998) writes that in this role at this time, women were to inculcate their children with civic virtue. This is another theme of the early years, the higher virtue of women because of their homemaker and reproductive roles.

Prior to this period, most health care was delivered by women (mothers and daughters). But in the first half of the nineteenth century, the medical industry was beginning to set a separate course as a (male-dominated) profession (see Starr 1982). There was competition for competing perspectives on medicine and a new focus on doctors' supervision of childbirth. Childbirth for a long time in the United States was a major source of sickness and death for women (Weisman 1998). Male physicians began to attend to childbirth and a very small number of women entered medical school (Weisman 1998).

The Popular Health Movement, advocated by higher income white women, argued that disease and death were not the result of decisions by God, but rather were preventable. Lifestyle changes could prevent many diseases (Weisman 1998). Another aspect of this movement was its emphasis on reproductive control, limiting the number of children women had. Abortion was used as a means of birth control, especially after 1840 (Weisman 1998).

The second period was in the latter part of the nineteenth century (Weisman 1998). This period was marked by a move toward outlawing both contraception and abortion. By the beginning of the twentieth century, abortion was illegal in the United States, though physicians could perform abortions to save the life of the mother (a position increasingly prominent a century later). More women became doctors, focusing on reproductive issues. Women were involved with charity and social movements. There was also a view of women that because of menstruation and childbirth, women were naturally unhealthy and suffered from psychological problems. Biological determinism, the idea that physiology affected both physical and social strength, was a prevalent view within the medical profession. Weisman (1998, 49–50) writes:

> Their [women's] normal biological functions—including menstruation and pregnancy—were defined by medical authorities as potentially debilitating, and both puberty and menstruation were viewed as dangerous transitions in women's lives. Energy had to be conserved to ensure the health of the reproductive organs and the safety of these biological processes.

Weisman (1998, 50) describes this as the "brain-uterus link." Women were seen as invalids. The increasing number of female doctors did not accept this biological determinist view.

The third period occurred during the Progressive era, in the early years of the twentieth century. During this period, women led social reform movements and focused particularly on infant and maternal mortality. Feminism had its early roots here. The social reform portion of this time consisted of both public and private efforts. The private efforts were the establishment of settlement houses in cities and education of mothers and pregnant women. Issues included breastfeeding and nutrition as well as hygiene. The public aspect led to the establishment of the Children's Bureau in 1912. This was followed by the passage in 1921 of the Sheppard-Towner Maternity and Infancy Act (Schlesinger 1967). The act provided for grants from the federal government to the states and then to communities. Prenatal care was set up with local physicians, as were home visits and child health clinics. The act expired in 1929. Though women had been given the right to vote, Schlesinger (1967) points out that there apparently was no such thing as a "women's vote." Further, the American Medical Association (AMA) opposed the legislation, largely on the grounds that it provided competition for doctors' services (Schlesinger 1967).

The other major element of this period was a movement to make birth control and abortion legal. Advocates such as Margaret Sanger argued that one of the major causes of mortality in women was too many pregnancies. Abortion would limit pregnancies, but birth control would also limit the use of abortion (Weisman 1998). Another argument was that women should have the right to control their bodies, which included the right to limit births and the right to sexual fulfillment. In earlier periods, women were thought to have weak sexual desires and sex was limited to achieving pregnancy. The first birth control clinic was opened in 1916 and Sanger founded in 1921 what would eventually become Planned Parenthood. Both movements focused on prevention and education (Weisman 1998). Obstetrics began as a medical specialty and women began delivering in hospitals. Midwives were becoming less important in childbirth.

Weisman (1998) observes that an important legacy of this period was the transformation of reproduction issues into services to be delivered by the medical system. Similarly, the Sheppard-Towner Act, though its existence was brief, set the stage for later legislation that was part of the 1935 Social Security Act and Medicaid in 1965.

The fourth period came in the activist period of the 1960s and 1970s (Weisman 1998). The Women's Health Movement grew along with other social movements of the period (civil rights, antiwar, and the larger women's movement). Women began demanding equal rights with men, including the right of self-determination. Abortion was one of the larger issues of this period, leading to the 1973 U.S. Supreme Court decisions of *Roe v. Wade* and *Doe v. Bolton,* though a number of states, including California (under Republican governor Ronald Reagan) and New York (under Republican governor Nelson Rockefeller) had very liberal abortion laws.

Contraception, particularly with the advent of the pill, became more widely available after the 1967 *Griswold v. Connecticut* decision (which allowed the distribution of birth control pills to married couples and also created the right to privacy that underlay the *Roe* decision) and the 1972 *Eisenstadt v. Baird* decision (which allowed such distribution to unmarried women) (Cushman 2000). Weisman (1998) notes that women's advocacy of oral contraception as early as 1951 led to the development of the modern pill. The fact that more women were entering the workplace, and had been since the end of World War II, and especially in the 1960s, also enhanced the need for the regulation of fertility.

One of the major events of this period was the publication of *Our Bodies, Ourselves* by the Boston Women's Health Collective (1976). The book was a manual, a guide to the female body, and its intent was to educate women about their bodies, and not just depend on (male) physicians for information and advice. It was also a celebration by women of their own body and sexuality. Related to this was the establishment by women of health clinics run by women and of free-standing birth clinics (Weisman 1998).

The passage of Title IX legislation made it easier for women to be accepted into medical schools. Another element of the movement of this time was the protection of women as subjects of medical experiments (Weisman 1998).

The final period is the 1990s. In 1989 came the first Supreme Court decision, *Webster v. Reproductive Health Services,* that limited the availability of abortion (Cushman 2000). Weisman points out that the controversy over the confirmation hearings of Clarence Thomas to the U.S. Supreme Court and charges of sexual harassment also contributed to activating women (on the Thomas hearings, see Mayer and Abramson 1994).

The focus of this period was two-fold, both having the underlying value of equality or equity (Weisman 1998). The first focus was on benefiting from medical research. Recall that in the previous period there was concern that women needed to be protected from medical research, especially that involving, directly or indirectly, reproduction. Women's advocates argued that women were not participating in medical research studies and that women's health issues were being neglected by such studies. Obstetrical issues were not an important component of the research agenda of the National Institutes of Health (NIH). And, perhaps the most interesting example deals with heart disease, the most common cause of death among both men and women in the United States. Heart disease in women turns out to be different from that in men. In two major trials, no women subjects were included (Weisman 1998). Weisman notes the irony of a third example. This was a study of human aging, whose title was *Normal Human Aging.* Although women were a majority of the elderly population, the study included no women during its first twenty years because, according to the researchers, bathroom facilities for women were not available when the study began. The title of the monograph, which implicitly equated normal with male, further incensed critics (Weisman 1998, 79).

Because of the advocacy of women's groups, funding for medical research has been redirected through the Women's Health Initiative (see below).

The breadth of the women's health movement that began in the 1970s was enormous:

> They [women's health activists] challenged the fundamental view of biology as destiny, refuted the depiction of women as mentally and physically fragile, and raised questions about hazards to women's health at home and in the paid labor force. They rejected the notion that women's health needs were limited to obstetrics and gynecology; sought to demedicalize pregnancy, menopause, and other aspects of women's reproductive lives; promoted access to birth control and sex education; contested restrictions on abortion; denounced population control and sterilization abuse directed against women of color; and began to make international ties with women in other countries concerned about women's health and women's social status. Taking on issues of sexuality and power as related to women's health, these activists vividly made clear the distinction between sex and gender, fought for more liberated, less restricted views of women's sexuality, supported lesbian rights, and broke the silence surrounding rape and domestic violence. (Fee and Krieger 1994, 1)

Health Status/Outcomes

In this section, we examine the health status of and health outcomes for women. As we shall see and have seen throughout this book, the status varies among women depending on race, ethnicity, and income. Let us begin with a profile of women. The numbers below reflect 2004 data, unless otherwise noted. We should note that in some respects women are healthier than men. Their life expectancy is longer than men and they are more likely to see a physician than men. On the other hand, women tend to experience more health issues than men (Weisman 1998).

Women, on the whole, report that they are in good health, but a little more than 20 percent report that they are in fair health. This is, understandably, related to age. Thirteen percent of women eighteen to forty-four report that they are in fair or poor health; the corresponding figures for women forty-five to sixty four and sixty-five and older are 23 and 31 percent respectively. Fourteen percent of women report that they have a medical or health condition that limits activity and 38 percent report a chronic condition that requires continual treatment. As before, older women are more likely to place themselves in these categories than younger women. The more common chronic conditions reported include arthritis, hypertension, high cholesterol, and osteoporosis (among older women) (Salganicoff, Ranji, and Wyn 2005). Minority women are more likely to report being in poor or fair health than white women. Twenty-nine percent of Latinas so report, as do 20 percent of African American women, compared to 13 percent of white women (Kaiser Family Foundation 2004a).

Minority women are more likely to report having chronic illnesses than white women. African American women report high levels of hypertension and arthritis, followed by Latinas, compared to white women. They also report higher levels of diabetes. However, Latinas and white women have higher levels of osteoporosis as compared to African American women (Kaiser Family Foundation 2004a).

Income is linked to health status. Women living in families with incomes less than 200 percent of the poverty line report higher levels of poor/fair health, medical conditions that limit activity, and chronic conditions that require continual treatment than women living in families with higher incomes. Likewise, race and ethnicity are linked to health status. African American women and Latinas report higher percentages in these categories than white women, though in some cases, the numbers for Latinas and whites are quite close (Salganicoff, Ranji, and Wyn 2005).

About 23 percent of women report suffering from depression and anxiety, compared to 11 percent of men. White women suffer from these psychological problems more than African American women, and low income women suffer from them at a 50 percent higher rate than higher income women (30 percent versus 20 percent) (Salganicoff, Ranji, and Wyn 2005).

Geography (which we consider in detail in Chapter 8) is related to health status. Women in rural areas tend to be in poorer health and tend to have greater barriers to health care than women and men in more urban areas (Health Resources and Services Administration 2005). The leading causes of death among women (2002 data) are heart disease (28.6 percent) and cancer (21.6 percent) (Health Resources and Services Administration 2005).

Another aspect of considering the health status of women is to compare them to men. Here we can examine the disparities in disease incidence and treatment. The first thing we should note is that the life expectancy of women exceeds that of men by about five years (Agency for Healthcare Research and Quality 2004). Cancer rates among men have been stable but have risen for women. The most common form of cancer among women is breast cancer. Screenings for breast cancer (mammography) is higher among whites, higher income, and more educated women than for minority women, lower income, and less educated women (Agency for Healthcare Research and Quality 2004). Women are more likely to get diabetes than men and pregnancy is a particularly susceptible time for contracting diabetes (Agency for Healthcare Research and Quality 2004).

Heart disease is a condition in which disparities appear to be quite great. Women with heart attacks are less likely to receive treatment than men and are more likely to have a second episode (Agency for Healthcare Research and Quality 2004). It is not clear why the disparity exists. One study found such disparities even among women covered by Medicare or private insurance, who were receiving care and had clear indications of heart disease (Bird 2007). One possibility is that the symptoms of heart disease in women differ from those of men. If the "male model" of heart disease is that one that doctors look for, then problems in women may be under-assessed and undertreated.

One health care issue of critical importance is the prevalence of HIV (human immunodeficiency virus) and AIDS (acquired immunodeficiency virus) among women, particularly minority women. HIV/AIDS has become increasingly evident among women, and has been labeled an epidemic (Kaiser Family Foundation 2001). The proportion of new HIV cases resulting from male homosexual behavior declined from 65 percent in 1985 to 43 percent in 2005. At the same time, the proportion of new HIV cases attributable to heterosexual contact rose from 3 percent in 1985 to 31 percent in 2005 (Kaiser Family Foundation 2007). Women accounted for 8 percent of new AIDS cases in 1985 and 27 percent in 2003 (Kaiser Family Foundation 2004b). AIDS is an important cause of death among young women. Most of the women with HIV/AIDS are women of color (Latinas and African Americans). This is especially true of African American women. They accounted for 63 percent of all new AIDS cases in 1999. The AIDS case rate for African American women is twenty-one times greater than for white women; the corresponding figure for Latinas is six times greater. Women of child-rearing age, particularly teenage girls, are especially vulnerable (Kaiser Family Foundation 2001). Additionally, lower income women were more vulnerable to contracting

HIV/AIDS than higher income women. The major means of transmission is heterosexual sex (Kaiser Family Foundation December 2004). This is a very efficient means of transmission. Also already having a sexually transmitted disease (STD) makes transmission of HIV more likely. HIV-infected women are more likely to develop the preconditions for cervical cancer than women who have not contracted the virus (Kaiser Family Foundation 2004b). Alarmingly, women who have contracted HIV/AIDS have difficulty accessing the health care system and obtaining effective treatment.

Access to Health Care

Lambrew (2001) argues that because women have both different and more needs for health care than men, health insurance is vitally important for them. One example of different and more health needs is reproductive care. Such differences mean that women need to regularly see a physician more than men. Health status is often affected by the ability to pay for health care, and that is usually a function of having health insurance. The number of women without health insurance (2002 data) is a bit less than men (14.4 percent versus 16.8 percent). White women are more likely to have health insurance than minorities and older women more likely than men (Health Resources and Services Administration 2005; Kaiser Family Foundation 2004a).The kind of health insurance coverage varies widely (2004 data). Twenty-nine percent of women obtain health insurance from their employer. Twenty-four percent of women obtain health insurance from employer-sponsored dependent insurance. Nineteen percent of women (older women) are on Medicare and 6 percent on Medicaid. Five percent purchase health insurance individually. While only about 14 percent of women lack health insurance for an entire year, about 27 percent lack it for part of the year (Salganicoff, Ranji, and Wyn 2005).

Both uninsured and insured women have more difficulty seeing a physician than men, but the differences are greater for the uninsured. Thirteen percent of women with insurance reported difficulty getting access to care as compared to 11.8 percent of men with insurance. Over 25 percent of women without health insurance reported difficulties compared to just under 21 percent of uninsured men (Lambrew 2001).

Lambrew (2001) reports that for women in the fifty to sixty-four age range (not yet eligible for Medicare) the differences in access between men and women are more pronounced. The access problem for all women of that age was 13 percent versus 7 percent of men of that age reporting access problems. For uninsured women in that age range, 29 percent reported access problems compared to 16 percent of men in that group (Lambrew 2001).

Again, race and ethnicity affect health insurance coverage. Latinas have the highest uninsurance rate (38 percent), followed by African American women (17 percent). The uninsurance rate among white women was 13 percent (Salganicoff, Ranji, and Wyn 2005). Minority women are more likely to be covered by Medicaid than white women. Twelve percent of Latinas and 17 percent of African American women are so covered (Kaiser Family Foundation 2004a).

We see similar trends when looking at access to health care. Women are more likely to have seen a doctor in the past year than men and older women more likely than younger women. Higher income women are more likely to have seen a doctor in the past year than lower income women and whites more than African American women or Latinas. Women with insurance are also more likely to have seen a doctor in the past year than women without insurance (Salganicoff, Ranji, and Wyn 2005; Kaiser Family Foundation 2004a). Minority women have difficulty seeing a specialist and difficulty in affording prescription drugs (Kaiser Family Foundation 2004a). Latinas in particular (31 percent) report not having a regular physician and are less likely to have a long-term relationship with a provider than white women. Both African American women and Latinas make more frequent use of health centers (Kaiser Family Foundation 2004a).

It also follows that minority women are less likely to make use of preventive services than white women. Because Latinas and African American women have higher rates of chronic diseases (see above), the lack of screening tests represents a real threat to their health. Disparities in breast cancer screening between Latinas and African American women, while smaller, still exist (Kaiser Family Foundation 2004a).

There are various reasons why women do not seek or delay seeking health care, not all of which are related to costs. Certainly, lack of insurance is one. In a 2004 survey, 19 percent of women without insurance indicated they had delayed seeking health care, and the rates were much higher for lower income than for higher income women. Other reasons for delay in seeking care include the inability to find the time, the inability to get time off from work to obtain the care, child care issues, and transportation issues. Again, these affected lower income women more than higher income women (Salganicoff, Ranji, and Wyn 2005).

More women than men report that they had a regular provider. The socioeconomic factors that we have discussed play a role here. Older women are more likely to have a regular provider than younger women, and white women more than African American women or Latinas. Higher income women are more likely to have a regular provider than lower income women. Insurance status might be the biggest factor. Only about 50 percent of uninsured women have a regular provider compared to 81 to 95 percent of women with insurance (depending on the kind of insurance) (Salganicoff, Ranji, and Wyn 2005).

Having health insurance is important. Those without health insurance are less likely to see providers than those with. Lambrew (2001, 2) points out the importance of insurance status: "Uninsured women are also 40 to 60 percent less likely to receive a mammogram or Pap smear and are significantly more likely to be hospitalized for avoidable conditions such as diabetes and pneumonia."

While the number of uninsured of both genders have increased over the years, the number of uninsured women has increased faster than men. In 1994, there were approximately 15.7 million uninsured men as compared to 13.1 million uninsured women. By 1998, there were 16.7 million uninsured men compared to 15.3 million uninsured women (Lambrew 2001). That represents a little over 6 percent increase for men and nearly a 17 percent increase for women. At that rate, there would be more uninsured women than men by 2006 (Lambrew 2001).

Lambrew (2001) points out the danger for married women in the insurance market. If wives are dependent on their husband's job-based health insurance, and wives are generally younger than their husbands when the husband retires and becomes eligible for Medicare, then the wife would lose her health insurance coverage. And women are more likely than men to have health insurance through spousal coverage. Patchias and Waxman (2007) note that employers are increasingly cutting back on spousal health insurance as a way of saving on employee health expenses.

Statistically, women are faced with two reinforcing problems. First, their incomes tend to be lower than men's. Second, they tend to make greater use of health care services than men. Much of this is due to the fact, stated above, that women suffer more from chronic health problems than men and also more from mental health issues (Patchias and Waxman 2007). The result is that women spend relatively more of their own income, out of pocket, on health care than men. One result of this is a tendency to avoid care because of the expense. Another result is greater problems paying for care and more health care debt (Patchias and Waxman 2007).

There are laws and programs that address the issue of women and health care disparities. Medicaid is perhaps the most important such program. Enacted in 1965, it provided for provider reimbursements for health care services to low income families, particularly women and children. Female-headed families make up a substantial portion of the poverty population in the United States. Considerable research points to increased access to health care on the part of Medicaid recipients (see Patel and Rushefsky 2006). Families enrolled in welfare programs were automatically enrolled in Medicaid.

Then came welfare reform. The old program, Aid to Families with Dependent Children (AFDC), originated with the passage of the 1935 Social Security Act. Because its payments were fairly modest and not adjusted for inflation, there was considerable unhappiness with it. One of the major complaints was that AFDC created incentives to stay on welfare and not become self-supporting. The political situation, such as Bill Clinton's promise to "end welfare as we know it" and the Republican congressional victories in 1994, led to significant change. The entitlement to federal assistance was ended and AFDC was replaced by TANF, Temporary Assistance for Needy Families. The emphasis was on reducing the welfare rolls and limiting the time for receiving assistance.

The linkage between Medicaid and TANF was broken. Those who applied for welfare were not told that they were eligible for Medicaid even if they were not eligible for or diverted from welfare. The question then is, what happened to women in these circumstances? One study, Handler et al. (2006), focused on what they call the "Medicaid Gap." The gap exists when low income women are not eligible for Medicaid until they become pregnant. Their study found that such low income women were significantly less likely (4.5 times) to have Medicaid coverage after welfare reform than before. The problem is that the lack of coverage extends to the early months of the pregnancy, when prenatal care is most important. Some of these women may have preexisting (chronic conditions) that remain untreated that might adversely affect the course of the pregnancy or the health of the baby.

Quality of Health Care

On average, a bit more money is spent on health care for women than for men, $3,644 in 2003 for women versus $3,550 for men. Hospital spending, the largest share of health care expenditures, is much higher for men than for women, $19,242 for men versus $11,000 for women for inpatient services and $2,030 for men and $1,638 for women for hospital outpatient services. Health care expenses for office visits, for medications, and for dental services are higher for men than for women (Health Resources and Services Administration 2006).

In general, the quality of care received by women has increased over time (Health Resources and Services Administration 2006). The annual series of reports, *Women's Health USA* published by the Health Resources and Services Administration, provides data on several quality indicators. The percentage receiving Pap smears for cervical cancer and chlamydia screenings are up since 2000. The timeliness of prenatal care and post-delivery checkups has increased. There has been some decline in mammograms for Medicaid recipients since 2003, likely reflecting state cutbacks in their Medicaid programs (Health Resources and Services Administration 2006).

One could also raise the question of the quality of care in reproductive health given the limitations placed on family planning clinics, such as Planned Parenthood, because of the abortion issue.

Possible Explanations for Health Care Disparities

Violence against Women

One issue that affects the health status of women and exacerbates the disparities in health outcomes between men and women is violence. Miller and Downs (2000) observe that there has been violence against women in all cultures over the course of human history. They also note that most of that violence is within families and that such violence has been accepted and even expected in some cultures.

Violence against females, unlike against males, tends to be inflicted by people known by the victim (Catalano 2006). For example, female victims knew the assailant in 64 percent of violent crimes and 73 percent in rape and sexual assault cases. Women victims were more likely than men (54.6 percent of cases versus 42.4 percent) to report violent crimes. However, only 38.3 percent of rapes/sexual assaults were reported to the police. The crime rate for violence against women has declined by 58 percent between 1993 and 2005 (this is in accord with the overall decline in crime rates) (Catalano 2006). Sexual assault crimes, of which women are the primary victims, have similarly drastically declined.

Intimate partner violence (IPV) can take four forms: physical violence, sexual violence, the threat of physical or sexual violence, and stalking (National Center for Injury Prevention and Control n.d.). It is estimated that there are about 5.3 million episodes of IPV per year. Alarmingly, about 44 percent of female victims of murder by an intimate partner had visited a hospital emergency room within the two years prior to their deaths.

Violence against women has important physical and mental health consequences (Macmillan and Kruttschnitt 2005; National Center for Injury Prevention and Control n.d.). Such violence can lead to depression and anxiety, a lower quality of physical health, poor self-esteem, and even post-traumatic stress disorder (PTSD), with symptoms such as sleep disorders and flashbacks (National Center for Injury Prevention and Control n.d.). Headaches and gastrointestinal problems may occur. Victims of violence may show other problems such as alcohol and drug abuse. Such violence may also explain the rising percentage of HIV sufferers that are women (Miller and Downs 2000). Other negative behaviors include engaging in high risk sex and negative food behaviors such as fasting or overusing diet pills (National Center for Injury Prevention and Control n.d.).

There are economic consequences to violence against women, especially IPV (National Center for Injury Prevention and Control n.d.). Women victims tend to be absent from their jobs (if employed), be unemployed, and be recipients of social services (that is, welfare). The direct and indirect health care costs of IPV exceed, according to one estimate, $8 billion per year (National Center for Injury Prevention and Control n.d.).

The National Center for Injury Prevention and Control (n.d.) lists a number of risk factors for being a victim of IPV (see Table 5.1). Note how many of the factors pertain to women.

Data on violence against women tend to be less than adequate. For example, a major research project funded by the U.S. Department of Justice and completed in 2005 (Macmillan and Kruttschnitt 2005; Tjaden and Thoennes 2000) used data from a 1995–96 study. Nevertheless, it is one of the best available studies. The researchers looked at patterns of violence against women: parental (including stepparent and foster parent), by other relatives, by partners (including ex-partners), dates, acquaintances (including supervisors, teachers, and ministers), and strangers. The variety of violent episodes included sexual assault, physical assault, and stalking.

While most women are not the victims of violence, when violence occurs the most frequent relationship involves parents and partners (Macmillan and Kruttschnitt 2005). The risk of physical violence is highest in relationships between parent and child. Miller and Downs (2000) find that there is a class relationship to violence against women. That is, violence against women is more likely in

Table 5.1

Risk Factors for Victims and Perpetrators of Intimate Partner Violence (IPV)

Risk Factors for Victims

Individual factors
Prior history of IPV
Being female
Young age
Heavy alcohol and drug use
High-risk sexual behavior
Witnessing or experiencing violence as a child
Being less educated
Unemployment
For men, having a different ethnicity from their partner's
For women, having a greater education level than their partner's
For women, being American Indian/Alaska Native or African American
For women, having a verbally abusive, jealous, or possessive partner
Relationship factors
Couples with income, educational, or job status disparities
Dominance and control of the relationship by the male
Community factors
Poverty and associated factors (e.g., overcrowding)
Low social capital—lack of institutions, relationships, and norms that shape the
    quality and quantity of a community's social interactions
Weak community sanctions against IPV (e.g., police unwilling to intervene)
Societal factors
Traditional gender norms (e.g., women should stay at home and not enter work-
    force, should be submissive)

Risk Factors for Perpetrators

Individual factors
Low self-esteem
Low income
Low academic achievement
Involvement in aggressive or delinquent behavior as a youth
Heavy alcohol and drug use
Depression
Anger and hostility
Personality disorders
Prior history of being physically abusive
Having few friends and being isolated from other people
Unemployment
Economic stress
Emotional dependence and insecurity
Belief in strict gender roles (e.g., male dominance and aggression in relationships)
Desire for power and control in relationships
Being a victim of physical or psychological abuse (consistently one of the strongest
    predictors of perpetration)
Relationship factors
Marital conflict—fights, tension, and other struggles

(continued)

Table 5.1 *(continued)*

Marital instability—divorces and separations
Dominance and control of the relationship by the male
Economic stress
Unhealthy family relationships and interactions
Community factors
Poverty and associated factors (e.g., overcrowding)
Low social capital—lack of institutions, relationships, and norms that shape the
    quality and quantity of a community's social interactions
Weak community sanctions against IPV (e.g., unwillingness of neighbors to
    intevene in situations where they witness violence)
Societal factors
Traditional gender norms (e.g., women should stay at home and not enter
    workforce, should be submissive)

Source: National Center for Injury Prevention and Control (n.d.)

lower than higher income classes. Additionally, pregnant women, especially from low income families, are more likely to be victims of violence than those from higher income families. Women with substance abuse problems also experience higher levels of violence (Miller and Downs 2000). Macmillan and Kruttschnitt (2005, 21) find the following factors related to greater risk of violence among women: "Age, race, low socioeconomic status, including unemployment, low educational attainment, low personal and household income, and poverty, and marital disruption."

In a telling commentary on the relationship between violence against women and health issues, a summary of 2005 legislation finds that such violence is linked to most of the health indicators in the *Healthy People 2010* report (Stewart 2005).

Miller and Downs (2000) examine the barriers to identifying women who have been victims of violence. One set of barriers is in the health care system. They argue that health care providers hesitate to ask about the possibility of violence. They cite a study suggesting that only 5 percent of IPV victims are identified as such in emergency rooms. Part of that is because the victims themselves do not mention it. Miller and Downs (2000) suggest several reasons why physicians do not report such violence. One of them is time constraints. There is considerable paperwork involved with reporting and testifying to a crime. They recommend routine screenings for women by medical personnel in various settings (family practice, obstetrics/gynecology, internal medicine, and emergency rooms).

Another barrier identified by Miller and Downs (2000) is the reluctance of women to identify themselves as victims of violence, particularly IPV. We saw above that only a little more than 30 percent of sexual assaults were reported to the police. Victims may fear further violence from the perpetrator, be uncomfortable talking about the violence with health care providers, and fear custody battles over children.

The major piece of federal legislation that addressed the issue of violence against women was the Violent Crime Control and Enforcement Act of 1994. Title IV of the act is what has come to known as the Violence Against Women Act (VAWA). The act has been reauthorized twice, once in 2000 (Victims of Trafficking and Violence Protection Act of 2000) and again in 2005 (Violence Against Women and Department of Justice Reauthorization Act of 2005).

VAWA's importance lies in recognizing the problem of domestic violence as a legitimate concern for women and the criminal justice system. Crimes such as interstate stalking and sexual assault became subject to federal jurisdiction. VAWA also helped develop a coordinated response among criminal justice agencies at all levels of government and provided support for shelters and support groups for abused women (National Task Force to End Sexual and Domestic Violence against Women 2005). The 2000 legislation strengthened VAWA, including adding intimate partner violence as a federal criminal act if it occurred across state lines. An important component of working to reduce domestic violence is to train health care providers to recognize symptoms of domestic violence. The 2005 legislation seeks to train providers and health-related professional schools in recognition. Transitional housing assistance was also included in the 2005 legislation (Laney 2005).

Not everyone is pleased with the legislation. Finney (2005) argues that VAWA is flawed in three important ways. First, the act assumes that only women are the victims of domestic violence. Finney says that men and women are equally victims and of those who are physically assaulted, men account for about one-third. Second, the major solution to domestic violence contained in the legislation is the breakup of the family and separating the wife from the abusive husband. Finney argues instead that what is needed is appropriate social services and support to keep the family intact and nonviolent. The third flaw is that the law uses public funds for police to arrest husbands, even if there was no physical abuse. His recommendation, which was not followed, was to not reauthorize the act.

Reproductive Issues

> It is hard not to recognize that most women, even those endowed with financial and other resources, have made reproductive decisions within the framework of existing public policies. In recent decades middle-class women have typically defined their relation to childbearing as a "choice." But federal, state, court, and corporate decisions about employment policies governing family leave, health insurance, and day care, for example, have all constrained or expanded the individual choices of even these women. Intensely private decisions about reproduction, including decisions about getting pregnant or not, are always shaped by public laws and policies. (Solinger 2005, 17)

Perhaps the most controversial of all issues regarding women, health, and disparities are those involving reproduction. Issues such as abortion and birth control directly impact the health of women. Men obviously have some interest in this area, either from a parental, spousal, or moral position, but it clearly affects women more than men.

As Solinger (2005) and others (see, for example, Weisman 1998) point out, the reproductive capability of women has shaped women's roles in society. Female black slaves in America were, especially after the end of the slave trade in 1808, seen as a valuable commodity and their childbearing was the only way to increase the slave population. Solinger (2005) quotes Thomas Jefferson, who penned the phrase "all men are created equal" in the Declaration of Independence, as viewing children born to slave women as adding to the capital of a farm. Women were seen as weak, tied to the home, and necessary for the survival of society because of childbearing. Further, until relatively recently, childbearing was a major cause of mortality among women of childbearing age. Consider the following statistics: the death rate from giving birth (maternal mortality rate) declined from 607.9 per 100,000 live births in 1915 to 12.1 in 2003 (Hoyert 2007). Pregnancy was seen as an illness.

Further, reproductive issues were seen at the heart of many social issues. Historically, there was concern that not enough white children were being born (Solinger 2005). The decline of the traditional family, defined as a husband, wife, and children, was attributed to both breakdowns in marriage, particularly among African Americans, as well as reproductive freedoms (and, some would add, the rise of the gay agenda). Illegitimacy as both a social problem and a cause of social problems is captured in the 1965 report by Daniel Patrick Moynihan on the Negro family and by the writings of Charles Murray.

In *The Negro Family* (Moynihan 1965), Moynihan attributes the declining status of the black community to two major factors. One is the continued existence of racism, which he estimates would remain a problem for a while. The other is the structure of the black family. Moynihan points to the very high rate of divorced black women, especially in the large cities, and the equally large illegitimacy rate. This leads to a series of bad outcomes or pathologies: increased dependence on welfare, poor education achievement, crime and delinquency, and alienation. The result is a matriarchical society. Moynihan (1965) writes:

> There is, presumably, no special reason why a society in which males are dominant in family relationships is to be preferred to a matriarchal arrangement. However, it is clearly a disadvantage for a minority group to be operating on one principle, while the great majority of the population, and the one with the most advantages to begin with, is operating on another. This is the present situation of the Negro. Ours is a society which presumes male leadership in private and public affairs. The arrangements of society facilitate such leadership and reward it. A subculture, such as that of the Negro American, in which this is not the pattern, is placed at a distinct disadvantage.

Murray takes the argument further and beyond African American families. A longtime opponent of public social welfare policies and a proponent of traditional values and the means to achieve those values, such as the stigma that used to be attached to illegitimacy, he wrote an influential article in 1983 grounding many social ills in the decline of the traditional family. Note in the following quote, how

Murray argues that white illegitimacy will produce the same social pathologies as black illegitimacy.

In raw numbers, European-American whites are the ethnic group with the most people in poverty, most illegitimate children, most women on welfare, most unemployed men, and most arrests for serious crime. . . .

But now the overall white illegitimacy rate is 22%. The figure in low-income working-class communities may be twice that. How much illegitimacy can a community tolerate? No one knows, but the historical fact is that the trendlines on black crime, dropout from the labor force and illegitimacy all shifted sharply upward as the overall black illegitimacy rate passed 25%. (Murray 1993)

Reproductive technologies enable women to control whether and when to bear children. Such technologies had profound influences on the health of women and their role in society (Solinger 2005). Finer and Henshaw (2006) examined the rate of unintended pregnancies in the United States, comparing 1994 and 2001 data. They found that the rate of unintended pregnancies had changed during this time period, with almost half of all pregnancies (49 percent) being unintended. They found that the unintended pregnancy rate was highest among the youngest females (eighteen to twenty-four), those who were not married, those with limited education (did not graduate from high school), and minorities. Fewer unintended pregnancies were aborted.

Finer et al. (2005) explored the reasons why women had abortions. A small group of women seek abortions because of health reasons (either their own or that of the fetus they are carrying; the latter refers to severe birth defects). The majority of abortions are to end unwanted pregnancies. The following were the most common reasons women gave for having an abortion: the timing was wrong, financial, feeling that the woman had finished her childbearing period, relationship issues or desire not to be a single mother, immaturity of the mother or already having young children, and interference with career and/or education (Finer et al. 2005, 114).

With ever more restrictions placed on the availability of abortion, one would expect there to be a decline in the number of abortions. Finer and Henshaw (2003) document that decline. They found that there was a 12 percent decline in the abortion rate from 1992 to 1996 and a five percent decline from 1996 to 2000. In addition, there are fewer providers offering abortion services, with the bulk of abortions being done in clinics. Over three-quarters of counties (87 percent) had no abortion providers, as was the case with many urban areas (31.2 percent).

The rate of abortions has varied over the years, with the rate increasing after the 1973 *Roe* decision and then declining after 1981. In 1973, the rate was 16.3 abortions per 1,000 women ages eighteen to forty-four (the prime childbearing years). The rate peaked in 1981 at 29.3 per 1,000 women. By 2002, the rate was just over 20 per 1,000 women (Guttmacher Institute 2006). The overwhelming majority of abortions (88.6 percent) occur within the first twelve weeks of gestation. Only 1.2 percent of abortions occur at the twenty-first week or later (Guttmacher Institute 2006).

Over time, the courts and legislatures have limited the availability of abortion. The original *Roe v. Wade* decision in 1973 developed a benchmark of when government could intrude into the decision to terminate a pregnancy. In the first three months, the state had no compelling interest in the decision. After the fetus reached viability, that is, could survive outside the womb, then the state could interfere. Prior to that the state could limit abortions to protect the health of the mother. The *Roe* decision was based on the value of privacy, established in a 1965 decision (*Griswold v. Connecticut*).

Following *Roe,* Congress, the courts and state legislatures enacted restrictions on abortion. In 1976, Congress passed the Hyde Amendment forbidding the use of the federal share of Medicaid funding to pay for abortions and gave states the option to forbid such use with their portion. Most states enacted such policies (American Civil Liberties Union 2004). This obviously impacted low income women. One study found that abortions paid for by Medicaid among low income women in the year following the enactment of the Hyde Amendment plummeted from 295,000 to 2,000 (Solinger 2005).

The Supreme Court issued rulings that limited the availability of abortion. In *Harris v. McRae* (1980), the Court ruled that there was no constitutional right to abortion, certainly no right to have government pay for one. It also said that *Roe* prohibited states from creating an "unduly burdensome interference" with the decision to have an abortion (quoted in Solinger 2005, 202; see also *Harris v. McRae*).

In 1989, the U.S. Supreme Court decided *Webster v. Reproductive Health Services.* The majority opinion, among other things, upheld a Missouri law that required the testing of a fetus to see if it were viable. In *Planned Parenthood v. Casey* (1992), the Court upheld *Roe* but permitted states to place restrictions on abortion, such as waiting periods and notification requirements. Further, the Court employed an undue burden standard to decide whether a restriction interfered with the decision to terminate. In *Rust v. Sullivan* (1991), the Court upheld a decision by the George H.W. Bush administration that banned funding for clinics that provided counseling or referrals relating to abortion (Solinger 2005).

States have enacted a series of restrictions on abortion availability. These include requiring that abortion be done by a licensed doctor, prohibiting abortion after viability and partial-birth abortion, placing restrictions on public funding, allowing physicians to refuse to perform abortions, counseling women seeking abortion (about mental health aspects, health consequences such as a possible link to breast cancer), and imposing waiting periods and parental involvement (for underage girls) (Guttmacher Institute 2007). South Dakota has one of the most restrictive abortion laws, though its 2006 law failed in a referendum (Simon 2006). Four states have laws that state that if *Roe* were overturned then abortion would be illegal in that state and over twenty others would likely pass legislation severely restricting abortion (Page 2007).

The issue of abortion raises important value questions and conflicts among different values. For those who oppose abortion, pro-life advocates, abortion is wrong because it results in the death (killing) of an unborn child. For many pro-life advocates, this is THE most important value. For those supporting the availability of abortion, the label is pro-choice. Here the emphasis is on the health and life of the mother as well as the ability of the mother to have control over her own body and control over decisions about reproduction.

The public has shown some division over the issue (as opposed to the heated arguments and activism of interest groups). A 2002 survey found a split, with 47 percent of those surveyed labeling themselves as pro-choice and 46 percent as pro-life. On the other hand, a majority of the public sees abortion as morally wrong, with 53 percent saying it is morally wrong and 38 percent saying it is morally acceptable (Public Agenda n.d.).

Presidents have also spoken on abortion, again showing a split in views. During his acceptance speech at the 1996 Democratic National Convention, President Bill Clinton expressed the ambivalence over this issue.

> We respect the individual conscience of every American on the painful issue of abortion, but believe as a matter of law that this decision should be left to a woman, her conscience, her doctor and her God.
>
> But abortion should not only be—abortion should not only be safe and legal, it should be rare. That's why I helped to establish and support a national effort to reduce out-of-wedlock teen pregnancy, and that is why we must promote adoption. ("President Bill Clinton Accepts His Nomination at the Democratic National Convention" 1996)

During the 2004 presidential debates, President Bush, speaking about possible vacancies on the U.S. Supreme Court, said that he would not appoint the type of person who had decided the *Dred Scott* case. On the surface, this appears rather odd. After all, the Dred Scott case involved the question of whether slaves were property or had rights when freed, an issue that has been settled since the Civil War. However, because pro-life advocates see the fight against abortion as analogous to the abolitionist (anti-slavery) cause, what the president was apparently saying was that he would never appoint someone who would uphold *Roe v. Wade* (Daily Women's Health Policy 2004).

President Bush did make good on his promise. His two appointees to the Supreme Court, Chief Justice John Roberts and Associate Justice Samuel Alito, voted to uphold the federal ban on partial birth abortions in April 2007, reversing a decision to overturn a similar ban in Nebraska (see Greenhouse 2007). In writing the majority opinion, Justice Anthony Kennedy emphasized that the federal government had a "legitimate and substantial interest in preserving and promoting fetal life" (Quoted in Greenhouse 2007). Kennedy made an argument that advocates of women's rights would likely have some difficulty with.

In describing the federal law's justifications, Justice Kennedy said that banning the procedure was in fact good for women, protecting them against terminating their pregnancies by a method they might not fully understand in advance and would come to regret later.

"Respect for human life finds an ultimate expression in the bond of love the mother has for her child," he said, adding: "It is self-evident that a mother who comes to regret her choice to abort must struggle with grief more anguished and sorrow more profound when she learns, only after the event, what she once did not know: that she allowed a doctor to pierce the skull and vacuum the fast-developing brain of her unborn child, a child assuming the human form." (Greenhouse 2007)

In challenging that perspective, Justice Ruth Bader Ginsberg asserted that such a view was paternalistic and was indicative of misplaced and discarded views of women's role (Greenhouse 2007; see also Stansell 2007 and Toner 2007).

There is an argument to defuse the abortion issue from liberals who generally support women's rights to choose. William Saletan, for example, argues that even supporters would acknowledge that abortion is bad (see also Baude 2006). Recall the Clinton quote from above. So what liberals should be supporting are ways to make abortion rare: contraception. He writes:

> The pro-choice path to those results is simple. Help every woman when she doesn't want an abortion: before she's pregnant. That means abstinence for those who can practice it, and contraception for everybody else. Nearly half of the unintended pregnancies in this country result in abortions, and at least half of our unintended pregnancies are attributable to women who didn't use contraception. The pregnancy rate among these women astronomically exceeds the pregnancy rate among women who use contraception. The No. 1 threat to the unborn isn't the unchurched. It's the unprotected. (Saletan 2006)

This is the other end of the argument over reproduction choices and equality: contraception. Saletan (2006) proposes more money for Title X programs that help with reproductive choices, greater insurance coverage for contraception, and education for teenagers, which would include abstinence as well as contraception education.

Related to this is the controversy over the "morning-after" pill or Plan B. The Food and Drug Administration has been hesitant to approve it (though it eventually did). Such emergency contraception (EC) is used when other contraceptive efforts fail (such as a condom breaking). One estimate is that the use of EC could prevent half of the nation's abortions (Kaiser Family Foundation 2005). Opposition to availability and use of such pills is twofold. First, opponents see it as an invitation for women to have sex because it would prevent pregnancy. Emergency contraception can also be used in cases of unprotected sex. Second, opponents see EC as essentially an abortion device (Kaiser Family Foundation 2005; see also Kaufman 2006). The Bush administration opposed allowing such pills to be sold over-the-counter but in 2006 the FDA approved such sales (Matthews and Martinez 2006).

Solinger (2005) argues that issues over reproduction have much to do with the status of women in society. Women, she argues, should be allowed to make their own reproductive choices without government interference. She concludes her survey of the history of reproductive politics by writing that reproductive justice requires both the right to safe and healthy pregnancies and the right not to reproduce. Only then will women have an equal status in society.

Medical Research Issues

One explanation for health disparities may be that women have been slighted in biomedical research. Hafner-Eaton (1993) pointed out that in 1990 only about 14 percent of research funding went specifically for women's health issues. The women's health movement lobbied for greater inclusion of women in clinical trials as well as more focus on women's health issues. One result was a 1985 report by a task force of the U.S. Public Health Service (Public Health Service 1985). Among other recommendations, the task force report recommended that "biomedical and behavioral research . . . be expanded to ensure emphasis on conditions and diseases unique to, or more prevalent in, women in all age groups" (Public Health Service 1985, 76). This was followed by a 1986 policy on the part of the National Institutes of Health (NIH) urging inclusion of women in medical research. In 1993, Congress passed legislation requiring inclusion of women (and minorities) in clinical research.

One can see the impact of these changes. Looking at NIH funding for Phase III clinical research (research involving human subjects) over time, in fiscal year (FY) 1994, 57.2 percent of the subjects were female. By FY 2005, that number had increased to almost 63 percent (National Institutes of Health 2007). A General Accounting Office (GAO, now Government Accountability Office) 2000 study reported that NIH had made considerable strides in including female (and minority subjects) (National Institutes of Health 2007).

A related effort was the Women's Health Initiative (WHI). WHI began as a fifteen-year study, housed in the National Heart, Lung, and Blood Institute within the National Institutes of Health. The focus of the initiative was on three health issues that particularly affected women: cancer (especially breast and colorectal), heart disease, and osteoporosis. The emphasis was on post-menopausal women. Much of the research, for example, testing the efficacy and consequences of hormone replacement therapy stemmed from the WHI.

"Feminization of Poverty"

A final explanation for health disparities of women as compared to men can be called the "feminization of poverty" (Rushefsky 2007). The data are reasonably clear that a greater percentage of women are poor than men, and that female-headed families tend to experience more poverty than male-headed or two-parent families. In 2004, 5.4 percent of two-parent families were in poverty, 13.5 percent of male-headed families were poor, and 28 percent of female-headed families were poor (U.S. Bureau of the Census 2006; DeNavas-Walt, Proctor, and Lee 2005). The median income for men in 2004 was $40,798 and $31, 223 for women. The ratio of income of women to men was 0.77, that is women earned about 77 percent as much as men. The poverty line in 2004 for a family of three (one householder and two children) was $15,219 (DeNavas-Walt, Proctor, and Lee 2005). Females of all ages made up about 56 percent of all those under the poverty line (2003 data) (U.S. Bureau of the Census 2006). One of the important things to keep in mind is that for many states, income at the poverty line is too high to qualify for Medicaid. Someone working full-time at a minimum wage job ($5.15/hour) would make $10,300 a year, again too high to qualify for many Medicaid programs.

An important question is why there has been this feminization of poverty. Gimenez (1994) offers a number of explanations (though she does not accept all of them). Single mothers generally have a difficult time and child support from the father tends to be minimal in many cases. Married women may outlive their husbands and when widowed may suffer economically. Finding good-paying jobs for many single mothers may be difficult. Welfare payments tend to be low (and temporary under the 1996 welfare reform). Poverty rates among minority women (black and Latino) are higher than for white women. By definition, lower class women are the ones often experiencing poverty or near-poverty conditions. Gimenez (1994) offers a Marxist approach, arguing that it is propertyless women (and men) who tend to be poor.

Conclusions

An emerging issue related to women and health care disparities is what has been called consumer-driven health care, or in President George W. Bush's terminology, "the ownership society" (Stobbe 2007; Hacker 2006; Patel and Rushefsky 2006). Health care costs continue to increase and businesses and governments are looking for ways to shift the costs from employer to employee.

Furthermore, consumer-driven health care has, as its fundamental principle, the idea that consumers of health care do not pay enough of their own medical expenses and therefore consume more than they would if they had to pay for it. This is what economists call a "moral hazard" (see Hacker 2006). Under one version of consumer-driven health care, which became part of the 2003 Medicare Modernization Act (see Patel and Rushefsky 2006), health savings accounts (HSAs) would be set up by individuals, similar to individual retirement accounts. The employee or consumer would deposit a certain amount of money in a tax-free savings account and then those funds could be used to pay for medical expenses. The consumer would also purchase a high-deductible health insurance plan to cover (much) of the remainder of health care expenses.

Apart from some fallacies with the theory (see Hacker 2006; Patel and Rushefsky 2006), HSAs are apparently something of a problem for more women than men. The reason for this, according to a 2007 study (see Stobbe 2007), is that women have many more routine medical needs than men, especially screenings for things such as breast and cervical cancer, pregnancy-related services, and so forth. According to the study, younger men who were participating in an HSA, under the age of forty-five, spent an average of about $550 a year. For women of a similar age, the average was over $1,200 a year. A greater percentage of women (55 percent) then men (around one-third) spent more than $1,050 a year. If the trend toward consumer-driven health care continues, than we should expect that women would be at a disadvantage.

The health status of women is affected by the confluence of race/ethnicity, socioeconomic class, and gender. On many measures of disparities, women come out on the short end. Minority women, especially blacks and Latinas, are further behind than white women.

Some of this is due to the perceived role of women in society (see the discussion on reproductive issues), and because some women are dependent on spouses or public programs for their health insurance. As public programs such as Medicaid in places such as Missouri and Tennessee are cut, and employer-provided health insurance is cut back in different ways, women suffer.

Efforts have been made to reduce the inequalities. Increased emphasis on women in clinical trials and the Women's Health Initiative are two examples. But much remains to be done before such disparities are narrowed or eliminated.

References

Adams, Abigail. 1776. "Abigail Adams to John Adams, March 31, 1776." Boston: Massachusetts Historical Society. Online at www.masshist.org/adams/apmanuscripts/apselected_1_text.html.

Agency for Healthcare Research and Quality. 2004. *2004 Healthcare Disparities Report.* Rockville, MD: U.S. Department of Health and Human Services.

American Civil Liberties Union. 2004. *Public Funding for Abortion.* July 21. Online at www.aclu.org/reproductiverights/lowincome/16393res20040721.html.

Barbour, Christine, and Gerald C. Wright. 2001. *Keeping the Republic: Power and Citizenship in American Politics.* Boston: Houghton Mifflin.

Baude, William. 2006. "States of Confusion." *New York Times,* January 22.

Bird, Choe. 2007. "Gender and Quality of Care for Heart Disease and Diabetes." Powerpoint presentation at Gender Disparities in Cardiovascular Care Congressional Briefing (May 21). Washington, D.C.: National Committee for Quality Assurance. Online at www.kaisernetwork.org/health_cast/hcast_index.cfm?display=detail&hc=2146.

Boston Women's Health Book Collective. 1976. *Our Bodies, Ourselves.* New York: Simon & Schuster.

Catalano, Shannan M. 2006. *Criminal Victimization, 2005.* Washington, D.C.: U.S. Department of Justice, Bureau of Justice Statistics.

Cushman, Clare. 2000. *Supreme Court Decisions and Women's Rights.* Washington, D.C.: CQ Press.

Daily Women's Health Policy. 2004. "Bush Reference to Dred Scott Case 'Subtle Nod' to Abortion-Rights Opponents, Antiabortion Advocates Say." October 14. Kaisernetwork.org. Online at www.kaisernetwork.org/daily_reports/rep_index.cfm?DR_ID=26234.

Declaration of Sentiments. 1848. Adopted by the Seneca Falls, NY, convention. Online at www.infoplease.com/ipa/A0875901.html.

DeNavas-Walt, Carmen; Bernadette D. Proctor, and Cheryl Hill Lee. 2005. *Income, Poverty, and Health Insurance Coverage in the United States: 2004.* Washington, D.C.: U.S. Census Bureau, Department of Commerce.

Fee, Elizabeth, and Nancy Krieger. 1994. "Introduction." In Elizabeth Fee and Nancy Krieger, eds., *Women's Health, Politics, and Power: Essays on Sex/Gender, Medicine, and Public Health,* 1–8. Amityville, NY: Baywood.

Finer, Lawrence B.; Lori F. Frohwirth; Lindsay A. Dauphinee; Susheela Singh; and Ann M. Moore. 2005. "Reasons Why U.S. Women Have Abortions: Quantitative and Qualitative Perspectives." *Perspectives on Sexual and Reproductive Health* 37, no. 3 (September): 110–18.

Finer, Lawrence B., and Stanley K. Henshaw. 2003. "Abortion Incidence and Services in the United States 2000." *Perspectives on Sexual and Reproductive Health* 35, no. 1 (January–February): 6–15.

Finer, Lawrence B., and Stanley K. Henshaw. 2006. "Disparities in the Rates of Unintended Pregnancies in the United States, 1994 and 2001." *Perspectives on Sexual and Reproductive Health* 38, no. 2 (June): 90–96.

Finney, Gordon E. 2005. "Fatal Flaws: VAWA 2005." *Washington Times,* July 19.

Friedan, Betty. 1996. *The Feminine Mystique.* New York: W.W. Norton.

Gimenez, Martha E. 1994. "The Feminization of Poverty: Myth or Reality?" In Elizabeth Fee and Nancy Krieger, eds., *Women's Health, Politics, and Power: Essays on Sex/Gender, Medicine, and Public Health,* 287–305. Amityville, NY: Baywood.

Greenhouse, Linda. 2007. "In Reversal, Justices Back Ban on Method of Abortion." *New York Times,* April 19.

Guttmacher Institute. 2006. *Facts on Induced Abortion in the United States.* New York: Guttmacher Institute.

Guttmacher Institute. 2007. *An Overview of Abortion Laws.* New York: Guttmacher Institute.

Hacker, Jacob S. 2006. *The Great Risk Shift: The Assault on American Jobs, Families, Health Care, and Retirement and How You Can Fight Back.* New York: Oxford University Press.

Hafner-Eaton, Chris. 1993. "Physician Utilization Disparities between the Uninsured and Insured: Comparisons of the Chronically Ill, Acutely Ill, and Well Nonelderly Populations." *Journal of the American Medical Association* 269, no. 6 (February 10): 787–82.

Handler, Arden, et al. 2006. "The Pre-Pregnancy Insurance Status of Public Aid Recipients in the Aftermath of Welfare Reform: Women in the Medicaid Gap." *Journal of Health Care for the Poor and the Underserved* 17, no. 1 (February): 162–79.

Harris v. McRae. Oyez: U.S. Supreme Court Media. Online at www.oyez.org/cases/1970-1979/1979/1979_79_1268.

Health Resources and Services Administration. 2005. *Women's Health USA 2005.* Rockville, MD: U.S. Department of Health and Human Services.

Health Resources and Services Administration. 2006. *Women's Health USA 2006.* Rockville, MD: U.S. Department of Health and Human Services.

Henry J. Kaiser Family Foundation. 2001. *Women and HIV/AIDS.* May. Menlo Park, CA.: Henry J. Kaiser Family Foundation.

Henry J. Kaiser Family Foundation. 2004a. *Racial and Ethnic Disparities in Women's Health Coverage and Access to Care Findings from the 2001 Kaiser Women's Health Survey.* March. Menlo Park, CA: Henry J. Kaiser Family Foundation.

Henry J. Kaiser Family Foundation. 2004b. *Women and HIV/AIDS in the United States.* December. Menlo Park, CA: Henry J. Kaiser Family Foundation.

Henry J. Kaiser Family Foundation. 2005. *Emergency Contraception.* November. Menlo Park, CA.: Henry J. Kaiser Family Foundation.

Henry J. Kaiser Family Foundation. 2007. *The HIV/AIDS Epidemic in the United States.* July. Menlo Park, CA: Henry J. Kaiser Family Foundation.

Hoyert, Donna L. 2007. *Maternal Mortality and Related Concepts.* Hyattsville, MD: National Center for Health Statistics. Centers for Disease Control and Prevent. U.S. Department of Health and Human Services. Vital Health Statistics Series 3, no. 33 (February).

Kaufman, Marc. 2006. "Plan B Battles Embroil States." *New York Times,* February 27.

Krieger, Nancy, and Elizabeth Fee. 1994. "Man-Made Medicine and Women's Health: The Biopolitics of Sex/Gender and Race/Ethnicity." In Elizabeth Fee and Nancy Krieger, eds., *Women's Health, Politics, and Power: Essays on Sex/Gender, Medicine, and Public Health* 11–29. Amityville, NY: Baywood.

Lambrew, Jeanne M. 2001. *Diagnosing Disparities in Health Insurance for Women: A Prescription for Change.* New York: Commonwealth Fund.

Laney, Garrine P. 2005. *Violence against Women Act: History and Federal Funding.* Washington, D.C.: Congressional Research Service.

Macmillan, Ross, and Catherine Kruttschnitt. 2005. *Patterns of Violence against Women: Risk Factors and Consequences.* Report funded by the U.S. Justice Department. Online at www.ncjrs.gov/pdffiles1/nij/grants/208346.pdf.

Matthews, Anna Wilde, and Barbara Martinez. 2006. "Plan B Shift Threatens to Deepen Rift." *Wall Street Journal,* August 25.

Mayer, Jane, and Jill Abramson. 1994. *Strange Justice: The Selling of Clarence Thomas.* Boston: Houghton Mifflin.

Miller, Brenda A., and William R. Downs. 2000. "Violence against Women." In Marlene B. Goldman and Maureen C. Hatch, eds., *Women and Health,* 529–40. San Diego: Academic Press.

Moynihan, Daniel Patrick. 1965. *The Negro Family: The Case for National Action.* Washington, D.C.: U.S. Department of Labor, Office of Policy Planning and Research. Online at www.dol.gov/oasam/programs/history/webid-moynihan.htm.

Murray, Charles. 1993. "The Coming White Underclass." *Wall Street Journal,* October 29.

National Center for Injury Prevention and Control. n.d. "Intimate Partner Violence." Washington, D.C.: Centers for Disease Control and Prevention. Online at www.cdc.gov/ncipc/factsheets/ipvoverview.htm.

National Institutes of Health. 2007. *Monitoring Adherence to the NIH Policy on the Inclusion of Women and Minorities as Subjects in Clinical Research.* Bethesda, MD: U.S. Department of Health and Human Services, National Institutes of Health.

National Task Force to End Sexual and Domestic Violence against Women. 2005. "The Violence Against Women Act: 10 Years of Progress and Moving Forward." Washington, D.C. Online at www.endabuse.org/vawa/factsheets/Overview.pdf.

Page, Susan. 2007. "'Roe v. Wade': The Divided States." *USA Today,* April 4.

Patchias, Elizabeth M., and Judy Waxman. 2007. *Women and Health Coverage: The Affordability Gap.* New York: Commonwealth Fund.

Patel, Kant, and Mark E. Rushefsky. 2006. *Health Care Politics and Policy in America.* 3rd ed. Armonk, NY: M.E. Sharpe.

"President Bill Clinton Accepts His Nomination at the Democratic National Convention." 1996 (August 29). PBS.org. Online at www.pbs.org/newshour/convention96/floor_speeches/clinton_8-29.html.

Public Agenda. n.d. *Abortion: People's Chief Concerns.* Online at www.publicagenda.org/issues/pcc_detail.cfm?issue_type=abortion&list=1.

Public Health Service. 1985. "Report of the Public Health Service Task Force on Women's Health Issues." *Public Health Reports* 100, no. 1 (January–February): 73–106.

Rushefsky, Mark E. 2007. *Public Policy in the United States: At the Dawn of the Twenty-First Century.* 4th ed. Armonk, NY: M.E. Sharpe.

Saletan, William. 2006. "Three Decades after *Roe:* A War We Can All Support." *New York Times,* January 22.

Salganicoff, Alina; Usha R. Ranji; and Roberta Wyn. 2005. *Women and Health Care: A National Profile*. Menlo Park, CA: Kaiser Family Foundation.

Schlesinger, Edward R. 1967. "The Sheppard-Towner Era: A Prototype Case Study in Federal-State Relations." *American Journal of Public Health* 57, no. 6 (June): 1034–40.

Simon, Stephanie. 2006. "South Dakota Scraps Abortion Ban." *Los Angeles Times,* November 8.

Solinger, Rickie. 2005. *Pregnancy and Power: A Short History of Reproductive Politics in America*. New York: New York University Press.

Stansell, Christine. 2007. "Partial Law." *The New Republic* 236, no. 4,813 (May 21): 12–14.

Starr, Paul. 1982. *The Social Transformation of American Medicine* New York: Basic Books.

Stewart, Kiersten. 2005. *Violence against Women Act 2005: Title V: Health Care Response.* Washington, D.C.: Task Force to End Sexual and Domestic Violence Against Women. Online at www.endabuse.org/vawa/factsheets/HealthCare.pdf.

Stobbe, Mike. 2007. "Study Says HSAs More Costly for Women." *Houston Chronicle,* April 5.

Tjaden, Patricia, and Nancy Theonnes. 2000. *Full Report of the Prevalence, Incidence, and Consequences of Violence against Women*. Washington, D.C.: U.S. Department of Justice, National Institute of Justice. Online at www.ncjrs.gov/txtfiles1/nij/183781.txt.

Toner, Robin. 2007. "Abortion Foes See Validation for New Tactic." *New York Times,* May 22.

U.S. Bureau of the Census. n.d. "Historical Poverty Tables." Washington, D.C.: U.S. Department of Commerce. Online at www.census.gov/hhes/www/poverty/histpov/hstpov1.html.

U.S. Bureau of the Census. 2006. *Statistical Abstract of the United States 2006*. Washington, D.C.: Department of Commerce.

U.S. Bureau of the Census. 2007. *Statistical Abstract of the United States 2007*. Washington, D.C.: Department of Commerce.

Weisman, Carol S. 1998. *Women's Health Care: Activist Traditions and Institutional Change.* Baltimore: Johns Hopkins University Press.

6

Children and Health Care

Children's health should be defined as the extent to which individual children or groups of children are able or enables them to (a) develop and realize their potential, (b) satisfy their needs, and (c) develop the capacities to allow them to interact successfully with their biological, physical and social environments.
(Institute of Medicine 2004 Report on Children's Health quoted in Haflon, DuPlessis, and Inkelas 2007, 316)

It was once said that the moral test of a government is how the government treats those who are in the dawn of life, the children; those who are in the twilight of life, the elderly; and those who are in the shadows of life, the sick, the needy and the handicapped.
(Humphrey 1977)

The extent to which a society protects its children reflects the magnitude of investment in its future.
(Starfield 2004, 165)

If there is a vulnerable portion of the population in any society it is children. The elderly, whom we consider in the next chapter, are also vulnerable and subject to inequalities as well. But many of them have assets to call upon. Many elderly can make decisions about their own lives; most children, especially younger children, cannot. The elderly vote; children do not. While there are very few uninsured older adults, there are millions of uninsured children.

In this chapter we examine the health of children in the United States and inequalities that exist among them. The usual suspects are to blame for the inequalities: the distribution of insurance coverage, ethnicity and race, socioeconomic class, language and cultural barriers, education, and so forth. As we shall see, while we have made progress, much more is yet to be accomplished.

History of Children's Health Care Policy

The history of health policy toward children is long and complex. The federal government's Maternal and Child Health Bureau (n.d.) has a sixty-six-page time line of public health–related policies toward children. Health policy in the United States has focused on two, not altogether coordinated, models (Patel and Rushefsky 2005). Both have affected the health of children. One is the preventive model, based on public health. Public policies in this area were sometimes focused on children (immunizations) but more often focused on the larger community. Early public health measures, such as sanitation, insuring the purity of the drinking water supply, fluoridation of the water supply (to prevent tooth decay), pasteurization of the milk supply, and so forth went a long way to reduce death and disease among children (Markel and Golden 2004). City and state health departments, and some private organizations, headed up this effort. Federal efforts came somewhat later (Markel and Golden 2004).

The other model of health care, which has dominated health care in the United States, is the curative or medical model (Patel and Rushefsky 2005). A thought experiment will make this point clear. Name a television series that focused on the medical care system. Now name one that focused on public health.

In the nineteenth century, under the curative model, health care for children was, obviously, a major responsibility of parents and other members of the family. To the extent that such health care involved the larger community, it was state governments and private agencies that had the sole role. President Theodore Roosevelt convened a White House Conference on Dependent Children. It recommended the creation of a Children's Bureau (Maternal and Child Health Bureau n.d.). That agency was established in 1912 (later renamed the Maternal and Child Health Bureau), for children with particular health needs (Golden and Markel 2007; van Dyck 2003). Golden and Markel (2007, 446) describe the Children's Bureau as "the world's first governmental agency to consider the problems of children." This then became the model for other countries to follow.

The early focus of the Children's Bureau was on infant mortality, looking for reasons for infant mortality and then providing information to families. The bureau also looked at special needs children ("handicapped, the homeless, the orphaned, and the delinquent"; Golden and Market 2007, 446) and created a set of local organizations to advocate for programs aimed at these types of problems.

The federal government really began its concern with child health in 1921 when Congress passed the Sheppard-Towner Infancy and Maternity Protection Act. This created a categorical grant program for states, "establishing the principle of public responsibility for child health (van Dyck 2003, 727). It also utilized a major method by which the federal government would create incentives for states to undertake certain activities: giving them money. The Sheppard-Towner Act had a visible and quantitative impact: "it supported 18,325 health conferences for mothers and babies, 2,978 permanent child health or diagnostic clinics (or both), 19,723 classes and the distribution of 21 million pieces of literature. More than four million infants and preschool children and approximately 700,000 pregnant women were served through the state programs" (Golden and Markel 2007, 447).

The bureau and the act were operating in a somewhat hostile environment. The bureau did not address child labor issues and avoided linking poverty and health status (Golden and Markel 2007).The law was repealed in 1928 after opposition by the Public Health Service, doctors, and the Catholic Church (van Dyck 2003).

The Great Depression created a window of opportunity for new social welfare legislation (Rushefsky 2007). Social Security and the welfare system (now Temporary Assistance to Needy Families) were created by the Social Security Act of 1935, the most important piece of social welfare legislation passed in the United States. Parts of the act addressed children's health needs. One part of the legislation created a grant program for pregnant women and children, especially crippled children. In the 1940s the Emergency Maternity Infant Care program created services for women and young children of low-ranking people in the military. Medicaid, enacted in 1965, has become a major source of health insurance for children. In the 1980s the Maternal and Child Health Services Block Grant combined a number of different programs. In the 1990s new programs, funded in large part by the federal government, focused on uninsured children and infant mortality issues (van Dyck 2003). The State Children's Health Insurance Program (SCHIP), passed in 1997, extended coverage to more lower income children.

More recent programs run through the Maternal and Child Health Bureau include a focus on reducing disparities in health care, emphasizing cultural competence, newborn screening, sudden infant death syndrome (SIDS), child care health and safety, emergency services, and working with families who have special needs children (van Dyck 2003).

Health Status/Outcomes

Halfon, DuPlessis, and Inkelas (2007) observe that in an important variety of ways the health of children in the United States is at its peak. Infant mortality rates have decreased significantly, the percentage of women having prenatal care has increased, and immunizations are widespread (Children's Defense Fund 2005; U.S. Department of Health and Human Services 2000). Having said that, they also find that while the more acute types of health issues have been reasonably successfully addressed, the more chronic ones have increased in prevalence. These include obesity, mental problems, developmental and speech problems in young children, and a variety of mental issues for school age children, such as attention deficit issues, behavioral problems, and learning problems.

The authors also find that the American health care system underperforms, with systemic problems such as "fragmented programs, disjointed and inadequate funding streams, inadequate performance monitoring, and the lack of a coherent planning framework" (Halfon, DuPlessis, and Inkelas 2007, 318). Further, the U.S. health

Table 6.1

Access and Quality Gaps in the Child Health System (in percent)

Access to Care

Children with special health care needs	12.6
Children without consistent health insurance coverage	14.9
Children who do not have a personal doctor or nurse	16.7

Quality of Care

Children with no preventive medical visit in previous year	22.2
Children with no preventive dental visit in previous year	28.0
Children ages 19–35 months receiving recommended series of vaccines	74.5
Children ages 12–18 years receiving needed mental health services	30.0

Source: U.S. Department of Health and Human Services (2005a,b).

care system underperforms compared to other countries. Here they are looking at such indicators as mental health problems, obesity, asthma, and infant mortality. There are significant disparities based on socioeconomic class, much greater than in other developed countries and, alarmingly, getting larger. In addition, the U.S. medical system is very much individual- rather than population-oriented and lacks, in opposition to developed countries, universal health coverage. Thus there are a variety of programs that cover children, those who have coverage, in the United States, public and private. Table 6.1 displays the gaps facing children in the U.S. health care system.

One important factor in understanding the health of the nation's children is the diversity within that demographic sector. According to the 1980 census, almost two-thirds of the country's children were white; the projection is that by the 2030 census that number will decrease to a little over 50 percent (Villarruel 2001). The fastest growing of the minority groups are Hispanics and Asians; most of the growth is native born, rather than immigrant; and Hispanics form the largest group of minority children (Villarruel 2001). Furthermore, the rate of uninsurance among immigrant children has been increasing (Parker and Teitelbaum 2003).

Obesity is a problem that is increasingly affecting children (as well as adults) (Homer and Simpson 2007). A study by Hedley et al. (2004) found alarming rates. Using data from the National Health and Nutrition Examination Survey (NHANES) from 1999 to 2002, they found that 16 percent of children six to nineteen were overweight and 31 percent were at risk for being overweight. For whites, a little under 14 percent were overweight and a little over 28 percent were at risk of being overweight. The numbers of blacks and Mexican Americans were, respectively, 20.5 percent and 35.4 percent for blacks and 22.0 percent and 39.9 percent for Mexican Americans (Hedley et al. 2004). The obesity numbers for adults is higher than for children. About 31 percent of adults are considered obese (Weight-Control Information Network n.d.). But obesity in children is of increasing concern.

Why is obesity a problem? According to the *Health People 2010* report, obesity can lead to a whole range of future health problems, including diabetes, cancer, heart disease, elevated blood pressure, and so forth. It is for that reason that reducing obesity is one of the major objectives of the report. The report notes that the prevalence of obesity has increased over the last forty years (U.S. Department of Health and Human Services 2000).

Another important health status indicator is infant mortality, which Starfield (2004, 165) observes is "the most common indicator of child health." Having stated that, the figures for the United States are not necessarily good. Twenty-four countries had lower infant mortality rates than the United States and the United States has had a slower decline in the rate than most of the developed countries (Children's Defense Fund 2005; Starfield 2004). According to the 2006 *State of the World's Mothers* (Save the Children 2006) report, the U.S. infant morality rate is two-and-a-half times higher than the Scandinavian countries, and three times higher than Japan's. Most of the problems of infant mortality in the United States are related to prematurity and low birth rate (see below) (Save the Children 2006). Interestingly, despite the relatively high infant mortality rate, the United States has more beds for neonates than other industrialized countries (Save the Children 2006). There are five major causes of infant deaths (Lohr 2007): birth defects, prematurity/low birth weight, sudden infant death syndrome, complications related to the pregnancy, and accidents and injuries.

Overall, infant mortality rates have decreased. However, for minority groups, this is not the case. The group with the highest infant mortality rate is blacks. Native American and Hispanics also experience high infant mortality rates, though there are variations within subgroups of these two ethnic populations (Lohr 2007; Villarruel 2001).

In April 2001, the Nebraska Governor's Blue Ribbon Panel on Infant Mortality issued a report that found that Nebraska's infant mortality rate was higher than the national average. More alarmingly, the report found that in the 1990–97 period, the infant mortality rate among blacks increased while the national average was decreasing ("Nebraska Makes Plans to Improve Infant Health" 2001).

Nebraska is hardly the only state with an infant mortality problem. Indeed, Southern states have the highest rates of infant mortality and some, such as Mississippi, have actually seen *increases* in the rate (Lohr 2007). Southern states have high rates of minorities and rural areas often lack providers (see Chapter 8) (Lohr 2007).

While infant mortality rates have generally declined, prematurity and low birth weights have increased (Alexander and Slay 2002). Survival of low birth weight babies have increased dramatically. (We should note here that both of Rushefsky's grandchildren were born premature, were in neonatal intensive care for weeks, and are progressing quite nicely.) Alexander and Slay (2002) offer a number of reasons for the increasing prematurity rates. These include more older mothers, more unmarried mothers, use of drugs and smoking, economic conditions, changes in reporting practices, increased use of ultrasound, increased number of multiple births, and increased use of reproductive technologies. Low birth weights vary by race. In 2004, 7 percent of white births were low birth weight, versus 6.7 percent for Hispanics (see Chapter 3 on the Hispanic paradox) and 13.4 percent for blacks (Annie E. Casey Foundation 2006).

Alexander and Slay (2002) distinguished between three types of risk factors. The first type are those that cannot be changed. These included previous prematurity or low birth weight deliveries, infertility problems, and gestational bleeding. The second set of factors are demographic, such as race, marital status, socioeconomic status, and environmental exposures. The third set are what they label as possibly changeable risk factors. These include smoking, use of illegal substances, weight gain, and diet.

There is some evidence that disparities in maternal and infant health have decreased a bit. Howell, Pettit, and Kingsley (2005) looked at four major metropolitan areas: Oakland, California; Marion County, Indiana; Denver, Colorado; and Cuyahoga County, Ohio. Using data from the National Neighborhood Indicators Partnership, they found declines in the teen birth rate, some declines in the prematurity rate, and declines in low birth weights and infant mortality. Interestingly, they found the declines highest in the most impoverished neighborhoods. Still the overall rates remain high. For whites, the infant mortality rate was 5.7 deaths per 1,000 live births, for Hispanics it was 5.8 percent, and for blacks it was 14.0 percent.

· Immunization is an area where there appears to be good news. Immunization rates are high and have increased for minority children, though there is still less immunization than is needed within minority communities (Villarruel 2001; U.S. Department of Health and Human Services 2000). Strine et al. (2003) found that immunization rates among American Indian and Alaskan Native children were lower than for the general population. Such children had risk factors such as being in lower socioeconomic families and have larger families. Nevertheless, the differences were small. Strine et al. (2003) attribute the better than expected immunization rate to trial health programs and Indian Health Service. Other programs that aided this group included the Vaccines for Children Program and the WIC program (the Women, Infants and Children program), the latter of which provides counseling as well nutritional assistance. They conclude (2048) that: "A precept of public health is the equitable distribution of preventive services benefits to all regardless of poverty, race/ethnicity, limited access, and so forth. The high immunization coverage estimates in a minority population with higher prevalence of several 'traditional' risk factors for underimmunization suggest that sufficiently targeted, community-based, culturally appropriate programs can affect racial/ethnic and other health disparities."

Hutchins, Jiles, and Bernier (2004) examine why disparities in measles vaccination were eliminated. They note first that there was a federal program created in 1963 to provide financial assistance to states, focusing especially on the polio vaccine. Early estimates of the disparities suggested gaps in the 12- to 26-percent range for a variety of vaccines, with a 14 percent gap for measles on average. The 1989–91 measles epidemic led to a renewed emphasis on vaccinations, which included target goals for specific preventable diseases. A dual strategy was developed. The first part was universal interventions. The second was targeted interventions aimed at specific sectors of the population. Table 6.2, from Hutchins, Jiles, and Bernier (2004), lists the interventions and their outcomes.

There are three observations to be made here. First, measles presents a public health problem in the sense that it is an epidemic. Second, it is easily preventable through a proven medical intervention. Third, and perhaps most important, is to examine Table 6.2 and all the interventions needed to deal with such a relatively easily treatable disease. Then think of what is needed to deal with more difficult problems that confront the health care system.

Of all the medical conditions affecting children, tooth decay (dental caries) is the most common, much more common than, say, asthma (Mouradian, Wehr, and Crall 2000). In the 1999–2002 period, 21.5 percent of children ages six to seventeen had untreated cavities. The percentage since the early 1970s has decreased. For eighteen to sixty-four-year-olds, the percentage was 23.8, also declining over the thirty year period (National Center for Health Statistics 2006).

One of the major problems with dentistry for children (pediatric dentistry), especially for low income children, is the availability of providers (Amschler 2003). Dentistry is one of the services provided for under Medicaid. However, it is perhaps the hardest service for eligible children to obtain. A 1997 study (cited in Lieberman and Paul 2002) found that inadequate reimbursement on the part of Medicaid was the single most important factor in refusal to provide services to Medicaid children. Paperwork, missed appointments, and limitations on covered services were also factors. A 1997 study found that fewer than 10 percent of the dentists in New York submitted reimbursement claims to Medicaid. As a result, fewer than half of Medicaid children receive dental services, and in some states the percentage drops to 30 percent (Lieberman and Paul 2002). Low income children in general have substantial unmet preventive dental needs (Kenney, McFeeters, and Yee 2005). When dentists can be found who will provide services to this population, their schedule is so busy that a year's wait for an appointment is not unusual.

The impacts of not having dental problems addressed are significant (Mouradian, Wehr, and Crall 2000). These include loss of school hours, restricted activity, and emergency room visits. Longer term impacts "include increased risk of premature labor and low birth weight in pregnant women with periodontal disease, and increased risk of cardiovascular disease and stroke in adults with periodontal disease (Mouradian, Wehr, and Crall 2000, 2626).

Mouradian, Wehr, and Crall (2000) estimate that routine dental care for children should constitute about 20 percent of the costs of health care. In the case of Med-

Table 6.2

Public Policy Interventions to Increase Vaccinations for Measles, 1989–2001

Intervention	Impact
Universal	
Second dose of measles vaccine	Reduced vaccine failures
Presidential priority	Increased attention and funding for childhood vaccinations
Increase funding for health departments	Strengthened immunization activities
Immunization action plans	Guided state immunization programs
Annual state survey of vaccine coverage	Measured state coverage of 19- to 35-month-old children
Extra funds for state immunization programs	Provided financial incentives for above-average performance
New standards for pediatric immunization practices	Improved vaccination services at the point of delivery
Quality improvement activities (AFIX) in clinics	Raised immunization coverage
Assessments of vaccine coverage (HEDIS) in MCOs	Stimulated improvements in coverage through measurement
State-based immunization registries of children	Tracked and measured vaccination status
State-based coalitions of organizations	Strengthened and extended existing immunization programs
Partnerships with national health organizations	Promoted and maintained immunizations as a priority
Research	Tested interventions/found reasons for low vaccine coverage
National public information campaign	Improved knowledge of the benefits of vaccination
Enforcement of laws/regulations for childcare centers	Achieved high vaccine coverage in childcare centers
Targeted	
Vaccines for children program	Entitled uninsured or underinsured children to free vaccine
Extra funding for urban-area health departments	Improved vaccine coverage for children in 28 urban areas
Annual assessment of vaccine coverage	Measured vaccine coverage in the same 28 urban areas
Local immunization action plans	Guided immunization programs in the 28 urban areas
Linkage of WIC and immunization activities	Screened 40 percent of all US births for immunization
Discounted vaccine prices for Medicaid programs	Enabled Medicaid programs to vaccinate
Higher reimbursement rates for Medicaid providers	Increased the number of Medicaid providers
Quality improvement (AFIX) in public clinics	Raised immunization coverage for low income children
More user-friendly hours for public clinics	enabled access to vaccination services of low income children
Partnerships with minority health organizations	Promoted and maintained immunizations as a priority
Special information campaigns	Improved knowledge of Spanish-speaking populations

Source: Hutchins, Jiles, and Bernier (2004, S147).

icaid, they point out, the actual numbers are 2 to 3 percent. A goal set in 2000 in the *Healthy People 2010* report was to lower the number of children with untreated cavities (Agency for Health Research and Quality 2005).

Mouradian, Wehr, and Crall (2000, 2628) point out that children with special health care needs (which can include those with Downs Syndrome, HIV, diabetes, and so forth) are at a particular risk if their dental needs are not taken care of: "The consequences from delays in access to oral care for children health care needs include postponed bone marrow and organ transplants, cardiac and other critical surgeries, failure to thrive, breathing difficulties, septicemia, brain abscesses, and other serious complications."

One of the major chronic diseases in childhood is asthma. Asthma is more serious for children than for adults and in many cases can be treated well with appropriate care (Akinbami and Schoendorf 2002). Using a variety of data sets available through the National Center for Health Statistics, Akinbami and Schoendorf (2002) find that the prevalence of asthma as well as asthma attacks among children increased in the 1980–2000 period. For example, the prevalence rate in 1980–81 was 36.8 per 1,000 children; in 1995–96 it was 68.6, an increase of over 86 percent (authors' calculations from Akinbami and Schoendorf 2002). Rates of physician visits, hospitalizations, and deaths due to asthma also increased during this period. Akinbami and Schoendorf (2002, 318) suggest that some of the increases may be due to what they called "diagnostic transfer," where other respiratory diseases were increasingly labeled as asthma. Another possible reason for the increases is environmental exposure, particularly in urban environments. But the evidence is mixed. Nevertheless, the increases in asthma are significant, though more recently they appear to have stabilized. The authors suggest that one reason for the plateauing is the increase in insurance coverage for children through the SCHIP program.

One rather large health category involves children with "special needs." Such children have chronic conditions (including those discussed above, but also including behavioral and emotional problems) that require help beyond that usually available to children (Campaign for Children's Health Care 2007). The Campaign for Children's Health Care (2007) estimates that 20 percent of families with children have at least one child that has special needs. This amounts to about 18.5 percent of all children, nearly 14 million children. More than half of these children did not receive the care that they needed because their families lacked health insurance. Some of these children live in families that have health insurance but the policies do not cover all the needs. These are the underinsured. Boys are more likely than girls to be in this category and older rather than younger children. About 40 percent of these children are covered by Medicaid or the State Children's Health Insurance Program (Campaign for Children's Health Care 2007).

Mental health is another area of inequalities among children. Children from minority groups and low income children have shown lower levels of academic success and lower cognitive functioning than majority children. While some, such as Herrnstein and Murray (1994), might argue that such differences are genetically based, Kramer, Allen, and Gergen (1995) found that children with less education, from lower income families, and from minority groups tended to do less well on cognitive tests. They also found that birth complications and health status sometimes were related to poorer performance on such tests.

An interesting inequality is in breastfeeding. Li and Grummer-Strawn (2002) point out that another goal of the *Healthy People 2010* report is to increase the rate of breastfeeding among mothers with small children (up to one year of age). Employing the Third National Health and Nutrition Examination Survey, they found that whites had more than twice as high a rate of breastfeeding as blacks or Mexican Americans. Their analysis also found that breastfeeding was lower among lower socioeconomic groups than for higher socioeconomic groups regardless of race or ethnicity.

Death due to injury is another area of disparities among children. Hussey (1997) points out that such deaths are the single most important cause of death for young people. She used the National Longitudinal Mortality Study combined with the National Death Index for the 1979–89 period (the most recent data at the time of her study). Hussey found that African American children had much higher levels of risk factors for death from injury than white children. These included living in a highly urbanized area, living in a female-headed family, low income, and low levels of education on the part of the head of household. She found that education and incomes were important homicide risk factors. The same was true of accidental injuries. Hussey suggests that changing the living environment of children through changes in parental behavior such as cessation of smoking, and smoke detectors, plus community prevention programs (such as violence prevention programs) could reduce deaths from injuries.

One important set of disparities concerns Latino children, the largest minority ethnic/racial group of children within the United States. Zambrana and Logie (2000) note that the Latino population in the United States is relatively young. About 35 percent of Latinos are under the age of eighteen, compared to 24 percent of whites. Flores et al. (2002) present a comprehensive discussion of Latino children's health. Their article is a summary of a report of the Latino Consortium of the American Academy of Pediatrics Center for Child Health Research. Flores et al. (2002, 83) write that "Latino children are a model population for evaluating effective approaches to improving the health of underserved and high-risk populations because they experience a disproportionate burden of health risk factors, morbidity, suboptimal health status, underuse of health services, impaired access to care, and health disparities." They also note that much about Latino children's health remains unknown because it has not been studied effectively.

Flores et al. (2002) then discuss a variety of health-related problems. There is a high risk of developmental and behavioral issues among Latino children (Zambrana and Logie 2000). Flores et al. (2002) cite studies that suggest that Latino children suffer from mental health problems at higher rates than whites or blacks, but are less likely to be hospitalized than either group for such problems. Mexican children in particular, and Latino children in general, suffer at higher rates than whites or blacks from dental problems (see also Burgos et al. 2005). They also find that Latino boys (first place) and Latino girls (second place) suffer from obesity. This is a major risk factor for diabetes.

Latino children have high rates of environmental-related diseases (Zambrana and Logie 2000). Thus asthma is prevalent at high rates among Latino children, especially Puerto Ricans. Flores et al. (2002) note that "Puerto Rican children have the highest prevalence of active asthma (11%) of any US ethnic-racial group of children, exceeding by far the prevalence for blacks (6%) and whites (3%), whereas active asthma is present in only 3% of Mexican American and 5% of Cuban American children." This is an appropriate place to note one of the major challenges in studying health care among Latino children (and Latinos in general). Latinos come from various places and there are differences in experiences between the different groups, such as the three major Latino groups mentioned here, Cuban, Mexican, and Puerto Rican.

Part of the reason for the exposure to environmental-related diseases among Latino children is their greater tendency to live in areas with environmental problems, such as landfills and toxic waste sites (Flores et al. 2002). Indeed, one interesting aspect of health disparities is a movement that combines concerns about environmental health and the civil rights movement, a movement known as environmental justice (see, for example, Bullard 2005). Flores et al. (2002) suggest that perhaps one reason for the disparities seen among Latinos is the greater exposure to environmental insults (for a discussion of environment and health see Patel and Rushefsky 2005).

An example of racial/ethnic disparities and the environment concerns lead (Children's Defense Fund 2005). This is more important for children than for adults. First, because adult body mass is much larger than that of small children, the same exposure will have a greater impact on children. Second, small children put everything they can find in their mouths. Third, lead exposure has an impact on mental and intellectual development. Lanphear, Weitzman, and Eberly (1996) found high levels of lead in the blood in black children as compared to white children. Their analysis found that housing conditions led to the greater exposure of black children. Black children were more likely to live in homes that had lead paint contamination. Dust in those homes was likely ingested by the children.

Research on Children's Health Problems

An important example of research on children's health problems is the Child Health Insurance Research Initiative (CHIRI). It began in 1999 by the Agency for Healthcare Research and Quality (AHRQ) of the U.S. Department of Health and Human Services (DHHS), the Health Resources and Services Administration (HRSA), and the David and Lucile Packard Foundation. The purpose of the program is to provide information for policy makers to help improve the quality of and access to health care services for low income children (Child Health Insurance Research Initiative 2007).

CHIRI has funded numerous studies, such as Brach et al. (2003) and Shone et al. (2003), on various aspects of SCHIP and other children's health programs.

Zambrana and Logie (2000) point out that the health of Latino children, especially subgroups, has been neglected. Much of the research has concentrated on the largest subgroup within the Latino community, Mexican Americans (Zambrana and Logie 2000).

Health Care Spending

Carasso, Steuerle, and Reynolds (2007) analyzed spending on children (not just on health care) in the federal government budget. Such spending ($333 billion) was about equal to 2.6 percent of the country's gross domestic product (GDP). By contrast, spending on the elderly equaled about 7.6 percent of GDP. Growth was faster in the elderly oriented programs. Social Security contains a cost of living provision, thus its spending goes up automatically (in addition to increases in the size of the eligible population). By contrast, spending on children usually increases when there are new programs. Even though much of federal spending for children has been geared to low income children, there is an interesting paradox. Real per capita spending on children for 2004 was $3,997 (again, looking at all programs, not just health); for the elderly the number was $19,405. Now compare the poverty rates in 2004: 13.1 percent for children and 6.8 percent for the elderly. Of course, one reason why the poverty rate for the elderly has decreased is because of federal programs such as Social Security and Medicare (see Chapter 7 and Rushefsky 2007). Considering only domestic spending, the share of federal spending for children has declined (Carasso, Steuerle, and Reynolds 2007). Carasso, Steuerle, and Reynolds (2007, 26) write that "despite frequent rhetoric from policymakers on the priority given to children, the federal budget makes fairly clear that children are less of a priority and more of an afterthought in the budget process."

Medicaid accounted for much of the growth in federal spending for children. In 2006, the federal portion of Medicaid spent on children was $40.8 billion and an additional $5.4 billion was spent through SCHIP (Carasso, Steuerle, and Reynolds 2007).

Pati, Keren, Alessandrini, and Schwarz (2004) examine the distribution of spending on social welfare programs by age groups. They found that more was spent on the elderly than on children: about $628 billion for the elderly versus $458 billion for children in 2000. Focusing on health care, public health programs for children (Medicaid, SCHIP, and Maternal and Child Health) cost about $28.5 billion versus about $219.5 billion (Medicare and Medicaid) for the elderly in 2000 (see also Meara, White, and Cutler 2004). An interesting comparison (using 2000 data) is that there are many more children (about 22 million) on Medicaid than elderly persons (4.6 million) (calculated from Patel and Rushefsky 2006 and Pati et al. 2004). There are about 4.8 times as many children as aged on Medicaid. But Medicaid spends over seven times as much per person on the elderly as it does on children. This does not count the large Medicare program established primarily for the aged. Pati et al. (2004) also note that the gap in spending between young and elderly increased from 1980 to 2000. There has also been some tendency for children to bear the brunt of cutbacks in spending during recessions, especially the two in the early 1980s and 1990s. The major reason for the gap in social welfare spending between the young and the elderly is the higher medical spending for the latter group (Pati et al. 2004).

Access to Health Care

There are health care disparities in access to health care, as Table 6.3 shows. The access of children to health care depends in large part on the presence of health insurance. Here is one area where children are advantaged. In 2004, 11.2 percent of those under the age of eighteen lacked insurance, compared to 15.4 percent of the total population (U.S. Bureau of the Census 2007). This understates the difference because the uninsurance rate among the elderly is very small (see Chapter 7).

Lack of insurance is particularly important when a child gets sick. According to a Families USA report (Sullivan and Stoll 2007, 8), "uninsured children have drastically different outcomes than insured children when hospitalized for severe, yet common, medical conditions. Differences in treatment, outcomes and discharge to rehabilitative care suggest that parents and physicians may be making unavoidable, tough choices about treatment for uninsured children. Sadly, elevated mortality rates for uninsured children mean that these choices can have tragic consequences."

For example, uninsured children with traumatic brain injury suffered twice the mortality rate as insured children and are much less likely to be released to rehabilitative care than insured children. The Families USA report presents data with similar findings for children suffering from general injuries, appendicitis, and ear infections (Sullivan and Stoll 2007).

Flores, Abreu, and Tomany-Korman (2006) find that Latino children have the lowest rate of insurance coverage (see also Zambrana and Logie 2000). They conducted a series of interviews with Latino parents in urban areas and found that it was not the ethnicity itself that was responsible for the low coverage for children. Rather, it was the high presence of the risk factors, for lack of insurance including citizenship status, low income, and having an older child.

Amschler (2003) notes that many of these children have dental care insurance through Medicaid or SCHIP. However, there is a shortage of dentists willing to provide services to this population (Mouradian, Wehr, and Crall 2000). Amschler (2003) also notes that part of the problem is a lack of demand for services on the part of this population. Those with less education may not be aware of the impor-

Table 6.3

Disparities in Child Health Care

	Race/Ethnicity			
	African American	Hispanic	White	All
Children with no preventive medical visit in previous year (%)	19.5	28.6	20.8	22.2
Children with no preventive dental visit in previous year (%)	33.6	39.1	23.0	28.0
Infant mortality rate (deaths per 1,000 live births)	14.1	5.9	5.8	6.9

	Family Income		
	<100% of poverty level*	≥400% of poverty level*	All
Children having both medical and dental preventive visits in previous year (%)	48.3	69.3	58.8
Children with moderate or severe health conditions (%)	11.4	5.7	7.9

Source: U.S. Department of Health and Human Services (2005a,b).
*The federal poverty level was equal to $18,400 for a family of four in 2003.

tance of taking care of the problem. Or they may not be aware that they qualify for public programs (Amschler 2003).

One possible contribution to relieving this problem and the disparities is to make use of school-based clinics. Cavities are easily treatable and preventive treatments exist that school-based services can use (Amschler 2003). In many ways, dental problems should be among the easiest to reduce. Yet children in low income families have much greater untreated dental needs than more affluent children. Minority children and poor children are also less likely to see a dental provider than more affluent children (Mouradian, Wehr, and Crall 2000).

While the percentage of childhood immunizations has increased, there are disparities in how well that has been done. Employing the National Immunization Survey, Chu, Barker, and Smith (2004) looked at immunization rates among young children in the 1996–2001 period. They found that the gap in immunization rates between whites and blacks and whites and Hispanics increased over the period, though it decreased between whites and Asians.

Specialty health care services also show disparities in access. Wang et al. (2004) sent questionnaires to otolaryngologists in Southern California. Most of the respondents said that they would not see children on California's Medicaid program, MediCal. The reasons for this low willingness to provide services to this portion of the population include burdensome paperwork and low reimbursements for services (both surgical and office).

An important problem associated with the health of Latinos, one that is difficult to research, is migrant children. Nearly all of the estimated one million migrant children in the United States are Latino (Flores et al. 2002). They suffer from even more problems than Latino children in general.

> These children receive inadequate preventive care; experience high rates of infectious diseases, including tuberculosis, parasites, and sexually transmitted diseases; have inadequate preparation for school entry and low rates of school completion; have impaired access to appropriate day care, forcing parents to bring them to the fields, where they have increased risks of pesticide exposures and injuries; work as farm laborers often in unsafe working conditions; and are at risk for nutritional disorders, such as anemia, diabetes, failure to thrive, and obesity. (Flores et al. 2002, 86)

Further, because of their less than permanent residence, it is difficult for them to become eligible for and receive benefits from SCHIP and Medicaid. Also because many of the children are from undocumented families, they are often not eligible for these programs (Flores et al. 2002).

Addressing Health Care Access Disparities

A variety of programs have addressed the issue of children's health and inequality. At the federal level, the Minority Health and Health Disparities Research and Development Act of 2000 set up the National Center on Minority Health and Health Disparities. The center has funded research in this area. The Closing the Health Gap Campaign was an initiative of Health and Human Services in 2001 (Beal 2004).

While most people who have insurance get it through an employer, that source of insurance, particularly for children, has declined as premiums continue to rise and companies try to reduce their costs either by shedding insurance entirely or shifting some (or all) of the costs to the employees (see Hacker 2006). The two large public programs discussed below, Medicaid and the State Children's Health Insurance Program, have filled in the void left by a lack of private insurance. Thus the proportion of insured children has stayed about the same, though the payer has shifted. These programs have truly been safety net programs for children (Zuckerman and Cook 2006).

Beal (2004, 172), however, observes that there is a "disparity in disparities" in the sense that there is much less research done on disparities among children than among adults. A literature review by the Institute of Medicine found fewer than 5 percent of studies focused directly on disparities among children (Beal 2004).

Medicaid

The most significant public program that provides health care for children is Medicaid. Sixty-five percent of children covered by a public health care program are enrolled in Medicaid, as compared to 35 percent covered by the State Children's Health Insurance Program (discussed below). In addition, there has been a shift in coverage by source since 1997 (Dubay et al. 2007). While about the same percentage of children had health insurance coverage in 1997 (74.3 percent) as in 2005 (77.1 percent), public programs have covered an increasing number of children. In 1997, 18.7 percent of all children were covered by public programs; by 2005 that number had increased to 27 percent. At the same time, private coverage of children declined from 64 percent in 1997 to 59.4 percent in 2005. The changes were most dramatic for lower income children (Dubay et al. 2007). This has been called crowding out, but Dubay et al. (2007) find that the major reasons for the shift have been premium increases and economic distress. Medicaid covers about 25 percent of children in the United States and a substantial proportion of births (Rosenbaum and Wise 2007).

One important feature of Medicaid, added in 1967, was the Early and Periodic Screening, Diagnosis and Treatment (EPSDT) program. Its purpose is to prevent health problems that were especially prevalent among low income children (Rosenbaum and Wise 2007). Rosenbaum and Wise (2007, 384) state the importance of EPSDT:

> This effort to articulate principles of financing that support a child development standard of care has never been equaled in other forms of health insurance. . . . The capacity to prevent many traditional threats to child health—particularly from acute infectious diseases—coupled with progress in screening for developmental and other disorders, have greatly intensified both the cadence and the context of early preventive services for children.
>
> Furthermore, the major reduction in acute illness among children has dramatically elevated the relative importance of treating chronic diseases and developmental conditions such as cystic fibrosis, asthma, sickle cell disease, and autism. These trends not only underscore the importance of screening, but also greatly increase the impact of organized, regionalized pediatric specialty care systems.

Despite the successes, there have been attempts, some successful, dating back to the Nixon administration and including the Clinton and George W. Bush administrations, to cut back on the screening program (Rosenbaum and Wise 2007). States were calling for the repeal of the program and administrations granted waivers. The Deficit Reduction Act of 2005 downgraded EPSDT as the standard of child health care.

Medicaid is also an important provider of services for children in the foster care system (Geen, Sommers, and Cohen 2005). There are over 800,000 children in foster care across the country at any given time. As Geen, Sommers, and Cohen (2005) point out, most of those children have suffered some sort of abuse (physical, mental, emotional, sexual) and have significant health care issues. However, many of those children do not receive the services necessary and required in many cases (about 30 percent of the cases) (Geen, Sommers, and Cohen 2005). On the other hand, foster care children account for a disproportionate amount of Medicaid spending. In 2001, Medicaid spent about $3.8 billion for a variety of services for foster care children; this amounts to $4,336 per foster child enrollee. Interestingly, states spent on average more per white child than for either black (22 percent) or Hispanic children (20 percent) (Geen, Sommers, and Cohen 2005; percentage calculations by authors). Medicaid spending on foster care children also differs dramatically by state. Arizona spends the least per foster care child, $1,309; Maine the most, $19,408. Average Medicaid spending per foster care child was $4,336 (all numbers are from 2001) (Geen, Somers, and Cohen 2005; for a discussion of fiscal disparities among the states, see Qiao 1999).

Children on Medicaid tend to have poorer health than those with private employer-based insurance or even those without any insurance. Medicaid and SCHIP cover about 28 percent of all children, yet about 58 percent of children on these public programs are described as in poor or fair health, about 47 percent have some type of activity limitation, and nearly 34 percent have special health care needs (Dubay et al. 2007).

Medicaid faces a number of issues over the next ten years or so. First, there are still a large number of children without any health insurance who are eligible for Medicaid (over four million) (Dubay et al. 2007). Fiscal issues (the high cost of Medicaid to the states) will limit outreach. Furthermore, the new citizenship requirement is a barrier to outreach (Dubay et al. 2007). There are also participation issues. Because Medicaid reimbursement is lower than either private insurance or Medicare, providers are reluctant to take on Medicaid patients. This is most obvious in the case of dental care, perhaps the greatest unmet need among this population.

A major problem with Medicaid is that there is instability in its coverage, one that has been increasing in recent years (Fairbrother, Emerson, and Partridge 2007). The major source of instability is that Medicaid is means-tested. That is, as we have seen above, there are income requirements for becoming and remaining eligible for the program. Those limits have changed over the years (see the discussion in Patel and Rushefsky 2006), in many cases increasing and more recently decreasing. Further, changes made by states have required more frequent documentation of eligibility on the part of Medicaid recipients. "There is inherent tension between targeting of funds [to make sure that the appropriate target groups and not others receive service] and ensuring continuity" (Fairbrother, Emerson, and Partridge 2007, 520).

Fairbrother, Emerson, and Partridge (2007) estimate that between 16 and 41 percent of children experience some gap in coverage, even if the gaps are fairly small. The authors note that instability in coverage causes several problems. The first and most important is that children who experience gaps in their coverage also experience less access to the health care system. They might not get all their medications and might miss out on prevention programs. Second, the continuing requirement to establish eligibility creates a tremendous amount of paperwork, which increases the administrative costs of Medicaid and SCHIP and makes them less efficient than otherwise. Third, quality of care might be impinged.

Another, related, problem is retention. Studies have shown that less than half of children on Medicaid stayed on Medicaid for an entire year. Some studies have shown the retention rate over a two-year period to be as low as 16 percent. States that have separate SCHIP programs have lower retention rates than combined Medicaid/SCHIP programs (see below) (Howell, Palmer, and Miller 2006).

One important concern is the relationship between welfare and Medicaid/SCHIP (both discussed below). The federal welfare program originated with the 1935 Social Security Act. (For a discussion of this legislation and welfare policies in general, see Rushefsky 2007). In 1965, Medicaid was created (along with Medicare; see Chapter 7) as an amendment to the 1935 act. SCHIP was added in 1997. But in 1996, welfare policy was reformed. The Work Opportunities and Personal Responsibility Reconciliation Act replaced Aid to Families with Dependent Children (AFDC) with Temporary Assistance to Needy Families (TANF).

As mentioned in Chapter 5, apart from the fundamental change in welfare policies, the 1996 legislation broke the linkage between welfare and Medicaid. Prior to 1996, those people enrolled under AFDC were automatically enrolled in Medicaid. After 1996 that was not the case. Not all applicants were told that they might be eligible for Medicaid even if they were turned down for welfare. And a substantial portion of this population did not know that they could apply for Medicaid without being on welfare (Lambrew 2007).

State Children's Health Insurance Program

One of the most important additions to child health care programs is the State Children's Health Insurance Program or SCHIP (sometimes referred to as S-CHIP or CHIP). It has its origins in the debates over health care in the early and mid-1990s. (For a discussion of health care policy in the 1990s, see Rushefsky and Patel 1998). President Clinton proposed the Health Security Act in 1993, but it never came to a vote in either house of Congress. Furthermore, partially as a result of the failure of the Clinton plan, Republicans gained complete control of the Congress for the first time in forty years. Following that came a series of battles about budget and social policy between the Republican Congress and the Democratic president. Out of these battles came SCHIP. SCHIP was added as Title XXI of the Social Security Act as part of the Balanced Budget Act of 1997. (For a discussion of the 1997 budget legislation, see Palazzolo 1999; for an extended discussion of the history of SCHIP, see Lambrew 2007).

SCHIP provides block grants to states, more generous (what is called an "enhanced match"; see Ryan 2007) than for Medicaid, to pay for medical services for uninsured children. States had the option of using the funds directly for Medicaid, setting up a separate program, or combining the two. Nineteen states chose to use Medicaid, fourteen states established separate programs, and the remaining thirteen states used combination programs (calculated from Patel and Rushefsky 2006). Forty-two states allowed children in families at or above 200 percent of the poverty line to participate in the program (Kenney and Yee 2007). About six million children are enrolled in SCHIP at some point during the year, which amounts to a little less than 8 percent of all children. Of those children who are eligible for the program, about 29 percent are actually in it (Kenney and Yee 2007). Enrollment in SCHIP has leveled off at the six million children figure, though some states such as Texas and Florida saw steep declines (Kenney and Yee 2007). For example, Texas saw a 10.1 percent decrease in SCHIP enrollment from 2001 to 2006 and Florida a 5.1 percent decrease. The largest percentage decrease was in the authors' home state of Missouri. The decline during this period was 34.8 percent (Smith et al. 2007). In actual numbers of children, Texas and Florida led the way.

The declines in enrollment in these states were policy related, that is, deliberate. For Texas, new policy required income verification every six months versus the old policy of every year. There were also problems with the consolidation of Medicaid and SCHIP under a single contractor. For Missouri, there were premiums for some SCHIP eligible families and "the end of presumptive eligibility for children in families between 150 and 225 percent of the federal poverty line (FPL)" (Smith et al. 2007, 10). In the case of Florida, there was a limit or cap placed on SCHIP enrollment and new requirements for proving new and continued eligibility (Smith et al. 2007). In later years, as the economy began to recover from the 2001 recession and state budgets saw surpluses, some of the states, such as Florida, reversed some of their policies (see Hill, Courtot, and Sullivan 2005). Another factor in declines and leveling off of SCHIP enrollment was the Deficit Reduction Act of 2005, which required proof of citizenship (Smith et al. 2007).

SCHIP contributed to the decline in uninsurance rates for children, especially for minority children (Kenney and Yee 2007). More children were covered under both SCHIP and Medicaid, which, Kenney and Yee (2007) suggest, meant that outreach programs were working.

Brach et al. (2003) observe that SCHIP was originally designed for children whose parents worked but did not have health insurance. They investigated who were the actual beneficiaries of the new program. They found that most of the children resided in families with income equal to or less than 150 percent of the federal poverty line. Many lived in single-parent families. Most parents of SCHIP children had limited education. Most children lived in families with at least one working parent and many with two working parents (see also Shone et al. 2003). Additionally, there was little crowding out. That is, most children who enrolled in SCHIP were not previously covered by private, employer-based insurance (Kenney and Yee 2007; Lambrew 2007; Sommers et al. 2007).

SCHIP has improved access to the health care system for enrolled children, especially children with chronic health care needs. At the same time, the impact of SCHIP on children's health is unclear (Kenney and Yee 2007).

Brach et al. (2003) found that most of the SCHIP children had a regular doctor. They summarize their findings about the needs of SCHIP children:

These findings suggest that SCHIP tends to enroll a population of children who were already connected to some degree with the health care system and were not predominantly disenfranchised children who lacked prior contact with the health care system. Nevertheless, a high proportion of all SCHIP enrollees . . . reported some kind of unmet health care need during the year before SCHIP. These included unmet needs for mental health care, specialty care, dental and vision care, and prescription medicines. (Brach et al. 2003, e502)

Brach et al. (2003) then focus on three subgroups. The first is children with special health care needs (CSHCN). Such children had a higher proportion of unmet needs than other children and made greater use of emergency and mental health services than other children. The second group consists of Blacks and Hispanics. They were highly represented among SCHIP, but differed from white children in having lower incomes (though all such children had low incomes), more single parent families, and poorer health (see also Shone et al. 2003). The third group is adolescents. Here the problem was risk behaviors on the part of this group and whether they received services to help prevent those behaviors. Males tended to get a bit fewer services, but in general those who exhibited such behaviors did receive services. In general, SCHIP appears to be serving the group it was intended for (Brach et al. 2003).

Brach et al. make several recommendations. First, they suggest that the stand-alone SCHIP programs have tended to resemble commercial insurance programs, accompanied with the kinds of limitations on services and benefits found in commercial programs. Such limitations are not allowed in Medicaid and need to be addressed. Second, there needs to be a broad range of provider networks, particularly given the diverse populations and needs of SCHIP children and their various developmental stages. Third, outreach programs need to be enhanced so as to increase the enrolled population targeted by SCHIP. The fourth recommendation is to increase the oversight of the quality of care for especially vulnerable populations.

SCHIP does face important issues. It was up for reauthorization in 2007. There is a dispute between the states and the federal government over SCHIP funding (involving whether states have used all of their funds). Thus the level of federal SCHIP funding is questionable. If federal funding does not increase above the baseline (about $5 billion a year), then states would have difficulty expanding the reach of SCHIP (Kenney and Yee 2007). It is not clear where extra federal funding would come from. Additionally, most states have spent more than their yearly allotments, creating shortfalls. There is also about $6 billion in federal SCHIP funding that has yet to be spent by states (Kenney and Yee 2007). If the federal government does not raise its spending ($5 billion a year), it is estimated that some two million children could lose coverage (Lambrew 2007).

A second important issue is participation. About two-thirds of the targeted children are participating in SCHIP. But barriers to enrollment, as have been enacted in states such as Florida, Missouri, and Texas, do affect enrollment. Kenney and Yee (2007) note that there are even more children eligible for Medicaid than for SCHIP, but because SCHIP reimbursements are higher than Medicaid, states may not make the effort to reach them. One of the issues related to reauthorization is whether to enhance participation by reaching out to eligible but uninsured children and by bringing higher income children into the program (Lambrew 2007).

Using the Medical Expenditures Panel Survey for 1996–2005, with a particular emphasis on the years 2001–5 (the period after the expansions of Medicaid and the creation of SCHIP), Hudson and Selden (2007) found that public coverage of children has increased and private coverage has decreased. It should be noted, because it has become part of the debate over SCHIP reauthorization, that there is an interest in the direction of the relationship. If public programs expanded and in response employer-provided insurance declined as a result, there is one set of implications. However, the decline in employer-provided insurance predates much of the 1990s expansions and the public programs grew in response.

The authors looked at three sets of children: those who were uninsured but eligible for public programs, those who would be eligible if the threshold for eligibility were raised ("expansion"), and those who would lose eligibility if the thresholds were lowered ("rollback"). Those in the first group, uninsured eligibles, were more likely to be Hispanic, older, in better health, have a single parent, and parents who did not have a job than the overall child population. Children in the "expansion" group tended to live in families with at least one full-time worker. The "rollback" group tended to be younger, Hispanic, in poorer health, and have a parent who worked full time (Hudson and Selden 2007).

A third issue involves the kind of care delivered and the benefit structure. Kenney and Yee (2007) note that much less attention has been paid to these issues than to participation. Despite these problems, Kenney and Yee (2007) conclude that SCHIP has been a success though changes are necessary to increase enrollment and reduce barriers.

Shone et al. (2003) found much the same results as Brach et al. (2003). Additionally, they point out that having insurance is not the same as having access to the health care system and that disparities among groups remained.

While public programs have reduced the number and percentage of uninsured children, there are still substantial numbers of those children. In 2005, some nine million children were uninsured and the rate had increased (Lambrew 2007). Part of the problem is that states are trying to cut back on spending on Medicaid and SCHIP. One of the barriers states have erected is income verification and paperwork requirements. Failure to fill out paperwork correctly can lead to ineligibility. Lambrew (2007) cites a study that in Washington State the overwhelming majority of children who lost coverage because of paperwork issues were in fact eligible for SCHIP. The state has since eased its requirements, but barriers remain.

School-Based Health Care

Another important source of health care for children is the public school system. It is an important source of mental health care for children, its public health focus has increased the immunization rate for children (because it is a requirement for enrollment), and it can also be used to address such children's health care issues as obesity (Lear 2007). A 2003 commission established by President Bush called for greater use of school-based health services for mental care (Lear 2007). Another factor emphasizing school-based health care is the No Child Left Behind Legislation (NCLB). NCLB focuses on improving student outcomes based on scores on standardized tests and provides a series of incentives (mostly negative, see Nichols and Berliner 2007) to achieve that goal. If poor health care, including mental problems, lack of insurance and access, and obesity, leads to poor test outcomes, then schools have an incentive to alleviate those problems (Lear 2007). Despite all these uses of the public education system for health purposes, Lear (2007, 410) describes it as a "'hidden system' of health care": "It is not operated by mainstream health care organizations. It is not commonly reimbursed by third-party payers, and its ways of doing business are rarely scrutinized in major health services research journals." Schools have a diverse set of health care providers and the number is growing: school nurses, health centers, counselors, psychologists, social workers, dental providers, physicians, HIV/AIDS counselors, and so forth (Lear 2007). Over $10 billion a year is spent on these programs. Much of the funding for these programs comes from local school district budgets, which are based on property taxes and state grants. Some states have provided additional funding for school-based health care programs. Federal support comes largely from Medicaid. About $2.3 billion for these programs comes from Medicaid (federal and state) (Lear 2007).

School-based health care programs face a number of issues. One is that the emphasis on achieving the goals under No Child Left Behind creates competition for education dollars. The high-stakes testing that NCLB emphasizes means that other programs, not just health care, get a secondary position (Nichols and Berliner 2007). A second issue is that, as with much of the health care system, fragmentation characterizes the financing and delivering of services. The question is, who is in charge? (Lear 2007). There are also questions as to who will continue to pay for these services, and there is political controversy over some of the services. Conservative groups in particular raise issues such as whether there will be counseling about reproduction and possible invasions of privacy from mental health services.

School-based health care programs represent one way to address the disparities in health care (and education) among America's children. The services are more likely to be used by low income and minority children than by higher income and white children. Much more attention needs to be paid to this "hidden" sector of the health care system. In a similar vein, Medicaid can be used to improve the health of children, and thus their readiness for school, through prevention programs such as EPSDT, mentioned above (Schor, Abrams, and Shea 2007).

Quality of Health Care

Beal (2004) finds that the quality of care that children receive may depend on their race or ethnicity. Black and Hispanic children may not get as good a quality of care as white children. She writes that some of this may be due to bias and poor care on the part of doctors, but that it may also be because of the nature of the larger system. She notes that Medicaid provider reimbursement is lower than for either Medicare or privately insured patients. This accounts for the lack of providers, say in dentistry, willing to take on Medicaid patients. There also tends to be underfunding. Beal (2004, 175) notes that the "interpersonal aspects of care" need improvement. This includes cross-cultural training of providers.

As noted above, asthma is an important childhood disease. As with other diseases, there are disparities among different groups. African American children appear to have a much higher incidence than whites. This appears to be especially true for attacks and deaths due to asthma. Akinbami and Schoendorf (2002) note that even when children do have a regular source of care, the quality of care is often less for black children than for white. Black children have lower quality of care and are less likely to have continued care for their asthma. They are also less likely to have appropriate therapies prescribed for them. Akinbami and Schoendorf (2002, 320) write that "some studies suggest that after adjusting for severity of disease, even greater disparities in health care utilization exist between poor and nonpoor children and between black and white children."

Mental health needs for children also show disparities in treatment. Kataoka, Zhang, and Wells (2002) looked at data from three national surveys for the 1996–98 period. Almost 80 percent of children who needed mental health services do not obtain them. The groups least likely to receive such services were those without insurance and Latino children. For children with unmet mental health needs, the risks of poor outcomes later in life increase. These include failure to find consistent work, depression, substance abuse, school failure, and suicide. Kataoka, Zhang, and Wells (2002) state that for Latino children, the unmet needs are even more consequential. Studies show that Latino children have higher rates of these poor outcomes than white children. They suggest that language and financial barriers play a role in the lack of mental health services.

Flores, Abreu, and Tomany-Korman (2006) note that even when Latinos receive health care services, the quality of the services they receive is often lower than for whites and blacks. For example, Latino children with gastroenteritis had fewer diagnostic exams than whites or blacks; those with asthma were much less likely than whites or blacks to receive nebulizers.

Possible Explanations for Health Care Disparities

As noted in other chapters, race, ethnicity, and income make a difference in health insurance coverage as well as health status. White children tend to have the highest coverage rates, with black, Hispanic, and Native American children having lower coverage rates (Schwartz, Hoffman, and Cook 2007). Another aspect is citizenship status. Children who are resident in the United States but not citizens tend to have higher uninsurance rates than children who are citizens. This is due to having lower incomes and also because they are not eligible for services (Schwartz, Hoffman, and Cook 2007).

Another aspect, to be discussed further in Chapter 8, is geographical distribution of insurance coverage. Children living in the southern states and to a lesser extent western states, tend to have higher rates of uninsurance than children in the Midwest or Northeast (Schwartz, Hoffman, and Cook 2007).

Pati et al. (2004) point out that social welfare spending on children is much lower in the United States than in most other countries. They also find that while the poverty rate among the elderly declined in the 1980–2000 period that they studied, children experienced more ups and downs. However, what is clear is that children (less than eighteen years of age) have the highest poverty rate of any age group (17.6 percent in 2005) and make up nearly 35 percent of those in poverty, though only about a quarter of the population is poor. Furthermore, poverty among children depends on the circumstances of their family structure. Female-headed families experience considerably higher poverty rates than two-parent families (or male-headed families) and young children in female-headed families experience a very high poverty rate, almost 53 percent (DeNavas-Walt, Proctor, and Lee 2006). As the Children's Defense Fund (2005, 33; see also U.S. Department of Health and Human Services 2000) notes, "health is strongly correlated with income."

This can be clearly seen in the statistics. We have previously shown disparities among whites, blacks, and Hispanics, such as in low birth weights/prematurity and infant mortality. Now consider the following. Eleven percent of white children are in impoverished families, compared to 29 percent of Hispanic children and 36 percent of black children. Twenty-seven percent of white children live in families where there is no full-time year-round worker, compared to 39 percent of Hispanics and 59 of blacks (Annie E. Casey Foundation 2006).

Patel (2001) points out that children living in poverty-stricken families are less likely to have health insurance than children in wealthier families. This takes into account Medicaid and SCHIP. Some families may not be aware that their children are eligible for these programs. Additionally, the income thresholds for Medicaid (less so for SCHIP) are below the poverty line. For non-working families, the average income threshold for Medicaid eligibility is 42 percent of the federal poverty line; for working families it is 65 percent (Henry J. Kaiser Family Foundation 2007). Bramlett and Blumberg (2007) find that children in two-parent families had better mental and physical health than children in other types of families. The one exception they find is that children in father-only families did as well as children in any other type of family.

Currie and Lin (2007) explore the relationship between income and the health of children using the National Health Interview Survey (NHIS) from 2001 to 2005. They estimate that a little under 19 percent of children, about 8.3 million, were poor. About 30 percent of those children were considered by their mothers to be in excellent or good health (compared to almost 87 percent of non-poor children). The rate of low birth weight was higher for the poor than for the non-poor. Poor children had higher incidences of chronic conditions such as asthma and mental conditions. Currie and Lin found that asthma, though not other chronic conditions, had a greater effect on poor children than on non-poor children.

A study by Alaimo et al. (2001) found that in the 1988–94 period, about 15 percent of children in low income families suffered food deprivation. Of course the usual factors were also present: low insurance rates, low education for head of household, lack of a regular physician, and so forth. They also had more health problems, such as ear infections and stomachaches. Alaimo et al. (2001) make two interesting findings. The first is that food-deprived children tend to have more health problems than food-sufficient children. The second is worth quoting: "Although food insufficiency disproportionately affects minority children and children living in single-parent families, the majority of food-insufficient children are non-Hispanic White, live in 2-parent families, and have at least one parent who is working" (Alaimo et al. 2001, 784).

Chu, Barker, and Smith (2004) offer several reasons for immunization disparities. These include lack of primary care (what they call fragmented care, including heavy reliance on emergency rooms), distrust of the health care system, and misunderstandings about benefits and risks of immunizations. They note that linking WIC vouchers with immunization information tends to improve the immunization rate among minorities.

Dovey et al. (2003) explore what they call the "ecology of medical care for children." To do so, they used the 1996 Medical Expenditure Panel Survey (MEPS). They found that medical care for children generally showed the same characteristics as that for adults, despite their expectations to the contrary. This was so because children had fewer chronic conditions than adults. They did find that the usual socioeconomic characteristics affected the use of medical services. They noted that this affected the use of physician services in the office more than other places for delivering medical services. Poverty, lack of insurance, ethnic minority status, lack of a family doctor, and having a head of household with limited education were related to lesser use of such services (Children's Defense Fund 2006). The same was true for insurance status (Patel 2001). Of course, one important inequality is insurance status. White children have higher insurance rates than minority children and higher income children have higher insurance rates than lower income children (Agency for Health Research and Quality 2005).

One interesting finding is that even if one accounted for insurance and socioeconomic status, there would still be disparities attributable to minority status (Children's Defense Fund 2005). There are several possible explanations for this. One, simply, is the history of discrimination in the United States, which particularly affects blacks. Blacks were systematically denied access to good housing and jobs and medical care (prior to the advent of the civil rights movement and the legislation it engendered). The Tuskegee medical experiments that began in the 1930s and continued into the 1970s, where black males who suffered from syphilis were observed but not treated (or told they had the health condition) even after cures were developed, created a sense of mistrust in the black community that partially explains some theories about AIDS and the reluctance to deal with it. Cultural and language barriers and the lack of sufficient minority health providers, especially surgeons, also contribute to the presence of disparities (Children's Defense Fund 2006).

Flores et al. (2002) examined the reasons for inequalities for the Latino population. They identify twenty-two such barriers to the health care system. These include some of the things mentioned above, such as lack of insurance, a regular physician, and poverty. They also include barriers to get to health care providers (transportation), and cultural and language issues.

Starfield (2004) examines why the health of U.S. children is poorer than that of children in other countries. She rules out two explanations. The first is the idea that the United States has a much more diverse population than say Sweden or Norway. Starfield points out that those countries are increasingly diverse as well. The second explanation ruled out is that Americans engage in riskier behaviors than people in other countries. Starfield notes that drinking and smoking rates are lower in the United States than elsewhere.

A third possible explanation is that there is more economic inequality in the United States than in other industrialized countries. Starfield (2004) states that such inequality is an important factor within the United States but less in other countries. A fourth possibility is that the United States has a relatively stingy social welfare policy compared to other countries (see Hacker 2002; 2006). As Starfield (2004) points out, the United States lacks a universal health insurance plan.

Conclusions

> The elimination of child health care disparities will require multiple interventions from various sectors in the health care system. (Beal 2004, 176)

> It is in the national interest to have healthy children. Healthy children are more ready and able to learn and, in the longer term, are more likely to become healthy adults who will contribute as a productive citizenry and workforce to the continued vitality of society. (Committee on Evaluation of Children's Health 2004, 1)

The health of the nation's children has improved over the years. At one time infections were the major cause of child morbidity and mortality. In a sense, those health issues, acute cases, were relatively easy to address. Identify the germ (or virus) and develop appropriate treatments, including an emphasis on antisepsis and development of antibiotics and vaccines. Further, public health efforts had a dramatic effect on children's health. These include such efforts as sanitation, pasteurization of milk, the opening of neighborhood clinics, and so forth (Markel and Golden 2004; see also the time line from the Maternal and Child Health Bureau n.d.).

More recently, however, the major problems have been chronic: diabetes, asthma, obesity, lack of insurance coverage, and lack of care (Committee on Evaluation of Children's Health 2004). The causes for this are many and varied.

Koplan and Fleming (2000), both of whom work at the Centers for Disease Control and Prevention (CDC), point to ten challenges facing public health. One is to eliminate the health disparities that we discuss throughout this book. A second is concentrate on the intellectual and emotional development of children. A third is to address the growing (no pun intended) obesity problem among children. A fourth, and related to the previous one, is to put more emphasis on exercise and proper eating. A fifth is enhanced concentration on mental health.

A major emerging issue related to the health care of children is the growing competition for health care resources. This manifests itself in two ways. First, health care costs in the United States continue to grow faster than the economy. This affects public and private programs. The cost increases lead those who pay for the care, particularly employers and governments (federal, state, and local), to look for ways to alleviate them. So the pressure exists not to expand programs at a time when the health care needs of children are increasing.

Second is the competition for dollars between children and the elderly, what is sometimes called the "Silver Tsunami" (Haflon, DuPlessis, and Inkelas 2007, 319). The baby boomer generation will be entering their elder years beginning in the late 2000s and early 2010s and, as we have already seen, they cost considerably more to care for than children. One difference between children and the elderly is that the elderly are a powerful political constituency that votes at a high rate. We can see this issue in Medicaid, where the spending on the elderly, a small proportion of the Medicaid population, is significantly larger than for children, a much larger proportion of the Medicaid population.

Having said that, there is some evidence to suggest that people put a priority on the health of children (and younger people in general) (Eisenberg and Freed 2007). Eisenberg and Freed (2007) speculate that there is a fairness component to this as well as the idea that children obviously have a much longer life expectancy than older people (these age preferences apparently also occur among the elderly). In addition, Eisenberg and Freed (2007) note that good health care and good care habits in younger years pay off in a longer and healthier life down the road.

Another important issue is retention rates for children in the Medicaid and SCHIP programs. Going from covered to uncovered and then covered again tends to disrupt the continuity of care for children (Howell, Palmer, and Miller 2006).

The public programs, Medicaid and SCHIP, have succeeded in reducing the number of uninsured children. When SCHIP was created in 1997, the uninsurance rate for children was 22.3 percent. By 2004 it had dropped to 14.9 percent (Lambrew 2007). Disparities based on race or ethnicity appeared to have declined somewhat because of SCHIP (Kenney and Yee 2007).

Some local governments have begun to address the problems of uninsured children. One county that has started an innovative program is Los Angeles (Hill, Courtot, and Wada 2006). The Healthy Kids Program has enrolled some 45,000 children in a fairly comprehensive benefits program that involves some cost-sharing on the part of the children's families. As with SCHIP, there is little evidence of crowding out of private insurance programs. Nevertheless, a good portion of children in the county still do not have insurance coverage. Other counties in California, such as San Mateo, are offering similar programs (see Howell et al. 2006).

Some efforts have been made to address the problems of pediatric dentistry availability (Lieberman and Paul 2002). The American Dental Association (ADA) has a yearly "Give Kids a Smile" day, where dentists provide free services to underserved children. This is a program that began in St. Louis, Missouri, in 2002 and has spread nationwide. It is sponsored by such corporations as Colgate Palmolive and Sullivan-Schein (see ADA web site at www.ADA.org).

A second front in the dentistry wars is the Reforming States Group, made up of government leaders. It recommended a model dental insurance plan for the SCHIP program, which has been implemented in Michigan and Alabama. The states dealt with reimbursement and billing issues, and dentists' participation in the program in those two states increased dramatically (Lieberman and Paul 2002).

The Children's Defense Fund (2006) made a number of recommendations for reducing the health care disparities among children. The first strategy is to focus on individuals. Here there is the need to make people aware of the disparities, and the underlying causes, such as poverty, and then how to gain access to the health care system. A second strategy is to strengthen the capacity of the community to understand disparities and the role of the various factors that lead to disparities. The third strategy is to increase the quality of and access to care. This includes creating cultural linkages, advocacy with health care institutions, and coordination. This would also involve collecting and disseminating information about programs and increasing the diversity of the health care workforce. The fourth recommendation is to advocate for public policy changes that would reduce disparities. The Children's Defense Fund recommends establishing more and stable community health centers, encouraging cultural competency among health care workers, and enforcing anti-discrimination laws.

Health care is unquestionably expensive to individuals and to the larger society. But poor health care is also expensive. We should be looking at increased spending on health care for children, especially low income and ethnic minority children, as investments that will pay off for the larger society in greater productivity and lower health care expenses (Children's Defense Fund 2005). If there is any part of the population that deserves greater investment it is children. And we should include all children with the goals of enhancing children's health and reducing disparities. Children are our future.

References

Agency for Health Research and Quality. 2005. *2005 National Health Care Disparities Report*. Rockville, MD: U.S. Department of Health and Human Services.
Akinbami, Lara J., and Kenneth C. Schoendorf. 2002. "Trends in Childhood Asthma: Prevalence, Health Care Utilization, and Mortality." *Pediatrics* 110, no. 2 (August): 315–22.

Alaimo, Katherine; Christine M. Olson; Edward A. Frongillo, Jr.; and Ronette R. Briefel. 2001. "Food Insufficiency, Family Income, and Health in Preschool and School-Aged Children." *American Journal of Public Health* 91, no. 5 (May): 781–86.

Alexander, Greg R., and Martha Slay. 2002. "Prematurity at Birth: Trends, Racial Disparities, and Epidemiology." *Mental Retardation and Developmental Disabilities Research Reviews* 8: 215–20.

Amschler, Denise H. 2003. "A Hidden Epidemic: Dental Disparities among Children." *Journal of School Health* 73, no. 1 (January): 38–40.

Annie E. Casey Foundation. 2006. *2006 Kids Count Data Book.* Baltimore, MD: Annie E. Casey Foundation.

Beal, Anne C. 2004. "Politics to Reduce Racial and Ethnic Disparities in Child Health and Health Care." *Health Affairs* 23, no. 5 (September–October): 171–79.

Brach, Cindy, et al. 2003. "Who's Enrolled in the State Children's Health Insurance Program (SCHIP)? An Overview of Findings from the Child Health Insurance Research Initiative." *Pediatrics* 112, no. 6 (December): e499–e507.

Bramlett, Matthew D., and Stephen J. Blumberg. 2007. "Family Structure and Children's Physical and Mental Health." *Health Affairs* 26, no. 2 (March–April): 549–58.

Bullard, Robert D. Ed. 2005. *The Quest for Environmental Justice: Human Rights and the Politics of Pollution.* San Francisco: Sierra Club Books.

Burgos, Anthony E., et al. 2005. "Importance of Generational Status in Examining Access to and Utilization of Health Care Services by Mexican American Children." *Pediatrics* 115, no. 3 (March): e322–e330.

Campaign for Children's Health Care. 2007. *Children and Youth with Special Health Care Needs.* Washington, D.C.: Campaign for Children's Health Care.

Carasso, Adam; C. Eugene Steuerle; and Gillian Reynolds. 2007. *Kids' Share 2007: How Children Fare in the Federal Budget.* Washington, D.C.: Urban Institute.

Child Health Insurance Research Initiative. 2007. Rockville, MD.: Agency for Healthcare Research and Quality. Online at www.ahrq.gov/chiri.

Children's Defense Fund. 2005. *The State of America's Children.* Washington, D.C.: Children's Defense Fund.

Children's Defense Fund. 2006. *Improving Children's Health: Understanding Children's Health Disparities and Promising Approaches to Address Them.* Washington, D.C.: Children's Defense Fund.

Chu, Susan Y.; Lawrence E. Barker; and Philip J. Smith. 2004. "Racial/Ethnic Disparities in Preschool Immunizations: United States, 1996–2001." *American Journal of Public Health* 94, no. 6 (June): 973–77.

Committee on Evaluation of Children's Health, National Research Council. 2004. *Children's Health, the Nation's Wealth: Assessing and Improving Child Health.*

Currie, Janet, and Wanchuan Lin. 2007. "Chipping Away at Health: More on the Relationship between Income and Child Health." *Health Affairs* 26, no. 2 (March–April): 331–44.

DeNavas-Walt, Carmen; Bernadette D. Proctor; and Cheryl Hill Lee. 2006. *Income, Poverty and Health Insurance Coverage in the United States: 2005.* Current Population Reports, U.S. Census Bureau, U.S. Department of Commerce.

Dovey, Susan, et al. 2003. "The Ecology of Medical Care for Children in the United States." *Pediatrics* 111, no. 5 (May): 1024–29.

Dubay, Lisa; Jocelyn Guyer; Cindy Mann; and Michael Odeh. 2007. "Medicaid at the Ten-Year Anniversary of SCHIP: Looking Back and Moving Forward." *Health Affairs* 26, no. 2 (March–April): 370–81.

Eisenberg, Daniel, and Gary L. Freed. 2007. "Reassessing How Society Prioritizes the Health of Young People." *Health Affairs* 26, no. 2 (March–April): 345–54.

Fairbrother, Gerry Lynn; Heidi Park Emerson; and Lee Partridge. 2007. "How Stable Is Medicaid Coverage for Children?" *Health Affairs* 26, no. 2 (March–April): 520–28.

Flores, Glenn, et al. 2002. "The Health of Latino Children." *JAMA* 288, no. 1 (July 3): 82–90.

Flores, Glenn; Milagros Abreu; and Sandra C. Tomany-Korman. 2006. "Why Are Latinos the Most Uninsured Racial/Ethnic Group of US Children? A Community-Based Study of Risk Factors for and Consequences of Being an Uninsured Latino Child." *Pediatrics* 118, no. 3 (September): e730–e740.

Geen, Rob; Anna Sommers; and Mindy Cohen. 2005. *Medicaid Spending on Foster Children.* Child Welfare Research Program, Brief no. 2 (August). Washington, D.C.: Urban Institute.

Golden, Janet, and Howard Markel. 2007. "A Historically Based Thought Experiment: Meeting New Challenges for Children's Health and Well-Being." *Health Affairs* 26, no. 2 (March–April): 445–49.

Hacker, Jacob S. 2002. *The Divided Welfare State: The Battle over Public and Private Social Benefits in the United States.* New York: Cambridge University Press.

Hacker, Jacob S. 2006. *The Great Risk Shift: The Assault on American Jobs, Families, Health Care, and Retirement, and How You Can Fight It.* New York: Oxford University Press.

Halfon, Neal; Helen DuPlessis; and Moira Inkelas. 2007. "Transforming the U.S. Child Health System." *Health Affairs* 26, no. 2 (March–April): 315–30.

Hedley, Allison A., et al. 2004. "Prevalence of Overweight and Obesity among US Children, Adolescents, and Adults, 1999–2002." *JAMA* 291, no. 23 (June 16): 2847–50.

Henry J. Kaiser Family Foundation. 2007. *Income Eligibility for Parents Applying for Medicaid by Annual Income as a Percent of Federal Poverty Level (FPL), 2006.* Online at www.statehealthfacts.org/cgi-bin/healthfacts.cgi?action=compare&category=Medi caid+%26+SCHIP&subcategory=Medicaid+Eligibility&topic=Income+Eligibility— Parents+in+Medicaid.

Herrnstein, Richard J., and Charles Murray. 1994. *The Bell Curve: Intelligence and Class Structure in American Life.* New York: Free Press.

Hill, Ian; Brigette Courtot; and Jennifer Sullivan. 2005. *Ebbing and Flowing: Some Gains, Some Losses as SCHIP Responds to Third Year of Budget Pressure.* New Federalism: Issues and Options for States, Series A, no. A-68 (May). Washington, D.C.: Urban Institute.

Hill, Ian; Brigette Courtot; and Eriko Wada. 2006. *Los Angeles Healthy Kids Program Gets a Healthy Start.* Health Policy Briefs, no. 19 (November). Washington, D.C.: Urban Institute.

Homer, Charles, and Lisa A. Simpson. 2007. "Childhood Obesity: What's Health Care Policy Got to Do With it?" *Health Affairs* 26, no. 2 (March–April): 441–44.

Howell, Embry; Dana Hughes; Genevieve Kennedy; Jennifer Sullivan; and Jamie Rubenstein. 2006. *Evaluation of the San Mateo County Health Initiative: Third Annual Report.* Washington, D.C.: Urban Institute.

Howell, Embry M.; Kathryn L.S. Pettit; and G. Thomas Kingsley. 2005. "Trends in Maternal and Infant Health Care in Poor Urban Neighborhoods: Good News from the 1990s, but Challenges Remain." *Public Health Reports* 120, no. 4 (July–August): 409–17.

Howell, Embry; Louise Palmer; and Dawn Miller. 2006. *Where Have All the Children Gone? Studying Retention in Child Public Health Insurance Programs in San Mateo, County, California.* Washington, D.C.: Urban Institute.

Hudson, Julie L., and Thomas M. Selden. 2007. "Children's Eligibility and Coverage: Recent Trends and a Look Ahead." *Health Affairs* web exclusive (August 16): w618–w629. Online at healthaffairs.org.

Humphrey, Hubert H. 1977. Quotation from *Congressional Record.* Online at www.brainyquote.com/quotes/authors/h/hubert_h_humphrey.html.

Hussey, Jon M. 1997. "The Effects of Race, Socioeconomic Status, and Household Structure on Injury Mortality in Children and Young Adults." *Maternal and Child Health Journal* 1, no. 4 (December): 217–27.

Hutchins, Sonja; Ruth Jiles; and Roger Bernier. 2004. "Elimination of Measles and of Disparities in Measles Childhood Vaccine Coverage among Racial and Ethnic Minority Populations in the United States." *Journal of Infectious Diseases* 189 (Supplement 1): S146–S152.

Kataoka, Sheryl H.; Lily Zhang; and Kenneth B. Wells. 2002. "Unmet Need for Mental Health Care among U.S. Children: Variation by Ethnicity and Insurance Status." *American Journal of Psychiatry* 159 (September): 1548–55.

Kenney, Genevieve; Joshua McFeeters; and Justin Yee. 2005. "Preventive Dental Care and Unmet Dental Needs among Low-Income Children." *American Journal of Public Health* 95, no. 8 (August): 1360–66.

Kenney, Genevieve, and Justin Yee. 2007. "SCHIP at a Crossroads: Experiences to Date and Challenges Ahead." *Health Affairs* 26, no. 2 (March–April): 356–69.

Koplan, Jeffrey P., and David W. Fleming. 2000. "Current and Future Public Health Challenges." *JAMA* 284, no. 13 (October 4): 1696–98.

Kramer, Rachel A.; LaRue Allen; and Peter J. Gergen. 1995. "Health and Social Characteristics and Children's Cognitive Functioning: Results from a National Cohort." *American Journal of Public Health* 85, no 3 (March): 312–18.

Lambrew, Jeanne. 2007. *The State Children's Health Insurance Program: Past, Present and Future.* New York: Commonwealth Fund Commission on High Performance Health Systems.

Lanphear, Bruce P.; Michael Weitzman; and Shirley Eberly. 1996. "Racial Differences in Urban Children's Environmental Exposures to Lead." *American Journal of Public Health* 86, no. 10 (October): 1460–63.

Lear, Julia Graham. 2007. "Health at School: A Hidden Health Care System Emerges from the Shadows." *Health Affairs* 26, no. 2 (March–April): 409–19.

Li, Ruowei, and Laurence Grummer-Strawn. 2002. "Racial and Ethnic Disparities in Breastfeeding among United States Infants: Third National Health and Nutrition Examination Survey, 1988–1994." *Birth* 29, no. 4 (December): 251–57.

Lieberman, William, and David P. Paul III. 2002. "Who Shall Care for the Children of the Poor and Uninsured? Pediatric Dentistry in the United States." *Hospital Topics* 80, no. 2 (Spring): 15–20.

Lohr, Kathy. 2007. "Mississippi Grapples with Rising Infant Death Rates." National Public Radio (June 21).

Markel, Howard, and Janet Golden. 2004. "Children's Public Health Policy in the United States: How the Past Can Inform the Future." *Health Affairs* 23, no. 5 (September–October): 147–52.

Maternal and Child Health Bureau. n.d. *History of Children's Health.* Washington, D.C.: U.S. Department of Health and Human Services. Online at www.mchb.hrsa.gov/timeline/text-only.html.

Meara, Ellen; Chapin White; and David M. Cutler. 2004. "Trends in Medical Spending by Age, 1963–2000." *Health Affairs* 23, no. 4 (July–August): 176–83.

Mouradian, Wendy E.; Elizabeth Wehr; and James J. Crall. 2000. "Disparities in Children's Oral Health and Access to Dental Care." *JAMA* 284, no. 20 (November 22–29): 2625–31.

National Center for Health Statistics. 2006. *Health USA 2006.* Hyattsville, MD: Centers for Disease Control and Prevention, U.S. Department of Health and Human Services.

"Nebraska Makes Plans to Improve Infant Health." 2001. *The Nation's Health* 31, no. 3 (April): 8.

Nichols, Len. 2007. "The Moral Case for Covering Children (and Everyone Else)." *Health Affairs* 26, no. 2 (March–April): 405–7.

Nichols, Sharon L., and David C. Berliner. 2007. *Collateral Damage: How High-Stakes Testing Corrupts America's Schools.* Cambridge, MA: Harvard Education Press.

Palazzolo, Daniel J. 1999. *Done Deal: The Politics of the 1997 Budget Agreement.* New York: Chatham House.

Parker, Emil, and Martha Teitelbaum. 2003. *Percentage of Immigrant Children without Health Insurance Is on the Rise.* Washington, D.C.: Children's Defense Fund.

Patel, Kant. 2001. "Down and Out in America: Children and Health Care." *Journal of Health & Social Policy* 13, no. 4: 33–56.

Patel, Kant, and Mark E. Rushefsky. 2005. *The Politics of Public Health in the United States.* Armonk, NY: M.E. Sharpe.

Patel, Kant, and Mark E. Rushefsky. 2006. *Health Care Politics and Policy in America.* 3rd ed. Armonk, NY: M.E. Sharpe.

Pati, Susmita; Ron Keren; Evaline A. Alessandrini; and Donald Schwarz. 2004. "Generational Differences in U.S. Public Spending, 1980–2000." *Health Affairs* 23, no. 5 (September–October): 131–41.

Qiao, Yuhua. 1999. *Interstate Fiscal Disparities in America: A Study of Trends and Causes.* New York: Garland.

Rosenbaum, Sara, and Paul H. Wise. 2007. "Crossing the Medicaid-Private Insurance Divide: The Case of EPSDT." *Health Affairs* 26, no. 2 (March–April): 382–93.

Rushefsky, Mark E. 2007. *Public Policy in the United States: At the Dawn of the Twenty-First Century.* 4th ed. Armonk, NY: M.E. Sharpe.

Rushefsky, Mark E., and Kant Patel. 1998. *Politics, Power & Policymaking: The Case of Health Reform in the 1990s.* Armonk, NY: M.E. Sharpe.

Ryan, Jennifer. 2007. *SCHIP Financing.* Washington, D.C.: National Health Policy Forum, George Washington University.

Save the Children. 2006. *State of the World's Mothers 2006.* Westport, CT: Save the Children.

Schor, Edward L.; Melinda Abrams; and Katherine Shea. 2007. "Medicaid: Health Promotion and Disease Prevention for School Readiness." *Health Affairs* 26, no. 2 (March–April): 420–29.

Schwartz, Karyn; Catherine Hoffman; and Allison Cook. 2007. *Health Insurance Coverage of America's Children.* Washington, D.C.: Kaiser Commission on Medicaid and the Uninsured.

Shone, Laura P., et al. 2003. "The Role of Race and Ethnicity in the State Children's Health Insurance Program (SCHIP) in Four States: Are There Baseline Disparities, and What Do They Mean for SCHIP?" *Pediatrics* 112, no. 6 (December): e512–e532.

Smith, Vernon; Jason Cooke; David Rousseau; Robin Rudowitz; and Caryn Marks. 2007. *SCHIP Turns 10: An Update on Enrollment and an Outlook on Reauthorization from the Program's Directors.* May. Menlo Park, CA: Kaiser Family Foundation, Kaiser Commission on Medicaid and the Uninsured.

Sommers, Anna; Stephen Zickerman; Lisa Dubay; and Genevieve Kenney. 2007. "Substitution of SCHIP for Private Coverage: Results from a 2002 Evaluation in Ten States." *Health Affairs* 26, no. 2 (March–April): 529–37.

Starfield, Barbara. 2004. "U.S. Child Health: What's Amiss, and What Should Be Done about It?" *Health Affairs* 23, no. 5 (September–October): 165–70.

Strine, Tara W., et al. 2003. "Vaccination Coverage of American Indian/Alaska Native Children Aged 19 to 35 Months: Finds from the National Immunization Survey, 1998–2000." *American Journal of Public Health* 93, no. 12 (December): 2046–49.

Sullivan, Jennifer, and Kathleen Stoll. 2007. *The Great Divide: When Kids Get Sick, Insurance Matters.* Washington, D.C.: Families USA.

U.S. Bureau of the Census. 2007. *Statistical Abstract of the United States 2007.* Washington, D.C.: U.S. Department of Commerce.

U.S. Department of Health and Human Services. 2000. *Healthy People 2010: Understanding and Improving Health.* 2nd ed. Washington, D.C.: Government Printing Office.

U.S. Department of Health and Human Services. 2005a, *Child Health USA 2005.* Rockville, MD: Health Resources and Services Administration, Maternal and Child Health Bureau.

U.S. Department of Health and Human Services. 2005b. *The Health and Well-Being of Children: A Portrait of the States and Nations 2005.* Rockville, MD: Health Resources and Services Administration, Maternal and Child Health Bureau.

van Dyck, Peter C. 2003. "A History of Child Health Equity Legislation in the United States." *Pediatrics* 12, no. 3 (September): 727–30.

Villarruel, Antonia. 2001. "Eliminating Health Disparities for Racial and Ethnic Minorities: A Nursing Agenda for Children." *JSPN Journal for Specialists in Pediatric Nursing* 6, no. 1 (January–March): 32–34.

Wang, Edward C., et al. 2004. "Inequality of Access to Surgical Specialty Health Care: Why Children with Government-Funded Insurance Have Less Access Than Those with Private Insurance in California." *Pediatrics* 114, no. 5 (November): e584–e590.

Weight-Control Information Network. n.d. *Statistics Related to Overweight and Obesity. National Institute of Diabetes and Digestive and Kidney Diseases.* Online at http://win.niddk.nih.gov/statistics/index.htm#preval.

Zambrana, Ruth E., and Laura A. Logie. 2000. "Latino Child Health: Need for Inclusion in the US National Discourse." *American Journal of Public Health* 90, no. 12 (December): 1827–33.

Zuckerman, Stephen, and Allison Cook. 2006. *The Role of Medicaid and SCHIP as an Insurance Safety Net.* August. Washington, D.C.: Urban Institute.

7

The Elderly and Health Care

Of all the chapters in a book on health care disparities, a chapter on the elderly population would seem to be the least necessary. Those sixty-five and over have the only public system of universal health care in the United States, a country notable for its lack of a national health care system. The elderly as a group have a low poverty rate and many have substantial assets; many have a pension in addition to Social Security. And the elderly as a group have enormous political power. Yet health disparities among the elderly remain.

The chapter proceeds as follows. The introduction will describe the elderly population in the United States, give a brief history of health care for the elderly, and a discussion of public (and private) programs aimed at the elderly. The next section will examine health disparities among the elderly, focusing on status and outcomes, access, and quality of care. The subsequent section will offer some possible explanations for the disparities. The conclusion will sum up the chapter.

The Elderly Population of the United States

Let us first look at the size of the elderly population (defined as sixty-five and older) and how it has changed over time. Table 7.1 presents the data. There are several important observations that can be made here. First, both the relative and absolute numbers of the elderly are increasing. In 1980, the elderly comprised a bit over 11 percent of the population. By 2005 they had increased to over 12 percent. Notice the projections for 2020 and 2050; by 2020 the elderly population is projected to be over 16 percent of the population. The enormous baby boomer generation (those born between 1946 and 1960) is responsible for this growth.

A second observation is the increase in the old-old, those eighty-five and over. Their relative size will increase from just under 1 percent of the total population in 1980 to over 2 percent in 2020. The third observation is the predominance of females in the elderly population, comprising, for example, over 68 percent of

Table 7.1

A Demographic Picture of the Elderly, 1980–2050

	1980		1990		2000		2005		2020*		2050*	
	Population (millions)	% of total population	Population (millions)	% of total population	Population (millions)	% of total population	Population (millions)	% of total population	Population (millions)	% of total population	Population (millions)	% of total population
Over 65	25.55	11.28	31.08	12.49	34.99	12.43	36.79	12.41	54.32	16.18	86.71	20.65
Over 75	9.96	4.40	13.04	5.24	16.6	5.90	18.15	6.12	22.85	6.80	48.76	11.61
Over 85	2.24	0.99	3.02	1.21	4.24	1.51	5.1	1.72	7.27	2.16	20.86	4.97

	1980	1990	2000	2005	2020*	2050*
Over 65, % female	59.69	59.81	58.82	58.11	n.a	n/a
Over 75, % female	64.46	64.80	63.25	62.09	n/a	n/a
Over 85, % female	69.64	72.19	70.99	68.43	n/a	n/a
U.S. median age	30.0	32.8	35.3	36.2	38.0	39.1

Source: Census Bureau (2007, p. 12–13).
*projected

Table 7.2

Racial/Ethnic Makeup of the Elderly Population, 2005 and 2015
(percent of elderly population and percentage change in growth)

	2005	2015*	Change in growth rate
Whites	87.3	85.5	24.6
African American	8.5	9.0	35.3
Hispanics	6.2	7.8	60.1
Asians	3.0	3.9	65.7

Source: U.S Bureau of the Census (2007, 15, 18).
  * projected

the over-eighty-five population in 2005. The final observation is that the median age of the U.S. population is increasing, from thirty in 1980 to just over thirty-six in 2005.

Table 7.2 presents data about the current and projected racial/ethnic makeup of the elderly population for 2005 and 2015. Note first that the elderly population is and will continue to be predominantly white. Second, that predominance is slowly decreasing. As the country becomes more ethnically and racially diverse, so too will the elderly population. Hispanics and African Americans (and to a lesser extent Asians) are a younger population than whites. The median age for the white population in 2005 was 37.6, compared to 30.9 for African Americans and 27.2 for Hispanics. Table 7.2 shows that the growth in the African American and especially Hispanic elderly population is larger than for whites. Mokdad et al. (2004), looking at population changes from 1990 to 2000, find that the white and African American populations are aging, but that the Hispanic population is getting younger. They attribute this to two reasons. First is the influx of Hispanic immigrants into the United States. Second, Hispanic mortality rates at younger ages are higher than for other groups. They conclude (Mokdad et al. 2004, 361) that "this underscores the need to develop and implement culturally sensitive prevention programs directed at various risk factors to target all ethnic groups. These programs should focus on the importance of disease prevention to eliminate racial and ethnic disparities in morbidity and mortality from chronic disease."

A little over 40 percent of the elderly have a disability, with disabilities increasing with age. Almost 30 percent of the young-old (sixty-five to seventy-four) are disabled, compared to almost 47 percent of those over seventy-four (authors' calculations from U.S. Bureau of the Census 2007).

We can also examine income data. Using 2004 data, the median income for all households was $44,389. For households where the head of the household was sixty-five or older, the median income was $24,509. The data also tell us that males do better than females. Males over sixty-five years of age had a money income in 2003 of $20,363 compared to $11,845 for elderly females (U.S. Bureau of the Census 2007).

Using 1996 data, a much smaller proportion of whites (67 percent) had incomes under $25,000 than African Americans (90 percent) or Hispanics (89 percent). A substantially greater proportion of whites (65 percent) had graduated from high school versus African Americans (37 percent) or Hispanics (30 percent) (Gornick 2000).

The data also tell us about the poverty rate for the elderly. We have already noted that the poverty rate among the elderly is relatively low. Examining 2004 data, the overall poverty rate was 12.7 percent. For children (under eighteen), the poverty rate was 17.8 percent. For the elderly, it was 9.8 percent, and a bit higher for those over seventy-five. But within this group we find the common disparities. The poverty rate for the white elderly population was 8.3 percent, 23.9 percent for blacks, 13.6 percent for Asians, and 18.7 for Hispanics (U.S. Bureau of the Census 2007; Pati et al. 2004).

Another indicator is net worth or wealth, which gives us a picture of the ability of the elderly to support themselves. The first thing we should point out, an obvious but important one, is that net worth tends to increase with age up to a point. After someone retires, net worth tends to decrease. The person is no longer working and is living off financial assets and pensions/Social Security. The better one does during the working years, the better financially off that person will be as a senior. Second, whites tend to have more net worth than African Americans or Hispanics (Weller and Wolff 2005). Average net worth for whites is over three times as much as for African Americans and Hispanics. Third, net worth, like income, tends to be skewed or unequal. That is, people at the higher end tend to have much more than people at the lower end. The wealth distribution is even more uneven than the income distribution among seniors (and the rest of the population, for that matter) (National Institute on Aging 2007). This is indicated by the average of net worth being higher than the median. Generally speaking, the data show that the mean is about three to four times higher than the median. The one interesting case is for minorities (of all ages), where the mean is six times higher than the median (authors' calculations from Bucks, Kennickell, and Moore 2006).

Wasow (2004) distinguishes between low wealth, median wealth, and high wealth people. The low wealth group has a little over $100,000, most of which is Social Security and a much smaller amount in personal savings. People in the high wealth group have nearly $1 million, almost half of which is in personal savings, about a third from private pensions, and the remainder from Social Security.

We can also examine the sources of income for the elderly (see Table 7.3) One very important source is Social Security. Social Security, along with Medicare, has helped reduce the poverty rate among the elderly. The poverty rate among the elderly has decreased from over one-third (35.2 percent) of the elderly in 1959 to just over 10 percent (10.2) in 2003 (Century Foundation 2005). We can also

Table 7.3

Sources of Income for People Sixty-five and Over (mean income for 2005)

Mean Income	$24,425
Percent from earnings	23.8
Percent from Social Security	38.1
Percent from pensions	17.6
Percent from income from assets	12.9
Percent from IRA/Keough/401	0.6

Source: Calculated from Employee Benefit Research Institute (2007).

see how dependent the elderly are on Social Security by looking at the percentage of total income accounted for by the program. For 21 percent of the beneficiaries (which includes more than the elderly), Social Security accounts for 100 percent of income. For another 13 percent, it accounts for 90 percent of income. For 31 percent of beneficiaries, it accounts for more than 50 percent of income. Simple arithmetic tells us that for only 35 percent of beneficiaries is Social Security less than 50 percent of total income (Century Foundation 2005; see also Weller and Wolff 2005). Women tend to rely on Social Security more than men for a variety of reasons: usually worked at lower paid jobs, interrupted work experience, less likely to have private pensions, and so forth. Women also live longer than men (see Table 7.1) and women make up the bulk of the older poor (Century Foundation 2005). Those at the upper income levels (the highest quintile) not only have more money but have a greater diversity of sources of income than those at lower levels. They have a larger stock of assets, bigger pension plans, and larger earnings (National Institute on Aging 2007).

A related point is that private pensions are diminishing. Less than half of workers (44 percent) have a private pension. On average, pensions (both public and private) account for just a bit over 18 percent of an elderly person's income (see Table 7.3). Most of those without employee pensions are people who work or have worked in smaller firms, are part-time, minorities, women, or work in non-unionized shops (Century Foundation 2005). In general, fewer companies have been offering pensions (Hacker 2006; Morris 2006). Companies are moving from defined-benefits plans (where the company promises to pay benefits to the worker [and perhaps the spouse] until death) to defined-contribution plans, where companies contribute to a plan or have a plan that employees contribute to or both. The contributions end when the worker retires. According to Hacker (2006), the median 401(k) account has about $13,000 (the mean has about $47,000). As we can see in Table 7.3, such plans produce a very small income for retired persons. Retirees with defined-contribution plans tend to be less satisfied with their retirement than those with the more traditional plans (National Institute on Aging 2007). To the extent that the retirement income of minorities and women has improved, it is because of changes in Social Security benefits. There is greater inequality in private pensions than in Social Security (Weller and Wolff 2005).

We can also examine retiree health benefits (Johnson 2007). Larger companies are much more likely to offer pensions to their retirees. But similar to what is occurring with private pensions, fewer companies of any size are offering retiree health benefits, and many that continue to do so are shifting more of the costs onto the retirees. Looking at seniors in 2005 who had worked in a place that offered health insurance during their working years, 34 percent had coverage from their former employer, 29 percent had Medicare, 4 percent were on Medicare or had military benefits, 5 percent were covered through a spouse's employer, and 1 percent had no insurance (an extraordinarily low figure) (Johnson 2007).

History of Health Care Policy for the Elderly

One can begin to get a sense of the elderly and health care by considering life expectancies. In 1900–1902 the life expectancy at birth of a white male was 48.2 years, for a white female it was 51.1 years, for all other males it was 32.5 years, and for all other females it was 35 years. Another way of looking at this is that the elderly comprised only about 3 percent of the U.S. population in 1870 (Fleming, Evans, and Chutka 2003). It was not until the turn of the twentieth century that age-related distinctions became important. Children went to school, adults went to work or bore children, and seniors were retired. Old age was characterized as "bounded by dependency, decay, and dementia" (Fleming, Evans, and Chutka 2003, 915). Old age often meant poverty and dependence on the very limited public (based on the British Poor Laws) and private services that existed at the time (Fleming, Evans, and Chutka 2003). It was not until after World War I that social movements to help the elderly were highly visible. Public-sector programs aimed at the elderly (and others) took off with the Great Depression and the New Deal programs of President Franklin Roosevelt.

By 1980, life expectancy had increased dramatically. For white males it was 74.8 years, for white females it was 80 years, for all other males it was 68.3 years, and for all other females it was 75 years (Infoplease n.d.). So here is the first of our disparities. Whites males have longer life expectancies than all other males (other ethnic and racial groups) and females have a longer life expectancy than males. Interestingly, the difference between white and African American life expectancy at age sixty-five *grew* in the period after the establishment of Medicare. The difference in life expectancy between white and African American males at age sixty-five was six-tenths of a year in 1970 and two years in 1990. By 1997, the difference had decreased a bit to 1.8 years (Gornick 2000).

A major reason for increases in life expectancies was the development of the health professions and their ability to cure and alleviate health problems. Hospitals became places for treatment rather than places for people to die. Because of these developments, the problems plaguing the elderly were less likely to be acute problems than chronic ones. But medical services have always been expensive.

Health insurance developed beginning in the 1930s (see Cohn 2007; Patel and Rushefsky 2006; and Starr 1982). The most affordable type of health insurance was employer-based. The reason is that insurance spreads the risks of having a catastrophic health care event across a large population. Insurance companies do not aggregate individuals. Each individual policy is considered in isolation from all others. Further, administrative costs are higher for individual policies than for group policies. There are also tax advantages to businesses that offer employee health insurance. Finally, group insurance provides some actuarial experiences of health events; individual coverage does not. Thus individual coverage is very expensive.

As health insurance developed, most people with health insurance were covered by their employers. But at retirement, health care benefits often disappeared. This was certainly the case for the elderly in the 1950s and 1960s. Cohn (2007, 90) notes that in the late 1950s, only about 40 percent of retirees had health insurance. Further, by the beginning of the 1960s, only about 7 percent of health care for the elderly was paid for by insurance.

Health care for the elderly arose out of the failure to pass a national health insurance (NHI) program during the Truman administration (Cohn 2007; Oberlander 2003; Marmor 2000; Starr 1982). NHI advocates turned to an incremental approach and targeted the elderly as the perfect group for a public health insurance program. First, the private sector did not provide much insurance for retired people. Second, the elderly were considered a worthy group. They had worked, but they did not have health insurance. And their health care needs were high (Cohn 2007; Marmor 2000).

The result of the effort was the passage of Medicare (and Medicaid) in 1965, abetted by the success of the Democrats (at both the presidential and congressional levels) in the 1964 elections. Medicare remains the major health care program for the elderly. The importance of Medicare is underscored by the decline in private employer-based health insurance coverage for retired workers. In 1988, about two-thirds of large firms offered such coverage (large firms are more likely than smaller firms to offer health insurance for current as well as retired employees); seventeen years later that percentage had been cut in half (Henry J. Kaiser Family Foundation 2007).

Medicare

Medicare has evolved significantly since its origin in 1965, most particularly in 1997 and 2003 (see Patel and Rushefsky 2006; Rushefsky 2004; Oberlander 2003). Its original structure consisted of two parts: Part A or hospital insurance, which covered hospital-based services, and Part B, or supplemental medical insurance, which was designed to cover physician and other outpatient services. The mix of covered services in Parts A and B has changed over the years. As of 2007, Medicare has a Part C, known as Medicare Advantage, where beneficiaries enroll in managed care organizations such as health maintenance organizations. Part D is the new prescription drug benefit (see Moon 2006; Patel and Rushefsky 2006; Oliver, Lee, and Lipton 2004; Rushefsky 2004).

An important aspect of Medicare is its cost-sharing provisions. For Part A, there is a deductible equal to the one-day cost of a hospital room. Part B requires premiums and has deductibles and co-payments. Medicare, using 2002 data, paid for less than 45 percent of expenses for beneficiaries. Other payment sources include retiree health care plans, Medicaid (see below), supplemental insurance policies (known as medigap plans), and out-of-pocket expenses. Retirees pay about 19 percent of their expenses (Cubanski et al. 2005).

There are gaps in Medicare coverage. Medicare pays for very little of long-term care and until recently did not pay for outpatient prescription drugs. Dental care is also not covered. Nevertheless, there is considerable evidence that Medicare has enhanced the health of the elderly, based both on ability to help themselves and life expectancy (Lubitz et al. 2001).

Medicaid

The companion program to Medicare, passed at the same time, is Medicaid. Unlike Medicare, which is a totally federally run program, Medicaid is a federal/state program. The federal government sets the ground rules and overall guidelines and makes payments to states for Medicaid services. It also requires a fairly comprehensive set of services. States pay the remainder of Medicaid costs, determine eligibility requirements, pay providers, and may include optional services and populations (see Patel and Rushefsky 2006).

Medicaid, unlike Medicare, was aimed at the poor and is similar to welfare (as Medicare is similar to Social Security) (see Rushefsky 2007, chap. 2). From our perspective, Medicaid acts as a supplemental policy for impoverished elderly people. All the elderly participate in Medicare. But of those, about 4.9 million in 2003 are also enrolled in Medicaid; they are known as dual eligibles (Holahan and Ghosh 2005). Depending on the elderly's financial situation, Medicaid can pay for the cost-sharing provisions of Medicare and can offer services that Medicare does not. Medicaid did not cover the cost of prescription drugs (prior to 2004), dental services, and, especially, long-term care (Holahan and Ghosh 2005).

There are disparities among those who are on Medicare alone and those who have other sources of health care insurance (Johnson 2006). More females (18 percent of the female Medicare population) are on Medicare only than are males (13 percent). Almost twice as many African Americans (27 percent) are Medicare-only as are whites (14 percent). Hispanics are in between at 20 percent. Those with less education are more likely to be Medicare-only than those with more education: 22 percent for those who did not graduate from high school and 10 percent for college graduates. Income levels are also related to Medicare. Eight percent of those whose income was four times the federal poverty line were Medicare-only compared to 25 percent whose income was less than the poverty rate.

This last point takes a bit of explanation. It would seem likely that those whose income is below the poverty rate would be eligible for Medicaid as well (dual eligibles), but for a variety of reasons, including citizenship status and state requirements, this might not be the case.

Disparities also exist for out-of-pocket spending. Goldman and Zissimopoulos (2003) looked at out-of-pocket spending among the elderly by income and wealth groups. Using the 1998 Health and Retirement Study, they found, first, that out-of-pocket spending tended to be concentrated among a small portion of the elderly. This can be seen by comparing average with median spending. If the average is higher than the median, the distribution is skewed. In this case, average out-of-pocket spending was $2,022 versus $920 for the median. Furthermore, those who were the sickest, not surprisingly, spent the most. The top 1 percent of the distribution spent out-of-pocket over $15,000 (Goldman and Zissimopoulos 2003).

Thirteen-and-a-half percent of the sample did not have some kind of supplemental coverage, with 6.7 percent of the highest wealth quartile lacking such cover versus 22.2 percent of the lowest wealth quartile. Those at the lower wealth quartiles were more likely to have Medicaid as a supplement, while those at the higher quartiles were likely either to have employer retiree insurance or to purchase a medigap policy (Goldman and Zissimopoulos 2003).

In the four-year period 1998–2002, median out-of-pocket spending among the elderly increased by about 38 percent, much of it in insurance premiums and the rest for direct payments to providers (deductibles and cost-sharing) (Johnson 2006). The trends among the different groups we have looked at are reversed for out-of-pocket spending. Whites, those with higher incomes, and those with more education, tended to spend more out of pocket than others (Johnson 2006).

Because the elderly tend to have more health needs (especially chronic needs) than children, Medicaid spends relatively more on the elderly than on children. Looking at 2003 data, there were almost 24 million children on Medicaid, compared to a little over 4 million elderly Medicaid beneficiaries, about six children for every elderly recipient. The elderly make up about 7.8 percent of the Medicaid population; children make up about 46 percent. However, the elderly account for about 25 percent of Medicaid spending, children almost 16 percent. The per-beneficiary spending for the elderly on Medicaid dwarfs that for children (U.S. Bureau of the Census 2007). Much of the spending on the elderly in the Medicaid program is for long-term care, precisely the service that Medicare does not much cover (Holahan and Ghosh 2005). In general, considerably more health care dollars are spent on the elderly than on children (Meara, White, and Cutler 2004).

A related observation is that we spend considerably more on the elderly than we do on children for all public programs. Including elementary and secondary education does not change this fact. Public spending for children in 2000 was about $459 billion in 2000, compared to about $629 billion for the elderly (Pati et al. 2004).

Disparities in Health Status, Access, and Quality of Care

Despite Medicare, Medicaid, medigap policies, and retiree health insurance programs (which are declining because of costs), there is a small number of uninsured elderly in the United States. Using data from the 2000 National Health Interview Study, Mold, Fryer, and Thomas (2004) found that there were some 350,000 elderly people who lacked health insurance. This amounted to a little over 1 percent of the elderly population (see also Okoro et al. 2005).

Mold, Fryer, and Thomas (2004) found distinct differences between the uninsured and the insured elderly. The uninsured elderly tended to be younger (sixty-five to seventy-four) and with a somewhat different marital status than the insured, less likely to be married, and more likely to be widowed. The usual racial/ethnic differences appear. The uninsured are more likely to be African American or Latino (Okoro et al. 2005). They were also more likely have been born outside the United States and less likely to be citizens of the United States.

The authors also examined the health characteristics of the uninsured and insured elderly. The uninsured were a little more likely to rate themselves as being in poor/fair health. They were less likely to have been hospitalized during the previous year and less likely to have had contact with a physician either by phone or through an office visit. The major reason for not having insurance was the high cost. Other reasons included not qualifying for Medicare or Medicaid, sometimes because the person was an illegal alien, sometimes because of a lack of information. Sometimes the person did not qualify for a public program because the person's income level was too high (for Medicaid) or because the person had not worked long enough in the United States (for Medicare) (Okoro et al. 2005).

Okoro et al. (2005) compared the insured elderly with the uninsured elderly on their use of health care services. Employing the Behavior Risk Factor Surveillance Survey, they asked whether there were differences in seeing doctors and for obtaining such preventive services as vaccinations and screenings. The uninsured were much more likely to have not seen a physician because of the cost than the insured (about five times as likely) and about three times as likely to have not had routine checkups.

The National Health Disparities Report (Agency for Healthcare Research and Quality 2006) identifies three health care disparities among the elderly, using data from the Medicare Current Beneficiary Survey. The first disparity is flu vaccination. The target immunization rate is 90 percent of the elderly. No group within the elderly met this target. However, elderly whites had a higher immunization rate than other ethnic or racial groups. Elderly African Americans had the lowest immunization rate, a little under 60 percent in 2002 (though a substantial increase from 1998). American Indians/Alaskan Natives were next, with nearly a 70 percent immunization rate (nearly the rate for whites) and also show a substantial improvement from four years earlier. Asian/Pacific Islanders show an increase from 1998 to 2002, but a decrease from 2000 to 2002 (apparently due to a concern in 2000 about a flu epidemic). Hispanics have a lower immunization rate than whites, approximately 57 percent versus about 72 percent. In addition, the Hispanic elderly immunization rate declined slightly from 1998 to 2002 (Agency for Healthcare Research and Quality 2006).

Economic class or income also is related to immunization rates among the elderly. The higher a person's income the more likely that person was to have gotten a flu shot. About 75 percent of the elderly at the highest income level received the vaccine in 2002, versus a little under 60 percent of those at the lowest income level (Agency for Healthcare Research and Quality 2006).

Sambamoorthi and Findley (2005) conducted a somewhat more sophisticated study of immunization rates. They looked at elderly people who never received immunizations and compared them to those who regularly did and those who did so episodically. Much greater proportions of Hispanics and African Americans were abstainers (never received immunizations). The researchers found little differences based on socioeconomic rank. Those with insurance were more likely to have received immunizations than those without. Interestingly, healthier seniors were less likely to have received flu shots than those who were in poorer health (that was true for physical as well as mental health). They (Sambamoorthi and Findley 2005, 475) note that "even after controlling for socioeconomic status, the gaps in rates of immunizations (never or inconsistent) between African Americans and whites remained, suggesting that it is not the socioeconomic disadvantage that contributes to the lack of preventive care among minorities." Other barriers include health literacy and having a usual source of care.

A second disparity contained in the *National Healthcare Disparities Report* (Agency for Healthcare Research and Quality 2006) concerned vision care. We see the same disparities among the elderly here as we saw with influenza vaccinations. Elderly with higher incomes were more likely to have had an eye exam than those with lower incomes, whites more likely than blacks or other racial groups (though the differences are smaller here), and whites more likely than Hispanics.

The third disparity contained in the report was access to health care. The particular question was whether the respondent delayed seeking care because of the cost of that care. Blacks were more likely to have delayed care than whites. The percentages are small. A little over 4 percent of whites delayed care versus around 5 percent for African Americans. Furthermore, the white percentage increased from 1998 to 2002 and decreased for African Americans. The comparisons between whites and Hispanics is similar. The income variable shows the expected findings. Those with higher incomes were less likely to delay care because of costs than those with lower incomes. Again the percentages of those delaying care are small, ranging from 2 to about 7 percent. The interesting finding is that such delays decreased for the lowest income group, but increased for the middle income group.

Elderly morbidity rates are related to income and race/ethnicity. Elderly whites with higher incomes have lower rates of diabetes, hypertension, and limited mobility, and self-report better health than those with lower incomes. This is generally true for Hispanic and African American elderly as well. The one exception is with diabetes. African Americans with higher incomes have higher rates of diabetes than those with lower incomes (Gornick 2000).

Another important disparity is in death rates. Among elderly males, mortality rates are higher for those with lower incomes than for those with higher incomes. This is true across racial lines. Death rates for elderly African Americans are higher at all income levels than for whites (Gornick 2000).

An area where gender plays a role (not covered in the National Health Disparities Report) is with the old-elderly population and particularly what can be called the frail elderly. Most—about two-thirds—of these older senior citizens with some sort of disability (physical or cognitive) are women (Johnson and Wiener 2006). Most of these women have limited income and wealth and many live outside of long-term care facilities (that is, nursing homes). This means they are either living with relatives or by themselves. Minorities such as African Americans and Hispanics are disproportionately represented among this group.

Education seems to be related to severity and number of disabilities. Those with a college education are less likely to have disabilities and to have fewer disabilities than those with less education. The same holds true for financial status. Indeed, many of these things are related. Those with less financial resources also have less education and are more likely to be widowed (Johnson and Wiener 2006).

Fitzpatrick et al. (2004) investigated whether Medicare beneficiaries perceived access barriers to care. They found that "older age, female gender, non-White race, lower income, and lack of complementary insurance were all significantly related to self-perception of problems with access to care" (Fitzpatrick et al. 2004, 1791). The authors speculate that there might be psychological barriers to care. That is, the perception of barriers might explain some of the racial disparities that are evident in much of the literature.

Another important disparity concerns the use of prescription medications. Here we can look at disparities between the elderly and the nonelderly and within the elderly population. We should also note that most of the research on prescription medications and the elderly predates the new prescription drug benefit (Part D) enacted in 2003 and fully implemented beginning in 2006. There is insufficient time to assess whether any disparities that existed prior to 2006 remain. But that will be part of the research agenda in the near future.

A careful study by Xu (2003, 211) notes that

> Cross-sectional comparisons of the elderly population and working-age adults (ages 18–64) serve two main purposes. First, they indicate the financial burdens associated with prescription drug use across different populations and provide quantitative measures of disparity. Second, they establish benchmarks for achieving the potential reform goals (that is, exactly how much disparity needs to be eliminated). Examination of cross-sectional disparity indicators can reveal the overall impact of Medicare reform within the elderly population and across various populations.

Xu (2003) used data from the Medical Expenditures Panel Survey for 1998. The first finding is that the elderly at all income levels spend more on prescription drugs than do the nonelderly. Elderly people spent an average of $537 in 1998 on prescriptions, representing about 3.5 percent of annual income. By comparison, nonelderly people spent an average of $192 on prescriptions, a little over 1 percent of income. The elderly also spent more of their own money (out-of-pocket expenses) for medications than the nonelderly.

Of course, the medical needs of the two groups are different. The nonelderly were more likely to rate themselves as in excellent or good physical and mental health and the elderly more likely to rate themselves as in poor or fair health. Over a large number of diseases, a greater proportion of the elderly had a variety of chronic diseases than the nonelderly. Financial disparities appeared to be greatest among those at the low income level but not eligible for Medicaid assistance (Xu 2003). Xu argues that after making adjustments for use or need, those at the higher end of the income scale were also disadvantaged compared to the nonelderly.

Overall, white Medicare beneficiaries were more likely to be without drug coverage than African Americans or Latinos, either for part or all of the year. Beneficiaries also differed in the source of prescription drug coverage prior to 2003. Overall, about 19 percent of beneficiaries lacked full-time prescription drug coverage in 2002. The percentages were fairly similar across racial and ethnic lines. Whites were much more likely than African Americans to have private coverage, which meant either a medigap policy that included prescription drug coverage or retiree coverage from an employer. African Americans and Latinos were much more likely than whites to receive their coverage from Medicaid (Henry J. Kaiser Family Foundation 2005).

A 2006 national survey (Neuman et al. 2007) was one of the first to examine the experience with the new Part D benefit. We can compare the findings of the study with the 2005 study mentioned above that looked at prescription drug coverage for Medicare beneficiaries in 2002. In 2002, about 19 percent of all beneficiaries lacked coverage. In 2006, that number had declined to 8.5 percent. In 2006, older seniors and women were more likely to be without coverage than younger seniors and men. Beneficiaries in rural areas were more likely (10.3 percent) to be without coverage than residents in urban areas (7.9 percent). In a reverse from 2002, racial and ethnic minorities were more likely to lack prescription drug coverage than whites (Neuman et al. 2007; Henry J. Kaiser Family Foundation 2005). Table 7.4 presents the racial ethnic and comparisons for 2002 and 2006.

Seniors with more education were also more likely to have prescription drug coverage in 2006: 6.4 percent of those who had some college education lacked such coverage versus 11.9 percent of those who did not graduate from high school. Income was also a factor, despite the low income subsidies contained in Medicare Part D: 13.7 percent of those with incomes under the federal poverty line lacked coverage compared to 6.6 percent of those with incomes greater than 200 percent of the federal

Table 7.4

Medicare Beneficiaries Without Prescription Drug Coverage, 2002 and 2006
(in percent)

	2002	2006
All	19	8.5
Whites	20	8
African Americans	18	11.6
Latinos	17	10.1
Asian	n/a	13.3
Other	n/a	11

Sources: Neuman et al. (2007); Kaiser Family Foundation (2005).

poverty line. Additionally, those who did not have prescription drug coverage in 2002 were also much more likely not to have it in 2006 (20.2) as compared to those seniors who had some drug coverage (1.1 percent) (Neuman et al. 2007).

Neuman et al. (2007, w637) summarize the characteristics of low income seniors with the drug benefit:

> Compared with enrollees having incomes above 200 percent of poverty, a higher percentage of Part D enrollees with incomes below 200 percent of poverty were age eighty-five or older, female, living in rural areas, and members of racial and ethnic minority groups. Lower-income Part D enrollees also had higher rates of health problems than their higher-income counterparts, reflected in the share reporting three or more chronic conditions and in the mean number of medications taken.

The 2006 survey also found that many low income seniors were not taking advantage of the subsidy provisions of the new program, thus having to pay a fair amount of their own money (out of pocket). The researchers also found that those with employer retiree or Veterans Affairs benefits had less out-of-pocket expenses than those in the private plans that characterize the new benefit (Neuman et al. 2007).

There are also disparities in the use of services on the part of Medicare beneficiaries. White rates of the following procedures are considerably higher than for African Americans: coronary artery bypass grafts, percutaneous transluminal coronary angioplasty, sonography of the carotid artery, thromboendarterectomy, and revascularization. The last is particularly important because some of the differences in cardiovascular treatment may be due to the differences in incidence. However, revascularization rates are still lower for African American than white patients with the same condition (Gornick 2000). Similar racial disparities were found for diagnostic procedures such as mammography. The mammography rate for white elderly females was about twenty-one percent higher than for African American elderly females.

Health Status/Outcomes

There is evidence that the elderly population today is healthier than previous generations of the elderly. Cutler (2001) presents several measures of this. First, the mortality
rate among the elderly is on a continual decline. Cutler cites statistics showing about
a 1 percent yearly decline in the mortality rate among the elderly since 1950. A second measure is the decline in the percentage of the elderly in nursing homes. Some
of this is due to increased state and federal regulations, and some due to increased
spending for home health care on the part of Medicare. But some is due to fewer
disabilities among the elderly, though as we have seen there are disparities here. A
third measure is dependency, the need for assistance in conducting activities of daily
living (ADL). Over time, various surveys have documented a decline in dependency,
though, naturally enough, dependency increases with age. A fourth, related measure,
is the decline in functional impairment among the elderly (Cutler 2001).

Cutler (2001) examines some reasons for this improvement in the health status
of the elderly. These include advancements in medical technology (including phar-
maceuticals), behavioral changes (such as a decline in smoking when the elderly
were younger), and more use of aids, such as canes, that prevent falls. Of course,
health status tends to decline with age among the elderly. According to the Health
and Retirement Study (National Institute on Aging 2007), about 78 percent of those
between sixty-five and seventy-four rate their health status as good, very good, or
excellent. For the middle group, seventy-five to eighty-four years old, about 63
percent so rate themselves. For the oldest group, eighty-five years of age and older,
only about 58 percent so rate themselves (National Institute on Aging 2007).

Gender differences on self-reported health status are small, but racial and ethnic
differences are large. About 25 percent of elderly Hispanics and African Americans
rate their health as excellent versus about 45 percent of elderly whites (National
Institute on Aging 2007).

A fifth explanation, very relevant to our concern with disparities, is socioeconomic status. Those who had more education, those who had more income, and
those who were more likely to have white-collar jobs (the categories overlap) are
less likely to become disabled. The elderly population is increasingly, if slowly,
taking on these characteristics. As Cutler (2001) points out, those with white-collar
jobs were less likely to have been subjected to injuries or exposure to hazardous
substances than those with blue-collar jobs. In addition, better educated people are
more likely to be knowledgeable about what constitutes appropriate healthy behavior
and are also more likely to seek medical services than those with less education.

There are disparities for several health conditions. These include hypertension
(where African Americans have higher rates than whites) and diabetes (African
Americans and Hispanics have higher rates than whites). In some cases, whites have
higher rates. For example, whites have higher rates of heart problems, pulmonary
problems, and cancer than Hispanics. Hispanics have less arthritis or strokes than
whites or African Americans (National Institute on Aging 2007).

As far as gender differences are concerned, a major difference is that elderly women have higher rates of arthritis than males. Related to this is that elderly women tend to have more limitations on daily activities (ADL) than men (National Institute on Aging 2007).

Davis and Lapane (2004) look at the characteristics of nursing home residents. Utilizing data from the 1999 National Nursing Home Survey of Current Residents, they found that minority males tended to be admitted to nursing homes at younger ages, perhaps because they were in poorer health than white males. Minorities also had fewer financial resources than whites and therefore were more likely to have their nursing home bills paid for by Medicaid, with whites more likely to have private insurance or to pay privately.

The authors make an important point about this. Medicaid reimbursement for nursing homes is lower than for those who privately pay. They suggest that the differences in reimbursement may lead to a delay in admission to a nursing home. They also found that residents of nursing homes where there were mostly public-paid residents tended to see greater declines in their ability to function (Davis and Lapane 2004). Members of minority groups in nursing homes tended to need more help than white nursing home residents.

Access to Health Care

We have looked at the elderly who do not have health insurance, a relatively small group, but one that fits the profiles we have seen throughout this book. However, there is an additional consideration to examine. What is the health status of the elderly who lack continuous coverage during the years prior to becoming eligible for Medicare?

It turns out, perhaps not surprisingly, that lack of coverage in early years has impacts on health in later years. The Health and Retirement Study divided respondents into three categories of insurance coverage prior to Medicare eligibility (looking at the 1992–96 period): those who were continuously covered, those who were covered some of the time (intermittently covered), and those who were continuously uncovered. The researchers cited in the National Institute on Aging report found that those who were continuously uncovered tended to have sharper declines in their health status than those who were continuously covered and more likely to have some disability that interfered with activities of daily living. Those who were intermittently covered tended to use fewer preventive services. A further finding of the research was that covering the previously uninsured tended to enhance reported health status (see citations in National Institute on Aging 2007).

A variation on the above studies compared the use of health services on the part of the insured and uninsured before and after getting on Medicare. The study found that the differences in the use of preventive services declined after both groups went on Medicare (National Institute on Aging 2007).

The Health and Retirement Study also looked at the use of health care services on the part of Medicare beneficiaries (2002 data). In general, the gender differences are small. A greater percentage of Hispanics than whites or African Americans did not see a doctor. A higher percentage of whites than African Americans or Hispanics had outpatient surgery. The biggest difference was in dental care. About 65 percent of whites saw a dentist in 2002, versus about 40 percent for African Americans and Hispanics (National Institute on Aging 2007).

Gornick (2000) found considerable differences in the use of services between whites and African Americans. Whites had a higher rate of office visits, seeing physicians, and seeing opthamologists. African Americans had higher rates of hospital inpatient use, emergency room use, and home health care or nursing home use. These findings are consistent with what we have discussed before. African Americans, of whatever age, are more likely to make use of emergency rooms as a source of regular care because they are less likely to have a regular doctor. This carries over, apparently, to old age, even with Medicare. Furthermore, because there is a tendency to postpone care, when they do seek care, they often are sicker and thus require hospitalization.

There are also differences related to socioeconomic status in the use of elective services. The more affluent are much more likely to make use of such services and the less affluent are more likely to go to emergency rooms. These income distinctions hold true within races (Gornick 2000).

Quality of Health Care

An example of quality of care is whether the population and subgroups within the population receive health screenings. Colon cancer is one of the most frequently diagnosed cancers and a very lethal type. Colonoscopies can screen for colon cancer and precursors and are considered very accurate. There are the typical disparities concerning this procedure. Ethnic and racial minorities receive fewer screenings than whites. Shih, Zhao, and Elting (2006) attribute the disparities to the costs of the procedure and to practice differences in different parts of the country. Their interest is whether having Medicare pay for the procedure reduced the disparities.

Shih, Zhao, and Elting (2006) point out that Medicare would pay for the procedure for those beneficiaries especially susceptible to colon cancer. But in 2001 Medicare widened the eligible population. Data from the National Health Interview Survey for 2000 and 2003 were employed to see if the new Medicare policy reduced these disparities. They first found that endoscopic colorectal cancer screenings among the Medicare population increased between 2000 and 2003. Second, the increases were greater for whites and African Americans than for Hispanics, who continued to have the lowest rate. They further found that women were more likely to have the screening than men and that the difference increased during this period. The lowest income elderly were less likely to have the screening than the next income group in 2003, though apparently not in the 2000 data.

The authors speculate about the low rates for Hispanics. They suggest that lack of knowledge about the benefit and Hispanic cultural factors might be responsible. Perhaps the most important factor is that the rate of colon cancer among Hispanics is considerably lower than for whites and African Americans. Thus, there is less perception of risk on the part of patient and provider (Shih, Zhao, and Elting 2006).

Shih, Zhao, and Elting (2006) observe that even with the expanded Medicare coverage of colonoscopies, there are still co-payments and deductibles. The patient cost-sharing could be as much as $240, an amount that might be difficult for poor or near-poor recipients to pay. Even the dual eligibles, discussed above, who had Medicaid coverage might still have to pay because nearly two-thirds of states did not cover the procedure through their Medicaid programs.

Basu (2005) examined whether there were disparities in the decision of whether to use a local or more distant hospital. Looking at data from New York State and New York City, Basu found, not surprisingly, that the senior elderly were less likely to travel to a distant hospital than the younger elderly. She also found that whites were more likely to travel than African Americans or Hispanics. When minorities did travel to a distant hospital it was more likely to be at a teaching hospital. Severity of illness did not change the findings much.

Bach et al. (2004) investigated whether there were differences in the quality of primary care received by black and white Medicare beneficiaries. Using a variety of data sets, the authors found that there were indeed disparities. Fewer physicians who treated black Medicare beneficiaries tended to be board certified compared to those treating white Medicare patients. Black Medicare patients also had less access to high-quality specialists and to technology such as the more sophisticated imaging devices, less access to nonemergency hospital admissions, and so forth.

The authors suggest that some of the discrepancies in quality of care may be due to the quality of the physicians they visit. For example, physicians who are not board certified are less likely to order necessary screenings. The physicians also seem to have less access to specialists and other services; this too could explain some of the discrepancies. They suggest that African American Medicare beneficiaries are limited in their access to more qualified physicians.

Sherkat et al. (2005) explored the relationship between use of doctor services and mortality differences among the races. The data, from the Medicare Enrollment Database and the Physicians Billing File for Part A and Part B of Medicare, followed Medicare beneficiaries in Tennessee from 1996 to 2002. They found that there is a difference in racial utilization of physician services for a variety of chronic conditions, including patients with multiple conditions. The mortality rate for African American Medicare beneficiaries is statistically significantly higher than for white Medicare beneficiaries. They also found that African American Medicare beneficiaries, despite seeing doctors less frequently than whites, had about the same cost as whites. The authors surmise that when African Americans seek physician services they are sicker than whites.

Gornick (2000) found two cancer-related differences in quality of care among

Medicare beneficiaries. In the first, whites were more likely than African Americans to have had localized cancers found. This means that cancers are more likely to be found in whites before they had spread (metastasized) as compared to African Americans. The largest difference was for corpus and uterine cancers (a 24 percent difference) and the smallest for lung and bronchial cancer (2 percent). The second and related difference is in the five-year survival rates. Overall, 58.8 percent of elderly whites survived five years after diagnosis, compared to 44.7 of African Americans.

Possible Explanations for Health Care Disparities

A number of possible explanations for disparities among the elderly can be dismissed. Gornick (2000) finds that there is little evidence that being in a fee-for-service system has an impact. She also notes that cost-sharing requirements also do not seem to be critical. Here she offers two pieces of evidence. First, there are disparities in use even among those who have supplemental insurance that covers mammography. Second, there are disparities in immunizations, even though Medicare covers them.

A second explanation that Gornick (2000) says does not fit the data well is genetic and biological differences. She notes that even after adjusting for severity and rate, disparities remain. A related explanation that has limited explanatory power is discrimination. Hospital admission rates are higher for African Americans than for whites. Moreover, she notes that there is an overlap in income as an explanation for the utilization of services. Thus some of what appears to be racial disparity might be the result of income disparities.

A very important explanation for the disparities we have documented in this chapter (and elsewhere throughout this book) is the relationship between health and income. The Health and Retirement Study shows that the higher one's income, the higher the level of self-reported health. This was also true for the relationship between health and wealth. Whites tend to have more income and wealth than minorities and men more women. The Health and Retirement Study did note that the differences between men and women in health status was smaller among married seniors (National Institute on Aging 2007). The correlation between health and wealth is even greater than for health and income (National Institute on Aging 2007).

Another explanation is family status. Data from the Health and Retirement Study (National Institute on Aging 2007) show that those who are married tend to report being in better health (both mental and physical) than those who are not. Moreover, disruptions of marital status tend to lead to income and wealth decreases and to be associated with more health problems. This appears to be particularly troublesome for minorities.

Another important explanation is that disparities among the elderly are influenced by disparities that occurred prior to age sixty-five. Sixty-five is not a magic number at which one's health suddenly declines. Rather one's health in old age is reflective of experiences at a younger age. One way to get at this is to examine those approaching sixty-five.

The near-elderly may be defined as those fifty-five to sixty-four. The percentage of males in this age group decreased in the 1970–97 period, while the percentage of females in this group increased. The size of this group is expected to increase (Pol, Mueller, and Adidam 2002). Because labor-force participation has decreased, many, though not all, members of this group may lack health insurance. The problem this creates, Pol, Mueller, and Adidam (2002) point out, is that those lacking such insurance may delay getting treatment, either preventive or for current health problems. They may try to wait until they turn sixty-five and become eligible for Medicare.

Our disparities show up here. Pol, Mueller, and Adidam (2002) and others (see references in the article) find that near-elderly African Americans and Hispanics are more likely to be without health insurance than whites. The authors point out an increase in the percentage of the elderly of the two minority groups and a decrease in the percentage of elderly who are white. Thus we should expect that, given the lack of health insurance among racial and minority near-elderly, as these groups turn sixty-five they will be in increasingly poorer health.

This is precisely what we find. McWilliams et al. (2004) utilized the Health and Retirement Study for 1992. They found that among the near-elderly, those with lower incomes were less likely to be insured. The same was generally true for wealth. Those without health insurance had higher mortality rates than those with insurance. Mortality rates by race or ethnic group were a bit intriguing. The usual results held for whites and African Americans. Those within those two groups who lacked health insurance had a higher mortality rate than those with insurance. For Hispanics, the results were the reverse. The mortality rate was higher for those with than for those without (McWilliams et al. 2004).

For those at the lowest income quartile, those without health insurance had higher mortality rates. The same was true for those at the three higher income quartiles, but the differences were smaller. For the lowest income quartile, the rates were higher for both insured and uninsured at the higher income levels (McWilliams et al. 2004). For the lowest income quartile, the uninsured had a 50 percent higher mortality rate than those with insurance. For the three higher income quartiles, the difference was 26.5 percent. Near-elderly with diabetes, heart conditions, or hypertension had higher rates of mortality than those without those conditions, for both insured and noninsured. And the differences were dramatic. The mortality rate for the uninsured with one or more of those conditions was about 50 percent higher than for those who had insurance. For those without the conditions, the mortality rate for the uninsured was only 20 percent higher than for those who had insurance (authors' calculations from McWilliams et al. 2004).

Hadley and Waidman (2006) take the exploration of the implications of the health of the near elderly to the next step. They ask the following questions:

> Does lack of insurance prior to age 65 result in people qualifying for Medicare in worse health than if they had been insured? If so, is public insurance spending through Medicare and Medicaid on newly enrolled beneficiaries greater than it would be if people had continuous insurance coverage prior to age 65? (Hadley and Waidman 2006, 429)

As with McWilliams et al. (2004) (and others), Hadley and Waidman use the Health and Retirement Survey and looked at those who were near-elderly in 1992. They found that health status prior to becoming eligible for Medicare greatly determined expenditures while on Medicare. For example, they found that those who rated themselves as in excellent health spent an annual average of almost $3,500 for the first three years under Medicare, whereas those who rated themselves as in poor health spent an annual average of over $12,000. Hadley and Waidman argue that because there is a linkage between access to health insurance and access to health care, extending health insurance to those near elderly who do not have health insurance might reduce subsequent morbidity while under Medicare.

Another possible explanation focuses on the characteristics of the beneficiaries. Gornick (2000, 35) states the case as follows:

> According to the framework of sociology, the traits and cultural propensities of individuals—such as attitudes, beliefs, behaviors, and preferences—range widely across population subgroups. Differing traits and propensities among the elderly may explain some of the disparities in the use of Medicare services. Beneficiaries have grown up in families that have had social and cultural experiences (stemming from family characteristics including race/ethnicity, education, and economic circumstances) that influence how a person perceives his or her situation . . . and that may influence the use of health care. At one end of the social and cultural experience are individuals with characteristics associated with a culture of poverty and at the other end are individuals with characteristics that reflect a culture of advantage.

Thus those experiencing poverty may have language issues or lack the ability to get to needed services. Education seems to be related to disparities. Those with less education make less use of services, have more health problems, and are less knowledgeable about treatments and so forth (Gornick 2000).

But Gornick says that the "culture of poverty" (35) is an insufficient explanation by itself for disparities. She also discusses the "culture of advantage" (36). People with good incomes, jobs, and education expect to get good health services and therefore make use of them. They are likely to seek knowledge (such as from the Internet) and are more able to make their way through the maze of health bureaucracies. Networking among the advantaged is a big help and something not usually available to less advantage people. An anecdote may help explain this.

One of the coauthors (Rushefsky) suffered a knee injury from a fall in January 2007 during an ice storm. He went to the emergency room at a local hospital, where nothing much was diagnosed, and was given a walker. He was told that if his knee did not get better in a week to see his physician. The next week he saw his physician (actually a physician's assistant) who ordered an MRI. The MRI was conducted later that week and the results showed damage to attachments to the knee. Rushefsky's doctor recommended that he see a surgeon and made an appointment with a noted knee surgeon for about a month later, specialists being hard to see on short notice. This was on a Friday. On Sunday, at a wedding at his local congregation, Rushefsky talked a member of his congregation who was also a doctor (and a former student). The friend noticed Rushefsky with a walker and a brace and asked what happened. By this time, Rushefsky had seen the MRI report. The friend was very concerned about waiting a month and said he knew the knee surgeon. He said he would call him the next day (Monday). Monday morning the knee surgeon called Rushefsky, said he had seen the MRI report, and told him that surgery was needed immediately. The next day, Tuesday, the surgery was conducted successfully. Rushefsky's knee was repaired about a month before his scheduled consulting appointment because of networking. Few impoverished people would be so lucky.

Gornick speculates as to other factors within the health care system. For example, she asks whether patients are more comfortable with providers more like themselves. She says there has been little research to see whether treatments differ because physicians do not think disadvantaged patients will follow the course of treatment.

The one danger in looking at the characteristics of beneficiaries as Gornick (2000) does is invoking the "blame the victim" explanation (Ryan 1976). This explanation places the blame for disparities, such as lack of knowledge or unwillingness to take the initiative, on the individuals themselves, rather than on larger social forces.

Conclusions

Among the different groups we have discussed in this book, the elderly should show the fewest inequalities or disparities in health care. They have what is effectively universal national health care through Medicare. Medicare is supplemented by Medicaid, employer retirement programs, and supplemental insurance. More recently, a prescription drug benefit program has been added to Medicare. Yet disparities remain.

Seniors with less income, less education, and from a minority racial or ethnic group generally show higher levels of health care problems and less utilization of health care services than those with more income, more education, and who are white. These are the same patterns we have seen in the previous chapters. An important distinction is that the differences appear to be fewer for seniors than for younger people.

Another important explanation for disparities is that health care problems that exist prior to turning sixty-five, the near-elderly, continue through the senior years. Thus an important way to reduce disparities among seniors is to reduce them among younger people. That might be the ultimate solution to the existence of disparities among the elderly.

References

Agency for Healthcare Research and Quality. 2006. *2006 National Healthcare Disparities Report.* Rockville, MD: U.S. Department of Health and Human Services.

Bach, Peter B., et al. 2004. "Primary Care Physicians Who Treat Blacks and Whites." *New England Journal of Medicine* 351, no. 6 (August 5): 575–84.

Basu, Jayasree. 2005. "Severity of Illness, Race, and Choice of Local Versus Distant Hospitals among the Elderly." *Journal of Health Care for the Poor and Underserved* 16, no. 2 (May): 391–405.

Bucks, Brian K.; Arthur B. Kennickell; and Kevin B. Moore. 2006. "Recent Changes in U.S. Family Finances: Evidence from the 2001 and 2004 Survey of Consumer Finances." *Federal Reserve Bulletin* 92, no. 2 (February): A1–A38.

Century Foundation. 2005. *Social Security Reform; Revised Edition.* New York: Century Foundation.

Cohn, Jonathan. 2007. *Sick: The Untold Story of America's Health Care Crisis—and the People Who Pay the Price.* New York: HarperCollins.

Cubanski, Juliette; Molly Voris; Michelle Kitchman; Tricia Neuman; and Lisa Potetz. 2005. *Medicare Chartbook.* 3rd ed. Menlo Park, CA: Henry J. Kaiser Family Foundation.

Cutler, David M. 2001. "Declining Disability among the Elderly." *Health Affairs* 20, no. 6 (November–December): 11–27.

Davis, Jullet A., and Kate L. Lapane. 2004. "Do Characteristics Associated with Nursing Home Residents Vary by Race/Ethnicity?" *Journal of Health Care for the Poor and Underserved* 15, no. 2 (May): 251–66.

Employee Benefit Research Institute. 2007. *EBRI Databook on Employee Benefits.* Washington, D.C.: Employee Benefit Research Institute. Online at www.ebri.org/publications/books/index.cfm?fa=databook.

Fitzpatrick, Annette L., et al. 2004. "Barriers to Health Care Access among the Elderly and Who Perceives Them." *American Journal of Public Health* 94, no. 10 (October): 1788–94.

Fleming, Kevin C.; Jonathan M. Evans; and Darryl S. Chutka. 2003. "A Cultural and Economic History of Old Age in America." *Mayo Clinic Proceedings* 78, no. 7 (July): 914–21.

Goldman, Dana P., and Julie M. Zissimopoulos. 2003. "High Out-of-Pocket Health Care Spending by the Elderly." *Health Affairs* 22, no. 3 (May–June): 194–202.

Gornick, Marian E. 2000. "Disparities in Medicare Services: Potential Causes, Plausible Explanations, and Recommendations." *Health Care Financing Review* 21, no. 4 (Summer): 23–43.

Hacker, Jacob S. 2006. *The Great Risk Shift: The Assault on American Jobs, Families, Health and Retirement and How You Can Fight Back.* New York: Oxford University Press.

Hadley, Jack, and Timothy Waidman. 2006. "Health Insurance and Health at Age 65: Implications for Medical Care Spending on New Medicare Beneficiaries." *Health Services Research* 41, no. 2 (April): 429–51.

Henry J. Kaiser Family Foundation. 2005. *A Profile of African Americans, Latinos, and Whites with Medicare: Implications for Outreach Efforts for the New Drug Benefit.* Menlo Park, CA: Henry J. Kaiser Family Foundation.

Henry J. Kaiser Family Foundation. 2007. *Medicare at a Glance.* Menlo Park, CA: Henry J. Kaiser Family Foundation.

Holahan, John, and Arunabh Ghosh. 2005. *Dual Eligibles: Medicaid Enrollment and Spending for Medicare Beneficiaries in 2003.* Washington, D.C.: Kaiser Commission on Medicaid and the Uninsured.

Infoplease. n.d. "Life Expectancy by Age, 1850–2004." Online at www.infoplease.com/ipa/A0005140.html.

Johnson, Richard W. 2006. *Health Insurance Coverage and Costs at Older Ages: Evidence from the Health and Retirement Study.* Washington, D.C.: American Association of Retired Persons.

Johnson, Richard W. 2007. *What Happens to Health Benefits after Retirement?* Center for Retirement Research Issue Brief (Series 7, February), Boston College.

Johnson, Richard W., and Joshua M. Wiener. 2006. *A Profile of Frail Older Americans and Their Caregivers.* Washington, D.C.: Urban Institute.

Lubitz, James, et al. 2001. "Three Decades of Health Care Use by the Elderly, 1865–1998." *Health Affairs* 20, no. 2 (March–April): 19–32.

Marmor, Theodore R. 2000. *The Politics of Medicare.* 2nd ed. New York: Aldine de Gruyter.

McWilliams, J. Michael; Alan M. Zaslavsky; Ellen Meara; and John Z. Ayanian. 2004. "Health Insurance Coverage and Mortality among the Near-Elderly." *Health Affairs* 23, no. 4 (July–August): 223–33.

Meara, Ellen; Chapin White; and David M. Cutler. 2004. "Trends in Medical Spending by Age, 1963–2000." *Health Affairs* 23, no. 4 (July–August): 176–83.

Mokdad, Ali H., et al. 2004. "Changes in Health Behaviors among Older Americans, 1990 to 2000." *Public Health Reports* 119, no. 3 (May–June): 356–61.

Mold, James W.; George E. Fryer; and Cynthia H. Thomas. 2004. "Who Are the Uninsured Elderly in the United States?" *Journal of the American Geriatrics Society* 52, no. 4 (April): 601–4.

Moon, Marilyn. 2006. *Medicare: A Policy Primer.* Washington, D.C.: Urban Institute.

Morris, Charles R. 2006. *Apart at the Seams: The Collapse of Private Pensions and Health Care Protections.* New York: Century Foundation.

National Institute on Aging. 2007. *Growing Older in America: The Health and Retirement Study.* Bethesda, MD: U.S. Department of Health and Human Services, National Institutes of Health.

Neuman, Patricia, et al. 2007. "Medicare Prescription Benefit Progress Report: Findings from a 2006 National Survey of Seniors." *Health Affairs* web exclusive (August 21): w630–w643.

Oberlander, Jonathan. 2003. *The Political Life of Medicare.* Chicago: University of Chicago Press.

Okoro, Catherine A.; Stacy L. Young; Tara W. String; Lina S. Balluz; and Ali H. Mokdad. 2005. "Uninsured Adults 65 Years and Older: Is Their Health at Risk?" *Journal of Health Care for the Poor and Underserved* 16, no. 3 (August): 453–63.

Oliver, Thomas R., Philip R. Lee, and Helene L. Lipton. 2004. "A Political History of Medicare and Prescription Drug Coverage." *Milbank Quarterly* 82, no. 2 (June): 283–354.

Patel, Kant, and Mark E. Rushefsky. 2006. *Health Care Politics and Policy in America.* Armonk, NY: M.E. Sharpe.

Pati, Susmita; Ron Keren; Evaline A. Alessandrini; and Donald F. Schwarz. 2004. "Generational Differences in U.S. Public Spending, 1980–2000." *Health Affairs* 23, no. 5 (September–October): 131–41.

Pol, Louis G.; Keith J. Mueller; and Phani Tej Adidam. 2002. "Racial and Ethnic Differences in Health Insurance for the Near Elderly." *Journal of Health Care for the Poor and Underserved* 13, no. 2 (May): 229–40.

Rushefsky, Mark E. 2004. "Ending Medicare as We Know It." Paper presented at the annual convention of the American Political Science Association, Chicago, IL.

Rushefsky, Mark E. 2007. *Public Policy in the United States: At the Dawn of the Twenty-First Century.* Armonk, NY: M.E. Sharpe.

Ryan, William. 1976. *Blaming the Victim.* New York: Vintage Books.

Sambamoorthi, Usha, and Patricia A. Findley. 2005. "Who Are the Elderly Who Never Receive Immmunization?" *Preventive Medicine* 40, no. 4 (April): 469–78.

Sherkat, Darren E., et al. 2005. "Explaining Race Differences in Mortality among the Tennessee Medicare Elderly: The Role of Physician Services." *Journal of Health Care for the Poor and Underserved* 16, no. 4 (November, Supplement A): 50–63.

Shih, Ya-Chen Tina; Lirong Zhao; and Linda S. Elting. 2006. "Does Medicare Coverage of Colonoscopy Reduce Racial/Ethnic Disparities in Cancer Screening among the Elderly?" *Health Affairs* 25, no. 4 (July–August): 1153–62.

Starr, Paul. 1982. *The Social Transformation of American Medicine.* New York: Basic Books.

U.S. Bureau of the Census. 2007. *Statistical Abstract of the United States.* Washington, D.C.: U.S. Department of Commerce.

Wasow, Bernard. 2004. *Policy for a Secure Retirement.* New York: Century Foundation.

Weller, Christian, and Edward N. Wolff. 2005. *Retirement Income: The Crucial Role of Social Security.* Washington, D.C.: Economic Policy Institute.

Xu, K. Tom. 2003. "Financial Disparities in Prescription Drug Use between Elderly and Nonelderly Americans." *Health Affairs* 22, no. 5 (September–October): 210–21.

8

Geography and Health Care

It is a maxim of business that success is based on "location, location, location." If you just have your business in a place where you can get customers, then your business is more likely to prosper. Place, or geography, is the subject of this chapter.

We have examined disparities from a number of different angles: race, ethnicity, gender, age, and income. And all of these factors come into play in this chapter as well. But place adds another dimension. Does access to health care, the health of residents, and the quality of care differ based on where one happens to live? The answer, in short, is yes.

There are, documented in the health care literature, variations in practices by geographic boundaries (see, for example, Baicker, Chandra, and Skinner 2005; Baicker et al. 2004; Wennberg 2004). This affects all the different groups discussed in previous chapters. The interaction of place with these other factors complicates understanding health care disparities.

The chapter proceeds as follows. In this introduction we will set forth the boundaries of geographic health care inequalities by exploring different geographical areas. We then look at health disparities of outcome, access, and quality of care based on geography. That is followed by a discussion of reasons for the disparities and attempts to reduce geographically based disparities. In this chapter we shall also explore the various other factors that create disparities.

A Health Care Geography

The *National Health Care Disparities Report* (Agency for Healthcare Research and Quality 2006, 182) distinguishes four geographical areas. The largest metropolitan areas are those with a million or more residents. Smaller metropolitan areas are those with less than a million residents. "Metropolitan urban areas" have 10,000 to 50,000 residents. And "noncore statistical areas" are the residual; none of the above.

Table 8.1

Defining Urban and Rural Areas

Category	Urban influence code*	MSA** status	Characteristics/ proximity	Population
Metro	1	MSA	Large (central and fringe counties)	1 million or more
	2	MSA	Small	Less than 1 million
Near-metro	3	non-MSA	Adjacent to large MSA	City of population of 10,000 or more
	4	non-MSA	Adjacent to large MSA	No city of population of 10,000 or more
	5	non-MSA	Adjacent to small MSA	City of population of 10,000 or more
	6	non-MSA	Adjacent to small MSA	No city of population of 10,000 or more
Near-rural	7	non-MSA	Not adjacent to MSA	City of population 10,000 or more
	8	non-MSA	Not adjacent to MSA	City of population 2,500–9,999
Rural	9	non-MSA	Not adjacent of MSA	No city or city of population less than 2,500

Source: Larson et al. (2004, 37).
* continuum from most urban to most rural; ** metropolitan statistical area

The U.S. Department of Health and Human Services divides the country into eight regions (Eberhardt, Ingram, and Makuc 2001). The northeast part of the country consists of the New England and the Middle Atlantic regions. The southern part of the country consists of the South Atlantic, the East South Central, and the West South Central regions. The midwest consists of the East North Central and the West North Central regions. And the western part of the country consists of the Mountain and Pacific regions.

Another way of classifying geographical areas is that adopted by Larson et al. (2004). They categorize the population into nine different geographical areas based on population. Table 8.1 shows the classification scheme.

Some of the disparities are regional, such as the Midwest or the South. Many of the problems of inequality and the literature focus on rural areas, the equivalent of the noncore areas, and inner-city areas. Baicker, Chandra, and Skinner (2005) point out that African Americans and Hispanics do not live in the same places as whites. So, for these groups (and the authors) geography is important.

One can look at health care disparities from three perspectives: compositional, collective, and contextual ("Editorial: Health in Rural America" 2004; Probst et al. 2004). The compositional perspective focuses on the characteristics of the population, the kinds of things we have been doing throughout this book. This would include race, ethnicity, gender, age (children, elderly), and income (or socioeconomic class). The collective perspective or effects come into play when there is a large concentration of people with certain characteristics. This is combined with the institutional/political and cultural contexts (Probst et al. 2004). The compositional effects or perspective is based on place, more particularly, "they derive from the special characteristics of rural areas" ("Editorial: Health in Rural America" 2004). We would extend this last notion to include inner-city urban areas, which have their own "special characteristics."

Murray et al. (2006) distinguish among what they call the "eight Americas." Using a variety of datasets, such as data from the Census Bureau, the National Center for Health Statistics, the Behavioral Risk Factor Surveillance System, and the World Health Organization (for international comparisons), we will examine the findings of the study below. Table 8.2 presents the definitions and descriptions of the "eight Americas." Note that these categories are only partially geographically based. They are also racially and ethnically based. There are also income characteristics, and in one case, high homicide rates. Population density is also a factor.

Gillanders, Buss, and Hofstetter (1996) argue that looking at disparities between urban and rural areas is too simplistic. Rather, in fitting in with the classification by Larson et al. (2004), they argue that we should look at a continuum from more to less rural. Gillanders, Buss, and Hofstetter (1996, 9) note that "rural areas are not typically dominated by either farming or wilderness as popularly perceived. Employment in 71% of 2,000 rural counties is concentrated in manufacturing, retirement, mining, government or federal lands."

Baicker, Chandra, and Skinner (2005, S44–S45) offer an alternative way of looking at geography. They argue that the best unit of analysis is the "hospital referral region" (HRR). Such a region is marked by a hospital that provides "end-of-life care" and cardiac care (S45). Another way of looking at that is that this is the market for these kinds of hospitals. Using this definition and data from Medicare, there are 306 such regions.

Racial and ethnic minorities are not evenly distributed around the United States. Probst et al. (2002, 2004) examine the distribution of minorities in rural areas. They find that rural African Americans tend to live in the southern states, with four such states accounting for half of that population and six states accounting for about three-quarters. There is a similar geographical concentration among rural Hispanics, this time in the southwestern United States. Texas by itself accounts for about 25 percent of rural Hispanics. Adding four more states brings the proportion to over 50 percent. Alaskan Natives and Native Americans tend to be clustered in five states. On the other hand, the number of Latinos in rural areas is growing, attracted by food processing plants. Fortunately, while businesses in rural areas tend not to offer health insurance, the food processing industry does offer such benefits (Blewett, Davern, and Rodin 2005). Baicker, Chandra, and Skinner (2005) find great variations in the proportions of African Americans in different areas. Some areas have as much as six times the proportion of African Americans as the national average.

Table 8.2

The Eight Americas

America	General description	Population (in millions)	Average income per capita	Percent completing high school	Definition
1	Asian	10.4	$21,566	80	Asians living in counties where Pacific Islanders make up less than 40 percent of total Asian population
2	Northland low-income rural white	3.6	$17,758	83	Whites in northern plains and Dakotas with 1990 county-level per capita income below $11,775 and population density less than 100 persons/km^2
3	Middle America	214.0	$24,640	84	All other whites not included in Americas 2 and 4, Asians not in America 1, and Native Americans not in America 5
4	Low-income whites in Appalachia and the Mississippi Valley	16.6	$16,390	72	Whites in Appalachia and the Mississippi Valley with 1990 county-level per capita income below $11,775
5	Western Native American	1.0	$10,029	69	Native American populations in the mountain and plain areas, predominantly on reservations
6	Black Middle America	23.4	$15,412	75	All other black populations living in counties not included in Americas 7 and 8
7	Southern low-income rural black	5.8	$10,463	61	Blacks living in counties in the Mississippi Valley and the Deep South with population density below 100 persons/km^2, 1990 county-level per capita income below $7,500, and total population size above 1,000 persons (to avoid small numbers)
8	High-risk urban black	7.5	$14,800	72	Urban populations of more than 150,000 blacks living in counties with cumulative probability of homicide death between 15 and 74 y greater than 1.0 percent.

Source: Murray et al. 2006. "Eight Americas: Investigating Mortality Disparities across Races, Counties, and Race-Counties in the United States." *PLoS Medicine* 3(9): e260. doi:10.1371/journal.pmed.0030260.t001

Population, income per capita, and education were calculated for race-county combinations from the 2000 U.S. census.
DOI: 10.1371/journal.pmed.0030260.t001

Rural areas are largely those with very small populations over large expanses of land.

Minorities in rural areas tend to be poorer than non-Hispanic whites. For example, the poverty rate among African Americans in rural areas is 34 percent versus 13 percent for the white population in rural areas. The same is true for Hispanics and Native Americans (Probst et al. 2002).

Probst et al. (2004) argue that the contextual factors have developed due to these concentrations. They note that having geographical concentrations, at least among rural blacks and likely urban, inner-city blacks, tends to raise disease and death rates.

Fluharty (2002) points out that rural areas are quite diverse. They differ "across space, circumstance, culture, and demography" (Fluharty 2002, 58). He notes that agriculture represents only a small portion of rural areas (about six percent [Cordes 1998] in terms of employment and residence). But he also notes that areas that are heavily reliant on agriculture face significant challenges. As a whole, rural areas thrived in the 1990s, with increases in employment, earnings, and so forth. While there was considerable job growth in rural areas, most of it has been in retail trade or services, accounting for almost two-thirds of the job increases (authors' calculations from Fluharty 2002, 59). As is generally true, those sectors are less likely to offer health insurance benefits than, say, manufacturing (Fluharty 2002). As Fluharty points out, low-wage employment dominates the job market and median incomes in rural areas are lower than in urban areas.

There are also higher rates of poverty in rural versus urban areas (or suburban areas) (Larson et al. 2004; van Dis 2002). Furthermore, Fluharty (2002, 61) writes that "particularly disturbing is the stark reality that rural poor families are more likely to be employed and remain poor." Similarly, child poverty is higher in rural versus urban counties as is the percentage of female-headed families. Twenty-three percent of rural counties are considered "persistent poverty-stricken . . . and are mainly in the South, core Appalachia, the lower Rio Grande Valley, and on American Indian reservations" (Fluharty 2002, 62). Rural areas also have a disproportionate number of elderly people. Nearly 19 percent of the population in rural areas is elderly (sixty-five and older), as compared to a little less than 11 percent in metropolitan areas. Many of these elderly people in rural areas are women (Larson et al. 2004). Levels of education also tend to be lower in rural areas (Larson et al. 2004).

Fluharty (2002) then turns to government issues. Rural areas receive substantial income transfers, about 20 percent of all income. Governments in these areas tend to be small and run by nonprofessionals. Also, these areas often lack technical support and suffer from a lack of Internet access. Additionally, when children finish high school, they often leave for other parts of the country, depriving rural areas of their skills and initiative. While change has taken place in rural areas, the same health care issues apparent during the Great Depression remain (Cordes 1998).

Disparities in Health Status, Access, and Quality of Care

One of the easiest disparities to investigate is mortality because deaths are publicly recorded. Murray et al. (2006), whom we discussed earlier in connection with the "eight Americas," focused on mortality rates and the differences in such rates among the eight groups. Asians had the highest life expectancy rate ("America 1," see Table 8.2), followed by "America 2," low-income, northland rural whites. The group with lowest life expectancy at birth is "America 8," urban blacks in high-risk counties. The biggest gap, 20.7 years, among the "eight Americas" was between Asian females and urban black males in high risk counties. The researchers found wide gaps in life expectancy within white populations. "America 2" has a considerably higher life expectancy at birth than the rest of the white population. They found that the "America 4" group, with an income about the same as the "America 2" group, had a life expectancy rate about the same as Panama and Mexico.

Disparities in access, outcome, and so forth vary depending on the region of the country. For example, infant mortality tends to be lowest in places near metropolitan areas. The highest infant mortality rates were found in inner cities in the Northeast and Midwest and very rural counties in the South (Eberhardt, Ingram, and Makuc 2001). The same was true for adults in the twenty-five to sixty-four age range.

Much of the material discussed below will focus on disparities between rural and metropolitan areas and inner city urban and metropolitan areas. But there are also disparities among metropolitan areas. Grossman et al. (2002) examined births among American Indians and Alaska Natives (AI/AN) in urban areas. Looking at data for 1989–91 period, they found considerable variation across the country using several different measures. The percentage of mothers receiving inadequate prenatal care varied from a low of 4.4 percent in Fayetteville, North Carolina, to a high of 29.8 percent in the Minneapolis–St. Paul, Minnesota, area. The percentage of low birth weight babies in this group varied from a low of 3.3 percent in Lawton, Oklahoma, to a high of 9.2 percent in the New York metropolitan area. The infant mortality rate varied from a low of zero in Lawton, Oklahoma, to a high of 27.17 per 1,000 live births in Yakima, Washington.

Murray et al. (2006) also looked at age groups within the "eight Americas." They found that the disparities in life expectancy were greatest for the middle groups (fifteen to sixty-four). The group of major concern was "America 8." "In these age groups [15–44, 44–64], blacks living in high-risk averse urban areas (America 8) have mortality risks similar to ones in the Russian Federation and sub-Saharan Africa" (Murray et al. 2006, 1520).

An additional rural disparity has been prescription drug coverage for Medicare beneficiaries. Until the passage of the Medicare Modernization Act in 2003, Medicare on its own did not have an outpatient prescription drug benefit. Prior to the act, beneficiaries could get coverage through an employee retirement health plan (less likely in rural areas where employee health benefits are relatively rare compared to urban and suburban areas), through Medicaid, through a supplemental plan (so-called Medigap plans) or through a health maintenance organization (HMO), which is also less likely in rural than in other areas. It should come as no surprise then that rural Medicare beneficiaries had less prescription drug coverage (more than one-third of such residents had no such coverage) than urban residents (about 18.8 percent) (National Rural Health Association 2005).

Baicker, Chandra, and Skinner's (2005) careful study documents geographic disparities. One such measure is use of procedures that are generally accepted and proven to be effective and cost-effective. These measures are:

> the administration of angiotensin-converting enzyme inhibitors, aspirin, and beta-blockers after heart attacks; mammograms for older women; influenza and flu vaccines; and eye exams and the evaluation of lipid profiles and HbA1c for diabetics. (Baicker, Chandra, and Skinner 2005, S46)

Within this group of procedures, the authors found geographic disparities, with some areas using these procedures at twice the rate of others.

The authors argue that there is a difference in disparities between areas and disparities within areas. They assert that racial segregation leads to disparities in health care. They use as an example one of the cost-effective procedures mentioned above, eye exams for people suffering from diabetes. They divided up the 306 HRRs by percentage of black population and found that the greater the proportion of blacks the less likely the residents were to get annual exams. Very importantly, the authors note that this was true for white residents in these high-proportion African American areas. They write that: "there *are* disparities in care within HRRs but that residential segregation increases racial disparities" (Baicker, Chandra, and Skinner 2005, S49; emphasis in original).

Their further analysis provides estimates of the impact of residence and provision by providers mentioned above. Using the same procedure as mentioned in the preceding paragraph, they estimate that 56 percent of disparities between races is due to where the races live and the other 44 percent is due to the different treatment the races receive (Baicker, Chandra, and Skinner 2005).

Rural Areas

> Simply stated, health care in rural American seems to be in a constant state of stress. (Basanta 2002, 37)

> These inequities in rural vs urban health care delivery are based in structural, economic and cultural differences." (van Dis 2002, 108)

The Agency for Healthcare Research and Quality (2006) identifies rural areas as a priority population. The health care disparities report lists five areas of disparities in rural areas where improvements are needed: helping children eat in a more healthy way, hospital heart attack deaths, pediatric asthma hospital admissions, timely care for illnesses or injuries, and increased access to health insurance (Agency for Healthcare Research and Quality 2006).

Basanta (2002) identifies a number of problems of rural health care that have been historically evident. These include the large number of people in rural areas lacking health insurance, the lack of providers in these areas, the precarious financial status of hospitals in rural areas, and the availability of health care technology. We will consider all these and others in the sections below.

Rural residents tend to engage in behaviors that adversely affect health as com- pared to suburban residents. There are higher rates of smoking and obesity and lower rates of exercise and healthy diets (Hartley 2004; see also Eberhardt, Ingram, and Makuc 2001). Hartley (2004) suggests that attempts to change such behaviors have been difficult with lower socioeconomic class people (low education and income) and suggests that there might be some cultural barriers to changing risky behaviors. Rural residence would include "culture, community, and environment" (Hartley 2004, 1676). Hartley also notes that there is variation in health issues depending on the region. For example, rural Northeast residents had high levels of dental issues. This was also true for residents in the South, regardless of degree of urbanization (Eberhardt, Ingram, and Makuc 2001).

There are also disparities in the distribution of health care providers (also dis- cussed below). About one-fifth of the population of the United States lives in rural areas. But only about 9 percent of physicians practice in those areas. Nurses are also in short supply, as measured per person (van Dis 2002).

In general, the smaller the community the lower the rate of providers in that community. For example, in large metropolitan areas, there were 304 physicians per 100,000 population (this is 1995 data), compared to 235 per 100,000 population in smaller metropolitan areas. The smallest and most rural communities had the lowest rate, 53 per 100,000 (Council on Graduate Medical Education 1998). Another way of looking at this problem is that adjusting for population size, which is what rates do, there are nearly six times as many physicians in the largest metropolitan areas than in the smallest rural areas. Obstetricians/gynecologists are readily abundant in urban (and suburban areas) but are much more difficult to find in rural areas. As noted below, the supply of family practitioners is about the same in rural and urban areas, but the rate of specialists is much higher in urban areas, with the largest gap in pediatrics (Council on Graduate Medical Education 1998).

The Council on Graduate Medical Education (1998) report addressed the reasons for the disparities in specialty providers. The major reason is the medical student's choice of specialty area. And the report found that the more specialized the training the less likely the new physician will locate in rural areas. The report notes that one reason for this is that specialists need a larger population to work with. For example, the report states that a family practice can serve an area of 2,000 people whereas a neurosurgical practice would need a service area with fifty times that number.

Heady (2002) points out the numerous characteristics of rural areas that create the kinds of problems and disparities that we are discussing. The major problem she finds is "low population densities" (Heady 2002, 110). This then leads to a whole slew of problems for the rural health care system (Heady 2002, 110):

"decreased patient volumes and diseconomies of scale, fixed overhead expenses, high percentages of subsidized and uninsured patients, disproportionately elderly populations, physician shortages, and decreased access for low-income patients." In addition, the racial makeup of rural areas—African Americans in some (mainly the South), Hispanics in others (mainly the Southwest), and Native American peoples in general—also leads to physician location decisions that exacerbate disparities. The Council on Graduate Medical Education (1998) also mentions the lack of amenities in these areas as a repellant force.

Having said that, an apparent paradox is that rural residents have a higher rate of hospital use than residents in metropolitan areas. The resolution to the paradox is that the relative lack of access to providers leads to delayed treatment for various illnesses. When the illness gets worse, the resident goes to the hospital (Eberhardt, Ingram, and Makuc 2001).

In the 1990s, states turned to managed care as a way to control the costs of their Medicaid programs. By 2003, a little over 59 percent of Medicaid recipients were enrolled in some type of managed care program (see Patel and Rushefsky 2006, 103–10). In some respects, this is a very high number, because in general the elderly and the disabled have not been required to enroll in such programs.

The question becomes: what has been the experience with Medicaid managed care, particularly in rural areas? Silfkin et al. (1998) examined state experiences with Medicaid managed care. They suggested four reasons why managed care penetration in rural areas might trail that in urban areas. The first, and most obvious is the smaller population and especially the low population density in rural areas. This is important because, following normal insurance risk principles, a larger and more dense population spreads the risk of very high health care costs. This is one reason why individual health insurance policies and small business health insurance policies are so expensive. A second possible, related reason is that commercial insurers have not entered rural markets in significant numbers.

The third reason is one we discussed earlier. Rural areas generally have fewer health care providers, particularly specialists, than urban and suburban areas. Thus there are fewer doctors to organize. A fourth reason is that mandating managed care enrollment could result in less choice of providers since managed care organizations (MCOs) seek to enroll some, but not all providers in an area. If a managed care organization enrolled all the providers in an area, there would be little point to having such a plan. So, access to health care providers could lessen (Silfkin et al. 1998).

To discover whether these arguments hold up, the researchers conducted interviews with officials in each state. They found significant differences between urban and rural counties. First of all, a higher percentage of urban counties (73.6 percent) had Medicaid managed care plans as compared to rural counties (57.2 percent) (Silfkin et al. 1998).

There were also differences in the type of managed care plans in urban versus rural counties. Urban counties were much more likely to have fully capitated managed health care plans than rural areas. Capitated plans are those that derive all or most of their funds from the state on a per person basis as opposed to a fee-for-service basis. That provides more opportunities for cost control. On the other hand, reflecting the lack of specialists, rural county Medicaid managed care plans were more likely than urban counties to have primary care case management (PCCM) plans, which are based more on fee-for-service and do not involve health maintenance organizations. Such plans involve considerably less risk to the organization and physicians than do partially or fully capitated plans (Silfkin et al. 1998). A third difference was that enrollment was more likely to be voluntary in rural counties than in urban counties. That is, if Medicaid managed care was available in a rural area, participants were often given the choice of whether to enroll in a fully capitated plan or a PCCM; urban residents were less likely to have that choice (Silfkin et al. 1998).

A follow-up survey (Silberman et al. 2002) found that Medicaid managed care penetration in rural areas had increased, though many of the same characteristics remained. Many more states had state-wide Medicaid managed care programs, which would make it more likely that rural counties were included. The percentage of rural and urban counties in 2001 with such programs increased over the 1997 figures, rising to 74.4 percent in rural areas and 85 percent in urban areas. Growth of such plans in rural areas was faster than, though still trailing, in urban areas.

One disturbing finding was that in the period between the two studies (1997–2001), some managed care plans pulled out of the Medicaid market because of costs. Silberman et al. (2002) found that while there were pullouts from urban areas, the pullouts had larger impacts in rural areas. They write that "plan pullouts created bigger 'holes' in rural areas since there were no other plans to pick up enrollees, and some counties returned to FFS [fee-for-service]" (261).

This was also a problem for rural residents on Medicare. From 1998 to 2000, Medicare HMOs (through what was then called Medicare+Choice and is now Medicare Advantage [Part D]; see Patel and Rushefsky 2006) were dropping their coverage, arguing that they could not afford the Medicare beneficiaries. In 2000, nearly a million Medicare beneficiaries were dropped. The impact on rural areas, as compared to urban areas, was pronounced. First, a much larger percentage of rural Medicare beneficiaries (32 percent) were dropped as compared to urban beneficiaries (about 15 percent). More critically, because of the lower managed care penetration in rural as compared to urban areas, many more rural beneficiaries (65 percent) had no HMO alternative to enroll in compared to urban beneficiaries (about 13 percent) (Boone 2000).

O'Neill (2004) investigated the impact of rural managed care, in this case among Medicare beneficiaries, on travel time to providers. He first notes the importance of distance. He writes that "patients who lived more than 20 miles from their admitting hospital have been shown to use fewer ambulatory services, to receive less high-technology procedures, and to have higher mortality rates in the year following hospital admission for cardiac treatment" (O'Neill 2004, 187). He notes that while managed care organizations offer important benefits to potential subscribers, such as lower or no copayments and supplementary benefits, a major drawback is the limitations mentioned above on provider availability (selective contracting), including physicians and hospitals.

Drawing on a variety of sources, O'Neill looked at 1998 data in Pennsylvania. He found that beneficiaries in Medicare HMOs spent more time traveling and had to go a greater distance to get to hospitals within the HMO system than enrollees in traditional fee-for-service Medicare. HMO enrollees were also more likely to have to go to an urban hospital and one outside their county of residence. Part of the problem, as discussed above, is the limited penetration of HMOs in rural areas as compared to urban and suburban areas.

Another problem that managed care presented to rural areas relates to the presence of the uninsured population. Managed care organizations are not required to serve the uninsured and thus to the extent that MCOs become an important provider of medical care, the uninsured may find their access actually decreases. Exacerbating this problem is the replacement of not-for-profit MCOs with for-profit ones, which are even less likely to provide unreimbursed care (Council on Graduate Medical Education 1998).

Not everyone agrees that disparities exist based upon place, or believe that if they do exist, the relationships are weak. Gillanders, Buss, and Hofstetter (1996) looked at counties in northeastern Ohio. They noted that health status tended to be better the closer a resident was to an urban area. But overall, the differences were small and on some measures were not statistically significant.

Similarly, Blazer et al. (1995) did not find many differences on a variety of measures for elderly residents in an urban and four rural counties in North Carolina. They found that if residents lived reasonably close to centers of medical care, then access, continuity, and transportation were not an issue. Cost, however, was more of an issue for the rural elderly than their urban counterparts.

Urban Areas

Inner-city areas also have issues related to access, outcomes, and quality that are long-standing. Brown, Wyn, and Teleki (2000) found, using 1998 data, that there was significant variation in uninsurance rates among the country's cities. The average uninsurance rates in metropolitan statistical areas (MSAs) was 19 percent, but 30 percent among those with low or moderate incomes. Akron, Ohio, and Harrisburg, Pennsylvania, had the lowest rates (7 percent uninsured) while El Paso, Texas, had the highest rate, with 30 percent uninsured overall and half of those with low and moderate incomes. There was also variation in employment-provided insurance coverage. The national average among the MSAs was 67 percent job-based coverage, and 45 percent among low and moderate income people. Milwaukee,

Wisconsin, had the highest overall coverage, at 84 percent, with El Paso the lowest, at 49 percent.

Brown, Wyn, and Teleki (2000) found that there were important differences on a number of indicators between MSAs with high rates of job-based coverage and those with low rates of such coverage. In the low-rate MSAs the unemployment rate was almost twice that of the high ones. Labor force participation was high in the high-rate MSAs. There were also more likely to be larger firms, particularly manufacturing firms, in the high-rate areas. Union membership was also higher in the high-rate areas. The poverty rate in the low-coverage areas was over twice as high as in the high-coverage areas.

The study also linked the lack of insurance with access issues. People in MSAs with high uninsurance rates were also more likely not to have a regular source of care, visit a doctor, or delay care. Brown, Wyn, and Teleki (2000, xiv) offer an explanation for the access issue: "public hospitals and community health centers—the safety net—are overwhelmed by uninsured residents in cities that have disproportionately large uninsured populations."

A 1979 study (Sixsmith and Goldman) attempted to estimate the health care costs of drug abuse. They examined inpatient charts from Harlem Hospital Center in New York for November 1976 period. One of the most arresting findings was that though the percentage of patients who were drug abusers or whose hospitalization was due to drug abuse was relatively small, their use of hospital resources was large. Length of hospital stay was over 75 percent higher than the entire sample population (authors' calculations from Sixsmith and Goldman 1979). Drug abusers who went for emergency services were more than twice as likely to be hospitalized as the overall sample population. They estimate the cost of drug abuse "in a community which is at high risk for health problems in general, and which has limited medical resources" (Sixsmith and Goldman 1979, 507) is wildly underestimated.

Access to hospital services in urban, inner-city areas can be as problematical as in rural areas, and, like the drug abuse issue discussed in the preceding paragraph, it is a problem with long roots. Gentry (1980) examined the situation in San Antonio, Texas, where the county was attempting to close the obstetrical unit in Robert B. Green Hospital and transfer it to a suburban area. Gentry writes that just trying to reach Green Hospital and another some fourteen miles away was difficult enough. With the possible switch, access for inner city residents would be even more difficult. Gentry notes that in the late 1970s a sizable number of inner city hospitals were closed. Opposition to such closures was based on civil rights, with the claim that they discriminated against minority communities.

Opportunity Agenda (n.d.) argues that geographic barriers are important within cities. Focusing on the nation's largest city, New York, the report says that easy access to hospitals is important because people in the local community rely on the hospitals for services. Hospitals, like schools, can often be anchors (1); other providers and clinics will locate near hospitals. If hospitals close in neighborhoods, then patients have to travel farther to get to another one, generally relying on public transportation. The study reports that travel time is related to receiving prenatal care. The shorter the travel time the more likely the mother is to get prenatal care. The report displayed data showing an inverse relationship between the availability of maternity hospital beds in a neighborhood and the rate of delayed prenatal care. The same was true for low birthweight babies. The report noted that hospital closures or the closing of maternity wards contributed to the problem.

An accompanying report (Opportunity Agenda n.d.) focused on primary care in New York City. The report noted the high penetration of primary care providers in high income communities and the low penetration of such providers in low income neighborhoods. The report states the theme of this chapter: "where you live affects your access to health care" (Opportunity Agenda (n.d., 1). Better access in low income communities could result in avoiding or reducing the prevalence of diseases. These kinds of diseases are called "ambulatory-care sensitive (ACS) conditions" (Opportunity Agenda n.d., 2). Such diseases include heart disease, diabetes, and asthma. As an example of the disparities of primary care within neighborhoods in New York City, an area in East Harlem had a primary care physician rate of 6 per 10,000 population. The more affluent residents of the Upper East Side in Manhattan had a ratio of 67 per 10,000, about ten times the rate. The Opportunity Agenda report also provided data for ACS conditions in the two neighborhoods. For the affluent neighborhood, the average rate was 269 conditions per 100,000 population, compared to 2,007 conditions per 100,000 population in the poor community. The same barriers exist for primary care as for hospital care: distance, lack of transportation, lack of insurance, and so forth.

One way of conceptualizing health disparities within urban areas is suggested by the phrase "urban health penalty" (Andrulis 1997; Prewitt 1997). The urban health penalty exists in the inner-city areas that feature high concentrations of low income people, often minorities. Andrulis (1997) defines the urban health penalty as "the confluence of circumstances such as poor nutrition, poverty and unemployment with deteriorating housing, violence and loss of services." He provides several examples of the urban health penalty. He compared the incidence of four medical conditions (AIDS, tuberculosis, syphilis, and gonorrhea) in the twenty-five largest cities in the United States with the overall population, using 1993 data. He found that the incidence rate (cases per 100,000 population) was higher in the cities than in the overall population, varying from a 20 percent difference for tuberculosis to a 152 percent difference for gonorrhea.

Other inner-city health problems included high rates of asthma hospitalizations, high substance abuse rates, and high rates of violence. In particular, Andrulis (1997) noted the health consequences for children: high infant mortality rates (especially for low income mothers), high teen birth rates, high levels of lead poisoning, low rates of child immunizations, and high homicide and suicide rates.

Another disparity affecting the inner cities is disability, the ability to function in daily life. Miller et al. (2005) distinguish between "frank" and "subclinical" disability. Frank disability is the inability to perform a task. Subclinical disability is difficulty in performing a task because of a health problem. Sometimes the result of a subclinical disability is not doing the task as often or finding some other way to perform it.

Miller et al. (2005) studied a sample of two communities in the St. Louis, Missouri, area. The inner-city area was considerably poorer and more racially and ethnically mixed than the suburban community. They found rates for both types of disabilities to be higher in the inner-city community. They also found that the rates were higher than for African Americans nationally. The study was limited to middle-aged African Americans in both communities. The authors admit that they do not know what the causes of the disparities were.

Inner-city urban areas also face maldistribution of provider issues, but in a different way from rural areas. This is captured in the following quote from a report by the Council on Graduate Medical Education (1998, 29): "Urban America is a juxtaposition of want and plenty, a place where sophisticated tertiary medical centers are near neighborhoods where people cannot get rudimentary health care." There are transportation barriers for residents who do not own cars. The inner cities also have concentrations of minority group members and high poverty rates. Physicians most likely to locate in inner-city areas are those who share the racial/ethnic makeup of those communities. The supply of minority physicians remains somewhat low.

Baicker, Chandra, and Skinner (2005) state that inner-city residents in theory should have access to high quality care because these areas may have high quality academic medical centers. However, they found that this did not work out well for African Americans because they tended to live in places where the quality of care was low. They note that because African Americans disproportionately live in areas with low quality care, there is often the mistaken judgment that racism is involved. However, they point out that white residents in the same areas also suffer from low quality of care. Geography is the problem.

The authors also noted the difficulty in puzzling out the disparities, because the size of disparities differs from one place to another and, most interestingly, differs among procedures.

The Council on Graduate Medical Education said that the reasons for the maldistribution in urban areas differ from the reasons in rural areas. For urban areas, the reasons include provider attitudes and perceptions about the community. Some of this, the report continues, arises from the fact that medical students are generally not exposed to the urban underserved and often come from different cultural and racial/ethnic backgrounds.

Another factor is working conditions. The quality of the facilities is often below what can be found in more affluent communities, staff ratios are lower, and the demand for services is high. The council report also noted that many of the health problems suffered by residents are extremely complex, often involving substance abuse and mental illness. This is reinforced by exposure to contagious diseases. Low reimbursements are also a problem (Council on Graduate Medical Education 1998).

Health Status/Outcomes

One area of health disparities is in HIV and AIDS incidence. Incidences of HIV and AIDS are disproportionately higher among minority populations (Latinos and African Americans), women (especially women of color), and residents in the southeastern United States (Nguyen and Whetten 2003). Additionally, the southern states suffer from geographic disparities. Nguyen and Whetten (2003) note that the incidences are much higher in the eastern than the western portions of North Carolina. They also observe that the population in this area tends to lack adequate transportation.

Another important sexually transmitted disease affecting the inner cities is syphilis. Baltimore has the highest rate of syphilis in the nation and the inner city is the predominant locus for the epidemic (Williams and Ekundayo 2001). Williams and Ekundayo (2001) investigated some of the reasons for the high incidence within inner-city Baltimore. These included low levels of education, low socioeconomic status, poor communications between patients and providers, the crack cocaine epidemic of the 1990s, and poor knowledge of the health issues involved.

Asthma is a chronic disease that especially affects poor, inner-city young people. Controlling for a number of factors, such as place of residence, gender, age, and so forth, African American children have higher rates of asthma than whites. Eggleston et al. (1999), after reviewing the literature on asthma incidence, find that for African Americans and Hispanics, geography, income, and race/ethnicity together produce the higher rates of both incident and death from the disease.

However, Eggleston et al. (1999) argue that exposure to environmental insults, such as allergens and pollutants, may be a causative factor and present a causal model of how that might work. They note that outdoor air pollution has decreased in cities even though the prevalence of asthma in the inner cities has increased. They examine studies looking at indoor air pollution in the inner cities and find some pollutants more prevalent in the inner cities than in the suburbs. These include cigarette smoke, particles, ozone, nitrogen dioxides, fungus and cockroach allergens, and mold (the last three might lead to greater sensitivity on the part of those exposed). They further suggest that pollutants and allergens interact. Their conclusion is that genetic susceptibility interacts with environmental exposure to produce the high rates of asthma in the inner cities.

One health problem that is predominant in inner-city areas is high blood lead levels among children, especially children living in older homes. Kassa et al. (2000) investigated blood levels in Toledo, Ohio. They found high levels of lead in the soil around homes and in play areas. The children analyzed also had high blood lead levels. They note that ethnicity or race is not a factor in these elevated blood levels. Rather, poverty and location (inner city) were the best predictors. While the blood levels declined after age four, the importance of elevated lead exposure cannot be downplayed. Elevated blood levels in children can lead to later health problems and also have negative effects on the ability to learn (Kassa et al. 2000; see also "Research Explains How Lead Exposure Produces Learning Deficits" 2007).

An important public health issue is death via intentional use of firearms, either via homicide or suicide. Branas et al. (2004) investigated differences in the intentional use of firearms for urban and rural areas, looking at the period from 1989 to 1999. During this time, over 367,000 such deaths were recorded. A little over half were suicides (54.4 percent) and the rest were homicides (45.6 percent). The suicide rate was higher for rural than urban areas, whereas, conversely, firearm homicide rates were higher for urban than rural areas. The more urban, the higher the homicide rate; the more rural, the higher the suicide rate. The overall rate of intentional firearms deaths was about the same in rural and urban areas.

Grisso et al. (1996) looked at injuries among African American women in the inner cities. The researchers looked at emergency room data as well as death certificates in the Philadelphia area from 1987 to 1991. They found a 29 percent increase in injuries among those age fifteen and older. They also found a 55 percent increase in injuries from violence (Grisso et al. 1996). This was a period during which crime rates, especially in the inner cities, was rising.

Weist and Acosta (2001) examined factors that predict whether inner-city children will become exposed to violence. They studied 217 high school students in Baltimore who had been referred to various programs. They compared a set of demographic factors, such as gender and race, with risk factors. The risk factors included life stresses, history of arrest, being held back in school, being in foster care, and substance abuse by parents. The risk factors were strong predictors of being exposed to violence. And the children, not surprisingly, had high rates of being a victim, or knowing a victim, or seeing violence. The stresses of life seemed to be the strongest predictor.

Guyer et al. (1994) investigated immunization rates among inner-city children in Baltimore. The characteristics of the sample, which they said mirrored the larger community in which the survey took place, included a very high proportion of minorities (African Americans accounted for about 90 percent of the sample), low age for mothers (the median was 22 years), low marriage rate (nearly 90 percent were unmarried), low education rates (significant numbers had not completed high school), and large majorities participating in Medicaid or WIC (Women, Infants and Children supplemental feeding program). While access to care was fairly high, most of that was through community health centers, HMOs, or hospital clinics.

Even given what seems like fairly good access to preventive care, immunization rates among this group of children were low (see also Stille and Christison-Lagay 2000). Guyer et al. (1994) point out that the national goal is to have 90 percent of children receiving all of their shots by age two. In this group, only half met that goal. Worse, there was a "drop off in immunization coverage" (Guyer et al. 1994, 56) after this age. Additionally, those children who missed immunizations in the very early years were even more likely to miss immunizations in later years. Steiner et al. (1996) found that immunization rates in rural and urban areas were about the same. However, in both settings, the rates were below those recommended by the federal government.

An example of an area where health problems flourish is inner-city Los Angeles. A May 2002 article in the *New York Times* (Sterngold 2002) reported on the situation ten years after the riots surrounding the Rodney King incident. The riots led to much burning and destruction in the inner-city areas, followed by rebuilding. Sterngold (2002) captures the problems of the inner city:

> Even by the poor standards of urban neighborhoods, experts say, the city's South-Central section and the surrounding areas stand out, with crippling levels of diabetes, lung cancer, asthma, obesity and heart disease. A largely Latino immigrant population is unable to find proper care for minor illnesses, much less for pregnancies.
>
> The situation is aggravated by the area's having the highest number of uninsured people in Los Angeles County, which itself has the highest rate of uninsured residents in the United States, about double the national average. In the South-Central neighborhood and its environs, 47.4 percent of adults have no health insurance, according to 1999 data, the latest available.

Other problems include a low rate of prenatal care and a high rate of homicides. Poverty rates are also relatively high.

Another problem in health outcomes is the prevalence of chronic diseases. Residents of rural areas tend to have higher levels of chronic diseases, such as heart and kidney disease, than residents in urban areas (Garkovich and Harris 1994).

Access to Health Care

An important indicator of access to health care is the presence of health insurance. Looking at 1993 data, Garkovich and Harris (1994) found that urban and rural areas had about the same percentage of insured residents. However, urban residents were more likely to have insurance through an employer and less likely to purchase individual insurance than rural residents. Garkovich and Harris (1994) attribute this to three reasons. First, rural areas tend to have more small business firms, which are less likely to offer insurance (see Patel and Rushefsky 2006). A related reason is the high cost of health insurance premiums, which makes health insurance less affordable for small businesses. The third reason is that insurance companies increasingly tend to experience rate businesses, that is, they adjust for risk. Because small firms have few employees, it is hard to spread risk. Garkovich and Harris (1994) report that " the current estimate is that small businesses pay up to 35 percent more than larger firms for the same benefits."

Hart-Hester and Thomas (2003) investigated the distribution of providers in Mississippi. They note that forty-five of Mississippi's eighty-two counties (that is, about 55 percent of all counties) are very rural (with less than 20,000 people per county). Yet about three-quarters of the counties (sixty-two) are labeled as having shortages of health professionals (health professionals shortage areas, or HPSA) and about 44 percent as having shortages of dental coverage. They also note that Mississippi has a lower rate of primary care physicians (43 per 100,000 people) than the nation as a whole (59 per 100,000 people). However, even given the under-average of primary care physicians in the state, Hart-Hester and Thomas (2003) found that within the state there was a maldistribution of health care workers.

The researchers found that nearly 60 percent of primary care doctors worked in only seven (8.5 percent) of Mississippi's eighty-two counties. As mentioned above, family practitioners are the ones most likely to provide services in rural areas. Thirty-six counties had five or fewer family practitioners, with six counties having none. They also found an aging population of family practitioners and various types of nurses (registered nurses, nurse practitioners), and that would likely exacerbate the access to services among the rural population in Mississippi.

Much of the delivery of health care services, especially in inner-city areas, comes from community health centers and other safety-net providers such as public hospitals (especially emergency departments) (Hurley, Pham, and Claxton 2005). The "lines of segregation are hardening, driven largely by the dictates of geography and channeled in part through growing disparities in access to physician care" (Hurley, Pham, and Claxton 2005, W5-572). Hurley, Pham, and Claxton see two trends leading to this hardening. The first is the massive increase in specialty services from hospital to outpatient provision. The second is the expansion by hospitals in relatively affluent areas. The authors (2005, W5-572) note the impact of these trends:

> Hospital expansions in affluent areas have the potential to worsen disparities when they reflect a differential investment of resources between poorer and wealthier communities. Institutions serving poorer populations begin with major disadvantages; they are less likely to have sufficient capital or the financial health to obtain debt financing to invest in new building. In New Jersey, for example, the suburban St. Barnabas and Atlantic hospital systems have ample ability to finance hundreds of millions of dollars' worth of expansion projects, while three inner-city hospitals serving lower-income populations had to close during the past two years, and more closures are anticipated in similar communities.

The expansion of facilities, both inpatient and outpatient, can exacerbate disparities in access to physicians. The new facilities provide new revenue streams and access to modern technology (Hurley, Pham, and Claxton 2005).

Another related issue is dental care, which we discussed in the chapter on children (Chapter 6). In Mississippi, sixteen counties had one or no dentists (Hart-Hester and Thomas 2003). Oral health care for children and the elderly population is a problem in both rural and urban areas. Access to mental health care is also difficult for those living in rural areas. There are psychologists in only about 39 percent of Mississippi's counties (Hart-Hester and Thomas 2003).

In addition, the use of mental health services by rural residents is less than for residents of metropolitan areas. The Office of Rural Health Policy (2005) attributes this to three reasons. The first is accessibility. The supply of mental health services is less than in more urban areas and so someone wishing to use those services has to travel some distance to more urban areas. The report notes that public transportation is not readily available in rural areas. This is a significant barrier. Another barrier is cost. Rural residents, in general, have lower incomes than more urban residents. The second factor is availability of services. Many rural counties have no practitioners and almost none have mental hospitals. The final factor is acceptability. There is a stigma attached to mental health problems that is likely greater in rural areas, with the importance placed on self-reliance, than in urban areas. Taken together, it is not surprising that suicide rates for children and adults are higher in rural than in urban areas.

Dental care is also an issue in inner cities. One study, conducted in 1993 and 1994, found that even when free dental care was made available for children, families did not take advantage of it ("Inner-City Children Passing Up Free Dental Care" 1994). In the study, which was conducted at an elementary school in Chicago, dentists examined students in November 1993. When dentists found cavities in a student, the parents were given the names of dentists who would see their children for free. The follow-up examinations in June 1994 showed that most students had not taken advantage of the free service. The author of the study, who taught second grade there said that "many students at the inner-city elementary level have never visited a dentist's office. Dental care appears to be a low priority, due to the lack of dental health instruction at school and in the home. Many students do not own toothbrushes, and others must share them with family members" (Susan Diamond, quoted in "Inner-City Children Passing Up Free Dental Care" 1994).

Pettinato et al. (2004) examined dental procedures among different geographical areas. Focusing on children on Medicaid in Virginia, they found that there were a significant number of dental care providers in the rural areas but they were more likely to be generalists than in the more urban areas. Further, the more rural the area, the more likely the dentists were to perform corrective procedures (for example, filling cavities, braces) than in more urban areas.

Zhang, Tao, and Anderson (2003) were interested in looking at population groups in rural areas, in particularly their access to care. Employing data from two services in the 1990s, they used four measures: "a regular source of care; a usual place of care; delaying medical care because costs; and health insurance status" (67). They found that proximity to an MSA was related to the four measures. Those near an MSA were more likely to be on public insurance than those farther from an MSA. The uninsurance rate was higher for the more rural areas than the more urban areas. Having a regular source and usual place tended to increase with age. Being in a less rural area and being older were correlated with a regular source of care, adjusting for sociodemographic factors and physician and hospital availability.

The authors found that younger people in rural areas had the worst access to care and the lowest health insurance rate. The middle-aged group were most affected by the cost of care, as were rural residents in general. The authors thought this was particularly distressing because this group was in the labor force and also had family responsibilities (Zhang, Tao, and Anderson 2003).

Rosenblatt (2004) finds that rural areas "import" both the people and the equipment needed to provide health services. Import, in this case, does not mean employing foreign health professionals. Rather, it means importing them from urban and suburban areas. Furthermore, there is a high percentage of family practitioners compared to specialists working in rural areas (specifically in small rural towns). Family practitioners in rural areas may have to act as specialists because of the scarcity of such physicians ("Don't Fall Sick on the Prairie" 1999). Related to this are two other factors that may exacerbate the problem. First is a decline in newly graduated physicians who are interested in family practice. Second, there is not much in the way of training (residency programs, medical schools) in rural areas. Thus, the problems of access to physicians in rural areas are likely to get worse. To see a physician, especially a specialist, may require considerable driving. It may also mean that residents of rural areas will tend to postpone seeking care until they are very sick ("Don't Fall Sick on the Prairie" 1999).

Rosenblatt also discusses hospitals in rural areas. Many of them were built after World War II through the National Hospital Survey and Construction Act of 1946, better known as the Hill-Burton Act. Readers of our *Health Care Politics and Policy in America* (Patel and Rushefsky 2006) will remember that Rushefsky's younger daughter, Leah, was born in such a hospital. Because rural areas tend to be poor, such hospitals are heavily dependent on reimbursements from Medicaid and Medicare. Medicaid reimbursements tend be low, and Medicare payments to hospitals in the 1990s were cut. Congress, Rosenblatt points out, tried to relieve rural hospitals from the cutbacks by categorizing hospitals so desiring as safety net or critical access hospitals.

Moreover, such rural hospitals are limited in both size and capability. "These hospitals have 25 or fewer beds, hospital stays averaging less than 96 hours, and 24-hour coverage in the emergency department . . . a reflection of their primary roles as providers of basic emergency and short-term services and as anchors for local health care systems" (Rosenblatt 2004, 1050). More complex care requires transferring to bigger hospitals in urban or suburban areas.

Halfon et al. (1997) investigated the relationship between Medicaid enrollment and access to health care services for Latino children in inner-city Los Angeles. They surveyed Latino families and their children in 1992 in South Central Los Angeles and East Los Angeles. They distinguished among families who were authorized or legal residents of the United States and those who were not, as well as those who were citizens. They found that those in the unauthorized group tended to be married and both parents were working in low-end jobs with few or no benefits compared to citizens. They also showed lower levels of education, higher levels of poverty, and lower levels of social support than the citizen group. Additionally, language barriers were higher for those in the non-citizen group, reflecting length of residence. Medicaid eligibility was greatest for children whose families were unauthorized. However, sustained enrollment in Medicaid was highest among children in the citizen group. They also had higher rates of having a regular physician, and were less likely to have visits postponed and to have private insurance.

The authors note that almost all the children in the survey were themselves U.S. citizens, even though most of the parents were not born here. They observe that the initiative passed in California in 1994 limiting access to publicly funded health services among illegal or unauthorized residents likely worsens the access situation for their children. Given the highly salient issue of immigration in America today, this could get even worse.

Wyn, Teleki, and Brown (2000) examined access issues among twenty-nine urban areas, focusing on low and moderate income groups, using data from the National Health Interview Survey for 1995–96. They found that nearly 20 percent of the population did not have a normal source of care, with Long Island, New York, having the smallest percentage of people without a usual source of care (about 10 percent) and Fort Worth, Texas, having the highest such percentage (about 39 percent). Another measure of utilization and access was whether respondents had seen a doctor in the previous twelve months. Here the difference between the lowest percentage reporting not having seen a doctor (14 percent in Philadelphia) and the highest so reporting (39 percent in Fort Worth and San Francisco) was enormous.

The authors also made a connection between having health insurance and having a regular physician. Those without health insurance, and here the authors are looking within metropolitan statistical areas (MSAs), were twice as likely not to have seen a doctor in the past year as those with a usual source of care. Similarly, people in MSAs with high uninsurance rates were less likely to see a doctor in the past year than people in low uninsurance rate MSAs (Wyn, Teleki, and Brown 2000). This last point seems to us to be very critical in light of what we have said earlier in this chapter. There are, apparently, concentrations of people in some urban areas that do not have very good access to the health care system. This is the "collective" perspective mentioned above (see Probst et al. 2004). It also fits in with the "eight Americas" view (Murray et al. 2006).

Murray et al. (2006) addressed the use of and access to health care services in their "eight Americas" study. "America 2" (see Table 8.2) had the highest health insurance coverage. The lowest was "America 5." Their measure of utilization was whether respondents had a routine medical exam within the previous year. The highest rates were in Americas 6–8, and the lowest in America 4.

Emergency medical services (EMS) is another part of the health care system with disparities. Unlike in urban areas, EMS in rural areas is provided largely by volunteers (Health Resources and Services Administration 2006). And, of course, the geographical area covered is large. Because of the longer distance, the cost per patient is about 200 percent more than that in urban services. Operating and purchasing an ambulance costs about the same in both rural and urban areas, but the reimbursement rates tend to be higher in urban areas (Heady 2002).

Another service where access is an issue is reproductive health care. Bennett (2002) points out that a combination of culture, economics, and distance limits reproductive freedom (autonomy is Bennett's term). The result of these factors is reinforcement of traditional roles of women and a lack of prenatal care. Access to a range of reproductive services, such as HIV/AIDS services, family planning, and emergency contraception is minimal in rural areas. Abortion services are much harder to obtain in rural than in urban areas. The authors recognize the value judgments that might be implied in the preceding sentences. Regardless of one's views toward abortion and other reproductive services, the fact remains that rural women have less access to them than women in urban or suburban settings.

As with rural areas, inner-city urban areas have access issues as well. Over five hundred metropolitan areas were considered underserved (Andrulis 1997). While there are many physicians in metropolitan areas, a much higher rate than in rural areas, the distribution of providers in those areas was uneven. The higher income metropolitan areas have a much higher rate of physicians than do inner-city areas (the "urban health penalty" mentioned above). Andrulis (1997) gives several examples, such as this one: "In Washington, DC, the more affluent northwest and related suburb of Bethesda, Maryland have a pediatrician/child ratio of 1/400, contrasting with the poorer southeastern areas of the city, where the ratio is 1/3700." That is, the ratio for the suburbs is more than nine times that for the inner city.

Andrulis (1997) notes that there are a set of disincentives to physicians to locate in the inner cities. These include the greater possibility of malpractice suits, environmental factors (such as crime and homelessness, drug abuse, and poverty) that overwhelm whatever physicians can do, characteristics of the residents (such as keeping appointments or following prescribed medical treatments), and the lower income of the population. Andrulis also notes that the scarcity of minority physicians hurts access to care.

One result of all of these factors is that often the source of primary care is the emergency room, a safety net for those who do not have regular access to a physician. One estimate, for 1992, was that over half of the emergency department visits were for non-emergency care. City hospitals become the access point for regular care, specialty care, and hospital admissions. Thus hospitals, especially public hospitals, provide the bulk of services for inner-city communities (Andrulis 1997). Grove, Lazebnick, and Petrack (2000) found that a sizable percentage of adolescents visiting an urban university hospital emergency department were there for nonurgent care, such as infections or injuries that could have been dealt with by a primary care physician. Most of the patients in the study were either on Medicaid or were uninsured. The authors also found that the hospitalization rate for this group was lower than is typical and follow-up referral was often not made. Because many of the patients at these hospitals cannot pay for their care, or are reimbursed at fairly low rates by Medicaid, they also experience financial problems. This leads to a decrease in services in the community, especially pre-natal and early childhood care (Andrulis 1997).

An example of an inner-city hospital that experienced considerable distress is Martin Luther King Jr. Harbor Hospital in Los Angeles. The hospital failed inspections by Medicare and in some cases negligence led to deaths. The result was that it lost all funding from the federal Centers for Medicare and Medicaid Services, the agency that runs Medicare and Medicaid (see Ornstein 2007).

Andrulis (1997) also notes the adverse affect the advent of managed care has had in inner-city communities. Medicaid has required most Medicaid recipients to join managed care organizations. By 2003, over 59 percent of Medicaid enrollees were in managed care organizations (Patel and Rushefsky 2006). However, managed care and Medicaid have not been an easy fit. Managed care works better with stable populations. However, because of legal changes (for example, cutbacks in Missouri and Tennessee in the 2000s) and changes within the population (such as getting a job or a change in marital status), Medicaid beneficiaries go on and off Medicaid. The result is considerable turnover in a managed care plan's Medicaid population. And because Medicaid reimbursement to providers is relatively low (compared to private insurance and Medicare), providers are less willing to participate, including in managed care plans with large Medicaid populations. Andrulis (1997) also states what became obvious in the middle and late 1990s. One has to have skills to navigate the maze that managed care has created. The subcultures of inner cities may be foreign to managed care personnel and residents may not have the education and so forth to get through the system.

Furthermore, managed care is a form of rationing (see Patel and Rushefsky 2002, 2006). While managed care organizations can provide a comprehensive set of services to its enrollees—indeed this was part of the original mission of predecessor types of organizations—its main purpose in the 1990s and 2000s was to control health care costs. The effect of cost control measures has been to cut services precisely to the population that needs more rather than less access. Additionally, Andrulis (1997) writes that managed care does not address fundamental problems of inner cities: "managed care programs that do not address the core problems in the community—consequences related to unemployment, poor nutrition and housing, crime, and other circumstances—may meet their 'Waterloo,' finding themselves repeatedly treating the same patients due to those circumstances. Such patient 'recycling' will boost costs, while the health status of those covered lives deteriorates further."

Quality of Health Care

An important measure of the health of a community is premature mortality (Mansfield et al. 1999). Mansfield et al. (1999) measured premature mortality at the county level. Their model of possible factors leading to premature mortality included community structure (such as unemployment rates, racial composition, income and education levels), medical care (hospital beds per 100,000 population, physicians per 100,000), and place. They distinguished among metropolitan counties (which include suburban areas), urban counties, and rural counties.

The authors found that the premature mortality rate was highest among rural counties, with urban and metropolitan counties about equal. Rural areas came out the lowest on many of the community variables. These included lower education levels, lower income, greater percentage of vacant housing, and so forth. Only on the percentage of female-headed females did rural areas not come out the worst.

Mansfield et al. (1999) also found that there were regional variations among counties, with states in the southern portion of the United States (southwestern and southeastern) showing considerably more premature mortality rates than other areas of the country. They also found some interactions among place and other variables. For example, counties with high percentages of African Americans and also high proportions of female-headed families had higher premature death rates in both metropolitan and rural counties. High and continuous unemployment rates in rural and urban counties tended to interact with high percentages of female-headed families.

Heart disease is another important marker of health. It is the major killer of both men and women. Graham-Garcia et al. (2001) report geographic disparities in cardiovascular disease (CVD) among African American women. They found the highest levels of CVD among African American women born in the southern part of the United States, with somewhat lower rates among those born in the northeastern states and the Caribbean. The South seems to have a relatively higher rate of mortality due to kidney failure, strokes, and heart disease. This is true on the state and county level. Other diseases where the South leads include hypertension (high blood pressure) and obesity. They summarize their 1997 study as follows (Graham-Garcia et al 2001, 59): "life for low-income, Southern-rural women is bleak, isolated, and lacking resources. These women experience limited access to health care, crisis-oriented health care, and difficult living conditions that jeopardize their perceptions of health status. Health promotion and disease prevention services are virtually nonexistent."

Wakefield (2002) points out that hospitals in rural areas are faced with considerable financial difficulties, enough so that conversions are occurring from the normal Medicare payment system to critical access hospitals, which pay on a different basis than Medicare's prospective payment system. She raises the question whether the financial exigencies facing rural hospitals affect the quality of care received by patients. She noted that quality of care tended to differ among rural areas. For example, one study she cited found that people living in more remote rural areas received better care than those living in rural areas near metropolitan counties, a somewhat counterintuitive result. She also observes that much more research has been done on quality and medical error issues in urban areas than in rural areas.

After reviewing the growing interest in the quality of care and efforts to reduce medical errors, Wakefield (2002) writes that the problems that face rural hospitals, such as financing and personnel issues, also likely affect efforts to improve quality. Wakefield (2002, 47) provides an example of these problems:

"prehospital emergency medical services in rural areas are often provided by volunteers who may have difficulty retaining knowledge and skill sets given low volume of emergency calls and who lack the medical oversight available through urban trauma systems."

Wakefield (2002) then reviews improvements suggested by agencies such as the Institute of Medicine to reduce errors and improve quality. One such suggestion is to increase the resources and the institutional and leadership commitment devoted to quality improvement. The Joint Commission on Accreditation of HealthCare Organizations (JCAHO) requires such a commitment. But, Wakefield points out, two-fifths of rural hospitals are not accredited by the JCAHO (itself an indicator of quality issues) and are subject instead to less strict state regulations.

Another aspect of quality improvement is the development of computer information systems. Again, this is a requirement of JCAHO that affects many but not all rural hospitals. Such resources, such as equipment, software, and personnel, place a strain on rural hospitals (Wakefield 2002). Bauer (2002), however, is more optimistic that the computer revolution will help change and improve health care in rural areas. He provides examples of potential changes brought about by "medical infomatics, telemedicine, and e-health" (77). These changes include those relating to online medical records, disease management, clinical research, professional education, materials management (supplies and equipment), human resources, and surgery.

The issue of managed care and rural areas also affects quality. Wakefield (2002) points out that Medicare managed care organizations had modest penetration in rural areas (and limited penetration within the Medicare population anyway; see Patel and Rushefsky 2006). Managed care organizations have an incentive to focus on and improve the quality of care. Thus the vast majority of Medicare beneficiaries in rural areas are in fee-for-service arrangements, and there seems to have been little effort within these arrangements to focus on quality (Wakefield 2002).

Rosenblatt, Casey, and Richardson (2002) looked at the supply and quality of personnel in public health departments in Alaska, Wyoming, and Montana. They found that the supply of such personnel in urban and rural areas in those three states was about the same. They did, however, find qualitative differences. Personnel in more rural areas (and here they are writing mostly about public health nurses) tended to be less well trained than their urban counterparts. They were also less likely to be full-time employees. There were also differences in the range of skills in the health departments, with rural departmental personnel having a smaller range of skills. Finally, there appeared to be little connection between doctors and dentists in the area and the rural health personnel.

Possible Explanations for Health Care Disparities

One explanation for the disparities is the distribution of medical providers. The study by Mansfield et al. (1999) demonstrates this. Looking at physicians, they found in the three types of counties examined (metropolitan, urban, and rural) that the rates differ dramatically by place. They found that metropolitan areas had the highest rate of doctors per 100,000 population (14.8), followed by urban counties (8.5), and rural counties (5.9). The national rate was 9.0.

There were also differences by whether the physician was a generalist (that is, family practitioner or internist) or a specialist. The overall national rate per 100,000 population was, for generalists, 4.4. The rate for metropolitan counties was 5.4, for urban counties it was 4.3, and for rural counties it was 3.9. For specialists, the rates were 4.0 for all counties, 8.3 for metropolitan counties, 3.6 for urban counties, and 1.7 for rural counties (Mansfield et al. 1999). Their findings are consistent with what we have pointed out earlier. There appears to be a reasonably sufficient supply of general practitioners in rural and urban areas, but specialists are harder to find in rural areas.

For rural areas, two parts of the infrastructure create barriers to health care that are somewhat less present in urban areas, and especially the more affluent suburban areas. The first is transportation. Rural areas lack mass transportation systems or even taxis that could get people who do not have their own cars to providers. Similarly, communications systems are much less well developed in rural areas. Internet access, especially high speed Internet access, is much less available in rural than other areas (Block 2005; see also Bell, Reddy, and Rainie 2004). Garkovich and Harris (1994) note that a significant number of rural residents in Kentucky do not have telephones. They point out the difficulties this presents for those with chronic diseases that require oversight. As we have seen, inner-city residents also have transportation problems even though, in theory, they are close to physicians, doctors, and safety-net institutions (that is, hospital emergency departments and community health clinics).

For both rural and inner cities, characteristics of the communities and the people who live in them explain many of the disparities. Both tend to be poorer than suburban areas, with lower levels of education. For rural communities, poverty and density combine to make health care resources relatively sparse. Medical providers, like other producers of services, seek places where they can make profits (this is true of even so-called not-for-profit health institutions). But the lack of a sufficient population makes that difficult. Rural areas also lack amenities that would attract providers. This becomes a reinforcing problem. Inner-city areas have similar problems. Because income is low, there is not a stable source of revenue for providers. The characteristics of inner-city dwellers may not correspond well with health providers (one reason why more minority doctors are crucial).

A more radical view for the existence of disparities, especially in the inner cities, is offered by Whiteis (2000). He first notes the increases in patterns of inequality within the United States and the high rates of poverty among children. He states that there is a relationship between socioeconomic status and health (wealthy is healthier; see article of that title by Pritchett and Summers 1996; we discuss this also in Chapter 9). Whiteis singles out segregation based on race and socioeconomic status as a major cause of the disparities (see also Massey and Denton 1993). Whiteis (2000, 259–60) writes that "inequality between social classes, rather than a low standard of living *within* any one class or group, represents the most significant predictor of health status across populations and geographic regions." He attributes the inequality to capitalism, the quest for profits, and the use of public resources to ensure private profits. He labels the conditions in the inner cities as "pathogenic" (Whiteis 2000, 265). Resources are withdrawn or kept from the inner cities, and those institutions that serve the inner cities, such as public hospitals and community health centers, face fiscal distress. Whiteis links poor economies and lack of political power with the pathogenetic conditions.

Conclusions

> Put in a global context, the disparities in mortality experiences among the eight Americas, each consisting of millions or tens of millions of Americans, are enormous. The eight Americas analysis indicates that ten million Americans with the best health have achieved one of the highest levels of life expectancy on record, 3 y better than Japan for females and 4 y better than Iceland for males. At the same time, tens of millions of Americans are experiencing levels of health that are more typical of middle-income or low-income developing countries. These poor levels of health occur in areas throughout the country. The health disparities among the eight Americas cannot be explained by single causes of death such as homicide or HIV. Nor are the largest sources of disparity in children and the elderly. The mortality disparities are most concentrated in young and middle-aged males and females, and are a result of a number of chronic diseases and injuries with well-established risk factors. (Murray et al. 2006, 1521)

The health care problems of urban and rural communities and their residents are not new. Rosen (1975) points out that such problems existed in the nineteenth century, and there were efforts to alleviate those problems. For example, in 1845 the New York Association for the Improvement of the Condition of the Poor proposed a plan that would open additional dispensaries or what we would call community health centers.

The presence of geographic disparities complicates the discussion of other kinds of disparities, especially those based on race/ethnicity or income. As Baicker, Chandra, and Skinner (2005) cogently point out, the disparities are not consistent and are more complex than a simple geographic explanation might imply. To them, the cause of disparities is the interaction of two large factors. The first is the unequal treatment by a given provider, whether a hospital or physician. The other is location. The two factors imply different sets of causation and, therefore, different ameliorative public policies.

References

Agency for Healthcare Research and Quality. 2006. *2006 National Healthcare Disparities Report.* Rockville, MD: U.S. Department of Health and Human Services.

Andrulis, Dennis P. 1997. *The Urban Health Penalty: New Dimensions and Directions in Inner-City Health.* Philadelphia: American College of Physicians.

Baicker, Katherine; Amitabh Chandra; and Jonathan S. Skinner. 2005. "Geographic Variation in Health Care and the Problem of Measuring Racial Disparities." *Perspectives in Biology and Medicine* 48, no. 1 supplement (Winter): S42–S53.

Baicker, Katherine; Amitabh Chandra; Jonathan S. Skinner; and John E. Wennberg. 2004. "Who You Are and Where You Live: How Race and Geography Affect the Treatment of Medicare Beneficiaries." *Health Affairs* (October 7): var33–var44.

Basanta, W. Eugene. 2002. "Rural Health Care Now and Tomorrow." *Journal of Legal Medicine* 23, no. 1 (March): 37–41.

Bauer, Jeffrey C. 2002. "Rural American and the Digital Transformation of Health Care." *Journal of Legal Medicine* 23, no. 1 (March): 73–83.

Bell, Peter; Pavani Reddy; and Lee Rainie. 2004. *Rural Areas and the Internet.* Washington, D.C.: Pew Internet and American Life Project.

Bennett, Trude. 2002. "Reproductive Health Care in the Rural United States." *MsJAMA* 2887, no. 1 (January 2): 112.

Blazer, Dan G.; Lawrence R. Landerman; Gerda Fillenbaum; and Ronnie Horner. 1995. "Health Services Access and Use among Older Adults in North Carolina: Urban vs Rural Residents." *American Journal of Public Health* 85, no. 10 (October): 1384–90.

Blewett, Lynn A.; Michael Davern; and Holly Rodin. 2005. "Employment and Health Insurance Coverage for Rural Latino Populations." *Journal of Community Health* 30, no. 3 (June): 181–95.

Block, Melissa. 2005. "Widening the Internet Highway to Rural America." *All Things Considered* National Public Radio (October 14).

Boone, Linda. 2000. "Hurting in the Heartland." *Modern Physician* 4, no. 9 (September). Online through EBSCOhost.

Branas, Charles C., et al. 2004. "Urban-Rural Shifts in Intentional Firearm Death: Different Causes, Same Result." *American Journal of Public Health* 94, no. 10 (October): 1750–55.

Brown, E. Richard; Roberta Wyn; and Stephanie Teleki. 2000. *Disparities in Health Insurance and Access to Care for Residents across U.S. Cities.* New York: Commonwealth Fund.

Cordes, Sam. 1998. "Health Care and the Rural Economy." *Forum for Applied Research and Public Policy* 13 (Summer): 90–93.

Council on Graduate Medical Education. 1998. *Physician Distribution and Health Care Challenges in Rural and Inner-City Areas.* Rockville, MD: Health Resources and Services Administration, U.S. Department of Health and Human Services.

"Don't Fall Sick on the Prairie." 1999. *Economist* 353, no. 8143 (October 30). Online through EBSCOhost.

Eberhardt, Mark S.; Deborah D. Ingram; and Diane M. Makuc. 2001. *Urban and Rural Health Chartbook. Health United States, 2001.* Hyattsville, MD: National Center for Health Statistics.

"Editorial: Health in Rural America: Remembering the Importance of Place." 2004. *American Journal of Public Health* 94, no. 10 (October): 1661–63.

Eggleston, Peyton, et al. 1999. "The Environment and Asthma in U.S. Inner Cities." *Environmental Health Perspectives* 107, supplement 3 (June): 439–50.

Fluharty, Charles W. 2002. "Refrain or Reality: A United States Rural Policy?" *Journal of Legal Medicine* 23, no. 1 (March): 57–72.

Garkovich, Lorraine, and Rosalind P. Harris. 1994. "Health and Health Care in Rural America." *Choices: The Magazine of Food, Farm & Resource Issues* 9, no. 3 (3rd quarter): 8. Online at EBSCOhost.

Gentry, Margaret. 1980. "The Inner-City Hospital Battle." *The Nation* 230, no. 10 (March 15): 301–3.

Gillanders, W.R.; Terry F. Buss; and C. Richard Hofstetter. 1996. "Urban/Rural Elderly Health Status Differences: The Dichotomy Revisited." *Journal of Aging & Social Policy* 8, no. 4: 8–24.

Graham-Garcia, Judy; Terri L. Raines; Jeannette O. Andrews; and George A. Mensah. 2001. "Race, Ethnicity and Geography: Disparities in Heart Disease in Women of Color." *Journal of Transcultural Nursing* 12, no. 1 (January): 56–67.

Grisso, Jeane Ann; Donald F. Schwarz; Carolyn G. Miles; and John H. Holmes. 1996. "Injuries among Inner-City Minority Women: A Population-Based Longitudinal Study." *American Journal of Public Health* 86, no. 1 (January): 67–70.

Grossman, David C., et al. 2002. "Disparities in Infant Health among American Indians and Alaskan Natives in US Metropolitan Areas." *Pediatrics* 109, no. 4 (April): 627–33.

Grove, Deanna Dahl; Rina Lazebnik; and Emory M. Petrack. 2000. "Urban Emergency Utilization by Adolescents." *Clinical Pediatrics* 39, no. 8 (August): 479–83.

Guyer, Gernard, et al. 1994. "Immunization Coverage and Its Relationship to Preventive Health Care Visits among Inner-City Children in Baltimore." *Pediatrics* 94, no. 1: 53–58.

Halfon, Neal, et al. 1997. "Medicaid Enrollment and Health Services Access by Latino Children in Inner-City Los Angeles." *JAMA* 277, no. 8 (February 26): 636–41.

Hart-Hester, Susan, and Charlotte Thomas. 2003. "Access to Health Care Professionals in Rural Mississippi." *Southern Medical Journal* 96, no. 2 (February): 149–54.

Hartley, David. 2004. "Rural Health Disparities, Population Health, and Rural Culture." *American Journal of Public Health* 94, no. 10 (October): 1675–78.

Heady, Hilda R. 2002. "A Delicate Balance: The Economics of Rural Health Care Delivery." *MsJAMA* 287, no. 1 (January 2): 110.

Health Resources and Services Administration. 2006. *Emergency Medical Services in Frontier Areas: Voluntary Community Organizations.* Washington, D.C.: U.S. Department of Health and Human Services.

Hurley, Robert E.; Hoangmai H. Pham; and Gary Claxton. 2005. "A Widening Rift in Access and Quality: Growing Evidence of Economic Disparities." *Health Affairs* (December 6): W5-566–W5-576. Online at healthaffairs.org.

"Inner-City Children Passing Up Free Dental Care, Researchers Find." 1994. *Nation's Health* 25, no. 1 (January). Online at EBSCOhost.

Kassa, Hailu; Michael S. Bisesi; Sadik A. Kuder; and Peter C. Park. 2000. "Assessment of a Lead Management Program for Inner-City Children." *Environmental Health* 62, no. 10 (June): 15–19.

Larson, Sharon L.; Steven R. Machlin; Alice Nixon; and Marc Zodet. 2004. *Health Care in Urban and Rural Areas, Combined Years 1998–2000.* Rockville, MD: Agency for Healthcare Research and Quality, U.S. Department of Health and Human Services.

Mansfield, Christopher J.; James L. Wilson; Edward J. Kobrinski; and Jim Mitchell. 1999. "Premature Mortality in the United States: The Roles of Geographic Area, Socioeconomic Status, Household Type, and Availability of Medical Care." *American Journal of Public Health* 89, no. 6 (June): 893–98.

Massey, Douglas S., and Nancy A. Denton. 1993. *American Apartheid: Segregation and the Making of the Underclass.* Cambridge, MA: Harvard University Press.

Miller, Douglas K., et al. 2005. "Inner City, Middle-Aged African Americans Have Excess Frank and Subclinical Disability." *Journal of Gerontology* 60A, no. 2 (February): 207–2.

Murray, Christopher J.L., et al. 2006. "Eight Americas: Investigating Mortality Disparities across Races, Counties, and Race-Counties in the United States." *PLoS Medicine* 3, no. 9 (September): 1513–24.

National Rural Health Association. 2005. *Protecting Rural Beneficiaries with a Medicare Prescription Drug Benefit.* Kansas City, MO: National Rural Health Association.

Nguyen, Trang Quyen, and Kathryn Whetten. 2003. "Is Anybody Out There? Integrating HIV Services in Rural Regions." *Public Health Reports* 118, no. 1 (January–February): 3–9.

Office of Rural Health Policy. 2005. *Mental Health and Rural America: 1994, 2005. An Overview and Annotated Bibliography.* Washington, D.C.: U.S. Department of Health and Human Services, Health Resources and Services Administration.

O'Neill, Liam. 2004. "The Effect of Insurance Status on Travel Time for Rural Medicare Patients." *Medical Care Research & Review* 61, no. 2 (June): 187–202.

Opportunity Agenda. n.d. "Geographic Barriers to Hospital-Based Health Care in New York City." Washington, D.C.: Opportunity Agenda. Online at www.opportunityagenda.org.

Ornstein, Charles. 2007. "A Troubled History: A Timeline of Problems at King Hospital." *Los Angeles Times,* August 10.

Patel, Kant, and Mark E. Rushefsky. 2002. *Health Care Policy in an Age of New Technologies.* Armonk, NY: M.E. Sharpe.

Patel, Kant, and Mark E. Rushefsky. 2006. *Health Care Politics and Policy in America.* Armonk, NY: M.E. Sharpe.

Pettinato, Frank C., II, et al. 2004. "Rural Versus Urban Analysis of Dental Procedures Provided to Virginia Medicaid Recipients." *Pediatric Dentistry* 26, no. 5 (September–October): 440–44.

Prewitt, Elizabeth. 1997. "Inner-City Health." *Annals of Internal Medicine* 126, no. 4 (March 15): 485–90.

Pritchett, Lant, and Lawrence H. Summers. 1996. "Wealthier Is Healthier." *Journal of Human Resources* 31, no. 4 (Autumn): 841–68.

Probst, Janice C., et al. 2002. *Minorities in Rural America: An Overview of Population Characteristics.* Columbia, SC: South Carolina Rural Health Research Center, Norman J. Arnold School of Public Health, University of South Carolina.

Probst, Janice C.; Charity G. Moore; Saundra H. Glover; and Michael E. Samuels. 2004. "Person and Place: The Compounding Race/Ethnicity and Rurality on Health." *American Journal of Public Health* 94, no. 10 (October): 1695–1703.

"Research Explains How Lead Exposure Produces Learning Deficits." 2007. *Journal of Environmental Health* 70, no. 3 (October): 58–59.

Rosen, George. 1975. "Medical Care for Urban Workers and the Poor: Two 19th Century Programs." *American Journal of Public Health* 65, no. 3 (March): 299–303.

Rosenblatt, Roger A. 2004. "A View from the Periphery: Health Care in Rural America." *New England Journal of Medicine* 39, no. 5 (September 9): 1049–51.

Rosenblatt, Roger A.; Susan Casey; and Mary Richardson. 2002. "Rural-Urban Differences in the Public Health Workforce: Local Health Departments in 3 Rural Western States." *American Journal of Public Health* 92, no. 7 (July): 1102–5.

Silberman, Pam; Stephanie Poley; Kerry James; and Rebecca Slifkin. 2002. "Tracing Medicaid Managed Care in Rural Communities: A Fifty-State Follow-up." *Health Affairs* 21, no. 4 (July–August): 255–63.

Silfkin, Rebecca T., et al. 1998. "Medicaid Managed Care Programs in Rural Areas: A Fifty-State Overview." *Health Affairs* 17, no. 6 (November–December): 217–27.

Sixsmith, Diane M., and Fred Goldman. 1979. "The Medical Cost of Drug Abuse in an Inner-City Community." *American Journal of Public Health* 69, no. 5 (May): 505–7.

Steiner, John F., et al. 1996. "Immunization Services in Rural Areas." *Journal of Family Practice* 32, no. 4 (October): 326–28.

Sterngold, James. 2002. "Los Angeles Inner City Beset by Chronic Health Problems." *New York Times,* May 3.

Stille, Christopher J., and Joan Christison-Lagay. 2000. "Determining Immunization Rates for Inner-City Infants: Statewide Registry Data vs Medical Record Review." *American Journal of Public Health* 90, no. 10 (October): 1613–15.

van Dis, Jane. 2002. "Where We Live: Heath Care in Rural vs Urban America." *MsJAMA* 287, no. 1 (January 2): 108.

Wakefield, Mary. 2002. "Patient Safety and Medical Errors." *Journal of Legal Medicine* 23, no. 1 (March): 43–56.

Weist, Mark E., and Olga M. Acosta. 2001. "Predictors of Violence Exposure among Inner-City Youth." *Journal of Clinical Child Psychology* 30, no. 2 (May): 187–98.

Wennberg, John E. 2004. "Practice Variations and Health Care Reform: Connecting the Dots." *Health Affairs* (October 7): var140–var144.

Whiteis, David G. 2000. "Poverty, Policy, and Pathogenesis: Economic Justice and Public Health in the US." *Critical Public Health* 10, no. 2 (June): 257–71.

Williams, P.B., and O. Ekundayo. 2001. "Study of Distribution and Factors Affecting Syphilis Epidemic among Inner-City Minorities of Baltimore." *Public Health* 115, no. 6 (November): 387–93.

Wyn, Roberta; Stephanie Teleki; and E. Richard Brown. 2000. "Differences in Access to Health Care among the Moderate- and Low-Income Population across Urban Areas." UCLA Center for Health Policy Research, Policy Brief (July).

Zhang, Ping; Guoyu Tao; and Lynda A. Anderson. 2003. "Differences in Access to Health Care Services among Adults in Rural America by Rural Classification Categories and Age." *American Journal of Rural Health* 11, no. 2 (April): 64–72.

———— 9 ————

Conclusions

Health and Inequality Reconsidered

Of all the forms of inequality, injustice in health is
the most shocking and the most inhumane.
(Martin Luther King, Jr., quoted in Prewitt 1997, 485)

There are several names that can be attached to what we have discussed throughout this book. One name or label is disparities. Another name often used is inequalities. We have used the terms inequality and disparity interchangeably. The Martin Luther King, Jr., quote above refers to injustice. Yet another term refers to vulnerable populations (see, for example, Mechanic and Tanner 2007). Each of these terms views a portion of the population as lacking something, in this case adequate health care. It may be the lack of access to providers, perhaps because of distance or race and ethnicity (the latter perhaps resulting from cultural barriers and the relative lack of minority providers). Sometimes it is a lack of finances and insurance. All show up in poorer health based on any number of indicators, such as visits to primary doctors, disproportionate representation in certain diseases, high levels of preventable illnesses, and so forth.

Whatever term is used, the problem has many dimensions as to both causes and solutions. On one level, this is a problem of morality (Mechanic and Tanner 2007). People differ in terms of how they view people who are on the low end of the socioeconomic scale. The debates over poverty and the causes of poverty are a good example (see Rushefsky 2007). Perhaps people are poor because they are lazy or perhaps because of racism or capitalism. The same debates exist over health care disparities. Mechanic and Tanner (2007, 1221) portray this debate as partly involving the perspective of "sinners versus victims."

John Rawls (1971) argues for a theory of justice based on the concept of fairness. Rawls offers two theories of justice. One is the "principle of equal liberty." The other is the "difference principle," which suggests that greater efforts are needed for those who have the least. Certainly in health care there are those who need more than others. Another related philosophical concept is distributive justice. Rawls's difference principle is based on this idea. It refers to the distribution of the burdens and benefits of whatever society produces. It suggests, again, that those who have less be given more help (for a discussion of distributive justice, see Lamont and Favor 2007).

The existence of health care disparities in the United States is unquestionable. The preceding chapters have documented it and provided some explanations for it. Reports such as the *Health USA* reports (see National Center for Health Statistics 2006; Eberhardt, Ingram, and Makuc 2001) present the data as do reports focusing more specifically on disparities, such as the *2005 National Health Care Disparities Report* (Agency for Healthcare Research and Quality 2005) and the Institute of Medicine study *Unequal Treatment* (Smedley, Stith, and Nelson 2002). The *Healthy People 2010* report sets as one of its goals the elimination of disparities (U.S. Department of Health and Human Services, 2000).

The federal government has agencies that focus on health care disparities and particular population groups that experience those disparities. The Centers for Disease Control and Prevention (CDC) focuses on these concerns with the goal of eliminating them. Its website lists the main factors that define the groups experiencing these disparities: "race/ethnicity, socioeconomic status, geography, gender, age, disability status, risk status related to sex and gender, and among other populations identified to be at-risk for health disparities" (Centers for Disease Control and Prevention n.d.). The *Healthy People 2010* report adds sexual orientation, income, and education as areas where the should be no health disparities. The U.S. Department of Health and Human Services has an Office of Minority Health and Healthcare Disparities (OMHD), an Office of Women's Health (OWH), the Administration for Children & Families, the Agency on Aging, and the Indian Health Service.

Explaining Health Care Disparities

Because there are so many different portions of the population with less than optimal health care, the causes are also multiple. We have discussed many of them directly and indirectly in the preceding chapters.

As is often the case with inequalities, those on the low end of the socioeconomic scale lack political power. Groups such as American Indians and Alaska Natives (AI/AN) are small in number, so small that it is hard to get data as good as those for other groups. If one looks at various indicators of political power, such as voting or representation in various legislative bodies (especially at the national level), they can hardly be seen. Children do not vote and so it should not be surprising that we spend less on children than we do on the elderly. Even within the Medicaid program, we spend much more on the elderly (and the disabled) than we do on children on a per person basis and totally, even though children outnumber the elderly. Of course, part of the reason for this is that children are generally healthier than the elderly and the last year of life consumes a considerable amount of health care. But the greater political power of the elderly helps explain, to some extent, why there are so few elderly who are uninsured. If this country has anything resembling universal health care, it is for the elderly through Medicare. Having money to contribute to election campaigns and to interest groups, which the elderly have for the most part and children do not, is also a factor.

Lawrence Jacobs (2005) offers three reasons (what he calls "trenches"; 42) why, politically, the move toward more equality in health care has been difficult. A couple of those reasons we have already addressed. The first is that interest groups, especially business groups, have inordinate influence on the American political system. The second is that those suffering disparities generally do not participate in the system and lack representation in policy-making institutions. The third is the weak state of organized labor in the United States. These combine to protect the status quo or give advantages to those with resources.

The Brookings Institution economist Henry Aaron offered several reasons why health care reform has failed, many of which are relevant to the causes of health care disparities (Aaron 2007). The first is that most people, about 84–85 percent of the population, have health insurance. Therefore they are not touched by the problem (though see the discussion below about the impact on the insured) and are afraid that change would hurt their health insurance status. A second reason is that reform, which in this case largely means increasing access to health care, involves redistribution, especially income redistribution. Some may have to pay more taxes or lose some services so that others can benefit. This is a difficult proposition in the United States, though not an impossible one.

A third reason offered by Aaron (2007) relates to governmental structure. Aaron argues that the nature of the Congress requires that there be significant support for change. An example of this was the huge Democratic majorities in Congress following the 1964 elections that created an environment in which Medicaid and Medicare could be enacted. Absent such large majorities, the potential to block action is enormous, especially in the Senate where the rules give advantages to those wishing to block change. Consider the events in 2007 when the State Children's Health Insurance Program (SCHIP) came up for renewal. Despite majority support for the program in both houses, President Bush's veto made it difficult to renew and expand the program.

A fourth reason why reform is problematic is that situations differ among the states. The proportion of minorities and types of minorities vary by state. Uninsurance rates differ by state, with Texas having nearly a quarter of its population uninsured and a few other states having less than half that amount.

An important factor brought up by Jacobs (2005) has to do with the concept of "rights" (see also Stone 2002). Jacobs distinguishes among three rights: civil, political, and social, the last of which is particularly important for our discussion. For example, if a person is eligible for Medicare, then that person has a right to receive services under the program. In the United States, unlike other Western, industrialized countries, there is no right to health care, though, as mentioned above, there are rights to services under government programs.

Another critical element touched upon in the various chapters is socioeconomic status, which is a combination of income, education, and occupation (Adler and Newman 2002). We will spend a few pages examining this factor. First, education and income are closely related (U.S. Department of Health and Human Services 2000). Second, education and income vary by racial and ethnic group, and by geography. Hispanics, African Americans, and AI/AN have lower levels of education and income than whites. They are also less likely to be employed in professional-managerial occupations. They also have, for the most part, poorer health status and outcomes with higher levels of diseases such as obesity, high blood lead levels, diabetes, asthma, and higher mortality rates (with the partial exception of the Hispanic paradox). This is because people with higher incomes are more likely to have health insurance and thus afford care, and are more likely to live in communities that have access to high quality health care.

This is the argument that Whiteis (2000) makes, though in a somewhat radical form. He attributes the socioeconomic differences to racial segregation and capitalism. Pritchett and Summers (1996) argue that wealthier people and groups tend to be healthier. But a related explanation is the existence of a market economy (see Cohn 2007; Relman 2007; Jacobs 2005).

The basic argument is that because the United States is largely a market economy, the behavior of people, groups, and institutions is often influenced by profit capabilities. If a geographic area or a particular group does not present such opportunities then the availability of service is likely to be limited.

Marmot (2002) found that there is an inverse relationship between income and mortality rates. Those with lower incomes had higher mortality rates and the relationship was fairly linear. Even adjusting for education, though the disparities were smaller, the same relationship appears.

Socioeconomic status may affect health in fairly indirect ways, working through a combination of four pathways (Adler and Newman 2002). One pathway is exposure to environmental insults, which tends to affect those of lower socioeconomic class and those in certain geographic locations. Exposure to lead is a good example of this, but not the only one. The environmental justice movement focuses on this concern (see Rushefsky 2007). A second possible pathway is through the social environment. Here Adler and Newman (2002) refer to how tightly connected a community and community institutions are. Social isolation is related to higher risks of premature mortality. More socially integrated communities, with a plethora of associations and clubs, tend to have lower homicide rates.

A third pathway is behaviors and lifestyle. People at the lower end of the socioeconomic continuum tend to engage in less healthy lifestyles than people at the higher end. For example, smoking rates are higher among people with less education and income (Adler and Newman 2002). There also tends to be less access to healthier and fresher foods in poorer communities than in more affluent ones (Jacobs 2005). The final pathway is that those at the lower end of the socioeconomic scale have less access to the health care system than those at the higher end.

Klick and Satel (2006) argue that there are myths associated with the idea of health disparities. They write that physician bias is not at the root of health care disparities. Rather, they see the interaction of socioeconomic status and residence (geography) as the important factors. They note that minority racial groups tend not to see the same medical providers as the more affluent and that the quality of medical providers in largely minority communities is low. So for them, class is much more important than race or racial prejudice.

They also make a particularly important point. While not denying that health care disparities exist, they believe they have been measured incorrectly. The typical measurement, they write, is relative measures comparing rates of the vulnerable with less vulnerable populations. It is also important to look at absolute increases in health status (such as mortality rates), which have improved for all groups.

Of course, not everyone accepts the relationship between income and health. Satel and Klick (2006) argue that income inequality is at best only weakly related to health care disparities. Their argument is that first, if there is a relationship, it is not linear. That is, the gains from greater income have a diminishing effect on greater health. Second, other factors, such as education and race/ethnicity, play a role, and when they are taken into account the impact of income on inequality disappears.

There are a couple of problems with this analysis. First, two years prior to this publication, one of the coauthors, Satel, co-authored a work (Eberstadt and Satel [2004]) that argued that class was more important than the other factors. So Satel, at least, contradicts herself. The other problem with their analysis is that many of the factors they control for are strongly related to each other and to income, as we noted before. Thus, statistically speaking, taking out those factors does not leave much room for income inequality to play a role. If they are all related, however, then income inequality is an issue.

One last source of disparities cannot go without mention. The disparities in the United States, whether among demographic groups or geographically based, are the result of inequalities that have existed in the past (Said, Thomas, and Fine 2003). The low status of women in American society is historically rooted, going back at least to Abigail Adams's reminder to her husband John, when the Continental Congress was considering breaking away from England, to "remember the ladies." The status of African Americans is a function of hundreds of years of slavery followed by active efforts, at least in the southern part of the country, to maintain their lower status during the Jim Crow period. Segregation of the races in housing and schools still exists, even if not sanctioned by law. The status of AI/AN has always been surrounded by contradiction. The status of Hispanics is affected by immigration issues but also by cultural ones. The legacy of the past lives on.

Addressing Health Care Disparities

There are efforts to reduce disparities. As indicated above, in 2000 the United States set a goal to eliminate disparities in its *Healthy People 2010* report. Also, there are a number of agencies within the federal government that focus on health care disparities. Several organizations in the private sector have also focused on health care disparities.

The American Medical Association (AMA) has programs designed to eliminate disparities. For example, the association recommends that providers review procedures within their own practices to make sure there are no inequalities. It also set up a commission, the American Medical Association/National Medical Association Commission to End Healthcare Disparities (information from www.ama-assn.org) to address these issues.

The major interest group of the insurance industry, America's Health Insurance Plans (AHIP), has also examined the issue with a number of publications. It details four activities focused on health care disparities: collecting data, competency training in cultural differences, quality improvements directed at disparities, and communicating the importance of decreasing disparities (information from www.ahip.org). And Families USA, a consumer/patient advocacy group, has a minority health resource center (online at familiesusa.org/issues/minority-health/resource-center).

Why Should We Care?

There are a number of reasons why we as a nation should be concerned about health care disparities. One is that it is in the interest of the insured. Pauly and Pagán (2007) argue and provide empirical evidence that even those with health insurance are impacted by those without it. Using data from the Community Tracking Study for 2003, they looked at three sets of indicators within communities that had high rates of uninsured and those with low rates of uninsured. They found, in general, that insured residents in the low uninsurance communities had greater access to health care than insured residents in high uninsurance communities. For example, insured people in the former communities were more likely to have seen a doctor, more likely to have had an exam, less likely to have problems getting a referral to a specialist, and more satisfied with their care than residents in the high uninsurance communities. So even though people have insurance, they do not necessarily have access. This is what are called "spillover effects" (Pauly and Pagán 2007, 1309). Pauly and Pagán (2007, 1312) argue that rather than just add more community health centers in underserved areas, it would be better to give the uninsured tax subsidies and let them use regular (as opposed to safety net) providers. This would help both the insured and the uninsured in the same communities.

Another reason is that health care is an instrumental good. People who are in good health are more productive citizens economically, sociologically, and personally. Society will be better off if its citizens are healthier. Perhaps the notion that wealthier is healthier works in reverse. Societies that are healthier are also wealthier. In addition, reducing health care disparities fits in with an important value of American society, equality. While, as discussed in Chapter 1, we can trace the American version of equality back to the Declaration of Independence, more recent times have seen the value achieve greater prominence.

And, finally, as the epigraph to this chapter asserts, reducing disparities would be just and fair.

Achieving a more just society, or reducing disparities, will not come easily. Comprehensive reform of the health care system, with the various interests embedded in society, is difficult. History has shown that. The American system of policy making is based on making smaller changes over a period of time. The name for this concept is incrementalism (see Rushefsky 2007; Lindblom 1959). Said, Thomas, and Fine (2003) argue that change is needed at three levels: patient characteristics, provider practices and characteristics, and systemic. Efforts are being made to make changes, but remedying the problem will take a long time.

> Although the diversity of the American population may be one of the Nation's greatest assets, it also represents a range of health improvement challenges—challenges that must be addressed by individuals, the community and State in which they live, and the Nation as a whole . . .
>
> Healthy People 2010 is firmly dedicated to the principle that—regardless of age, gender, race or ethnicity, income, education, geographic location, disability, and sexual orientation—every person in every community across the Nation deserves equal access to comprehensive, culturally competent, community-based health care systems that are committed to serving the needs of the individual and promoting community health. (U.S. Department of Health and Human Services 2000, 16)

References

Aaron, Henry. 2007. "Why Has Health Care Reform Failed?" *New York Times,* November 6.

Adler, Nancy E., and Katherine Newman. 2002. "Socioeconomic Disparities in Health: Pathways and Policies." *Health Affairs* 21, no. 2 (March–April): 60–76.

Agency for Healthcare Research and Quality. 2005. *2005 National Healthcare Disparities Report.* Rockville, MD: U.S. Department of Health and Human Services.

Centers for Disease Control and Prevention. n.d. "Health Disparities." Online at www.cdc.gov/omhd/Topic/HealthDisparities.html.

Cohn, Jonathan. 2007. *Sick: The Untold Story of America's Health Care Crisis—and the People Who Pay the Price.* New York: HarperCollins.

Eberhardt, Mark S.; Deborah D. Ingram; and Diane M. Makuc. 2001. *Urban and Rural Health Chartbook. Health United States, 2001.* Hyattsville, MD: National Center for Health Statistics.

Eberstadt, Nicholas, and Sally Satel. 2004. *Health and the Income Inequality Hypothesis: A Doctrine in Search of Data.* Washington, D.C.: AEI Press.

Jacobs, Lawrence R. 2005. "Health Disparities in the Land of Equality." In James A. Morone and Lawrence R. Jacobs, eds., *Healthy, Wealthy, and Fair: Health Care and the Good Society,* 37–62. New York: Oxford University Press.

Klick, Jonathan, and Sally Satel. 2006. *The Health Disparities Myth.* Washington, D.C.: AEI Press.

Lamont, Julian, and Christi Favor. 2007. "Distributive Justice." Edward N. Zalta, ed. *Stanford Encyclopedia of Philosophy* (Spring 2007 edition). Online at http://plato.stanford.edu/archives/spr2007/entries/justice-distributive.

Lindblom, Charles. 1959. "The Science of Muddling Through." *Public Administration Review* 19, no. 2 (Spring): 79–88.

Marmot, Michael. 2002. "The Influence of Income on Health: Views of an Epidemiologist." *Health Affairs* 21, no. 2 (March–April): 31–46.

Mechanic, David, and Jennifer Tanner. 2007. "Vulnerable People, Groups, and Populations: Societal View." *Health Affairs* 26, no. 5 (September–October): 1220–30.

National Center for Health Statistics. 2006. *Health, United States, 2006.* Hyattsville, MD: U.S. Department of Health and Human Services.

Pauly, Mark V., and José A. Pagán. 2007. "Spillovers and Vulnerability: The Case of Community Uninsurance." *Health Affairs* 26, no. 5 (September–November): 1304–14.

Prewitt, Elizabeth. 1997. "Inner-City Health." *Annals of Internal Medicine* 126, no. 4 (March 15): 485–90.

Pritchett, Lant, and Lawrence H. Summers. 1996. "Wealthier Is Healthier." *Journal of Human Resources* 31, no. 4 (Autumn): 841–68.

Rawls, John. 1971. *A Theory of Justice.* Cambridge, MA: Belknap Press of Harvard University Press.

Relman, Arnold S. 2007. *A Second Opinion: Rescuing America's Health Care.* New York: Public Affairs.

Rushefsky, Mark E. 2007. *Public Policy in the United States: At the Dawn of the Twenty-First Century.* 4th ed. Armonk, NY: M.E. Sharpe.

Said, Ibrahim A.; Stephan B. Thomas; and Michael J. Fine. 2003. "Achieving Health Equity: An Incremental Journey." *American Journal of Public Health* 93, no. 10 (October): 1619–21.

Satel, Sally, and Jonathan Klick. 2006. The Health Disparities Myth. Washington, D.C.: AEI Press.

Smedley, Brian D.; Adrienne T. Stith; and Alan R. Nelson. Eds. 2002. *Unequal Treatment: Confronting Racial/Ethnic Disparities in Healthcare.* Washington, D.C.: National Academy Press.

Stone, Deborah A. 2002. *Policy Paradox: The Art of Political Decision Making.* 2nd ed. New York: Norton.

U.S. Department of Health and Human Services. 2000. *Healthy People 2010: Understanding and Improving Health.* 2nd ed. Washington, D.C.: U.S. Government Printing Office.

Whiteis, David G. 2000. "Poverty, Policy, and Pathogenesis: Economic Justice and Public Health in the U.S." *Critical Public Health* 10, no. 2 (June): 257–71.

Index

About the Authors

Kant Patel, Ph.D., is professor in the department of political science at Missouri State University in Springfield, MO. He has published numerous articles and books in the area of health care politics and policies. He has published articles in journals such as *Journal of Health and Social Policy, Evaluation,* and *Health Professions,* among others. Dr. Patel has coauthored (with Mark Rushefsky) several books including, most recently, *The Politics of Public Health in the United States* (M.E. Sharpe, 2004). Their other books include *Health Care Policy in an Age of New Technologie*s (M.E. Sharpe, 2002), *Health Care Politics and Policy in America,* 3rd edition (M.E. Sharpe, 2006), and *Politics, Power and Policy Making: The Case of Health Care Reform in the 1990s* (M.E. Sharpe, 1998).

Mark E. Rushefsky, Ph.D., is professor in the department of political science at Missouri State University in Springfield, MO. He has published numerous articles, chapters, and books in the field of public policy, concentrating on health policy. The fourth edition of his *Public Policy in the United States: At the Dawn of the Twenty-First Century* was published in 2007 (M.E. Sharpe). Dr. Rushefsky has coauthored (with Kant Patel) several books, including *The Politics of Public Health in the United States* (M.E. Sharpe, 2004), *Health Care Policy in an Age of New Technologie*s (M.E. Sharpe, 2002), *Health Care Politics and Policy in America,* 3rd edition (M.E. Sharpe, 2006), and *Politics, Power and Policy Making: The Case of Health Care Reform in the 1990s* (M.E. Sharpe, 1998). He is also the author of *Making Cancer Policy* (State University of New York Press, 1986).